D0427948

IMPERIAL GERMANY, 1871–1914

Economy, Society, Culture, and Politics

1. Germany in 1914: political and economic. Reproduced with permission of Cambridge University Press from V.R. Berghahn, *Modern Germany*, Cambridge 1987, p. 2.

IMPERIAL GERMANY, 1871–1914

Economy, Society, Culture, and Politics

V. R. Berghahn
Professor of History, Brown University

Berghahn Books
Providence • Oxford

Published in 1994 by

Berghahn Books
Editorial offices:
165 Taber Avenue, Providence, RI 02906, U.S.A.
Bush House, Merewood Avenue, Oxford OX3 8EF, UK

Library of Congress Cataloging-in-Publication Data
Berghahn, Volker Rolf.
Imperial Germany, 1871-1914: economy, society, culture, and politics / V.R. Berghahn.
p. cm.
Includes bibliographical references and index.
1. Germany – Economic conditions – 1888-1918. 2. Germany – Politics and government – 1871-1918. 3. Germany – Social conditions – 1871-1918. 4. Germany – Intellectual life – 19th century.
I. Title
HC285.B395 1994 94-20683
943.08'3 – dc20 CIP

British Library Cataloguing in Publication Data
A CIP catalog record for this book is available from
the British Library.

ISBN: 1-57181-013-7
1-57181-014-5 pb

Printed in the United States.

To Marion

Contents

Introduction

The German Empire, which was founded by Otto von Bismarck in 1871 and collapsed at the end of World War I, has been the focus of unusually intensive research during the past three decades. In good measure, this development has been due to the controversy which the Hamburg University historian Fritz Fischer unleashed during the early 1960s concerning the origins of that war. His hypotheses shifted attention away from the history of the Weimar Republic and the Third Reich back toward the pre-1914 period, while raising the question of continuity and discontinuity in modern German history "from Bismarck to Hitler." [1] However, although referring to Fischer has become a standard way of introducing recent historical writing on the *Kaiserreich*, his work is no more than a partial explanation for the rich scholarly harvest which forms the basis of this attempt to present a comprehensive history of German society between the founding of the Second Empire and the outbreak of the First World War. Our understanding of this period has also been expanded by debates whose scope went far beyond Fischer's original concerns. Above all, the historiography of this period benefited enormously from the pluralization of perspectives and methods which the discipline of history experienced internationally. If political history continued to be at the center of academic teaching and research during the first two postwar decades, since then economic, social, and cultural history have expanded in many directions. Indeed, what characterizes historical writing around the world today is its methodological and thematic diversity. There may still be "fashions," but their influence is no longer comparable with the hegemonic position which political and diplomatic history once enjoyed.

These developments have also provided us with a more colorful and sophisticated understanding of modern German history. Today historians are researching topics about which virtually nothing was known only a few decades ago. Anyone with the courage to write a history of the period 1871-

1. See F. Fischer, *Germany's War Aims in the First World War* (London 1969); idem, *War of Illusions* (London 1973); idem *From Kaiserreich to Third Reich* (London 1986); J.C.G. Röhl, ed., *From Bismarck to Hitler* (London 1970).

1914 during, say, the 1950s, would have found it impossible to synthesize developments in the country's economy, society, and culture in ways which, at least theoretically, are available today. This dramatic change poses a great and daunting challenge. Those critical readers of this study who believe that fragmentation has become the hallmark of the modern age will presumably lose no time in pointing out that the age of historiographical synthesis is over. I continue to think, however, that we can and, indeed, should attempt to write the history of an entire society in a given epoch, rather than merely the history of its microscopic parts. At the same time it would be naive to think that the richness of contemporary research opens up the possibility of producing a perfectly well-balanced textbook. Any general text is bound to take positions on past and current controversies; it will deal with open and perhaps unresolvable questions. Where I have done so, I hope I have been fair, and that I have provided enough historiographical context without dubbing a particular argument I happen to disagree with as "wrong" – a method which Thomas Nipperdey resorted to in his highly acclaimed *Deutsche Geschichte, 1866-1918.*[2] Indeed, it seems more honest to me to clarify at the start the most important premises that run through subsequent chapters, as I certainly would not wish to mislead the reader into believing that this is a text with all the "right" answers.

The Fischer debate initially centered around the decision-making processes in July 1914 that triggered World War I, but subsequently turned toward the underlying causes of that catastrophic conflict. Ensuing research challenged firmly held convictions that the basic principles of German foreign policy between 1871 and 1914 had been exclusively determined by the country's exposed geographical situation "in the middle of Europe" and by the primacy of foreign policy considerations [3] According to this older view, both Otto von Bismarck, the first Reich Chancellor, and his successors had been haunted by the nightmare of hostile foreign coalitions. The historian Eckart Kehr was the first to counter this in the early 1930s by arguing that domestic politics took "primacy" over external pressures. Thirty years later, in the 1960s, Kehr's arguments were rediscovered and elaborated.[4] If, Kehr argued, Germany's diplomatic situation just before the outbreak of the war was quite

2. T. Nipperdey, *Deutsche Geschichte, 1866-1918* (Munich 1990/91).

3. H. Boockmann, ed., *Mitten in Europa* (Berlin 1984). See also D. Calleo, *The German Problem Reconsidered* (Cambridge 1978).

4. E. Kehr, *Battleship Building and Party Politics in Germany* (Chicago 1975); idem, *Economic Interest, Militarism, and Foreign Policy* (Berkeley 1977); V.R. Berghahn, *Der Tirpitz-Plan* (Düsseldorf 1971).

desperate, the roots for this predicament go back to the 1890s. It was at that time that the Kaiserreich initiated a tariff and armaments policy which permanently antagonized Russia and Britain, the two major powers to the east and west. Both now moved to contain the ambitious and volatile German monarchy. However, according to Kehr, the Reich government's decision to embark upon a huge naval build-up and a policy of higher agricultural tariffs around the turn of the century was not a defensive response to an increased foreign threat at this time; rather it resulted from a domestic pact which agriculture and industry had entered into against the perceived threat of a growing working-class movement that had begun to demand, ever more persistently, changes in the distribution of wealth, power, and influence inside Germany.

It was Hans-Ulrich Wehler, above all, who applied the "primacy of domestic politics" view to the Bismarckian era. (5) Like his successors, Bismarck, too, was assumed to have been driven not by a *cauchemar des coalitions*, but by the nightmare of a threatening social revolution; hence he attempted to deflect foreign policy dangers to the periphery of Europe by conducting a comprehensive policy of peace toward the outside world. The first Reich Chancellor hoped that, by claiming that Imperial Germany was a satiated power, he would be free to consolidate the internal power structures of the newly created monarchical state; and when the success of this policy proved ephemeral, he tried to divert attention from the domestic difficulties by embarking on a policy of colonial expansion. But his aim was still to block all shifts in the existing imbalance of power, an imbalance that blatantly favored the monarchy and the social and political forces supporting it.

It did not take long for the "Kehrite" view (6) to be challenged in turn by the diplomatic historians. The latter objected to the idea of seeing foreign policy as part of a more comprehensive "history of society" (Gesellschaftsgeschichte) and reasserted the autonomy, if not the dominance, of a "political history in modern perspective" (7) which, in effect, was a return to the

5. H.-U. Wehler, *Bismarck und der Imperialismus* (Köln 1969); idem, *The German Empire, 1871-1918* (Leamington Spa 1985).

6. See W.J. Mommsen, "Domestic Factors in German Foreign Policy before 1914," in: *Central European History*, 1973, 3-43; see also H.-J. Puhle, "Zur Legende von der Kehrschen Schule," in: *Geschichte und Gesellschaft*, 1978, 108-19.

7. A. Hillgruber, "Politische Geschichte in moderner Sicht," in: *Historische Zeitschrift*, 1973, 529-52; K. Hildebrand, "Geschichte oder Gesellschaftsgeschichte?" in: *Ibid.*, 1976, 329-57; *idem*, "Staatskunst oder Systemzwang?" in: *Ibid.*, 1979, 624-44.

positions of the 1950s. Like their predecessors, they insisted that foreign policy, operating, as it was forced to, in an anarchic international system and wedded to the principle of Social Darwinist power politics, had a dynamic of its own. In other words, scholars like Andreas Hillgruber and Klaus Hildebrand refused to accept Wehler's notion that foreign policy was a mere extension of domestic politics and in the 1970s revived alternative paradigms to interpret the history of the Kaiserreich and the origins of World War I. By the 1980s, these scholars no longer viewed the containment of Germany in the last years before 1914 as the backlash of the ambitious foreign and naval policies initiated by Germany at the turn of the century; [8] they now interpreted the world war as a consequence of the inability of the other great powers, notably Britain, to accommodate the dynamic and politically unpredictable Hohenzollern monarchy within the existing international system. This view of the outbreak of World War I was therefore very different from the one espoused by Fischer and Wehler. All powers were once again given an equal share of the responsibility. The much-vaunted "normality" of the German case among the history of the western industrial societies had been reestablished.

At the same time it is true that even scholars like Wehler never accepted Fischer's view that German policy before 1914 represented an aggressive "grasping for world power", which the Reich government was supposed to have prepared ever since the War Council of December 1912. [9] In this respect they found themselves in rare agreement with diplomatic historians like Hildebrand and Gregor Schöllgen in their perception that Germany's plunge into war in 1914 amounted to a *Flucht nach vorn*, a flight forward from the impasse that the country had faced [10] The Kaiser and his advisers did not exacerbate the crisis after the assassinations at Sarajevo in an exuberant mood, seizing the opportunity to assume Germany's leading position among the great powers; rather they made their fateful decisions pessimistically in the face of a seemingly desperate situation of turmoil and isolation both at home and abroad. In searching for the causes of this impasse, some scholars have highlighted the incompetence and pathological learning which, they

---

8. K. Hildebrand, *Deutsche Außenpolitik, 1871-1945* (Munich 1990); G. Schöllgen, ed., *Escape into War?* (Oxford 1990).
9. F. Fischer, *War* (note 1), 231ff.; J.C.G. Röhl, "An der Schwelle zum Weltkrieg," in: *Militärgeschichtliche Mitteilungen*, 1977, 77-134.
10. See V.R. Berghahn, "Das Kaiserreich in der Sackgasse," in: *Neue Politische Literatur*, 1971, 494-506; idem, *Germany and the Approach of War in 1914* (London 1973, 2nd ed. 1993); H.-U. Wehler, *Empire* (note 5).

believed, permeated the decision-making processes within the Prusso-German monarchy. Others have taken a more structuralist approach and related the seemingly evermore insoluable problems of the German Empire to the inexorable advance of long-term processes. They saw industrialization, urbanization, and the increasing participation of the "masses" in politics as the cause of the impasse of 1914. What united the two theoretical camps was the conviction that the country had sunk slowly into a "polycratic chaos," becoming less and less governable. [11]

Finally, there occurred within this broader interpretive framework a revival of an older debate concerning the basic character of the 1871 Constitution and its reformability. This time, however, the issue was not so much whether the "personal rule" of Emperor Wilhelm II amounted to a degeneration of a political system that was basically sound;[12] rather the question was whether the Prusso-German political system reached the verge of collapse as a result of a growing constitutional crisis that could be traced back to the Bismarckian period. [13] Against this latter interpretation Manfred Rauh argued that the Kaiserreich found itself on the path to a major constitutional change and experienced the beginnings of a silent parliamentarization.[14] The center of political power, he maintained, was shifting from the monarchy toward the Reichstag, the democratically elected national assembly. Looking back on this particular debate, it may be said that Rauh's position has not become accepted.

More serious and more profound in its impact on the direction of research has been the challenge that the Kehrites have faced from a group of younger British historians. [15] Although, as confirmed social historians, they too had

11. H.-U. Wehler, *Empire* (note 5), 192.

12. See, e.g., E. Eyck, *Das persönliche Regiment* (Zürich 1948); E. Fehrenbach, *Die Wandlungen des deutschen Kaisergedankens* (Munich 1969); E.R. Huber, *Deutsche Verfassungsgeschichte seit 1789*, vol. 3, Stuttgart 1963; J.G.C. Röhl, *Germany without Bismarck* (London 1967).

13. See H.-U. Wehler, *Empire* (note 5); M. Stürmer, ed., *Das kaiserliche Deutschland* (Düsseldorf 1970).

14. M. Rauh, *Föderalismus und Parlamentarismus* (Düsseldorf 1972); idem, *Die Parlamentarisierung des Deutschen Reiches* (Düsseldorf 1977).

15. See R.J. Evans, ed., *Society and Politics in Wilhelmine Germany* (London 1978); G. Eley, *Reshaping the German Right* (New Haven, Conn. 1980); D. Blackbourn, *Class, Religion and Local Politics in Wilhelmine Germany* (New Haven 1980).

little time for Hildebrand's and Schöllgen's return to a "primacy of foreign policy," they began to criticize the type of elite history "from above" that Wehler and others had been writing. In their view, the history of the German Empire could not just be seen as the history of small manipulative groups dominated by the landowning Junker class and the archconservative representatives of heavy industry. These younger historians believed that anyone who wished to understand the development of the German Empire, especially after 1890, should focus on the autonomous self-mobilization of new social groups "from below" and their growing involvement in Wilhelmine politics.

The advantage of this approach, which was clearly indebted to the perspectives of popular history first developed in Britain by E.P. Thompson, [16] was that attention began to shift toward the intensive study of living conditions, life-styles, and daily experiences of the lower classes. As the interest in the "grass-roots" history of German society grew, fresh research into these topics began to broaden the discipline. The door to Alltagsgeschichte (the history of daily life) had been opened. It was Geoff Eley who soon expanded his early critique into a more fundamental challenge by questioning the viability of the *Sonderweg* hypothesis that was underlying the Kehrite view, but also much of Anglo-American writing on modern German history [17] This basically pessimistic interpretation had postulated a German divergence from the West and had drawn a more or less straight line from the Third Reich back to the late nineteenth century, where the roots of later disasters were to be found. These disasters were thought to result mainly from the inability of the country's elites to read the signs of the times and to put the country on a more viable track toward modernity. Eley – in rejecting the *Sonderweg* argument and asserting that Germany, by undergoing its own "bourgeois revolution", had in fact taken a path quite similar to that of the West – now openly proposed to "depathologize" the course of German history. He added that in his view the one-sided emphasis on the dominance of preindustrial elites and their manipulation of the "masses" had obscured a much more interesting and colorful historical reality. In this way he countered the Kehrite view with one that stressed the self-articulation and independence not only of the industrial proletariat, but also of the lower middle class. Above all, Germany, too, began to leave the old agrarian order behind and develop the foundations of an industrial capitalism which undermined the hegemony of the traditional agrarian elites. Slowly but steadily, modernity

16. E.P. Thompson, *The Making of the English Working Class* (London 1963).

17. G. Eley and D. Blackbourn, *The Peculiarities of German History* (Oxford 1984).

overwhelmed the antimodernist opposition spearheaded by the Prussian Junker class. Eley proposed to discard the older paradigm of the "failure of German liberalism" and to study instead divergent forms of Western bourgeois modernity as well as its dangers and its pathology.[18]

If the ways in which Wehler and others responded to Eley's revisionism were shrill, this may partly have been because the latter had meanwhile received much applause from a number of West German critics of the Kehrites who had their own reservations about the *Sonderweg* concept.[19] Thus Thomas Nipperdey had been protesting for some time against a type of historical writing that seemed to relish focusing on the alleged continuities "from Bismarck to Hitler" and arrogantly sat in judgment over the Wilhelmine grandfathers.[20] He reiterated instead the Rankean principle that every epoch is immediate, if not to God, at least to itself and should be treated as such. The Wilhelminians, he added, did not know the future and should not be made responsible for later catastrophes. It cannot be said that Eley was particularly happy about the succor he received from Nipperdey. Above all, his position on the *Sonderweg* debate which raged throughout the 1980s has remained ambiguous. It seems significant that a collection of his articles on the subject appeared in 1986 under the title *From Unification to Nazism*;[21] more importantly, he has recently been pushing for a "normalization" of modern German history only to the extent that he now speaks of a "bourgeois revolution" comparable to the Meiji Restoration in Japan. That is a position which the Kehrites may be perfectly happy to accept.[22]

Regardless of such incongruities, the "British" controversy has had a major impact on the analysis to be found in subsequent chapters. The results

18. G. Eley, *From Unification to Nazism* (London 1986).

19. See H.-U. Wehler, "Deutscher Sonderweg oder allgemeine Probleme des westlichen Kapitalismus?" in: *Merkur*, 1981, 478-87; J. Kocka, "Der deutsche 'Sonderweg' in der Diskussion," in: *German Studies Review*, 1982, 365-79. See also the summaries of the debate in: R.G. Moeller, "The Kaiserreich Recast?" in: *Journal of Social History*, 1984, 655-83; R. Fletcher, "Recent Developments in West German Historiography," in: *German Studies Review*, 1984, 423-50; J.N. Retallack, "Social History with a Vengeance?" in: *Ibid.*, 451-80.

20. T. Nipperdey, "Wehlers 'Kaiserreich'," in: *Geschichte und Gesellschaft*, 1975, 539-60. See also idem, *Gesellschaft, Kultur, Theorie* (Munich 1976).

21. As in note 18.

22. G. Eley, "In Search of the Bourgeois Revolution," in: *Political Power and Theory*, 1988, 105-33, esp. 118.

of recent research in the field of social and cultural history certainly make it imperative to highlight the progressive pluralization of German society in this epoch. However, if the element of a gradual evolution of diversity is to be emphasized, we cannot also ignore the slow formation of class lines, the "pillarization" of the *Kaiserreich*, and the emergence of larger political and ideological blocs. What follows revolves around the dual concepts of pluralization and polarization and in the process constantly asks the question of who the winners and losers were in this development. In trying to arrive at an overall judgment of the modernity of the German Empire and its ability to change and adapt politically to the diversification of its society, economy, and culture, it seems particularly instructive to look at the losers. This is particularly true of the situation of minorities, whose history – studied in considerable depth by the "new" social historians – is given due attention in this book. Overall, it is my hope that a synthesis of recent research, i.e., a history of German society in all its aspects, offers an opportunity to clarify not merely the contradictions, but also the broader lines of development during the years from the founding of the empire to the outbreak of World War I. In this sense, this book is also an attempt to explain, not so much why Germany ended up with Hitler in 1933, but rather why she went to war in 1914. This, while not wishing to deny the continuities in modern German history from the *Kaiserreich* to the Weimar Republic and the Third Reich, seemed to me to be an assignment that was difficult enough.

A final word about the structure of this book. As a glance at the table of contents will show, it is not conceived in the tradition of a grand chronological narrative. Rather it is thematically organized and, while each part follows a basic chronology, individual sections are also designed to provide a quick overview of a particular topic. Part V, which traces the major events in the field of domestic and foreign policy, is relatively brief. A more detailed analysis of the topics described here may be found, at least for the Wilhelmine period, in my *Germany and the Approach of War in 1914.* [23] I confess that I do not like to make such cross-references and wish I had as much space as Nipperdey was given by his publisher. He had no less than 1,745 pages at his disposal to cover the years 1866-1918. Finally, I hope that the statistical tables in the appendix will be found useful and informative. For easier use, their numbers appear in parentheses within the text, while cross-references in the footnotes together with the index should help the reader find the relevant passages in other parts of the book where the same theme is

23. V.R. Berghahn, *Germany* (note 10).

presented from a different angle. The book was written in the late 1980s without an army of assistants and a string of sabbaticals. However, I did receive many very perceptive comments from Klaus Bade, Keith Bullivant, Ute Frevert, Robin Lenman, Uta Poiger, Mark Ruff, and Hanna Schissler. I am most grateful to all of them and to the authors of many excellent studies both in German and in English with the help of whose arguments I have tried to develop a comprehensive interpretation of my own. Marion, my wife, was another gentle critic whose own neglected research on German-Jewish identity greatly helped me in dealing with the problem of minorities in German society. There is another reason, however, for why this book is dedicated to her. As the founder of a very successful and highly regarded academic press with a major list in German Studies she showed great strength and courage in adversity last year when her partners, for reasons of their own, forced her out. I was therefore very happy to take my manuscript from Berg Publishers to Berghahn Books, her new and serious venture, and not, as some readers might suspect, my vanity press.

Part I: Economy

1. Economic Sectors and Structural Change

A. Agriculture, Industry, Commerce, and Services

It is of fundamental importance for an understanding of Germany's economic development in this period that the upward trend in economic growth that began before the founding of the Second Empire continued, in principle, until the eve of World War I. There were, it is true, ups and downs and there were also setbacks. But although these were perceived by contemporaries as severe depressions, we can now see, with the benefit of hindsight, that they were in effect periods of *retarded growth*, not reversals of the general trend. The Net Domestic Product (NDP) provides a particularly clear gauge of these shifts. It rose moderately from the 1860s onward, before shooting up quite steeply beginning in the 1890s. By 1890 it had reached a level of 20 billion reichsmarks (RM), and by the outbreak of World War I the figure had more than doubled again. Knut Borchardt, it is true, has warned that the poor state of the statistical material undermines the reliability of many of the detailed figures,(1) but the task here is to discover the macroeconomic trend, and that is discernible enough. The relative prosperity of the German national economy is also reflected in the fact that the additional millions of people which the population explosion of the late nineteenth century had produced were overwhelmingly absorbed by the labor market without a drastic decline in living standards. Although income differentials remained large, in the long run a majority of Germans even enjoyed a higher living standard. Admittedly, the overall improvement was helped by the emigration of some 1.8 million people who left the country during the third wave of the nineteenth century (1880-1893).(2)

---

1. K. Borchardt, "The Industrial Revolution in Germany," in: C.M. Cipolla, ed., *Fontana Economic History of Europe*, vol. 4/1 (London 1973), 78.

2. See below pp.44ff.

The contribution which the different sectors of the economy made to the national prosperity varied considerably, however. If we take the respective shares of the Gross National Product (GNP), we find that until the 1880s agriculture retained its lead at 35-40 percent over industry's 30-35 percent. Thereafter the primary sector (agriculture, forestry, fisheries, and market gardening) went into relative decline. By 1913 that sector's share was less than 25 percent, while the share of industry, mining, crafts, putters-out, and domestic manufacture amounted to 45 percent. Meanwhile the share of the commercial and service sector hovered, more or less continuously, slightly above 30 percent.

These changes were indicative of a structural transformation, related to the Industrial Revolution, that all European countries, sooner or later, began to experience during the eighteenth and nineteenth centuries. However, it would be erroneous to speak of a simple shift from an *Agrarstaat*, a nation based on agriculture, to one defined by its industrial base (*Industriestaat*). Klaus Bade's notion of a metamorphosis from an "*Agrarstaat* with a powerful industry to an *Industriestaat* with a strong agrarian base" is probably more accurate here. [3] It is also for this reason that we do not immediately turn to an examination of the process of German industrialization, but focus, in the first instance, on agriculture as the older sector of the economy. Indeed, up to a point it was the emergence of an agrarian capitalism in the first half of the nineteenth century that helped to pave the way for industry. Nor did mechanization and rationalization remain exclusively confined to the factory system. If agriculture saw an quantitative expansion of its production in the second half of the nineteenth century, this development was no longer due primarily, as in the past, to an extension of land utilization, but to increased productivity (tables 1-2, 4).

Indeed, between 1903 and 1905 the increases for animal products and agricultural produce were once more quite steep, before taking another dip toward 1914. In 1870 total agricultural output, after deducting seeds, animal feedstuffs, and wastage, reached 4,080 million marks in current prices. A peak was achieved in 1912 with 12,348 million marks, after which the total declined to 11,740 million a year later. Considering that the number of those employed in agriculture vacillated only slightly between 1895 and 1905

3. K.J. Bade, "Transnationale Migration und Arbeitsmarkt im Kaiserreich: Vom Agrarstaat mit starker Industrie zum Industriestaat mit starker agrarischer Basis," in: T. Pierenkemper and R. Tilly, eds., *Historische Arbeitsmarktforschung* (Göttingen 1982).

between 9,788 million and 9,926 million (table 23), the above figures reflect productivity gains, which were stimulated in part by increased demand due to a fast rising population, but also by the more widespread use of fertilizer, better irrigation, improved winter feeding methods, and the advance of agricultural machinery. While there were some 268,000 simple threshing machines and 75,500 steam threshers in Germany in 1882, their number had expanded to 947,000 and just under 489,000 respectively by 1907. The number of mowers rose from 19,600 to 301,000 during the same period. In the 1860s, Germany had been an exporter of grain, until it was hit by the overproduction crisis of the 1870s when American and Russian competitors appeared on the world market. For several decades Germany's grain-growers huddled behind the protective tariffs walls which, at their prompting, the government had erected after 1879. But after the turn of the century the *Kaiserreich* once again became a grain exporter.

Still, not even these favorable developments were able to solve the structural problems of German agriculture during this period of continuous industrialization. Time and again, industry proved more dynamic and productive than agriculture, a fact supported by the employment figures of the time. In 1913, it is true, agricultural employment reached its peak at 10.7 million (table 23). But by this time industry (including crafts) had already overtaken the agricultural sector and now employed some 11 million people. This was an impressive change, also considering that the national economy, in which 18.6 million people had found employment in 1875, provided a livelihood for 31.3 million in 1914. Between 1900 and 1914 alone almost six million Germans found work for the first time, most of them in industry and in the tertiary sector. While many of them came from the major cities, where there were high birth rates, the rest were long-distance migrants, mainly from the agricultural northeast and the surrounding rural areas. Millions of people left agriculture hoping for a better life working in industry in the cities (tables 34-37).

The economic superiority of industry emerges even more impressively if we look at the expansion of production and employment in individual branches and their investment activities. In 1865 mining employed some 209,000 people; thirty years later there were 432,000. By 1913, this work force had doubled again to 863,000 (table 23). The metal-producing industries tripled their workforce between 1875 and 1913 from 150,000 to 398,000. Metal manufacturing saw similar increases. The textile industry employed some 926,000 in 1875, a figure which declined slightly to just under 900,000 by 1913. However, the clothing industry witnessed an increase in its workforce from a little under 1.1 million to over 1.5 million. The construction industry also registered a remarkable growth from 530,000 workers in 1875 to 1.63 million in 1913. The most impressive growth rate was experienced by the chemical industry, where employment increased from 65,000 to 290,000 during the same period.

If we follow Rolf Wagenführ's calculations, the annual industrial growth rate between 1866 and 1872 was 4.5 percent.[4] During the years 1873-1890, which came to be seen as the period of the "Great Depression," the average rate was still 3.0 percent per annum, a figure which then leapt back to 4.5 percent between 1890 and 1913. After the founding of the German Empire, the growing demand for raw materials and energy led to a further rise in coal production from 47 million tons in 1880 to 191 million in 1913 (table 6). Germany was now in third place in coal production, behind Britain and the United States. Meanwhile iron and steel saw even greater production increases. In this field, Germany moved into second place before World War I, outproducing the British (table 5). Demand for iron and steel was particularly strong in railway construction. During the 1850s, the length of track in central Europe had almost doubled to 11,326 kilometers. Close to another 8,000 kilometers were added in the following decade, only to be outdone by the addition of 9,000 kilometers in the first five years after the founding of the *Kaiserreich.* After this, the growth of the network proceeded at a slower pace, reaching a total of 61,000 kilometers by 1910, of which just under 12,000 kilometers of track had been laid since the turn of the century. The length of the road system also doubled.

During the boom period after the founding of the German Empire, the so-called "*Gründerboom*", railways had been the leading branch of German industry. Thereafter they lost this role to other branches, above all to steel, machine tools, and to the new industries of the "second Industrial Revolution" (especially electrical engineering and chemicals). In 1861 some 8,647 machines had been manufactured in Prussia. In 1875 their number had risen to almost 36,000. Later automobiles and electrics experienced their first boom period. By 1907 Germany had close to 26,000 cars and 1,211 large trucks. During the next five years alone these figures rose to 83,000 and 9,700 respectively. Unlike the steel and automobile industries, the chemical industry had a very wide range of products. In addition to the steep rise in the workforce, already mentioned above, two statistics strongly reflect the success of this branch. To begin with, its average annual growth rate was 6.2 percent;

4. R. Wagenführ, *Die Industriewirtschaft* (Berlin 1933), 13.

secondly, so impressive was the expansion of the most successful chemical companies that no fewer than twelve of them ranked among the hundred largest German enterprises a mere twenty years after their first boom period. Concentrating increasingly on the production of synthetic materials, German chemical companies quickly reached a leading position on the world market for dyes and pharmaceuticals. In 1900, Germany's share in dyes was 90 percent of world production. Another good indicator of basic structural changes affecting the national economy is provided by net investment rates. After 1870 the figure usually hovered around 10-11 percent for agriculture (table 7). With the exception of a period of retarded growth between 1875 and 1879, the share of industry was at least three times that figure, finally reaching a mark around 43 percent between 1905 and 1913. At the time of the founding of the *Kaiserreich*, capital invested in industry came to just under 10 billion marks in current prices; the figure for 1913 was over 85 billion. At the same time, industry also overtook agriculture in the return on capital.

In view of the rapid overall growth of industry, it was almost inevitable that the tertiary sector, or service sector, would benefit. The connection is most clearly discernible with respect to commerce and banking.[5] The abolition of customs barriers when Germany became unified, and the *Gründerboom*, are very directly reflected in the expansion of the financial institutions. With regard to commerce it must be remembered that Germany by the late nineteenth century had become one of the major trading nations of the world. In 1880 products (including foodstuffs) were exported to the tune of 2.9 billion marks, among them finished goods worth 1.4 billion. By 1913 exports had risen to just under 10.1 billion marks. Among these, the share of finished goods was worth almost 5.4 billion; that of semi-finished goods, 2.1 billion. However, the balance of trade remained marginally negative for most years before 1914, reflecting the country's great appetite for raw materials (table 8). All in all the German Empire became an exporter par excellence of high value-added goods which it promoted on the world market through repeated export offensives. Meanwhile capital exports reached 23.5 billion marks by 1914, reflecting the growing importance of banking. Nevertheless, the tertiary sector never employed as many people or enjoyed as high a share of the NDP as the industrial sector did. While the number of jobs grew in commerce, banking, and insurance, the figure for domestic servants declined sharply, even if – as will be seen – there were not merely economic, but also social reasons for this (table 23).

---

5. See below pp. 25ff.

B. Wealth and Incomes

The macroeconomic processes that have been described so far had inevitable consequences for the structure of wealth and income in the *Kaiserreich*. The differences were most striking in respect to wealth. In 1896/97 the top 10 percent of the Prussian population owned no less than 59 percent of all personal assets. By 1911, this share had increased further to 63 percent. These disparities, which were only in part due to income differentials, provided the critics of the existing social order with plenty of ammunition. The long-term structural changes that worked against agriculture and favored industry can also be traced in this particular field. The developments of the late nineteenth century demonstrated ever more clearly that ownership of factories carried with it greater productivity and higher profits than could be achieved by the owners of agriculturally used landed property. Land prices were high in the 1860s in the wake of the agricultural boom but declined during the following two decades and recovered only marginally thereafter. Only those who held land in areas with expanding cities saw their property values rising sharply. Selling landed property was frequently also made difficult or even impossible because of legal restrictions (e.g., the strict inheritance rules to which estates held as a *Fideikommiß* were subjected) and high mortgages. Nevertheless, in the mid-1880s there were close to 18,000 estates of over one hundred hectares in the eastern provinces of Prussia (table 3). Among the wealthiest estate owners were the Pless (83 estates with 70,139 hectares), the Henckel von Donnersmarck (58 estates with 38,388 hectares), and the Schaffgotsch (939 estates with 31,011 hectares).

Many landowners were thus sitting on assets whose value was considerable, if declining. Inheritance restrictions made it difficult for quite a few of them to realize their assets. If, on top of it all, the owners were ignorant of financial affairs or too conservative to adapt to the changing conditions of the marketplace, estates and farmsteads could quickly become a burden whose weight was further increased by mortgage debts. Only through rationalization could the individual farmer hope to cope with the impact of the above-mentioned structural crisis of agriculture. Some were astute enough to turn the corner. Many more did not prove competent to operate in the capitalist marketplace with success. They now had to tighten their belts if they hoped to retain their property and to save it from the great "butchery of the estates" that was going on. Between 1885 and 1900, some 5,000 large estates went into bankruptcy. A telling example of the anguish that this engendered is the case of Udo Count Stolberg-Wernigerode, a descendent of an ancient noble family. In the middle of the 1890s he had to sell his townhouse in Berlin because he could no longer afford the high overhead costs of running it. Such experiences reinforced a sense of bitterness and led to political activism. [(6)] As Elard von Oldenburg-Januschau, a Prussian *Junker* and Conservative deputy in the Reichstag, put it in 1904, "being poor" (as large numbers of Germans then were), was "no misfortune"; but he had no doubt that *falling* into poverty constituted one. [(7)] A way of life, so it seemed to many, was simply obliterated.

On the other hand, those who had invested their money in industry and commerce no doubt found the long-term increase in their wealth very satisfying, provided they had spread the risk and were good at exploiting market opportunities (table 7). To be sure, there were also those who found that the risks they had taken had been too high. They could easily lose all their assets unless they had limited their liability in compliance with the provisions of the Commercial Code of 1861. Anyone who was shrewd and lucky enough to survive recurrent recessions or the difficult early phases of building a business could look forward to a bright future, especially if he had hitched himself to one of the growth industries. It is difficult to know exactly how much wealth the individual was able to gain from dealings in industry, commerce or finance at this time. The statistics provided by the Inland Revenue Service presuppose a considerable trust in the taxpayer's honesty. Bearing in mind these methodological problems, the Prussian Inland Revenue Service counted 1,600 individuals in 1896 with an annual income of over 100,000 marks. That year there were also 9,265 individuals who declared incomes between 30,500 and 100,000 marks. (Table 17) This was a gigantic sum at a time when the average annual income from wages and salaries was around 740 marks (table 14). By 1912 the number of individuals in the two above categories had increased to 4,456 and 20,999 respectively. If in 1896/97 some 5,440 Prussian taxpayers were listed as millionaires, their number had grown to 9,349 by 1911.

That those who were making their money in industry were doing very well is also reflected in the impressive homes they built for themselves. In 1873 the Villa Hügel of Friedrich Krupp, the Prussian "Cannon King", was completed, overlooking Lake Baldeney south of Essen in the Ruhr area. As somber as it was ostentatious, the building had close to 270 rooms. Even Benjamin Disraeli, the British Prime Minister and a man not easily impressed by imperial splendor, was moved to speak at length of a lavish

6. See below pp. 226ff.
7. Quoted in: P.-C. Witt, *Die Finanzpolitik des deutschen Reiches von 1903 bis 1913* (Lübeck 1970), 60n.

reception which he attended at the palatial residence of Gerson Bleichroeder, Bismarck's private banker. [8] Walther Rathenau, who together with his father Emil was the driving force behind the rise of the Allgemeine Elektricitäts-Gesellschaft (AEG, General Electrics) and who by 1909 had business links with no fewer than eighty-four other large companies, acquired a stately home, *Schloß Freienwalde*, near Berlin, and there were others like him who bought up time-honored country homes which had once been in the hands of aristocratic families. However, it is not even necessary to inspect these manifestations of rising prosperity. It is sufficient to walk through the Hamburgian suburb of Pöseldorf today, through *Bismarckallee* in Bad Godesberg on the Rhine just south of Bonn or through Berlin-Dahlem to look at some of the *Jugendstil* villas to gain an impression of the wealth that the industrial and commercial bourgeoisie began to accumulate from the late nineteenth century onward. Of course, not everyone who had started in a small workshop or as a retailer made the jump into big money. For many of the self-employed it remained a hard struggle. They lacked capital, initiative, or simply good luck. And many craftsmen stubbornly put out goods that machines could produce much more cheaply. Although they formed associations for their economic self-protection and occasionally succeeded in obtaining government help, capitalist competition proved time and again to be too much for the less efficient. If, on the other hand, a small workshop was able to become a supplier to a larger enterprise or to move into new business like electrical installation or precision tool making, a firm base for further expansion might be reached. In the meantime the existence of most members of this so-called Old *Mittelstand* of artisans and small shopkeepers remained precarious. Accordingly, the share of the self-employed declined from 25.4 percent to 18.8 percent between 1882 and 1907 (table 22).

The New *Mittelstand* of white-collar employees in industry and commerce, whose share of the workforce rose from 4.7 percent to 10.7 percent during the same period, presented a different picture. According to Prussian statistics, the number of those who earned 900-3,000 marks per annum increased from 2.5 million to 6.8 million between 1896 and 1912, an increase of 167 percent (table 16). To be sure, not all of them saw their salaries go up. At Maschinenfabrik Esslingen in the southwest, for example, white-collar employees received around 1,800 marks per annum. During the boom year of 1900, salaries averaged around 4,151 marks, but between 1910 and 1912 they declined to 3,500 marks (table 14). The electrical engineering firm of Siemens paid its white-

8. See F. Stern, *Gold and Iron* (London 1977), 478.

collar employees around 2,800 marks in 1895, but barely more than 2,620 marks per annum in 1912. Civil servants were not only well provided for in their retirement, but also witnessed an improvement in their annual incomes from an average of 1,306 marks in 1870 to 2,607 marks in 1913 (table 14). During that year Bavarian public servants even achieved an average of 2,823 marks. At the time of the founding of the *Kaiserreich* postal employees, who had civil service status in Germany, earned 698 marks per annum; in 1913 the figure had more than doubled to 1,550 marks. During the Wilhelmine period the head of a provincial district (*Landrat*) could expect an annual income of 3,300-4,800 marks. On top of this he would be given some 6,000 marks in expenses, from which he had to pay his assistants and entertainment. At the turn of the century the famous physicist Max Planck received, as full professor at Berlin University, a salary of 4,400 marks to which was added a housing allowance of 900 marks per annum. His membership in the Academy of Science entitled him to another 900 marks for expenses. This was a little below the average salary of some of his colleagues. Meanwhile, in 1884, the great majority of physicians practicing in Berlin earned up to 3,000 marks per annum.

All these statistics must be seen in context, however. They were average incomes, and by 1914 the average annual earnings of the German population as a whole (including top earners) had barely reached 1,334 marks (table 16). In 1912 there were some 8.2 million working men and women in Prussia who took home less than 900 marks per annum and who, except for a few pieces of furniture, did not have any assets (table 18). This represented no more than a 5 percent decrease on the same category for 1896. It means that well over half of all the taxpayers of Prussia, where two-thirds of the total German population were living, belonged to the lowest income group and that these people participated in the wave of prosperity during the two decades prior to World War I only in a very limited way. In 1870 the average annual income of industrial workers and craftsmen was 506 marks (table 14). Twenty years later, they earned 711 marks, and finally in 1913 this figure increased to 1,163 marks. Miners, who belonged to the labor elite, saw their wages rise from 767 marks in 1870 to 1,496 marks in 1913. The average wages paid in agriculture mirrored the general economic difficulties of this sector. Annual earnings here (including forestry and fisheries) were a mere 350 marks in 1870. This figure increased to 417 marks by 1890 and to 682 marks by 1913. In addition land laborers and servants had free room and board.

A high percentage of these servants were young women whose remuneration varied considerably (tables 29-31). In any case, however, it was lower than the wages of their male counterparts. Many of them therefore moved into the cities to seek employment as domestic servants with middle-class families. Housework was often onerous and the workday was long. In Berlin an *Alleinmädchen* could expect 100-250 marks per annum, and Berlin was the city with the highest wages. If the woman decided to find a job in industry, she could expect better pay and more leisure time but suffered even greater wage discrimination in comparison with men. There are a few statistics relating to gender-specific wage differentials in Stuttgart in southwest Germany. The average weekly wage there for men was 22 marks, for women a mere 9.57 marks, i.e., 43 percent of the rates for men. In some other occupations the share was as low as 36-37 percent. Wage scales also reflect these inequalities. Thus no more than 1.1 percent of the males earned below 12 marks per week, but 70 percent of the women did. In the professions (for example, in teaching) discrimination was equally blatant, and in comparison with men, women were also less frequently promoted. (9)

All statistics that have been quoted so far merely relate to nominal incomes and therefore provide a quite incomplete picture of the economic situation of millions of people. They must be correlated with the development of prices. Taking the period 1871-1914, it can be said that the living standards of the majority of the population increased slightly, and certainly there was no recurrence of the mass pauperism that central Europe had seen before the onset of the Industrial Revolution. To this day we do not have reliable calculations of real (i.e., inflation-adjusted) wages for the period from the founding of the *Kaiserreich* up to 1914. Some scholars have spoken of increases of 92 percent, others of 37 percent. In the 1880s the index of real wages dipped repeatedly. It recovered in the 1890s, and in the last years before 1914 wages and salaries kept just ahead of the rate of inflation. The figures that D.V. Desai has calculated give a more favorable overall picture (10) (table 13).

More importantly, averages tend to veil the difficulties which many families experienced, especially in times of recession. This becomes all too evident if we compare the above-mentioned average wages with the figure which the Reich Statistical Office issued as a minimum living standard, i.e., 1,300 marks per annum. For the city of Bochum in the Ruhr industrial

9. See below pp. 67f.

10. A.V. Desai, *Real Wages in Germany, 1871-1913* (Oxford 1968). See also T. Pierenkemper, "The Standard of Living and Employment in Germany," in: *Journal of European Economic History*, 1987, 66.

district, we also have a list of welfare recipients (table 71). According to this document, twenty among every one thousand inhabitants required permanent assistance, while another 20 on average needed help on a temporary basis. [11] Meanwhile many families who did not rely on welfare slipped below the poverty line. These conditions can also be reconstructed from a number of family budgets that have been found (table 67). At the time of the founding of the German Empire, workers spent some 60 percent of their income on food and drink. After the turn of the century, the figure was closer to 40-45 percent. In 1907/8 a skilled worker needed no less than 51.5 percent of his annual wages for food, 16.8 percent for rent, 11.2 percent for clothing, and 4.2 percent for heating and light. Once the sums for personal hygiene, insurance, and leisure had been deducted, there remained a mere 1.1 percent for emergencies. If unemployment or illness struck, the larger items had to be cut back – with far-reaching consequences for housing and the nutritional standards of the whole family. [12] In this respect the consumption power of the middle classes was not only considerably bigger, but their greater ability to put aside savings also prepared them better for harder times.

The figures presented above appear to confirm the introductory statement that the German national economy experienced a period of overall growth up to 1913/14. But we have also found that there were ups and downs and even underlying structural problems. Furthermore, different social groups were very differently affected by these developments. Finally, there were not only sectoral, but also regional shifts. The next section will deal with this set of issues.

2. Booms, Depressions, and Regional Developments

A. *Gründerboom*, "Great Depression," Expansion and Recession (1896-1914).

The ups and downs in the German national economy which have just been mentioned hinted at the importance of conjunctural factors. Although the macroeconomic trend was upward, the economy was prone to overheat or to sputter from time to time. The very long waves in the development of the world economy since the Middle Ages are relatively well researched. More immediately relevant for the history of the *Kaiserreich* are the more short-

11. See below pp. 247ff.

12. See below pp. 59ff.

term vacillations which have been studied by Wassili Kondratieff and Arthur Spiethoff among others. [13] They have identified two phases during the late nineteenth and early twentieth centuries. The first phase began with an upswing which occurred between the years 1844-51 and 1870-75. There then followed a slowdown which came to an end only two decades later, to be replaced by the second upswing phase which was sustained, with various smaller vacillations, until just before World War I.

Economic and social historians have worked particularly intensively on the years 1874-79 to 1890-95, which have become known as the "Great Depression." However, most experts agree today that these years were less a depression than a period of retarded growth. Nor was it a general decline across the board. Industries were hit unevenly, some sooner and others later, as the former were beginning to recover. The statistical data which have been put forward to demonstrate these realities have not undermined, however, the argument that contemporaries nevertheless *perceived* the years 1874-79 to 1890-94 as a "Great Depression." This is an important point to bear in mind and helps to explain people's political responses in this period.

Within these more extended ups and downs in economic activity there occurred in turn briefer economic fluctuations. In this context, the so-called *Gründerboom* that took off just before the founding of the Second Empire in 1871, is of interest. The year 1866 was the last one to see a mild recession and a credit crunch. Thereafter, the economy began to pick up very quickly, for which several factors were responsible. Prussian leaders succeeded in unifying Germany and violently ousted Austria from the German Confederation. This, in turn, allowed the Ruhr, the industrial heart of Prussia, to exert a powerful economic influence on the southern German states. A few indices, like the rapid expansion of the railway network, have already been mentioned. [14] Pig iron production, which in 1866 had reached 1 million tons, had similarly experienced a 50 percent increase by the time of the founding of the German Empire (table 5). Coal production stood at 26 million tons in 1870 – a 114 percent increase since 1860. Other indications of an impending boom can be found in feverish investment activities and in the growth of the banking industry. Railroad stocks were doing so well that some companies were able to pay dividends of up to 8 percent; the Berlin-Magdeburg Railroad Company was even able to pay 20 percent. Commerce and the chemical

13. See H. Rosenberg, *Große Depression und Bismarckzeit* (Berlin 1967), 1ff.

14. See above pp. 2ff.

industries also began to flourish. For the moment agriculture was not doing badly either. There was strong demand for cereals, meat, milk, and eggs, and their production went up (table 1).

All this prosperity was nothing in comparison with the boom that set in after 1870/71. During the next four years the same number of ironworks and machine manufacturing companies were founded as "in the seventy years since 1800." [15] The capital sunk into these and hundreds of other stock-holding firms amounted to 2.8 billion marks, thus surpassing by 400,000 marks the total of investments made in the previous two decades (table 7). During the twenty years before 1870 the coal and iron industries had attracted some 69 percent of investments, followed by textiles (16 percent). The share of metal manufacturing and chemicals was a mere 8.5 and 2.0 percent respectively. The years 1870-74 witnessed a marked shift in these shares. Coal and iron shrank to 38 percent, textiles to 6.5 percent. Metal manufacturing now attracted 22.5 percent, while chemicals more than doubled its share to 4.5 percent. Some companies in the industrial centers of unified Germany had more orders than they could take. In Essen, Krupp expanded his work force between 1870 and 1873 from 7,000 to 12,000. In 1846 the "Cannon King" had had a mere 140 workers. However, the upswing was much more subdued in the textile industry than elsewhere, and it is important to bear in mind a highly differentiated picture. As before, banks played a key role during the *Gründerboom*, and not just in the channeling of French reparations payments, which no doubt provided an additional economic stimulus. No less than 103 banks were registered on the stock market between 1871 and 1873. The bigger ones among them fared so well that they were able to pay dividends of between 12.5 and 20 percent (table 9). The average dividend payments between 1870 and 1872 were 12.49 percent, implying an equivalent yield of 8.64 percent. The industrial boom coincided with favorable conditions in agriculture. The value of cereal production rose continuously from 1.698 billion marks in 1870 to 2.692 billion marks four years later (table 1). Meat production went up by 50 percent.

But the crash, which ushered in the period of retarded growth from 1874/79 to 1890/94, was not far away. The coal industry was hit hard from the start. The index of its prices fell from 116 points in 1873 to 49 in 1879. Prices for textiles meanwhile fell by a mere 23 percent, while other branches of industry tried to balance the decline in their domestic markets by

15. H.-U. Wehler, *Bismarck und der Imperialismus* (Cologne 1969), 57.

increasing exports. Accordingly the volume index for German foreign trade rose from 17.7 to 24.9 points between 1873 and 1878. Other companies resorted to price fixing with their competitors and began to form cartels. [16] Work forces were reduced, in some cases quite drastically, and production was further rationalized. This explains why the number of blast furnaces fell from 379 to 210 between 1873 and 1879, whereas iron production, which had reached its peak of 2.2 million tons in 1873, never slipped lower than just under 2.0 million tons. Indeed by 1879 it had almost climbed back to the 1873 figure, and it continued to rise slowly throughout the 1880s. Similarly coal production only once fell below the 36.3 million tons of 1873, i.e., in 1874. It then hovered between 37.5 million and 39.5 million tons, until in 1879 it reached just over 42 million tons. Thereafter the slow growth continued during the 1880s.

These figures have led Reinhard Spree to argue that the "Great Depression" first started as a trend reversal in heavy industry which began to affect the consumer industries only from 1876 onward. [17] Beginning in 1877, the economy stabilized itself, albeit on a lower level of production, employment, and profitability. Spree also believes that the banking crash has been exaggerated. This may be true for the retrospective analyst who looks at the available statistics. On the other hand, it must be remembered that 73 of 139 credit institutes had to close their doors and that the number of bankruptcies also rose in other branches. The stock-market reacted nervously and some 444 stock-holding companies saw their prices almost cut in half. In the late 1870s, most of large banks barely paid more than a dividend of 6 percent (table 9). Holders of shares in Berliner Handels-Gesellschaft did not receive any dividends between 1876 and 1878. Not everyone had enough in the kitty to absorb losses. Above all, the psychological impact of this period should not be underestimated. Businessmen experienced setbacks; they heard what was happening to their friends and competitors or they read about the crisis in the papers. The cumulative effect of all this influenced the economic climate for years to come; much of the optimism of the early 1870s was gone; people were less inclined to invest in risky ventures; above all, they complained loudly and constantly about the low prices and the allegedly unfair practices of the competitors.

---

16. See below pp. 29ff.

17. R. Spree, *Die Wachstumszyklen der deutschen Wirtschaft von 1840 bis 1880* (Göttingen 1978), 352ff.

The depth of these feelings explains why the basic mood showed no marked change when the economic situation improved for a brief period in the early 1880s. The next slowdown followed in 1886-1890, though it was less dramatic than that of the 1870s. If the NDP had been negative during the previous ten years, in 1886 it edged back to 0.6 percent, rising to 4.0 percent in the following year and reaching 4.2 percent and 4.7 percent in 1888 and 1889 respectively. Yet even then the business world did not regain its former bullish mood. Those who had capital to invest put it into bonds and securities. Investments beyond the borders of the Reich became more popular and should probably also be seen in connection with the clamor for the acquisition of a larger colonial empire. [(18)]

Although the "Great Depression" loomed ominously in the minds of entrepreneurs and businessmen, it is much more directly reflected in the agricultural statistics of the period. Here the downturn after the years of prosperity in the early 1870s worked in conjunction with a structural crisis which, as has been mentioned, was related to the fact that the wealth-creating capacity of industry simply proved so much greater than that of agriculture. Despite a continued population growth, the worth of grain production declined from its 1874 peak of 2.7 billion marks by about 20 percent in the years thereafter (table 1). Meanwhile meat production stagnated, while the total worth of milk and egg production oscillated around the 1874 level. Unlike similar indices in the industrial sector, these figures barely saw an improvement during the temporary upswing of the early 1880s. A glance at net investment figures confirms this picture of stagnation (table 7). In comparison with figures from 1865 to 1869 they had declined by more than half to 10.3 percent as early as 1874, and until 1895 they never went above the average of 11.5 percent. Even during the most gloomy years, the rate in industry was more than three times this average. It was clear that, faced with poor results, the agricultural sector lacked the means to modernize and thus to increase its prospects for the future.

In the early 1890s, the end of the "Great Depression" finally appeared on the horizon. In 1891 the Net Domestic Product (in 1913 prices) had once more slumped to 0.0 percent. However, it reached 4.1 percent in the following year and 5.0 percent in 1893. Thenceforth the economy experienced an upswing which lasted until 1913. It was interrupted in 1900/1 and 1907/8 by two brief, though serious slumps. The seriousness of the first one is reflected in a decline of the NDP to -2.3 percent. It unleashed a loud call for government

18. See below pp. 228ff.

help, above all in the shape of more orders of warships. [19] Similar pressures arose in 1907/8, but in both cases the recession was overcome fairly rapidly.

As during the *Gründerboom* and the "Great Depression," the stock market became the most sensitive barometer of the state of the economy. During the second half of the 1890s, gains in share prices had been made virtually everywhere. The expansion of the Imperial Navy acted as a boost to the prices of many steel and ship-building companies, which then suffered considerable losses again during the 1900/1 recession. There followed another bull market which began in the middle of the decade and then continued after 1909, punctuated by the second decline of 1907/8. New problems became visible just before the outbreak of the First World War. While stock market figures are telling, the period of prosperity can also be traced through investment levels in the industrial sector (table 7). In 1896 they reached 2 billion marks (in current prices) and climbed to 3 billion marks in 1898. After the turn of the century, the average was below the level of 2 billion marks for several years, before rising again to an average of just under 2.8 billion marks between 1904 and 1906. Following a peak of 3.7 billion marks in 1907, the average until 1911 levelled out once more at around 2.3 billion marks. The highest level of the entire prewar period was finally achieved in 1912 at 4.0 billion marks.

Many of these investments could not have been made without resort to the capital market. The issue of new shares may serve as a convenient guide to the measure of industrial growth in this period. And indeed, total stock holdings increased by just under 6 billion marks to over 16 billion marks between 1895 and 1913. After the recession of 1907/8, Germany saw another "strong increase in the issue of industrial shares" in 1909, [20] with lower levels in the following two years. But this did not affect profitability or the level of dividends. The year 1912 was the last year before World War I with high rates of growth and investments, accompanied by the issue of many new shares. It was a sign of a possible further reversal of the prewar trend that the volume of trade in industrial shares witnessed a tangible decline thereafter. A contemporary explanation of this may be found in the following comment in the *Volkswirtschaftliche Chronik*: "Conjunctural influences can be recognized clearly here. It shows at the same time that banks, in view of strongly rising inflation and unfavorable stock market conditions, found it more difficult to

19. E. Kehr, *Der Primat der Innenpolitik* (Berlin 1970), 146f.

20. R. Kroboth, *Die Finanzpolitik des Deutschen Reiches während der Reichskanzlerschaft Bethmann Hollwegs und die Geld- und Kapitalmärkte* (Frankfurt 1986), 82.

convert short-term loans to industry into stocks and long-term loans. This is also why they held back with making new loans". [21]

How well German industry had been doing between 1895/96 and 1912/13 may also be gauged from the fact that iron production doubled and steel production trebled during this period (table 5). By 1893 Krupp had twenty-four thousand workers; in 1912 he had as many as sixty-eight thousand. The production index for textiles reached 63.0 points in 1900 and rose to 102.9 in 1912, before declining to its standard level of 100 a year later. We have already mentioned the ascendancy of the industries of the second Industrial Revolution. [22] Cars were manufactured in larger and larger numbers. If the production index for the chemical industry had reached 42.5 points at the turn of the century (1913 = 100), it had almost doubled by 1910 (table 6). Similarly commerce could look back in 1912/13 on a twenty-year era of almost continuous growth, which took it from 60.9 index points in 1895 to 100.0 in 1913. Banking, which had a major share in the upswing of the national economy, grew from 22.8 index points in 1895 to 100.0 in 1913; credit cooperatives achieved an even larger growth from 16.5 in 1895 to 100.0 in 1913.

As has been mentioned, agriculture participated in this prosperity. Total production increased, and yet it was unable to exploit opportunities in the same way as the other two sectors (tables 1, 2, 4). Existing gaps grew wider. It could not raise enough capital for long-term investments and it remained more vulnerable to the ups and downs in the economy (table 7). Thus the recession of 1900/1 resulted in a sharp decline in wheat production from 3.2 million tons to 2.0 million tons, which a simultaneous 12 percent increase in potato production could hardly compensate for. Once this recession was over, a moderate growth in agricultural production was restored, but it was undermined by occasional years of underproduction. Meat production developed along similar lines. Finally, the unemployment figures, which were at that time more systematically collected than previously, provide a rough guide to how the economy was faring (table 21).

B. Regions and Regional Shifts, Infrastructural Change

Just as the sectors and branches of the German economy experienced the macroeconomic movements differently, the same can be said for the country's various regions. In agriculture, regional variations were determined by

21. Quoted in: *Ibid.*, 85.

22. See above pp. 4ff.

the size of the units of land, the quality of the soil and local inheritance laws. In 1878, the total agricultural area was 36.7 million hectares, of which 25.8 million had been taken under the plow. The rest was made up of grasslands, fruit plantations (10.5 million hectares), vineyards (0.13 million hectares), and gardening (0.4 million hectares). In the nineteenth century, the line of primogeniture ran east of a demarcation sharply along the west coast of Schleswig-Holstein to the Dutch border and the Lower Rhine. Here it turned east into Thuringia (with the exception of parts of Hesse), before making another turn through Franconia, finally dividing Baden and Württemberg from Bavaria in the south. By the measure of the above-mentioned criteria, the region east of the river Elbe from Mecklenburg to East Prussia may be regarded as a contiguous agricultural region. This was the land of the large-scale estate owners, whose sandy soils were best suited for cereal and potato crops. [23] This area also contained woodlands that as late as 1905 made up some 46.4 percent of landed property in Prussia. Although this region had been opened up to market-oriented methods of management, it remained rooted in many ways in practices and attitudes that were precapitalist. [24]

As far as the northwest of the Reich is concerned, Schleswig-Holstein may be seen as a region that was structured differently from the territories east of the Elbe. Particularly along the North Sea coast, freehold farmsteads of five to fifty hectares predominated, specializing in meat production and dairy farming (table 3). The fertile soils of Dithmarschen, just north of the mouth of the Elbe were well suited for cabbage and sugar beet. In the eastern parts of Schleswig the soil became sandier again, and farmers concentrated on animal husbandry. The arable land was used "primarily for the production of animal feedstuffs." [25] There were also a number of large estates near the Baltic Sea coast; but most of the so-called *Geestbauern* had small farms, situated like those of Holstein in a landscape of hills and woods.

There were many regional similarities between Schleswig-Holstein and the northern Rhineland, the Province of Westphalia, and the areas stretching further east towards Hanover and Celle, known as the North-German Basin. The rich soil in the west, it is true, becomes sandier soil in the regions further east around Magdeburg; but there were few large estates here and agriculture was devoted to dairy farming as well as the production of cereals,

---

23. See above p. 6.

24. See below pp. 23ff., 147ff., 56f.

25. R. Heberle, *Landbevölkerung und Nationalsozialismus* (Stuttgart 1963), 93.

potatoes, and beetroot. In the Rhineland and in Westphalia a mere 1 percent of all farmsteads were larger than fifty hectares. Small farmers were also to be found in large numbers in the entire Rhine valley region further south to the Swiss border and eastward in Württemberg. Unsuited geomorphically for large-scale agriculture, the family enterprises along the Rhine and its tributaries (Nahe, Main, and Neckar) specialized in wine and fruit production. Animal husbandry and dairy farming, as well as the production of grain and hops prevailed further east in Franconia and Bavaria. The region had a number of large estates, but the majority of peasants did not have more than one to ten hectares of land. Hesse and Thuringia also had mostly smallholdings with forestry as an important element in this mountainous region. Finally, mixed patterns of agriculture were to be found in Saxony, which at the same time was one of the oldest industrial regions of central Europe.

Since the eighteenth century, if not before, the kingdom of Saxony and, further to the east, the Silesian territories had been a center of textiles which for a long time had been organized on the basis of cottage industries. Here underemployed peasant strata had adopted cottage industry-style production. Raw materials were provided by putters-out, merchant capitalists who also saw to the marketing of the end products. As early as the late eighteenth and early nineteenth centuries, many villages in the Eichsfeld east of Göttingen, in the Thuringian Forest, and in the uplands along the rivers Elbe and Oder in Saxony and Silesia had a high percentage of weavers and spinners. Slowly, with the advent of larger power looms and steam engines, these industries underwent a process of concentration, leading to the building of factories which housed dozens of workers under one roof. However, many of the old putting-out networks did survive into the 1870s. The decline of the textile industry thereafter was partly made good by the rise of the chemical industry, which developed around Halle-Merseburg and Leipzig and, in conjunction with the exploitation of the region's lignite deposits, transformed the area into the industrial heart of Central Germany.

Once Berlin became the capital of the Reich, however, there arose further north not only a commercial and financial center, but also a competitor. Berlin became home to many companies in the field of metal manufacturing and electrical engineering. Yet neither Berlin nor Saxony, and even less Hamburg, a focal point of ship-building and metal manufacture, were able to compete with the industrial region along the rivers Rhine and Ruhr, as well as the Wupper River Valley and the Siegerland. However severely its heavy industries had first been hit by the "Great Depression," the Ruhr, which had a long tradition of coal and iron production, benefited from the growing importance of the metal industry. Technological developments, moreover, made possible the mining of the deeper-lying coal deposits of the so-called Emscher Zone to the north. It also proved advantageous that the Rhine provided a major waterway and that western Europe and many of Germany's important trading partners were within easy reach. Further south, Frankfurt emerged as a center of manufacturing, thanks to, as in the case of Berlin, the city's long-standing position as a hub of commerce and finance. Among the older industrial regions, mention must also be made of the upper and lower Neckar River Valley. In Stuttgart and Neckargemünd, there was a long tradition of metal manufacturing. Further north on the banks of the Rhine and at the mouth of the Neckar, Mannheim and Ludwigshafen attracted the flourishing chemical industry. Munich, the Bavarian capital, never achieved the significance of Berlin or Frankfurt as an industrial center. Apart from Augsburg, however, the region around Nuremberg established itself as a manufacturer of toys and metal goods.

Location was obviously an important factor in the success of a particular industrial region. But in view of the continued growth of the German economy – more slowly during the "Great Depression" and rapidly thereafter – it is difficult to speak of the decline of any one region, only of a strengthening of one region over another. The region of Rhine and Ruhr unquestionably gained a dominant position which it defended until after World War II. Saxon industry tried to overcome its locational handicap at the end of the nineteenth century with the building of the *Mittellandkanal*. The project ran into the bitter opposition of the agrarians, to whom the canal was not a waterway for the transport of raw materials and finished goods to and from Saxony, but an avenue for a flood of cheap grain imports from North America. Building canals and making rivers navigable became an important state activity so that shipping grew from 1.6 billion ton/kilometer in 1870 to 17.8 billion in 1913. Meanwhile the railroads were of even greater importance for all industrial regions. It is no accident that the first German railroad was opened between Nuremberg and nearby Fürth in 1840. Other lines soon followed between Munich and Augsburg in Bavaria and between Magdeburg and Dresden via Halle and Leipzig in Saxony. By 1912 over 60,000 kilometers of track had been built. In 1870 the railroads transported 5.3 billion ton/kilometer of goods; by 1913 this figure had risen to 67.7 billion. The comparable figures for rail passengers increased almost tenfold between 1871 and 1913. Wolfgang Schivelbusch has written about this "industrialization of time and space" and about the impact of the railroads upon the mentalities of the people of that time.[26] Thenceforth, distances that seemed huge began to shrink. Remote villages suddenly were brought into the orbit of cities. Fresh fruit and vegetables reached the markets of the densely populated industrial regions. Timekeeping became standardized. In 1893, Central European Time was introduced for the whole of the Reich.

Road traffic also proliferated. In the countryside and the villages carts and coaches remained the most important means of transportation. The first horse-drawn streetcar in Berlin began carrying passengers in 1865. By 1881 Siemens had developed an electric tram which ran between Berlin and nearby Lichterfelde. The city of Wuppertal in the west erected the *Schwebebahn* which, suspended from pylons, ran above the meandering river Wupper. In 1896 Berlin opened the *Hochbahn*, a commuter system on elevated tracks. Bicycles enjoyed a rising popularity toward the end of the nineteenth century. From the middle of the 1890s onward, automobiles became the rage for those who could afford them. The slow expansion of paved overland roads promoted bus and motorized postal services. These were able to reach the more remote parts of the country which the railroad companies had bypassed. To be sure, this was not yet the age of mass motorization. Germany remained behind the United States, France, and Britain in the number of cars per capita. Passenger cars remained luxury items, custom-made, primarily in small workshops.

The building of railroads and the advent of automobiles also benefited postal services. The invention of the telegraph and later of the telephone further accelerated and facilitated communication in unprecedented ways. In 1872 the German postal service handled around 972 million messages of all kinds. By the turn of the century, this figure had risen to 5.7 billion. In 1913 the number of letters and parcels alone handled by the Reichspost amounted to 5.9 billion. In 1872 some 12 million telegrams were sent; in 1910 it was four times that number. Similarly the number of telephones quickly increased after the turn of the century. In 1910, Germany had 1 million telephones, and the exchanges connected some 1.8 billion calls.

Under British leadership the telegraph network was greatly expanded, integrating German industry and commerce into the world economy. The above-mentioned growth in exports and imports (table 8) stimulated not only ship-building, but also commercial shipping. Until the mid-1880s the transport capacity of the tall ships continued to be larger than that of steamboats.

26. W. Schivelbusch, *Railway Journey* (Oxford 1987).

By 1910 the latter had a combined space of 2,185,890 BRT (register tons), and it doubled once more to 4.4 million BRT by 1913. By then the total for tall ships had declined to around 440,000 BRT. Technological developments, like the invention of the steam turbine and later, large diesel engines, further enhanced the position of the German commercial fleet. Norddeutscher Lloyd and Hamburg-Amerika-Paketfahrt Aktien-Gesellschaft (HAPAG) became the two major shipping companies. In 1913 no less than thirty-three large passenger steamers and freighters of over 10,000 BRT had been put into service, and several of these had a capacity of over 50,000 BRT. Germany now held second place behind Britain among the world's commercial fleets.

All in all it may be said that the expansion of communications is a good example of the modernizing impulses that stimulated the German national economy before 1914. Although structural changes, the ups and downs in the economy, and geography affected some branches and sectors negatively, overall the *Kaiserreich* gave the impression of strength and vitality. Only agriculture fell more and more behind – with consequences that we will investigate in later chapters. [27]

3. The Organization of Industry

The evolution of capitalist industrialization and urbanization is inseparably connected with the phenomenon of increased organization within industry, a development which affected both the economy and all other spheres of life in the second half of the nineteenth century. We first turn to the organization of the various local and national markets.

A. Labor Markets, Capital Markets, and Cartels

There was a marked increase in the number of working men and women between 1871 and 1913 from 17.3 million to 30.9 million (table 28). This amounted to an average annual growth rate of 1.2 percent. However, considerable imbalances developed due to the migrations from agriculture into industry and the tertiary sector. [28] Moreover, the absolute figures listed above must be correlated with the employment rate which was partly determined by the country's age structure, the percentage of working women, the age of entry into the labor market, and the average retirement age (tables 27, 29). Until 1880 the employment rate vacillated around 43-44 percent, rising

27. See below pp. 44ff., 201ff., 216ff., 226ff.

28. See below pp. 44ff.

to no more than 46 percent by 1913. The fact that the percentage of the population between the ages of fourteen and sixty-five remained more or less constant at 63 percent in the decades prior to 1914 is partly responsible for this small increase.

Similarly the percentage of the work force comprised of women remained at around 30 percent, notwithstanding the loss of workers from agriculture to industry as well as changes within the tertiary sector, where the number of domestic servants declined, while that of female office workers ("white-blouse" occupations) increased [(29)] (tables 29-31). Furthermore, the decline of child labor and the extension of education and training for young people must be taken into consideration when we look at the relative stability of the employment rate. Reasonably reliable calculations of unemployment figures exist only from 1887 onwards (table 21). But these statistics refer only to industry and crafts, so that the actual figures were certainly somewhat higher. In 1887 the unemployment rate was below 1 percent, but hovered around the 4-percent mark a year later. There was another decline in 1890 and 1891 before it reached a peak at roughly 6 percent in the following year. Later, at the end of the 1890s, the rate levelled off again at a little higher than 1 percent. It reached a high of 7 percent during the recession of 1901/2, when over 630,000 persons were unempoyed. After this date the statistics which the trade unions had kept were complemented by official records. Above all, the rate stabilized at between 2 percent and 4 percent until 1913. In the last year before the war some 350,000 unemployed were once more on the books, a statistic which was seen by some as another sign of a reversal of the economic trend. These developments, coupled with the steady stream of people looking for employment, put pressure on the labor market to become better organized.

Agriculture – except in the case of pure family farms – had for a long time hired its laborers on a daily basis every morning in accordance with demand. But the massive flight to the cities and into industry moved the estate owners to offer steadier employment conditions, which gave them the advantage of firmer social control and, in the age of mass politics, control over the land laborers' voting behavior. [(30)] Faced with a scarcity of labor, the large-scale landowners in East Elbia were forced to rely, moreover, on migrant workers. Most of these workers were Poles from the Russian parts of former "Congress Poland" who were sent back at the end of the season. These employment practices increased tensions with the Tsarist Empire, especially

29. See below pp. 66ff.

30. See below pp. 210ff.

toward 1914; they also undermined the anti-Polish Germanization policies of the Prussian government.[31] In any case, as early as the 1890s the agricultural chambers in the east began to organize regional labor exchanges. In 1903, with the support of the Prussian Ministry of Agriculture, the nationalist Society of the Eastern Marches (HKT) and the Pan-German League temporarily appeared on the scene. Finally in 1905 the Central Office for German Land Laborers was founded, which, after considerable bureaucratic wrangling, ultimately succeeded in 1908/9 in centralizing the existing systems of labor exchanges. Via this system, and also through innumerable private agencies, well over 500,000 migrant workers came to Germany every year, most of them Poles.

It does not require much imagination to visualize what social and openly racist prejudices these very poorly paid "*Pollacken*" encountered. Their situation as third-class laborers was reinforced by political and ideological problems.[32] At this point it must suffice to note that it was rather an odd agricultural labor market which emerged in the east and in which the workers – indigenous ones included – had virtually no rights. Industry could not have survived with this kind of a system. Cottage industries were suited only for certain types of jobs. Factory production and the handling of fairly complex machines required workers who could not simply be hired on an ad hoc daily basis. Although industrial workers remained virtually without legal protection against dismissal, the employers' interest in uninterrupted production demanded that most factories acquire a core of skilled workers, and these in turn could insist on greater job security than agriculture was able to offer.

These circumstances affected the organization of the nonagricultural labor markets. At first the employers merely kept lists which were designed to prevent the hiring of Social Democratic "agitators."[33] Later, employers developed and ran exchanges, organizations which acted as intermediate agents between the employers and those looking for work. The government also began to assume a role in this field. Thus local authorities organized exchanges through which domestic servants and unskilled laborers were placed. Although the employers, particularly those in mining and the metal industry, were able to preserve their predominance in this area, the

---

31. See below pp. 110ff.

32. See below pp. 232f.

33. See K. Saul, *Staat, Industrie, Arbeiterbewegung im Kaiserreich* (Düsseldorf 1974), 51ff.

government did gain a foot in the door. The government's role became fixed in the Placement Law of 1912, indicating that those looking for work were no longer completely at the mercy of the employers. The introduction in the 1880s of a social insurance system had enhanced the material and legal position of the workers, even if Bismarck had his own political considerations when he devised this system. [(34)] In short, there was a close connection between the growing demands of modern factory production and the organization of the labor markets. The same is true of the organization of the capital markets.

The capital requirements of the national economy, the rise of the banks, and the changing needs of employers and the public administration have already been mentioned. In organizing the capital markets, banks were bound to assume a key role, and not just because private bankers were personally liable and share-holding institutions operated under limited liability. The latter were able to expand their capital basis considerably during the *Gründerboom* and thus gained levers to influence the national economy as a whole. However, it is the model of the "universal bank" – developed from the concept of the French *crédit mobilier* institution – that was fundamental to the increased power of the German banks. As the name indicates, "universal banks" were not just credit institutions that attracted savings accounts and then provided short-term loans to whoever was deemed creditworthy. Unlike their British and American counterparts, German banks were allowed to act as brokers on the stockmarket and even to acquire and sell shares for their own gain. Indeed, they could engage themselves in virtually all financial matters. They could acquire a stake in an industrial or commercial enterprise and then exercise their voting rights at the annual meeting of shareholders. These organizational and legal conditions explain why German credit institutes were less interested in short-term high profits, but in the long-term health of those companies in which they had a direct or indirect interest. Whereas British banks rarely offered more than an overdraft facility, German banks made a long-term commitment to the firms of their choice.

And so a close relationship developed between banking and industry as a result of which expanding and successful enterprises were able to base their investment planning on strategic projections. Ever since Rudolf Hilferding published his famous book before World War I, the argument could be heard that "finance capital" had gained the upper hand in this relationship. More

34. See below pp. 250ff.

recent research indicates, however, that it was a more evenly balanced, genuine symbiosis which both sides nourished as mutually beneficial and without a constant desire to dominate. The rise of joint-stock companies like the Deutsche Bank, Commerz- und Disconto Bank, and Dresdner Bank was certainly promoted by their links with rapidly growing firms like Siemens and Allgemeine Elektricitäts-Gesellschaft (AEG), although some companies, particularly in the chemical industry, also reinvested a large share of their profits. Private bankers, because of unlimited liability requirements and other factors, may have had to be more cautious, but their role in the organization of Germany's capital markets should not be underestimated. Many of them worked in the field of industrial investments or floated lucrative public loans, often as agents of foreign governments. The wealth which Gerson Bleichroeder accumulated not only for his most famous client, Otto von Bismarck, but also for himself was generated by a long string of successful transactions on the capital markets of Europe.

Among the large banks, Deutsche Bank's growth was particularly impressive. Its share capital, which included that of several larger regional banks, amounted to 691 million marks by 1911. It had reserves of 238.5 million marks. Siemens & Halske and Norddeutscher Lloyd were among its major customers. Deutsche Bank, in cooperation with Berliner Handels-Gesellschaft and Bankhaus Delbrück, Leo & Co., supported Emil Rathenau in building up his AEG empire. Its top executives were represented on the supervisory boards of other important industrial and commercial enterprises. In the southwest Darmstädter Bank, in conjunction with Schaafhausener Bankverein, mediated agreements in 1905 between Badische Anilin- und Sodafabriken (BASF), Bayer, and Agfa, three of the up-and-coming chemical firms. Meanwhile Dresdner Bank promoted the further expansion of Saxon industry, but also of the Felten & Guilleaume Cable Works in Cologne. Other well-known big banks were engaged in the mining and steel industries.

Given their commitments to industry, most larger banks were more interested in attracting major investors than small savings from ordinary people. The latter, whose cumulative wealth was everything but insignificant, were courted by communal savings banks (*Sparkassen*). These customers were not interested in risk papers like stocks, but wished to have their funds securely invested for their retirement. Accordingly, the amounts held by these institutions trebled in the decade after 1870. At the time of the founding of the *Kaiserreich* Saxony alone had no less than 144 savings banks with some 517,105 accounts. They held a total of 131.1 million marks. Twenty years later the number of savings banks had risen to 229 with 1.7 million accounts and

602.6 million marks. In 1914 the total for Saxony was 361 institutions holding a little over 2 billion marks. In 1913 the customers of all savings banks had entrusted to them some 19.7 billion marks. This was four times the amount that was held by the eight largest joint-stock banks (table 19).

To be sure, individual savings banks often remained so tiny and bound to their locality that they could do no more than provide small loans. On the other hand, the credit needs of artisans, shopkeepers, and farmers were often considerable, especially in economically hard times. This is where cooperative banks came in. They were credit associations whose members shared, through the capital they had put in, the cooperative's profits and losses. They could also obtain loans at favorable rates. The great popularity of this type of credit institution is reflected in its membership figures. In 1870 they had 314,656 members; by 1913 this number had increased to over 800,000. The total number of these associations doubled to 1,500 during the same period. A separate system of cooperatives developed to cater to the credit needs of agriculture, three quarters of which belonged to the Reichsverband der landwirtschaflichen Genossenschaften, the rest to the Raiffeisen-Verband. The latter was more centralized and offered its members other services besides loans.

With the indebtedness of agriculture rising under the impact of the "Great Depression" and the above-mentioned, more general structural crisis of this sector, the traditional system of lending continued. This entailed private loans at often very high interest rates. This kind of lending had a bad reputation, though not always justifiedly so. Of course, there were many cases in which the usurer unscrupulously exploited the plight of a particular peasant. But equally there were many lenders who would not immediately confiscate the property the moment the borrower was in arrears with his payments. This and the fact that many usurers were non-Jews did little to prevent the fanning of anti-Semitic resentments in many rural areas on which politicians then tried to capitalize. [35] Finally, mortgage banks grew up in the second half of the nineteenth century as an alternative to the credit associations. Like the universal bank, this type of credit institution was modeled on the French example. Mortgage banks operated under strict legal rules which were further strengthened at the turn of the century and which did not allow them to help in any emergency. Moreover, the lending activities of these banks shifted increasingly from the rural to the urban market. Due to the country's demographic explosion, there arose a growing demand for mortgages to finance city housing. Builders were as a rule also able to offer better securities

---

35. See below pp. 102ff.

than farmers, whose properties were frequently overburdened with other mortgages.

Founded in 1875, the Reichsbank stood at the top of this highly diversified financial system with responsibility for currency and interest rate policies. Reichsbank shares were held by private investors who had little influence, however, on its policies. The bank's president was appointed by the Kaiser. The banknotes issued by it were increasingly backed by the country's gold reserves, by 1913 up to 45 percent. The base rate was held as low as possible to promote economic growth. Yet however well the German banking system may have been equipped organizationally and by law to support the expansion of industry and commerce, the available capital resources always remained tight and in fact became even scarcer toward 1914. The serious indebtedness of agriculture propelled too much capital into a sector that was structurally weak and declining. The growing borrowing needs of the public sector proved an even greater drawback. The rising costs of armaments, which began in the late 1890s with the Kaiser's ambitious naval program, bloated the Reich budget. But the federal states and local government became no less reliant on the capital market to cover their deficits, which they found more and more difficult to remove by politically sensitive tax increases. [36] Ultimately the capital markets suffered from the fact that Germany – where a more broadly based wealth was a recent phenomenon – did not stand on as firm a financial basis as did Britain. In no other area is this weakness evidenced more clearly than in the German hesitancy to make foreign investments on a larger scale, even when this seemed desirable for both economic and strategic-political reasons. Even in the years of prosperity before 1914, the pie was simply too small to cater for all those needs, private and public, at home and abroad.

Finally, there were the commodity markets which, in organizational terms, underwent a major change which was to have consequences for the development of Germany's industry and commerce well beyond the lifetime of the *Kaiserreich*. According to liberal-capitalist theory these markets were to be exclusively subject to the laws of supply and demand. These laws supposedly determined the movement of prices and the volume of production. The market was thus endowed with a self-healing capacity which would correct temporary imbalances in supply and demand by making an adjustment in prices or production respectively. Another advantage was said to lie in the

---

36. See below pp. 196ff., 272ff.

mechanism of competition in the open marketplace that would result in the disappearance of weak enterprises. The slowdown of the 1870s with its many bankruptcies demonstrated that there was some truth in this argument. Prices slumped and many firms that had been founded in the heady days of the *Gründerboom* lacked the financial strength and stamina to survive until demand picked up again and the economy righted itself. Faced with such hard times, businessmen had been inclined many times before to throw their professed support for the principle of competition overboard and to seek protection against the vagaries of the market. They banded together to stabilize prices and production in the hope that this would accelerate the turn-around of the economy. And as before, foreign competitors were the first against whom one formed a common front.

In the face of the protectionist tendencies that were never far from the surface in the developing German industrial economy, it is not surprising that demands for higher tariff walls were made soon after the end of the *Gründerboom.* Business became organized. Associations were founded whose lobbyists began to exert pressure on the government and Reichstag deputies. [37] As a result of this agitation, industrial and agricultural tariffs were introduced in 1878/79 and increased in subsequent years, as the "Great Depression" appeared to many to show no signs of abating. While tariffs impeded foreign competition, many businesses had moved beyond this in the meantime. They began to help each other, concluding agreements among themselves over prices, conditions and production. These horizontal agreements between independent firms (known as cartels) were undoubtedly, as initially conceived, responses to a perceived emergency. In 1875 there had been no more than 8 cartels, confined to a few branches of industry. By 1887 the total had risen to 70, and by 1895 there were 143. Cartel agreements were binding contracts in civil law and a violation of one could be made the subject of court litigation. Trying to break out of the discipline of a cartel therefore became expensive, quite apart from the threat of other sanctions by the remaining cartel members against the offending company. Furthermore, refusing to join a cartel could lead to costly ostracism by the majority.

Naturally, if cartels were products of a crisis situation, they should have been disbanded when the recovery came after 1895. But in the meantime many cartel associations had begun to live a life of their own. Many members so appreciated the stability that they provided that they preferred the arrangement to a renewed exposure to competition in the open marketplace.

---

37. See below pp. 222ff.

This was particularly true of those weaker firms for whom cartels with price-fixing policies and exact production quotas provided a lifeboat even in better times. Moreover, traumatized by the long period of retarded growth, cartel members sought protection not only against competition in a period of boom, but also against future recessions. Accordingly, the expansion of cartel organizations continued after 1895. By the turn of the century the number of agreements had again doubled to 300. In 1910 there were some 673 cartels. However, the degree of cartellization varied considerably from branch to branch. It was highest in mining, followed by the paper, iron, and cement industries. In relation to the value of its output, the potash industry was fully cartellized, followed by the paper industry (90 percent) and coal (82 percent). In the iron and cement industries, cartellization reached just under 50 percent and was still rising. The degree of cartellization in car manufacturing and electrical engineering, on the other hand, was a mere 10 percent. Virtually no cartel agreements existed in the chemical industry.

Apart from conditioning their members to behave in an anticompetitive way, cartels were also fostered by the organizational structures that had developed since the 1870s. In order to safeguard coordinated sales of their products and also to control their members, sales associations (so-called syndicates) had been established. They looked after the marketing and selling of the production quotas that a cartel had agreed upon. Once in existence, it proved difficult to abolish such organizations. Finally, in 1897 the Reich Court rendered an important decision which permitted horizontal agreements between independent firms and thus confirmed that breaches of cartel agreements could be made the subject of civil suits. As a result of this decision, a very different legal framework developed in Imperial Germany from that of the United States, for example, where, in line with dominant liberal ideology, cartels were deemed detrimental to competition and to the interests of the consumer. They were outlawed and breaches criminalized by the Sherman Act of 1890. Notwithstanding the exceptions that were ratified in later years, the organization of business in the United States thenceforth occurred within a different legal framework from that of Germany, where cartels were in principle allowed. American industry logically developed in the direction of oligopolistic competition. Although Germany also experienced before 1914 a concentration movement which led to ever larger enterprises, cartellization – which promoted the survival of smaller and weaker firms – generally led to increased prices. In fixing their prices, cartels had to calculate them on the basis of the profitability of their weakest members. Ultimately, the consumer therefore had to pay and the benefits of mass production were not passed on, as America's Henry Ford had begun to advocate. German industry developed into a well-organized, authoritarian producer capitalism.

Cartels probably slowed down the emergence of mass consumption in the *Kaiserreich*, but they did not prevent it. Just as in France, Britain, and the United States, department stores and nickel-and-dime stores began to proliferate, selling cheap mass-produced goods to a growing urban industrial working class. Still, although reliable figures are lacking, the impact of price reductions was so small that improvements in living standards could, in the face of inflation, only be reached by fighting for higher wages. The pursuit of an expansionary wage policy on the part of the workers and their organizations, the trade unions, was further stimulated by developments in the markets for agricultural produce. Price increases in this sector were not fueled by cartels but through high tariffs. After a lull in the 1890s, the tariff laws of 1902, which primarily affected cheap foreign grain imports, once again adversely affected the budgets of millions of low-income families. This in turn lent additional force to wage demands promoted by a working class that had meanwhile begun to organize.

B. The Development of Enterprise, Labor Conflicts

Today, when over 40 percent of all working men and women are employed in enterprises with over one thousand laborers and office employees, it is not easy to visualize the structure and organization of German industry during the early 1870s. Then the overwhelming majority worked in companies that had no more than five people (tables, 22-23, 25-26). This high percentage, which was primarily due to the continued importance of crafts in this period, declined to 40 percent by 1895 and to 30 percent by 1907. Meanwhile there was an increase in enterprises employing between eleven and one thousand men and women. In 1895 there were over 1.5 million artisans, of whom some 532,000 were self-employed and almost twice as many (983,000) employed in a workshop.

It is difficult to overestimate the consequences of this concentration movement in industry for the organization of work, for industrial relations, and for the general climate that developed in German industry. At a most basic level, there was a continuation of the patriarchal values which had defined the internal structure and the atmosphere in the workshops before the Industrial Revolution. In a small enterprise, it was still possible for the master and/or owner to have a knowledge of all aspects of the production process and to be in constant control. He held disciplinary powers and supervised sales and the keeping of the accounts. The advantage of this type of small-scale organization was that relations were more personal and that many masters and owners felt directly responsible for the welfare of their workers. Once an enterprise had one hundred or two hundred employees, a limit had often been reached at which it was impossible for the employer to maintain a patriarchal role. Work became more differentiated and divided, although it remained hierarchically organized. Still, there now developed several levels of command.

Hand in hand with this went a growing bureaucratization which Jürgen Kocka traced when he studied the expansion of Siemens, the electrical engineering firm. [38] Krupp and men like him tried to uphold the image of the ever-present entrepreneur; but even in Krupp's heavy industrial empire personal relations inexorably became more anonymous. By 1913, he had around 77,500 men and women on his payrolls. Siemens & Schuckert trebled its rolls between 1882 and 1907. Research and Development, stockpiling, production, sales, and financial control evolved into separate spheres. Specialized knowledge was required in all of them, thus promoting the rise of the expert. This resulted in a further differentiation which was particularly visible in the production sphere and was partly also related to the impact of mechanization. With the transition from workshop to factory, artisanal expertise was undermined by the use of machines. It was sufficient to have workers who were familiar with a few basic operations, and among whom many were women. They were supervised by a small number of skilled workers and foremen whose task was to secure uninterrupted production. And the more the technical expertise of the latter increased with the growing complexity of the production processes and the pressure to integrate the various elements into a well-functioning, efficient enterprise, the more they emerged as a separate category from the majority of the work force. Together with other highly qualified experts in Research and Development, marketing, sales, and finance, they became the new group of white-collar employees. By 1912, Siemens had some 12,502 of these, with 44,400 blue-collar laborers involved with the actual manufacturing of goods. The rise of the white-collar employee had important societal, political, and ideological consequences which will be dealt with later. [39]

The emergence of large enterprises also affected the role of women in the labor process. Women had been economically active before the advent of industrialization. They had made a major contribution to the peasant family economy and, during the period of proto-industrialization, to those scores of

38. J. Kocka, *Unternehmensverwaltung und Angestelltenschaft* (Stuttgart 1969).

39. See below pp. 123ff., 224ff..

families who turned to manufacturing in their cottages. The rise of the factory, which employed both men and women, triggered an important change (table 29). Until now women had enjoyed a considerable degree of economic equality with men. Industrial labor, however, resulted in a marked differentiation in pay between men and women. For the entrepreneurs this situation was not only profitable, but it also helped them to create jobs which required fewer skills than previously more tolerable to their major laborers since women were moved into a position even worse than their own. This is a partial explanation for why many men supported discrimination against women in the workplace. It must also be remembered that these men had grown up in the milieu of the patriarchal family where women had traditionally occupied an inferior social position. One consequence of this mechanism was that the promotion prospects of women also remained low. Thus, unless they became organized to voice their grievances, the factory system imposed on them the double burden of their class and their gender. Nor did women who worked in the offices beyond the production lines fare any better. The emergence of the differentiated large enterprise had led to the creation of many new positions in the sphere of sales, marketing, and accounting. But most women entered these offices as secretaries and assistants, and their promotion prospects in competition with men were similarly severely restricted. Their pay was also unequal, and they had to struggle against massive patriarchal prejudice on the part of their superiors.[40]

Whatever the structured inequalities and new hierarchies that were created in the wake of the rapid growth and more complex organizations of industry – and however much employers may have promoted the differentiations between blue-collar and white-collar employee, between male and female worker – employers also hoped to secure their domination and control of people and work processes. The earlier model of an "absolute monarchy" was increasingly replaced by the bureaucratic principle in which the orders came from a management board. But insofar as industry under the Hohenzollern monarchy tried to copy an organizational model, it was that of the Army and in particular of the Prussian General Staff. Entrepreneurs admired the Prusso-German Army for its clear lines of command and its legendary efficiency. And this happened at a time when industry and commerce were moving toward definitions of rationality and profitability that pertained to all aspects of a company's life. The relative popularity of the General Staff model was enhanced by the conservative influence of heavy industry, which

40. See below pp. 66ff.

was able to retain its ideological and political leadership position even after the economic rise of the industries of the second Industrial Revolution.

Hand in hand with organization and bureaucratization came stress on competency, loyalty, and reliability. These qualities were increasingly seen as no less important than the willingness to take risks and the demonstration of a brilliant business sense. Certainly, the stability of the work force became an major consideration in the management of human resources. With the upswing in the economy after 1895 there was increased competition for well-qualified people, and this also explains why loyalty and identification with the company became important. Employees who, instead of coming up through the ranks, moved in from the outside and then turned into ambitious climbers were viewed with suspicion. Careers were made by internal promotion and therefore people tended to advance slowly. It is also true that after the trauma of the long period of retarded growth, employees had a strong desire to gain job security. This attitude fostered a "civil service" mentality which neatly complemented the organizational aims of the employers. In the end, some white-collar employees were even called "civil servants" because, after a certain number of "service years" they could no longer be fired. Like public officials, they could only be transferred to other departments or be forced into early retirement.

It was in this atmosphere that new work rules flourished. To be sure, like the factory codes of the early phases of industrialization, they were designed to fix entrepreneurial rights and powers of control; yet they contained a number of new elements. Although in many cases milder versions of the disciplinary clauses for blue-collar workers remained in force, there were other clauses which specified entrepreneurial obligations and rights of the employees, an indication that a company constitutionalism began to develop. The emergence of such elements did not just grow from inside the company. There were also external influences. Thus 1891 saw the ratification of a Labor Protection Bill that obliged enterprises with more than twenty workers to introduce a labor code. Beyond the traditional catalogue of disciplinary penalties, these codes were supposed to contain regulations which specified the modes of wage payments, hours of work, and rest breaks for employees.

The Labor Protection Law even gave employees an opportunity to elect a workers' committee until a new code was introduced through which they could communicate their ideas to their employer. Considering that entrepreneurs continued stubbornly to refuse to enter into any kind of negotiations with their workers, the idea of transforming such committees into permanent bodies for the discussion of wage and welfare questions tended to make little headway before 1914. Although this was their declared *raison d'être*, trade unions were even less acceptable to employers as workers' representations. In the face of a widespread hostility toward unions, the recognition of workers' spokesmen progressed only slowly. By 1905 some type of active committee apparently existed in no more than 10 percent of all companies with over 20 workers. However, there were a few pioneers, like Daimler Cars. In this company a workers' committee was at least permitted to hear individual workers' complaints against a wage increase that the management wanted to impose. During the last year before World War I, trade unions in some companies even got involved in wage negotiations. Thus Bosch, the Stuttgart electrical engineering firm, began to deal with a workers' committee whose elected representatives were members of the German Metal Workers' Union (DMV). Such arrangements could not in all cases prevent the outbreak of strikes. However, like Bosch, other employers also saw the benefits of an official recognition of workers' organizations. The flow of production was less likely to be disrupted without warning. Compromises could be forged. Workers were more motivated and loyal when they felt that they were listened to. Some enterprises even proved too weak to resist pressure from their organized work force. If there had been no more than 51 negotiated wage agreements in 1891, by 1913 their number had increased to 10,885, covering 1.4 million workers in 143,000 enterprises (table 10). The rate of participation was particularly high in graphics (50.8 percent of the workers covered) and in construction (46.8 percent). In the chemical and textile industries, on the other hand, these percentages were as low as 4.3 and 1.9 percent respectively. Other companies that remained hostile to trade unions tried to organize their own works committees (*Werkvereine* – "Yellow Trade Unions"). With the huge rise in trade union membership, this movement did gain some momentum before 1914. It is no doubt a reflection of the growing polarization of pre-1914 industrial relations and politics that yellow unions were quite vigorously promoted by the employers. Polarization was also mirrored in the wave of strikes that hit German industry at this time (table 11). In these circumstances, employers saw it as one of their most important tasks to support the founding of docile works committees. In a few large companies in the shipbuilding, machine tool, and chemicals branches these committees had over one thousand members by the spring of 1914.

Whenever negotiations between employers and workers' representatives occurred during the upswing after 1895, it was not just the traditional topics of wages and working conditions that were put on the table, but also the question of rationalization. Toward the end of the nineteenth century a movement had gathered momentum, especially in the United States, that, connected with the name of Frederick Taylor, initiated a further stage in the process of systematizing and organizing production. These American ideas, which, for the period after the turn of the century, must also be related to Henry Ford's experiments with standardization and assembly-line production, came to be hotly debated in German industry. True, many German entrepreneurs did not think that the developments across the Atlantic, which were oriented toward mass production, were widely applicable in Europe. Nevertheless, some of them began to introduce "Taylorist" and "Fordist" methods.

These experiments required the cooperation of the workforce, and Bosch accordingly entered into discussions on these matters with the local branch of the Metal Workers' Union. In the long run the adoption of the "Bosch Tempo" in a company that had a reputation as a liberal employer introduced a further element of tension into labor relations there, and just before World War I the firm had a major strike over this matter on its hands. An interesting case is also presented by the experience of the Hamburg shipbuilding industry. Following a strike in 1900, it became clear how much control the DMV had been able to retain during the dispute. This led the employers to seek closer cooperation with the union in subsequent years. It was partly due to changes in ship-building technology and work organization that this accord was torn up by disaffected workers who staged spontaneous strikes and refused to follow the union's lead. Many employers watched these proceedings with a certain amount of glee. To them, the strikes confirmed their rejection of all attempts to institutionalize industrial conflict through cooperation with the unions. They continued to adhere to the time-honored practices of rigid control from above and of fighting unions tooth and nail. Toward 1914, as the situation in the *Kaiserreich* became more generally polarized, hostility toward unions, whose membership had by then reached over 2.4 million, was rising so rapidly that calls for a renewed proscription of the working-class movement became louder. Given the size of that movement, such a ban would have entailed considerable risks for law and order — the Reich government therefore refused to respond to the pressure from the employers. The growing importance of the unions, which should not be confused with a similar growth in power, is also reflected in the wave of strikes which reached a very high peak during the last years before the World War I.

After the lapse of the anti-Socialist laws in 1890, a number of major conflicts between workers and employers occurred during that decade. However, until the turn of the century their number and the number of workers involved in them remained relatively small. The Hamburg Dock Strike of 1896/97 was perhaps an exception to this rule, mobilizing at its peak more than 17,000 workers. There was a steep increase in conflicts in 1905-6; in 1906 alone, over 3,500 strikes and lockouts took place, involving around 350,000 workers. A second wave of strikes, which began in 1910, culminated in 1913 in a number of particularly large and bitter disputes. The high figure for lockouts indicates that the employers often took a hard line (table 11). Nevertheless, despite the steep rise in labor conflicts, there was also an increase in the number of disputes that ended peacefully. Moreover, Britain and France experienced an even higher number of strikes. Consequently Germany's international competitiveness was not undermined and, as the continued growth in production and productivity of those years showed, the economic effect of the strikes was less tangible than the employers claimed. The latter never tired of painting very gloomy pictures about the future of German industry and, indeed, the country as a whole, as it faced the allegedly lethal threat of Social Democracy. However, the successes of German industry and its changing organizational structures must also be seen in the context of the rise of applied science and technological innovation with which the following section is concerned.

C. Industrial Research and Applied Science

One of the most distinctive features of the Industrial Revolution was the development and application of the great technical inventions since the eighteenth century. The invention of the steam engine was probably the most important among them. Textile machinery also became ever more sophisticated and efficient. Gasoline and diesel engines were invented. The great breakthroughs in electrics, precision optics, and chemistry must be included in this picture of the rapid expansion of science and its application. By the late nineteenth century, the *Kaiserreich* held a leading position in an international process of research and innovation. Earlier on, German industry had participated in this process by importing machinery or engineers, mainly from Britain, or by copying innovations seen in visits to the industrial centers of western Europe. After the beginning of the twentieth century, as has just been noted, there was a growing interest in what the Americans were doing. However, the number of patents that were approved demonstrates, if nothing else, that German science and industry were increasingly making their own contribution to the process of technological innovation. In 1880, some 2,542 patents were registered for all sectors, including agriculture (among them 74 in electrics and 186 in chemicals). Twenty years later, this figure had risen to 6,449 (among them 590 in electrics and 940 in chemicals).

By 1913 the annual total was at 9,471 (among them 1,164 in electrics and 1,394 in chemicals).

Many of the patent applications came from individuals who experimented with their ideas in basements and garden sheds. But with the increasing organization and division of labor within rapidly expanding companies, Research and Development departments were added in which trained scientists developed the next generation of products. Earlier on, the example of Siemens had not been untypical where Werner Siemens, one of the pioneers of electrical engineering, with his co-workers at his side, worked in a small workshop trying to put his ideas to industrial use. As late as 1884 a "college-trained manufacturing engineer" at the firm of Ganz & Cie, "who had just introduced himself to the company's director, was caught and taken away by the head of the embryonic electro-technical department to become, within the nick of time, a successful electrical engineer." [41] In 1870, BASF, Hoechst, and Bayer had no more than ten university-trained chemists. Twenty years later there were 207 among a total work force of 123,000 (1.6 percent), and by 1910 the total was 651 among 240,000 employees (2.7 percent).

The rising demand for R & D personnel raised the question of training. Up to the 1880s, Siemens had a virtual monopoly in training people in electrical engineering. To the company this training amounted to a major investment. Its management therefore did not like to see its engineers, many of whom moreover had gained a deep insight into the secrets of the firm's research and organization, move over to the competition. In these circumstances it was fortunate that the state had become involved for some time not only in the schooling of the young, but also in their subsequent training. The advance of industry further reinforced the economic and political calculations which had driven the expansion of the school system and tertiary education. A state-of-the-art knowledge of the sciences was obviously indispensable in fields such as electrical engineering or chemistry. Only an academic institution could provide this knowledge.

A glance at government expenditure on the sciences and humanities demonstrates the importance that was attached to this notion. In Prussia, the largest German state, funding rose continuously and it shot up steeply after the turn of the century, when the Germans proudly began to claim a leading position (*Weltgeltung*) among the industrial nations. By 1914 annual expenditure had reached 50.1 million marks, up from 2.5 million marks in 1850

41. J. Kocka, *Unternehmensverwaltung* (note 38), 275.

(table 12). Prussia was surpassed by Baden and Saxony in its spending on these fields, both in terms of percentage of the total budget and per capita figures. The overall expenditure for schools and institutions of the tertiary sector in the Reich reached 1,378 billion marks in 1913, almost ten times what had been allocated in 1870. The percentage rise of the budgets for scientific research in the Reich and the federal states was even higher. Meanwhile a controversy had begun as to whether these funds should be invested into the development of the sciences at universities whose influence in the tertiary sector was dominant. But the universities were themselves hesitant. To some extent the older humanities faculties were responsible for this, since many of their members did not wish to share the budget with expensive sciences and also looked down upon their colleagues in chemistry or physics. They had an even stronger aversion to the applied sciences where research was turned into commercially usable technical products. This prejudice against "commercialism" in the academy was later extended to economics and business studies whose research results were expected to benefit industry and economic policy-making. In the end the applied sciences were completely rejected by the universities as "non-scientific." They established themselves in Polytechnical Schools that were later elevated to Technical High Schools (*Technische Hochschulen,* TH).

These institutions reacted to their hostile critics by emphasizing, next to a practical training, the importance of theory. Such concessions could not prevent the rift with the universities from widening. [42] The scientists and engineers working in industrial laboratories were among those who argued against this separation. Defining their work as a "cultural profession," they advanced the hypothesis that "a highly developed *Kulturstaat*" must "comprise *all* important cultural tasks" among which "the first role" belonged to technology. [43] Meanwhile the Technical High Schools and the Business Schools (*Handelshochschulen*) emerged as vital centers of training and research. Agronomy also firmly established itself and was taught at separate institutes. The German system of tertiary education was studied closely abroad and was seen by some as the key to the country's technical and economic achievements.

The first TH was opened in Munich in 1868, followed two years later by the TH Aachen. By the late 1870s several other Polytechnical Schools that

42. See below pp. 170ff.

43. Quoted in: F.R. Pfetsch, *Zur Entwicklung der Wissenschaftspolitik in Deutschland* (Berlin 1974), 140f.

had existed since the 1830s were elevated to the status of Technical High School. THs now existed at Dresden, Braunschweig, Darmstadt, Hanover, and Berlin. Karlsruhe and Stuttgart followed suit in 1885 and 1890 respectively. The fact that most THs were founded during a period of retarded economic growth has led to the argument that the incentive to improve the technological infrastructure is particularly great during hard times and that investments thus have an anticyclical effect. In any case, the THs were a resounding success. Around the turn of the century some 11,000 students were enrolled with them, compared with 33,000 in the universities (table 52). During the two decades following the founding of the German Empire public expenditures for tertiary education made up almost 60 percent of the total budget for education. This figure then dropped to an average of 54 percent and, just before World War I, to only 50 percent. At the same time the THs, relying on their newly won prestige, succeeded in increasing their budget share of 5 percent for 1850-1880 to 10 percent between 1880 and 1914. To these must be added the governmental support that went into science and applied science research in the private sector. By 1914 this sphere attracted some 11 percent of resources, if agronomy and related disciplines are included, even 19 percent. These percentages are all the more remarkable since little external money was available for research in the humanities and social sciences outside the universities. Nor should it be overlooked that the public purse in some cases provided no more than 20 percent of budget for the THs. In other words, these model institutions could not have survived without donations and funded projects from industry.

Just how far the promotion of science, which was economically motivated and devoted to application, had gone before 1914 may be gleaned from a comparison with expenditures for military research. In the early 1880s, these latter items still occupied first place, but fell back later. As far as the promotion of the applied sciences was concerned, the role of the state changed in another respect as well. The founding of the former Polytechnical Schools had been due almost exclusively to the initiative of politicians and higher civil servants who were motivated by what they believed to be the beneficial effects of these institutions on the economy and by what they had learned about French policies. In the second half of the nineteenth century, the government functioned less as an initiator, but responded to the demands of industry. Now the spokesmen of the latter became the dynamic element. This applies even more so to the development of Business Schools for the training of commercial experts. Thus the *Handelshochschule* at Cologne, founded in 1901, was the brainchild of Gustav von Mevissen an influential native industrialist, who had first conceived of the idea in 1879. In Frankfurt, the local chamber of commerce and the Polytechnical Society had a similar role in the opening of a business school there. In Berlin the local merchants were behind the establishment of such a school in 1906.

All these initiatives grew from the fertile soil provided by a number of private organizations, clubs, and academies which devoted themselves to the proliferation of scientific and technical knowledge. In this respect, too, the late nineteenth century saw a significant shift vis-à-vis the humanities. Soon there was barely a scientific or medical field (or a combination of both) which did not have its own regional or national association. The history of the *Physikalisch-Technische Reichsanstalt* (PTR) in Berlin shows how strong the interest of industry and commerce in applied research had become. [44] Werner Siemens had been the first to promote the idea when, in a memorandum, he directly linked scientific research with technical progress, industrial growth, and international technical leadership. Long negotiations with the government ensued, considerably changing the mission of the projected PTR. The original aim had been to improve the state of precision engineering with the financial help of the state. When the Institute was finally founded, its research brief was much broader, and by 1914 its ordinary budget, which had been 100,000 marks in 1887/88, had grown sevenfold.

The Kaiser Wilhelm Society had similar origins.[45] As chemistry began its meteoric rise, its prominent representatives, Professors Ernst Fischer, Wilhelm Ostwald and Walther Nernst, began to dream of a chemical research institute like the PTR. With the support of the chemical industry, they lobbied the Reich government to found such an institute. But with public finances rapidly deteriorating after the turn of the century, the plan was finally turned down in February 1906. If, the government replied, a chemical research institute was so important, the prosperous chemical industry might dip into its own pockets. At the end of 1907 the Secretary of the Reich Treasury still refused to make funds available for 1909 or 1910. At this point another solution was developed with the help of the famous theologian Adolf von Harnack, who had direct access to the Kaiser: the monarch would make a personal public appeal to send donations for a prospective Kaiser Wilhelm Society (KWG). It was under the roof of this society that a number of

44. *Ibid.*

45. R. Vierhaus and B. vom Brocke, Hg., *Forschung im Spannungsfeld von Politik und Gesellschaft* (Stuttgart 1988); J.A. Johnson, *The Kaiser's Chemists* (Chapel Hill 1990).

research institutes would then be created outside the university system, to be financed through the KWG. After much hemming and hawing, the necessary millions were finally collected and the society was officially founded in January 1911. Within this framework there later emerged an institute for chemistry, followed by institutes for biology, coal research, and work psychology. These were all supposed to conduct basic research as well as to develop applications in close cooperation with industry.

The infrastructure of tertiary education, which emerged ever so slowly and centered on the THs, research institutes, and scientific societies, was charged with the training of highly qualified people. These men would either continue their work within this framework or move into the R & D departments of the large industrial enterprises to turn inventions into new products. No doubt this system was important for the rise of Germany in the international economy. As competition in the world markets became more intense, both Britain and the United States began to study German tertiary education and research closely. [46] Conversely, as we have seen, German industrialists observed the activities of their counterparts, particularly in America. They expected that the major challenges would come from across the Atlantic and not from Britain, which they perceived as a declining power. This, after all, was an age when leadership in scientific knowledge was equated with power advantages in the global competition for markets.

---

46. G. Hollenberg, *Englisches Interesse am Kaiserreich* (Wiesbaden 1974).

Part II: Society

4. Demographic Structure and Development

A. Population Growth and Patterns of Migration

Population growth and urbanization are inseparably connected with the process of industrialization in central Europe. All three processes unfolded at an even more rapid pace after the founding of the *Kaiserreich* than before. According to the first census in the new Reich, taken in 1872, the total population at that time was a little over 40 million (table 34). This figure had grown to 56 million by the turn of the century. In 1913 the population was 67 million. If some 206,000 foreigners lived in Germany in 1871, their number had risen to around 1.3 million by 1910. Most of these immigrants came from eastern Europe (table 40). Germany also contained a fluctuating number of seasonal land laborers and an unknown number of illegal immigrants. We should also mention the approximately 3 million Germans who emigrated overseas between 1871 and 1911. Overall the population rose by 58 percent during those years.

The reasons for the demographic explosion are to some extent to be found in a noticeable increase in the average life expectancy and a decline in mortality. During the decade following the founding of the German Empire, life expectancy from birth was on average a mere 37 years (35.6 years for men and 38.5 years for women) (table 58). During the first decade of the twentieth century, these figures improved to an average of 44.8 years for men and 48.3 years for women. In 1910 the age structure had the shape of an almost perfect pyramid (table 55). Only 5 percent were over 65 years of age, whereas some 35 percent had not yet reached the age of 15. Meanwhile mortality rates began to decline. If, of 1,000 men and women born during the decade after the founding of the *Kaiserreich* no more than 297 women and 248 men could expect to reach the age of 65, the figures for those born in the decade 1901-1910 had improved to 435 and 361 respectively (table 59). While mortality rates among adults and children witnessed a tangible downturn throughout the period, mortality rates for infants (i.e., for babies under a year old) remained high for a long time and registered a marked decline only after the turn of the century (table 60). Indeed, the deterioration of the situation for infants which had occurred during the two decades before the creation of the German Empire continued for more than twenty years thereafter. It was only in 1885 that infant mortality declined to the level of 1850. Still, the improvements which the other age groups experienced saw to it that the surplus of births over deaths rose steadily to just under 15 per 1,000.

A baby boom hit the country in the 1870s, followed by two decades of relatively high birth rates. Although the birth rate began to decline after the turn of the century, it was still above the (also declining) mortality rate, thus securing a continued population growth. Put into figures, the growth rate was 1.22 percent during 1875, the first year of the early baby boom. It slowed down to under 1.00 percent during the economically pessimistic years of the 1880s, then rose again from the mid-1890s to between 1.31 and 1.5 percent. There was a sharp drop from 1.21 percent in 1912 to 0.65 percent a year later. This decline is probably less related to the political and economic difficulties of the immediate prewar period than to a more long-term trend toward lower birth rates which also affected other industrial countries. Finally, it is important to note that the number of live births per thousand inhabitants as well as of deaths per thousand inhabitants (discounting stillbirths) remained high. While the surplus had reached a peak of 14.8 per thousand between 1896 and 1900, from 1911 to 1913 it was still at 12.1 per thousand.

It is hardly surprising that the growth of the population was unevenly distributed between different regions (tables 34-35). In 1871 some 31 percent of all Germans had been living in the east, including Berlin and Brandenburg. By 1910, only 29.9 percent of Germans lived in the east. Southern Germany experienced an even sharper decline from 23.8 to 20.8 percent during the same period (table 41). Meanwhile central Germany registered a small increase in the percentage of Germans who lived there, with the most marked population growth occurring in the west. In 1910, 23.1 percent of all Germans lived there, up from 19.0 percent in 1871. The population increased in all regions, but if one takes a closer look at individual provinces in the east, it emerges that the growth rate was a mere 13.2 percent in East Prussia; but it reached 131.9 percent in Westphalia and 150.8 percent in Berlin. Among the urban areas with the highest growth rates were Chemnitz (268 percent), Cologne (282 percent), Dortmund (271 percent), Essen (438 percent), and Kiel (468 percent) (tables 36-37). The population of Dortmund grew fivefold between 1871 and 1910. The most staggering demographic explosion probably took place in the Ruhr town of Hamborn, whose population had been 4,260 in 1890 and was 101,703 twenty years later. The population density in inhabitants per square kilometer also increased everywhere. But whereas the growth in East Prussia was from 49 to 56, Westphalia's was from 88 to 204, and Saxony's from 171 to 321. All this meant that the population density for the Reich as a whole rose from 75 to 120 inhabitants per square kilometer.

Although the low figures for East Prussia and the large increases for Westphalia and the cities were to some extent the statistical reflections of the changes in the birth rate, another factor must be added to explain the often huge rises, i.e., the migration movements. These assumed such enormous proportions that in the end some 54 percent of the population no longer lived at their place of birth (table 42). Only a small number of these migrants went overseas; people who had been born in eastern Germany constituted the largest group, comprising 35 percent of the total. This and the fact that the wave of emigrants was particularly large between 1880 and 1893 indicate that economic and sociopolitical reasons may have been a prime factor, and it is interesting to consider what might have happened, at a time of retarded economic growth and rising fears of a revolutionary upheaval, if this valve through which some 1.8 million Germans were able to leave the country had not been available.[1] Most of these people left with their families. Only after 1890 was there an increase in the number of individuals between the ages of twenty-one and fifty who left without their families. The share of peasants and land laborers had been at a high 34 percent of those who left in 1870-74; it then dropped continuously to 20 percent in 1880-84 and 14 percent in 1890-92. Meanwhile the share of workers rose from 18 percent of the total in 1871-74 to 30 percent in 1880-84 and was still at 27 percent in 1890-92. Most emigrants who went overseas settled in North America, around 2 percent went to Brazil and 1.3 percent moved to Australia. There was a sharp decline after 1893 when the number of emigrants dropped below the 30,000 mark, after a peak of over 127,000 during the period 1880-1893.

The number of foreign migrant workers in Germany was well over 1 million before 1914. Among them Polish seasonal workers constituted the largest group with over 250,000 individuals. They were employed mainly during the summer to fill the manpower gaps that had arisen on the large estates in the east, only to be sent back in the winter. As has been previously mentioned, these practices, whose psychological impact on Russia was exacerbated by

1. K.J. Bade, *Population, Labour and Migration in 19th and 20th Century Germany* (Oxford 1987).

ruthless Germanization policies of the Prussian government and by tariff wars, contributed to strained relations with the Tsarist Empire.[(2)] Less insecure and unsteady were the lives of those Germans who migrated to urban centers from the immediate rural vicinity. At the beginning they constituted the largest section among the migrant population, although exact statistics are difficult to come by. However, it is fairly certain that many migrants – and women more often than men – tried to find factory work in one of the nearby cities. Some became daily commuters; others found accommodation in the town during the week and returned to their families on the weekends or during harvesttime. In the long run, however, those who migrated longer distances are more important to an understanding of the huge changes in the country's demographic structure. Only by taking these migrants into account can we explain why some eastern regions became depleted of people, while some cities had to cope with a population explosion. By 1907 no less than 55 percent of all internal migrants had moved to these cities. Almost everywhere, these migrants made up over 50 percent of the population, outnumbering those who had been born locally (table 42). Around 30 percent of the approximately nine million long-distance migrants lived in the forty-two cities of Germany at this time. In some of these places, especially in the Ruhr area, the newcomers formed colonies of their own which became known as "New Masuria" or "Little East Prussia". Around 60 percent of the long-distance migrants were unmarried men, so that by the turn of the century rural Prussia had come to have a surplus of women. But it also happened quite frequently that the whole family moved at a later date. Nor did many of the migrants from the east ever completely lose contact with their kin back "home".

Up until 1880, total demographic losses in the eastern provinces (East and West Prussia, Posen, Silesia, Pomerania, and Mecklenburg) amounted to just under 570,000 men and women. A decade later another 1.135 million had been subtracted from the total. By 1900, the population had decreased by another 1.7 million, and by the time of the 1907 census the 2 million mark had been reached (table 41). Losses were also considerable in a few limited areas in Hesse and Franconia as well as in the Black Forest and Lower Saxony. For many of those who found a first abode in one of the industrial cities, this was only the beginning of something like a nomadic existence. Although our knowledge of this aspect of life at that time is still very incomplete, further moves within the same city or from one city to another evidently became part of the lives of millions of men, women, and children. In economically hard

2. See below pp. 110ff., 232ff.

times, many workers and their families were forced to leave their accommodations, as they could no longer afford rising rents. For years many unmarried men and women lived without fixed address by being taken in as lodgers (*Schlafgänger*) with working-class families. During recessions, people left their homes because they had lost their jobs; during an economic upswing they packed their few belongings because they had heard that a firm in a neighboring city was paying higher wages. We will analyze in connection with our examination of housing conditions what this nomadic life meant for families and children.

B. Town and Country

The movement of millions of people from the rural to the industrial regions of Germany is also reflected by the changing size of the communities (table 36). In 1871 some 63.9 percent of the population still lived in communities of under 2,000. By 1890, this figure had declined to 53 percent and, by 1910, to 40 percent. At the other end of the scale, the share of towns with over 50,000 inhabitants rose from 8.9 percent in 1870 to 26.7 percent in 1910. At this time, cities with populations of over 100,000, whose share in the above category had been a mere 4.8 percent in 1870, now held 21.3 percent of the population. However impressive the growth of the big cities, the importance of the provincial towns must not be underestimated. In 1910, just under one-third of the German population still lived in such towns, and the population of purely rural regions still was around 21 million. Similarly the share of communities with 5,000 to 20,000 inhabitants increased between 1871 and 1910 from 11.2 to 14.1 percent. Daily life in these towns, which attracted at most small industrial enterprises, saw little change. As for larger towns, it seems best to differentiate between "old" and "new" communities; for although older settlements did not grow 'organically' in this age of hectic building, they at least had a clearly identifiable inner city. In the "new" towns the incorporation of surrounding settlements often prevented any systematic planning. Up until 1910, some 19 percent of the growth of the big cities was due to such incorporations. In comparison with 1850, the average area occupied by such cities had grown from 20.9 square kilometers to over 42 square kilometers sixty years later. Nor were the "new" towns melting pots of populations, even if they often displayed a greater social homogeneity than the "old" towns. Indeed, the towns' architecture mirrored the patterns of social stratification. Or one merely had to look at the dress of the local population to know which part of town one was in. [3] What the towns and cities of all categories had in

3. See below pp. 123ff.

common, though, was their "youthfulness". In 1890 the share of children under fifteen in towns of up to 20,000 inhabitants was highest at 345 per thousand. It was a high 292 per thousand in the cities. Meanwhile the number of inhabitants between the ages of fifteen and forty rose to 474 per thousand in the cities; in small towns, it was 417 per thousand. The proportions were reversed among those who were over sixty years of age (68 per thousand in small towns; 57 per thousand in cities).

Meanwhile the share of the elderly increased in the rural areas, which had lost the most people to migration. Whoever travelled in eastern Germany saw a countryside as it had always been: "Sandy flat soils, covered by much grain, barley, beetroot, and potatoes, just a few rural marginal industries like breweries, schnapps distilleries, sugar factories, a silo belonging to an estate or to an agricultural cooperative here and there, few towns, a few stately homes with their parks, surrounded by villages in traditional low-level architecture, all of them connected by gravel roads, or more rarely by cobblestone surfaces, lined by gnarled fruit trees." [4] The way in which these contrasts between town and country were ideologized during the Wilhelmine period, if not before, is one of the more fascinating chapters of German social and intellectual history. The rapid and uncontrolled expansion of the cities produced a critique of urbanism which was advanced not only by agrarian politicians, defending the values of rural life, but also by bourgeois intellectuals. On the other side of this debate there were those who defended the city as a cultural center and the source of the achievements of Western civilization and who could not conceive of a better form of communal living. Insofar as they admitted that there might be a dark side to urban life, they believed that this could be remedied through reforms. They founded movements devoted to the improvement of housing conditions. [5] The idea of generously spaced garden cities was born. Some reformers advocated suburban housing estates with allotments. There were also numerous proposals to improve the infrastructure: schools, hospitals, playgrounds, waterworks, electricity, sewage, mass transport.

Many of the urban reform associations were born from a fear of the growing industrial proletariat that would one day come out of their ghettoes and slums to turn the bourgeois world upside down. This was even more true of the growing movement which rejected urban living. To its members, cities were a cancer of vice, illness, degeneration, and the disintegration of traditional values. They saw asphalt jungles with high crime rates and the

4. M. Stürmer, *Das ruhelose Reich* (Berlin 1983), 68.

5. A. Berger-Thimme, *Wohnungsfrage und Sozialstaat* (Frankfurt 1976).

"subversive" activities of the "revolutionary" working-class movement. Fear of socialism mixed with anti-Semitism, antisecularism, illiberalism, anti-industrialism, and other resentments and formed a common front against the modern age. The city became the scapegoat for all existing evils. The panacea was not the reform of the city and its infrastructure, but the return of its inhabitants to the country. The rejection of the city was thus complemented by a romantic vision of rural life that was promoted with increasing aggressiveness toward 1914. The village community was a world in which healthy and self-reliant humans lived a happy life and in which tradition and the respect for custom still mattered. It was only from this solid base that the perceived social crisis could be tackled and salvation and renovation would come.

Since this ideology also involved a new appreciation of the "farming estate", it is not surprising that "*Agrarromantik und Großstadtfeindschaft*" [6] gained many adherents in the rural regions of pre-1914 Germany, while industrialization and urbanization continued inexorably. This theme was taken up not only by farmers' associations, but also by provincial poets and writers. Meanwhile the officer corps, worrying about the influx of possibly unreliable recruits who had been exposed to socialist ideas in the cities, began to support the argument that recruits from the countryside provided better "soldiers' material" in comparison with the emaciated young men from the industrial centers. [7] As the bourgeoisie was progressively also seized by a fear of the proletariat and the presumed power of its growing organizations, back-to-the-land ideas also took hold there. Theologians, social scientists, physicians, hygienists, anthropologists, social workers, and intellectuals soon filled the pages of the provincial press with their articles and recipes. They were picked up not merely by artisans and small-town professionals, but ultimately also by well-to-do burghers in the big cities, as they read in their morning papers about the disquieting events that had occurred in other parts of their city during the previous night. Clearly they lived in a period which produced not only a welcome industrial prosperity, but also alarming manifestations of decadence and crisis.

5. Social Stratification and Inequalities

A. Basic Issues

If the demographic explosion and the migration of millions of people during the period of all-pervasive industrialization tells us quite a lot about the

6. K. Bergmann, *Agrarromantik und Großstadtfeindschaft* (Meisenheim 1970).

7. See below pp. 257ff.

condition and the development of German society between 1871 and the outbreak of World War I, a look at social mobility will deepen our understanding. Like other complex societies, that of the *Kaiserreich* did not merely consist of 65 million atomized individuals. There were social groups that operated within a horizontal as well as vertical structure. The examination of wealth and income moreover provides a first indication that inequalities existed and that the situation of some groups in society was better simply because they possessed superior economic resources in comparison with others. [8] The question to be investigated here is whether social stratification was very finely layered or whether it is possible to recognize the emergence of larger blocs. Ultimately, we will have to find an answer to the question of whether German society came to assume the shape of a class society. By this we mean a society which is divided into numerically large groups whose members find themselves in a similar position as regards "the provision with goods, their exterior life situation, and their inner existential predicament" (Max Weber). Conversely, the members of such a group differentiate themselves from those of other groups that exist as identifiable blocs of privilege or underprivilege within a pyramid of social inequality. In short, the question is whether we can discover, beyond a differentiation by dozens of occupational groups, the formation of classes which were separated by recognizably bolder dividing lines.

The answer to this question, which is obviously vital to an understanding of how German society functioned, is sought here by way of a detour. The first step represents an inquiry into social mobility, i.e., the ways in which individuals and groups moved up and down the social pyramid. Changes in the occupational structure and in marriage patterns will be taken as yardsticks here. The results of historical research on mobility will then be complemented by an analysis of two other basic factors of human existence, i.e., health and housing. The detour will then be extended into an examination of gender, generations, religion, and minorities in prewar Germany, all of which are also relevant to an exploration of social inequality in that society. Only after this will we return to the question of how the basic character and structure of the society of the *Kaiserreich* might be most convincingly defined.

B. Social Mobility

Millions of men and women who lived in the Second Empire hoped to improve their economic and social situation through occupational mobility.

---

8. See above pp. 6ff.

The expansion of the economy, the growing differentiation and complexity of most spheres of life, and the inflation of the administrative apparatus resulted in a considerable quantitative growth of jobs and positions. As we have seen, white-collar employees emerged beside the blue-collar workers as industry and commerce slowly moved toward larger units of organization. [9] These employees ultimately grew by an annual average of almost 5 percent (table 22). By 1907 they made up some 6 percent of all those employed in industry. In the meantime, civil servants experienced an annual growth of 3 percent. In Prussia alone the number of middle-ranking civil servants grew from 40,000 in the middle of the nineteenth century to 250,000 in 1907. In 1876, some 13,700 physicians were practicing in Germany; by 1913, their number was 34,136. The number of Prussian officers quadrupled to over 20,000 between 1860 and 1907. The number of noncommissioned officers was 87,000 in 1905. The additional number of school teachers also outpaced the rapid expansion of the population, expanding their ranks by almost 43 percent in the two decades after 1891. In 1901, over 146,000 primary school teachers taught in the Reich. By 1911, their number had increased to 187,485 (table 44). During the previous year some 4,000 professors worked in the tertiary sector, thanks primarily to the expansion of the sciences and applied sciences. The artisans experienced a drop in self-employment between 1849 and 1895, which hints that downward mobility threatened this particular group. But new opportunities offered themselves to well-qualified employed craftsmen who were upwardly mobile. However, their road to higher income and status was not as wide as that for white-collar employees and civil servants.

This does not mean to say that all groups were fully open to recruitment "from below". Among white-collar professionals self-recruitment was high and acceptance of social climbers slow in coming (tables 45-47). In the Prussian province of Hanover, 33.6 percent of the attorneys had fathers who had likewise been in this profession. The fathers of the next 28.7 percent were higher civil servants or university-trained, and 13.3 percent of the Hanoverian attorneys were the sons of middle-ranking or lower civil servants. The majority of higher civil servants came from the upper classes. However, considerable differences between Prussia and the south German states developed in this respect. In Bavaria and Baden, for example, civil service recruitment from the middle class amounted to 29-35 percent between 1876 and 1918. Meanwhile access to the diplomatic service remained very restricted (table 48). The Hamburg shipping magnate Albert Ballin once

9. See above pp. 31ff.

called the German Foreign Office a "club" where entry depended on high birth. [10] Accordingly, close to 69 percent of the higher civil servants were noblemen. Self-recruitment was also the dominant pattern in the Army and the Navy. Officers in this category made up 34 percent of the Army in 1909, declining to 28 percent by 1913. [11] Also during the same year, some 37 percent of officer aspirants were sons of higher civil servants. The fathers of another 11 percent were large-scale landowners and the fathers of 15 percent were entrepreneurs. Among 550 Prussian and Württembergian generals who served between 1871 and 1914, 182 (33 percent) were of bourgeois background. 131 of them ultimately received a noble title. As for the Navy, an analysis of the crew of 1907 shows that a mere 22 (11 percent) came from an aristocratic background. Some 90 emerged from academic middle-class families. Another 52 had fathers who had been officers; 34 came from families with backgrounds in industry and commerce, and 10 originated from landowning or professional families. Among the teachers in higher education, 73 percent were upper middle or upper class between 1860 and 1889. This figure declined to 64 percent between 1890 and 1919.

The share of the upper bourgeoisie among entrepreneurs hovered around the 67-percent mark throughout this period. The rate of self-recruitment was around 50 percent. Among the 175 leaders of Westphalian heavy industry, 95 came from industrial families and 47 from "traditional" occupations (landowners, officers, civil servants, mining officials). The fathers of another 12 were in academic professions, and 10 were engineers or craftsmen. Dolores Augustine, who has studied the careers of 502 very wealthy businessmen, found that 76.7 per cent of them were not of noble birth. [12] Only some 36 came from the old nobility, whereas 14.7 percent had inherited their title. Between 1871 and 1918 a mere 7 businessmen had a title that could not be passed on. These figures obviously raise problems for the argument that this group became part of the upper class during the *Kaiserreich*.

The social origins of high school teachers and of doctors have been reconstructed on the basis of the composition of the student body training in the respective disciplines (table 46). Here recruitment from the upper strata was extensive, but in some regions the percentages of upwardly mobile middle-class students were equally high. As in the case of white-collar employees

10. Quoted in: L. Cecil, *Albert Ballin* (Princeton 1967), 123.

11. D. Bald, *Vom Kaiserheer zur Bundeswehr* (Frankfurt 1981), 21.

12. D.L. Augustine-Perez, "Very Wealthy Businessmen in Imperial Germany," in: *Journal of Social History*, 1988, 299-321.

and civil servants, members of the lower strata hardly ever "made it". Social climbers who had risen into the middle-ranking civil service and white-collar employment frequently came from the lower middle class, if the example of Euskirchen in the Rhineland is any guide. Among the sons of skilled workers from the Eßlingen area in Württemberg between 5 and 13 percent moved up into the civil service, while some 30 to 40 percent of them became craftsmen. Among primary school teachers, horizontal recruitment was apparently the dominant pattern and only in Baden did lower-class applicants find the door to this profession to be a bit more open (table 45).

Figures on high school graduates and college students offer an indirect guide to mobility rates. In 1873, some 27.1 percent of all high school graduates had moved directly into a career. Thereafter high school came to be seen more and more as a preparation for university. The number of graduates rose rapidly until 1914 by 159 per cent (table 52). The tertiary sector suddenly found itself inundated with students (table 52). Critics began to warn that an academic proletariat was being nurtured here. The effect of the discussions that ensued and the countermeasures that were taken was that the universities and THs largely remained institutions for the training of the elite (table 51). It was difficult enough for students of lower-class background to withstand the psychological, financial, and academic pressures of the high school system up to the *Abitur*, the exit examination. They encountered further obstacles if they decided to go to college, not the least of which were financial. State aid was more difficult to come by. In 1887-88 the number of recipients of scholarships had been 20 percent. By 1911, this figure had declined to around 10 percent. In short, the tertiary sector offered a few opportunities for more upwardly mobile students from the lower middle class, and virtually none for working-class children. Among the students at Bonn University between 1865 and 1914, some 19.2 percent had higher civil servants as their fathers and 8.3 percent of them were professionals (table 53). An additional 24.4 percent originated from the propertied middle class. On the other hand, 48.7 percent were sons of white-collar employees, artisans, farmers, and low-ranking officials. A mere 0.2 per cent came from lower-class backgrounds. In 1905, some 54.2 percent of the students in Baden had lower-middle class fathers. In Prussia this figure was as much as 60 percent in 1911-12. Such percentages should not be underestimated when it comes to assessing rates of mobility in Wilhelmine Germany. But it is equally important to note the very small share of lower class students. This is where barriers proved insurmountable for all but a few.

We will talk in a moment about other formal and informal obstacles – including social and political prejudices and the practice of giving retired noncommissioned officers preferential treatment in the lower civil service – that faced upwardly mobile people, especially those from the lower class. For the moment, however, we will investigate patterns of upward and downward mobility at the bottom of the social pyramid now that a better idea has been gained of movements higher up on the social scale. In this respect we are relatively well informed about a few industrial towns. Thus David Crew has followed the changes in occupational mobility among workers and employees in Bochum between 1880 and 1890 [13] (table 43). His statistics indicate that of those who had occupied unskilled and semiskilled jobs in 1880 some 87.1 percent still worked in the same category ten years later. A mere 6.9 percent had been able to climb to the position of skilled laborer or craftsman. Although immobility among skilled men was lower during the same period (78.8 percent), it would be mistaken to assume that they did better; for of the remaining 21.4 percent some 11.3 percent had been forced to move down the social scale. By the turn of the century the picture had improved somewhat for both unskilled/semiskilled and for skilled men. Among the former some 21 percent had now achieved skilled positions; among the latter, 23.6 percent had become white-collar workers. But these figures must be juxtaposed with the 15.5. percent of skilled workers who had moved down to a lower position.

Studies that have looked at the national picture have arrived at somewhat lower figures than Crew's. For reasons that will be discussed later, mobility among working-class women was even more stagnant, and their dispiriting experience must be included when we consider the basic character of German society. As far as social mobility was concerned, this was a society that was relatively immobile at the top and at the bottom. There was a good deal of upward mobility within the broad spectrum of the middle class. Even if intergenerational mobility is taken into account, workers rarely achieved more than the small step upward within the larger bracket of the working class. [14] What was left to them was horizontal mobility, the opportunity to move into other occupations in the hope of being able to improve their material situation in times when labor was scarce and companies were competing for hard-working personnel. Most unskilled laborers, including many women, did not even have this opportunity, so that only a special type of

13. D. Crew, *Bochum* (Frankfurt 1980), 87ff.

14. J. Mooser, *Arbeiterleben in Deutschland* (Frankfurt 1984), 118

upward mobility existed at the bottom of the pyramid, if the rural parts of Germany are included. In the context of the huge migrations to the cities it has already been mentioned that many land laborers from the east left their jobs in agriculture because they saw better prospects in industry but this was also done by short-distance migrants. For many, perhaps after a difficult initial period, the move brought benefits and in this sense the migratory phenomenon may perhaps also be discussed under the rubric of social mobility. It was a mobility that occurred within the lower class, but not much beyond it. We will examine in a moment what the virtual vertical immobility meant for the "exterior life situation and the inner existential predicament" of the industrial working class, male and female. [15]

C. Marriage Patterns

The continuing importance of the link between town and country, which commuters and short-distance migrants in particular never severed, is also reflected in what has been called connubial mobility. Like occupational mobility, marriage patterns provide a deep insight into the degrees of openness of a particular society, especially at the upper and the lower end of the social pyramid. The hour of truth has arrived whenever a daughter of "good" family background wants to marry the upstart. Unfortunately we are much less informed about questions of connubial mobility than we are about occupational mobility. Reliable figures exist about the number of married people as a percentage of the total population. In 1871 some 51 percent of all Germans over the age of fifteen were married. By 1910 the figure had risen to 54 percent.

There are a few disparate statistics relating to marriage patterns among the lower strata in the regions of Bielefeld in Westphalia and Eßlingen in Württemberg. The figures for the latter town indicate relative openness. Two-thirds of the local textile and metal workers there married daughters of craftsmen, and a smaller number married the daughters of peasants. In many cases occupational mobility went hand in hand with connubial mobility. In Bielefeld, on the other hand, no more than 4 percent of the unskilled laborers and 9 percent of the skilled men succeeded in marrying into artisanal families. Somewhat higher was the share of unskilled and skilled workers who married a peasant woman. These figures must be compared with those 48 percent of the unskilled laborers and 27 percent of the skilled men who married into land laborers' families. Equally high (48 percent) was the share

15. See below pp. 57ff.

of skilled workers in Bielefeld who married working-class women. Among the unskilled, the figure was 35 percent. As far as the latter group is concerned this share nearly doubled by 1910, while it rose to 59 percent among the skilled men. In the meantime marriages with daughters of land laborers declined to 18 percent among the unskilled laborers and to 11 percent among the skilled ones. Around the turn of the century, some 80 percent of the industrial workers in Chemnitz in Saxony married their female counterparts, and another 7 percent married local domestic servants. All these figures seem to indicate that, even taking account of the many variations in these patterns, industrial workers increasingly married among themselves.

Whereas statistics on connubial mobility for the lower middle class and middle class of this time remain scarce to this day, there are data on very wealthy businessmen. Over 50 percent of their wives were daughters of other businessmen and a further third came from very wealthy entrepreneurial families. Around 10 percent originated from the upper middle class groups of higher civil servants and professionals. Marriage links with noble families were rare. Although there are signs that mobility through marriage was more frequent than it was in the lower classes, horizontal patterns predominated. Even if the desire to marry upward was strong, parental pressure and the well-known argument that the prospective husband would not "fit into the family" led to the cancellation of many wedding plans. Conversely, fewer barriers presumably existed against a daughter-in-law who did not quite come from the "right" social background. The danger of "mismatches", whether on the male or the female side, was, of course, often avoided because parents saw to it that the social life of eligible children took place in the proper circles.

This maxim was even more valid at the top of the social pyramid which in monarchical Germany was occupied by the nobility and the courts of the federal states. Here being of equal birth was actually a "juridical category" and not just a social requirement, and as such it had an "extraordinary influence upon the objective social position and the social self-image", especially of the ruling houses and the high nobility. [16] To be sure, their family laws were quite varied and in most cases open to marriage links with the lesser nobility. Exceptions were even possible in the case of marriages with women of bourgeois background, and such exceptions included elevation to the nobility. The lesser nobility was not so strict regarding equal birth as a *sine qua non*. In these circles connubial mobility was more likely to encounter social,

16. H. Gollwitzer, *Die Standesherren* (Göttingen 1964), 263.

rather than legal obstacles. Thus the ancient nobility felt superior to the new nobility or, even more so, to members of the upper bourgeoisie who had been ennobled. On the other hand, this hauteur was not so powerful as to prevent "social linkages or even the blending of aristocratic groups with parts of the upper bourgeoisie". [17] Thus it happened time and again that close family alliances were forged among the upper strata, giving the nobility access to bourgeois wealth and, in turn, providing the upper bourgeoisie with the prestige of having become part of the "first estate". Still, the important point is that such marriage links remained the exception. Marriage "into non-noble circles was generally regarded with displeasure, unless they were represented by non-noble or recently ennobled higher civil service families, and, depending on the status of the bride, it could mean the end of an officer's career." [18] If it was a marriage for the money of a non-noble heiress, such a match was "excused after the raising of many eyebrows." No such excuses were accepted if an officer wanted to marry into a Jewish family. And so it was in the end that only "a relatively small stratum of the upper bourgeoisie" fostered its relations with "parts of the nobility."

D. Life Expectancy and Health

In connection with the question of population growth in the *Kaiserreich* it has already been noted that mortality rates declined noticeably after the turn of the century. The birth rate also declined, but not as dramatically as the mortality rate, so that the population continued to grow. So far only averages have been mentioned. We must now ask about the health of different social groups and about inequalities in the face of illness and death. Infant mortality (i.e., deaths within the first twelve months) provides particularly telling illustrations that the averages veiled considerable inequalities (table 61). Various fluctuations notwithstanding, until the turn of the century this rate was over 30 percent among the often illegitimate babies of domestic servants. It was 22 to 24 percent among unskilled workers and 14 to 17 percent among the self-employed, white-collar employees, and civil servants. Disregarding a brief increase in 1911, infant mortality declined tangibly and across the board after 1900. Yet chances of survival within the first twelve months for a baby born to a civil service family remained three times higher than for a child of a domestic ser-

17. J. Kocka, "Bürgertum und bürgerliche Gesellschaft im 19. Jahrhundert," in: idem, ed., *Bürgertum und bürgerliche Gesellschaft im 19. Jahrhundert,* vol. 1 (Munich 1988), 65.

18. W.E. Mosse, "Adel und Bürgertum im Europa des 19. Jahrhunderts," in: J. Kocka, ed., *Bürgertum* (note 17), vol. 2, 289, also for the following quotations.

vant and twice as high as for the infant of an unskilled laborer. The rates were also lower for skilled workers so that a dividing line arose which, for once, put the latter into a category closer to the middle class.

It was due to these developments that average mortality rates decreased between 1876 and 1913 by 7.7 percent for men and 6.2 percent for women. If these averages are broken down by age and region, it becomes clear that Prussian city-dwellers between the ages of ten and fifteen, as well as their twenty-to-twenty-five-year-old counterparts, remained below the average (table 60). However, for Prussian city-dwellers over the age of thirty, the rate declined more slowly than the average for the whole of that state. This has led Reinhard Spree to assume that the latter groups had begun to suffer from a higher incidence of illness, a weaker immune system, and more generally from getting worn out by long hours of hard work, all of which reduced their life expectancy. [19] Since many of them were prone to fall ill with particular diseases and in some cases even to die from them, it appears that it was not just the life chances of infants that depended on position in the social pyramid. Men and women over thirty who worked in the industrial centers of Prussia were similarly subject to this rule. The spread of tuberculosis (TB) is the most striking example of this.

According to rough estimates, 600,000 to one million Germans suffered from TB of the lungs before World War I. In many cases the illness was fatal. Reich statistics show that in 1887 some 44 percent of all deaths were due to nine types of diseases, among which the share of TB was 14 percent. Another 11 percent died from acute infections of the respiratory tract, while 9 percent died of diseases to the digestive tract. By 1904, 37 percent of Germans died of these diseases, an increase of 3 percent. In 1913 the share of TB and other fatal diseases of the respiratory tract stood at 33 percent. More importantly, that these were diseases of the industrial lower classes is demonstrated by the fact that the death rate was higher in the cities than in rural areas, and that white-collar employees, civil servants, and self-employed individuals were less affected by them than unskilled workers were. Successes in the treatment of TB which were achieved before 1914 did little to change the ratios. True, by 1913 the number of patients had risen to 50,000 and the amount spent on their treatment had reached 16 to 18 million marks. But those who participated in these programs comprised at most a mere 8 percent of all those who should have been treated, and the most needy were presumably among the other 92 percent.

---

19. R. Spree, *Health and Social Class in Imperial Germany* (Oxford 1988), 39.

Furthermore it would be a mistake to deduce that once TB could be successfully treated, the decline in the overall mortality rate was the result of more knowledgeable doctors and improved healthcare. Although, disregarding wide regional discrepancies, the share of physicians per 100,000 population increased from 35 in 1885 to 51 in 1913, and although the number of hospital beds grew by 250 percent (tables 60-70), it is widely accepted today that the decline in mortality was more decisively influenced by non-medical factors. Among them were changes in nutritional standards and housing conditions. However, these factors too were related to the system of social stratification and, as in the case of health, illness, and death, they must be studied to gain an understanding of prevalent patterns of social inequality in the *Kaiserreich*.

E. Nutrition

As has been shown on the basis of statistics for the eastern provinces of Prussia, there exists a fairly close connection between life expectancy, health, and proper nutrition. [20] Thanks to the general rise in real incomes and living standards in Imperial Germany, many more families could begin to think of better eating and drinking. But again, given the large income differentials, not all Germans were equally well nourished. The improvement of the transport system, had – as we have seen – resulted in a greater availability of fresh fruit and vegetables in the urban centers. But such produce was expensive and so was meat and many imported foods (*Kolonialwaren*). Only the more prosperous and wealthy strata could actually afford these goods on a regular basis. To be sure, if the per capita consumption of meat grew from an annual 25 kilograms to 51 kilograms between 1870 and 1910 and that of sugar from 6 kilograms to 18 kilograms, the lower classes, too, had a share in these increases (table 20). And yet, the differences in food consumption between them and the middle and upper classes were very tangible.

This means that for many working-class households the greatest nutritional improvement was putting enough food on the dinner table. The decline in the number of children also exerted a favorable influence. Civil servants and white-collar employees had begun to limit the size of the family to an average of three children even before 1905 (table 64). At this time the averages in agriculture and mining, for example, were still as high as five children. But lower-class persons who married in 1910 had an average of at least one child less than their counterparts who had married ten years before. In the meantime civil servants and white-collar employees had limited the number of their children to an average of a little over two. Higher real wages and smaller

20. R.A. Dickler cited = *Ibid.*, 147.

families certainly helped to create a situation where, as had often been the case before, the wife no longer had to eat the scraps after she had just about managed to supply enough food for her husband and their children. Enough food usually meant large quantities. Working-class meals were also rich in calories and this was rarely the healthiest kind of nutrition. At a time when the workday was still ten to twelve hours, six days a week (table 15), meals frequently contained animal fats, but few vitamins and minerals. Thus up to 90 percent of the energy intake in lower-class families consisted of potatoes, bread, pastries, and animal fats.

Walther Hoffmann's calculations provide a rough guide to the development of food consumption in Germany.[21] Up until 1874 the average intake of calories was around 90 percent of the daily requirement. Between 1875 and 1879 the German population reached the 100-percent level. There was a renewed drop to 95 percent during the 1880s, but from the 1890s onward the daily intake finally surpassed the requirement for good, at least until World War I. Indeed, just before 1914 it was close to the 120-percent mark. A focus on the consumption of specific food items provides another indication of the general improvement in nutritional standards. Thus it appears that fewer potatoes and more sugar were consumed. Wheat consumption increased, while rye consumption stagnated. Meat, though primarily reserved for the wealthier strata, increasingly also appeared on the tables of the lower classes. The per capita consumption of pork quadrupled between 1850 and 1910, constituting 60 percent of meat consumption, if sausages are included. It is probable that working-class families had meat once or twice per week, but it was rarely the more expensive parts. The consumption of cabbage and root vegetables also saw an increase, and by 1914 some 1 million units of canned food were produced in some thirty-two factories in the Reich. Fresh fruit remained a luxury for the lower classes, although the acreage for growing it doubled between 1878 and 1898.

If consumption of these items fluctuated, it was not only because of varying harvest levels and prices, but also because of developments in income and in the labor markets. As we have seen, periods of increased unemployment and temporary work continued after the "Great Depression", and they usually hit the lower classes hardest. As late as 1907, some 80 percent of the private consumption of a working-class household was taken up by necessities (food, clothing, rent, and heating). The remaining 20 percent was divided

21. W.G. Hoffmann, *Das Wachstum der deutschen Wirtschaft seit der Mitte des 19. Jahrhun derts* (Berlin 1965), 659.

between purchases of household goods (6.1 percent), personal hygiene (2.8 percent), education and entertainment (5.9 percent), and miscellaneous expenditure (2.0 percent). The percentages which J.S. Roberts has calculated largely tally with these figures, but his research is additionally interesting for its comparisons with the household budgets of civil servants and teachers [22] (table 67). Thus the 522 working-class families of his sample spent 80.6 percent of their annual income on food, clothing, rent, and heating, leaving 19.4 percent for the rest. By contrast, the respective averages for his 218 middle-class families were 72 percent and 28 percent. This meant that working-class families had little room for manoeuvre, if struck by serious illness or unemployment. Inevitably, nutritional standards also suffered in such times of crisis. This is when belts were tightened, often at the expense of the health of the family and of the mother in particular, who would in most cases come last.

A seemingly contradictory connection between infant mortality and breast-feeding habits demonstrates, however, how difficult it is to make a straight link between life expectancy and nutrition. According to the statistics, mortality rates for infants who were not breast-fed by their mothers increased by 300 percent. At first glance, this nutritional factor might explain the above-mentioned high mortality rates for lower-class children (table 61). The complicating factor is that working-class children were apparently more frequently breast-fed than infants in the upper strata (table 63). The survival chances of the upper-class babies were increased by the better general care and attention they received, though not by as much as they might have been had they been breast-fed. In other words, upper-class infants became victims of deeply ingrained cultural traditions, so that infant mortality rates here moved against the general trend and remained higher because of an ignorance about the benefits of breast-feeding. Conversely, cultural traditions in this case inadvertently worked to the advantage of lower-class infants. Once the benefits of breast-feeding had been advertised more widely, the rates for upper-class infants began to decline more steeply. What is not included in the undoubtedly welcome discovery of the benefits of breast-feeding is the question of its effect on the health of lower-class mothers. It may be surmised that, if their health was often poor, this was not just because of more frequent pregnancies and of letting others eat first at dinnertime, but also because breast-feeding was a drain on their bodies.

---

22. J.S. Roberts, "Drink and Working Class Living Standards in Late 19th Century Germany," in: W. Conze and U. Engelhardt, eds., *Arbeiterexistenzen im 19. Jahrhundert* (Stuttgart 1981), 79.

F. Housing

However useful changes in the nutritional standards of the German population may be for gauging social inequalities, the study of housing patterns is no less instructive. Here, too, the question arises of what were the dividing lines that may tell us something about the basic principles along which the *Kaiserreich* was organized.

The huge population movement from the countryside into the towns and cities confronted local governments and the construction industry with unprecedented problems. [23] Two of these problems were the supply of water and the building of sewage systems. Improved knowledge of the causes of epidemic diseases like cholera and typhus increased pressures on town planning departments to improve their infrastructure. The massive outbreak of cholera in Hamburg in 1892 had once more underscored the importance of a modern infrastructure. Accordingly, much was already being done. In 1895, around 87 percent of all towns over 10,000 inhabitants had a central water supply (table 66). For small towns (5,000 to 10,000 inhabitants) the figure was 62 percent, with communities of 2,000 to 5,000 inhabitants trailing far behind at 38 percent. The 1890s also saw a considerable rise in the number of waterworks, although around 1900 only 52 percent of all towns were connected to this type of water supply. The regional differences are even more striking. The non-Prussian states made remarkable strides; meanwhile some 60 percent of the population continued to depend on tanks and pumps in the largest federal state.

With regard to sewage systems, most towns did develop active building programs before 1914. Nevertheless, barely more than 66.5 percent of the Prussian population living in communities of over 2,000 was linked to such a system. As in the case of water supply, city dwellers were largely better provided for than the rest of the country. These facts mirrored inequalities which affected different strata in the same way and which cannot easily be subdivided. It is a different matter when we examine the proliferation of flush toilets. Certainly with regard to Berlin, about which we have the best information, it is possible to make a strong connection between the quality of housing in different parts of the city, the number of toilets, and mortality rates (although the latter, as has been noted, depended also on other factors). Since there was also a high correlation between districts with a large number of inhabitants per heatable room and those with a large number of communal toilets halfway down the stairwell of an apartment bloc, the question of residential culture is also raised.

---

23. See below pp. 244ff.

The size of a family's accommodations was closely connected with its overall purchasing power. In agriculture no major changes occurred in this respect. The estate owners continued to live in their often impressive homes, many of which had been built or extended in better times. Those among them who were not satisfied with their seclusion in the countryside, who preferred the alternative of an urban life-style and perhaps even had contacts at the court of their state, would, if they could afford it, acquire a town residence. Peasants lived in a wide variety of houses ranging from the spacious and well-equipped *Gutshaus* to the hovel, which had only one room. Many of these hovels did not even contain the most basic household goods. Wealthier peasants, on the other hand, took pride in taking the homes of their noble neighbors or the interior styles of town residences as their model when it came to furniture and draperies. In many farmhouses in Central Europe, whether large or small, animals lived under the same roof. If the family could afford servants, they would be put up in small rooms next to or above the stables.

As for urban dwelling, it has already been mentioned in connection with the question of wealth and income that many prosperous burghers built their ostentatious villas in the suburbs of the large cities. Closer to the center of cities, *Mietspaläste* ("rental palaces") were built, offering prestige accommodation for members of the upper bourgeoisie, professors, and higher civil servants who could not, or did not want to, buy property. These apartments had salons, dining rooms and libraries. Bedrooms and rooms for the children and domestic servants would be at the end of long corridors. Balconies and staircases were also lavishly laid out. Of course, owning one's own home was an aim that an increasing number was able to realize for themselves. But for millions of others it remained but a fancy dream. From the residential "palaces" downward many types of apartments could be found. At the bottom of the scale ranked those tiny one- or two-room spaces into which the *Mietskasernen* ("rental barracks"), as they were called, were divided. These houses had narrow stairwells and dark backyards. In 1871 there existed in Berlin close to 14,500 of such blocks, half of which had one to ten separate apartments; a similar number had between eleven and fifty. Forty-nine blocks contained between fifty-one and one hundred apartments. In 1895, about 53 percent of Munich's working-class families lived in accommodations that had one room, in some cases with an additional kitchen or chamber (table 65). But the occupancy of two rooms did not necessarily mean that conditions were less cramped. As we have seen, working-class families had on average more children than those of civil servants and white-collar employees. Worse, in order to be able to pay rents which rising demand for housing in the wake of the migration to the cities had pushed sky-high, between 10 and 20 per cent of working-class families took in lodgers to help pay for the apartment (table 68). According to a survey conducted in Berlin in 1880, some 39,298 households (15.3 percent) had overnight lodgers (*Schlafgänger*), while another 18,318 (7.1 percent) had full-time lodgers (*Einmieter*). Some 8,000 households offered a bed either to two male overnight lodgers or to a male and a female one. A few cases have been reported in which the number of *Schlafgänger* totalled ten or even thirty-four people. It is not too difficult to visualize what this meant for the day-to-day life of a family, for marital relations, or for the upbringing of the children. Such apartments were also hotbeds for infectious diseases. Nor should the effects on the life of the lodgers be ignored. In 1893, some 25 percent of the Ruhr miners lived as *Schlafgänger* and many of them were lucky to share the bed, after a long workday, with no more than one other person. And if the rent which these men and women paid became too small to cover the family's weekly dues, the search for cheaper accommodation began. Again it was presumably the working wives, the children, the chronically sick, and the elderly who suffered most from such conditions.

For economic and social reasons, but also for political ones, some employers started to build company housing. Krupp was one of the pioneers of this idea, and he also knew how to hold "his" workers to loyalty and a puritanical lifestyle with the help of strict rules. Other firms copied his model. By 1914 the Ruhr mining companies had a total of some 82,000 company-owned apartments, whose rents were often one-third of the going rate on the free market, and sometimes even less. Finally there emerged another type of lower-class accommodation, the workers' colony – estates built on the fringes of the Ruhr cities or in the rural spaces between them. These colonies multiplied quickly, especially in the northern parts of the Ruhr district, housing in some cases over 50 percent of the work force of a particular mine. Compared with the overcrowded "rental barracks" of the big cities, the colonies, despite the strict rules imposed by the owners, had many obvious advantages. The housing units were smaller; the individual apartments a bit more spacious. The backyard was large enough for the growing of vegetables. There was usually a sports field at the center of the housing complex. At the same time – as has been convincingly argued – [24] these settlements

24. F. Brüggemeier and L. Niethammer, "Lodgers, Schnapps-Casinos and Working-Class Colonies in a Heavy-Industrial Region," in: G.G. Iggers, ed., *The Social History of Politics* (Leamington Spa 1985), 257f.

promoted the opposite of what their industrial owners had envisaged. They created a strong sense of a common fate among the inhabitants. There emerged a cultural infrastructure and a milieu which was important for the formation of a working class. This does not imply that the feelings of solidarity which were forged by the conditions in the "rental barracks" of the cities were any less significant in promoting a sense of cohesiveness between a group of people who had discovered how much they had in common with their neighbors not just with respect to their exterior life situation, but also in terms of their inner existential predicament. Certainly the city was not a melting pot of all the different social groups that settled in them.

If one surveys the material that has been presented so far, one is certainly struck by the variety of social life and life-styles that could be found in Imperial Germany. Here we have millions of men, women, and children who were differentiated not only by divergent backgrounds, talents, occupations, socioeconomic situations, cultural tastes, and opportunities for development, but also by divergent hopes and expectations. And yet these inequalities are marked in crucial places by common features. Inequality existed in the workplace and without. We have noted this by looking at occupational and connubial mobility. As has been seen, it also made a difference with regard to health and life expectancy whether a child was born into a lower-class family or one headed by a civil servant. The same held true of nutrition and housing. There were also uniformities that sharpened the dividing lines between the social strata. In most cases, social groups who in a cumulative way experienced similar life conditions found themselves thrown together. However, before we address the question of whether these structures were those of an industrial class society and whether the class character of German society prior to 1914 became its most basic criterion in the face of which all other inequalities became secondary, it is necessary to turn to other areas of social inequality.

6. Women and Men

For a long time research into patterns of social inequality during the *Kaiserreich* focused on the broad spectrum of social strata. More recently, the discussion has been broadened and considerably enriched by the expansion of the history of gender and the family. The history of classes was primarily concerned with reconstructing the situation of millions of men and women at the lower end of the social scale. Women's history, by contrast, is interested in the situation of no less than half the population, and increasingly also in the interaction between the two sexes in all spheres of life. Some of the handicaps from which women suffered have already been mentioned in our examination of inequalities in the workplace and of income. [25] If women were more poorly paid than men, what then was their situation in an increasingly industrial society in which place of work and residence had become separated more sharply than had been the case in agrarian societies?

The overall employment rate for women hovered around the 30 percent mark between 1882 and 1907. Put in absolute terms, in 1882 there were 7.79 million working women out of a total of 23 million. By 1907 this figure had risen to 9.74 million out of 31.26 million. The employment structure underwent similar changes during this period (tables 29-31). In 1882 "helping family members", most of whom were female, amounted to 40.7 percent. Some 15.5 percent of the agricultural laborers were women. By 1907 these shares had declined to 35.2 and 14.5 percent respectively, following a general trend toward work in industry. The share of domestic servants also declined. Meanwhile the rates for women working in industry rose from 17.9 percent in 1882 to 18.3 percent in 1907. It must be added that the statistics for "helping family members", most of whom were in small-scale agriculture, crafts, and domestic industry, are rather incomplete. This type of female labor was particularly widespread in southern and southwestern Germany.

In industry, the share of women in textiles and clothing was especially high, although it declined toward 1914. The home-based textile industries met with a similar fate. Food, including breweries and sugar manufacturing, was the third-largest industrial employer in 1907, and in this sector women made up 24.7 percent of the labor force – a quadrupling since 1882. Women were least common in the metal industries and in machine tools. In 1907 a mere 3.3 percent and 2.0 percent respectively of all women laborers worked here. In relation to the male work force the shares in these industries were 6.3 percent and 4.8 percent respectively. Only in cities like Duisburg and Dortmund in the Ruhr area were these percentages a little higher. Regional differences in female industrial labor can also be discerned. In the Saxon textile town of Plauen, nearly half the work force was female. In cities like Barmen, Krefeld, and Elberfeld it was at least a quarter or more. Women also shifted away from textiles toward electrical engineering, a new and thriving branch whose rationalization policies resulted in a growing demand for unskilled and semiskilled women.

A marked rise finally occurred in the tertiary sector (table 29). The expansion of consumption increased the demand for shop assistants. While many

25. See above pp. 9ff.

smaller shops could rarely afford more than one employee, the emergence of the department store created jobs in much larger numbers. As has been mentioned, the rise of the white-collar employee was accompanied by a growth in "white blouse" occupations. In the proliferating public services women found employment as secretaries and receptionists. In 1882 no more than 7.7 percent of all working women were involved in the tertiary sector. By 1907 the share had increased to 14.6 percent.

Reference must finally be made to a relatively small group of women who, unlike most of the female laborers discussed so far, as a rule did not come from lower class backgrounds. Before 1914 there were very few female doctors, lawyers, or academics in Germany, since the required professional training for a long time remained closed to them. But a start was made when opportunities to attend high school and to obtain the *Abitur* were expanded. At the time of the founding of the *Kaiserreich* most girls, whose parents wanted to give them a better education beyond the primary level, went to private schools. In 1872 there were also some 165 high schools for girls, which were supported by the state or by local government and in which instruction was mostly in German, French, mathematics, needlework, and religion. The range of subjects offered was based on the assumption that the task was to equip these girls, most of whom were of bourgeois or upper-class background, to become better future mothers, not to train them for professional careers.

Consequently most girls left these schools without the certificate that institutions of advanced learning required. Only a few institutes were specifically geared to prepare their pupils for the *Abitur*, the state-supervised final examination. Individual teachers, like Helene Lange, made a stronger academic orientation of the curriculum their concern. Because of this, a growing number of women succeeded after 1890 in passing the necessary examinations. After this breakthrough, the universities had a much harder time upholding their traditional refusal to admit women. However, their policies were marked from the start by contradictions and a lack of uniformity which made the exclusion of women appear evermore absurd. First there was the tug-of-war over the admission of women as auditors. Saxony and Bavaria had granted this privilege even before the founding of the German Empire. Prussia did not follow suit until the 1890s, and even thereafter admission rules varied considerably from university to university. The admission figures showed that interest in academic study was by now considerable (table 54). In 1896/97 some 223 female auditors were registered in Prussia; nine years later the figure had increased to 1,669. Meanwhile, some southern states had continued to handle admission in a liberal fashion and began to experiment with the idea of allowing women to enroll as full-time students. This in turn exerted pressure on Prussia to abandon its restrictive practices. When the last barriers finally fell in 1909, the number of female students rose quickly. Just before World War I, some 7.44 percent of the Prussian student body was female. The Reich total was 4.8 percent. A mere 7.1 percent of the female students were Catholic, whereas the share of Jewish women studying was more than twice that figure.

These developments were accompanied, almost inevitably, by the question of whether women could take university examinations and to which subjects they should be admitted. This in turn unleashed a debate on whether they were actually capable of scholarly inquiry. Not a few scientists, lawyers, and medical professors openly expressed their doubts about this. Paul Möbius even went so far as to publish a pamphlet in 1900, in which he discussed the alleged "physiological feeblemindedness of women". But for others, as well, no argument was too primitive to be launched against the onslaught of female high school graduates who wanted to go to university. It made little difference that a few foreign women had successfully passed their examinations as early as the 1870s at places like Göttingen and Leipzig. Nor did it help that women had long been admitted to foreign universities, above all in Switzerland, where they had obtained higher qualifications in the sciences as well as in the humanities. Some had even received doctorates. Around 1900, there were twenty female physicians who had passed their qualifying examinations in Switzerland and had subsequently opened practices in Germany. What kinds of emotional hurdles women had to overcome is demonstrated by the case of the famous physicist Max Planck, who – in this respect rather more liberal than many of his colleagues – had allowed women to attend his lectures as early as 1897. Nevertheless, he continued to hold the view, widespread at the time among men and women, that the natural role of the woman was as mother and housewife and that this alleged law of nature could not be ignored without serious detriment to individual and society.

The expansion of the school system, however, opened the door early on for pedagogically inclined single women who wanted to become teachers. This career could be pursued without the *Abitur* certificate by studying at one of the pedagogical institutes. Even many men who were otherwise hostile to female professionals found it plausible that girls were best instructed by women. Thus it happened that Prussia had some 3,896 female primary schoolteachers as early as 1875. Their number more than doubled to 8,380 by

1891 (table 44). Twenty years later, there were over 24,000 women teaching next to 91,600 males. Similarly the growth of girls' high schools required more female teachers. Some 9,100 of them worked in these schools around the turn of the century. Meanwhile the question of pay, which at all levels was higher for men than for women, generated much controversy. Similarly the fact that female teachers who married were required to terminate their careers was bound to cause bitterness. There was also the problem of equal promotion rights, which were time and again denied to women. Conflicts also broke out over access to further training and qualifying examinations which would allow women to ascend the career ladder in tandem with their male colleagues. Men were also in the forefront of the opposition to an incipient, female-dominated preschool movement, which they protested on the grounds that six was the appropriate age for starting an education. Meanwhile fresh opportunities arose for women, usually of lower middle-class background, who decided to go into the nursing profession. Here, too, special training was required, and the work was no doubt more interesting than factory manufacture. Before World War I, 55 percent of healthcare workers were women. On the other hand, the few actresses and artists who made it to the top were statistically insignificant, though they acted as role models. Even if the most prominent among them earned high honoraria, there was no question that their male colleagues received more, and this was equally true of women in the legal and medical professions. Although they were also disadvantaged when it came to promotions, these women nevertheless achieved a higher level of job satisfaction than female laborers, secretaries, and shop assistants.

Ultimately women working in the factory were just as much without a vocation or some kind of career perspective for the future as their male counterparts. But in order to fully appreciate the special difficulties which the former encountered, we must present yet another set of statistics, relating to their marital status. In 1907 agriculture still had the highest share of married women, i.e., 54 percent. Their share in industry rose from 31.1 percent in 1895 to 32.9 percent in 1907. Some 44.7 percent of domestic servants were married, closely followed by women in the tertiary sector (44 percent). For the year 1875 we also have for Prussia a breakdown by age group. According to this table, some 25.1 percent of women between the ages of sixteen and eighteen were laborers, of whom 0.6 percent were married (table 33). Of the eighteen- to twenty-five-year-olds, who made up 43 percent of the total, no less than 88.6 percent were unmarried. Only among women above the age of twenty-five was the percentage of those who were married considerable, i.e.,

56 percent. This means that most female factory workers in various branches of industry were young and unmarried (table 32). Workers in home industries present a different picture, as most were married or widowed. These were at the same time the industries with the lowest pay rates and without promotion prospects. Whatever other handicaps these women workers may have labored under, work in home industries offered certain logistical advantages, especially for women with small children. All in all they constituted a badly exploited group whose work was moreover subject to sharp seasonal vacillations.

In terms of pay and prestige, however, the unmarried female servant working in agriculture was probably at the bottom of the pile. The only escape for her was to move into the city where positions as domestic servants to the well-to-do were available. In terms of city work, being a maid was pretty much the pits. The workdays were long and included Sunday. Chambers were often no more than cubbyholes. Since room and board were free, domestics rarely received more than a small allowance. There was also the supervision by the "mistress of the house" who was frequently very strict. On the positive side was the fact that these women had left worse conditions in agriculture behind them. Each immediately had a roof over her head and usually enough to eat. Employers were not invariably exploitative. Maids could expect to inherit unwanted clothes from the mistress who might also be generous in other ways. Finally, these women also gained insight into the organization of the household which would be useful later on once they were married.

With the decline in the number of domestic positions, many women who arrived in the cities as commuters or long-distance migrants went straight into the factory. Some returned to their parents at night, if these lived nearby; others lodged with working-class families. There were also shelters for young female workers. At least pay was better than for maids. Those women who did not commute did not have to hand over their earnings to their parents. They had money to spend, while the reduction of work hours gave them more leisure time. In the 1880s the workday for female textile workers was still twelve to thirteen hours (table 15). After the turn of the century, the eleven-hour workday became more typical in the textile industry. In other branches it even decreased to ten hours and in 1910 a law was put into effect that prescribed this length for all industries. Nightshift work was banned and pregnant women became protected by law against dismissal. If the factory was some distance away, all these improvements still meant an exhausting daily routine. But at least Sunday was completely free, and when Saturday work hours were reduced to eight, the evening of that day was similarly available for leisure pursuits. Beyond this, few of these working-class women succeeded in moving up into the group of white-collar employees. Income improvements could perhaps be achieved by moving to jobs in other companies which paid higher wages and offered better benefits.

And many unmarried female factory workers did try to enjoy their Sundays. They went with their friends and colleagues to dance halls or beer gardens, where they would meet single men many of whom had also migrated from the rural parts of the country. Social contact might lead to sexual relations, which caused bourgeois social critics to utter dark warnings about the alleged decline in morals. But any attempt to understand the sexual behavior of young working-class men and women would fail if we applied the yardsticks of these critics. Civil servants, white-collar employees, craftsmen, wealthy businessmen, and the nobility expected their daughters to preserve their virginity until marriage. To become pregnant with an illegitimate child was deemed a violation of family honor. Of course, different standards applied to "young gentlemen". Ever so discreetly, they would be encouraged to sow their oats during their bachelor years. The codes were again different for female laborers, maids, and – at least in some regions – agricultural servants. Certainly they were less restrictive than those for women from the middle and upper classes. If, having met at some dance, a young couple warmed to each other, the relationship frequently led to sexual intercourse. It also happened, especially in economically harder times, that female factory workers or domestic servants would slip into occasional prostitution. In 1873, the number of prostitutes under police supervision in Berlin was 2,224. The share of female factory workers among them was 16 percent, while domestic servants and shop assistants made up another 42 percent. By 1890, the figure had risen to 4,039, and contemporary estimates of the actual numbers of prostitutes were many times higher. Around 1909, the Berlin total was thought to be 40,000, contributing to a high percentage of illegitimate births. Nationally the figure, according to some estimates, was as high as 350,000 in 1914. Overall the share of illegitimate births compared with the total number of births varied considerably from city to city. In Munich it was as high as 31.6 percent, in Dresden 20.5 percent, in Berlin 12.3 percent, and in Cologne a mere 9.8 percent.

It would be mistaken to reduce an interpretation of such percentages to a lack of morals among the lower classes. Even when illegitimate children were born, they often were the result of a stable relationship which knew genuine love, emotional relief, and mutual support. If such relationships did not last, this was due to many circumstances, but not as a rule to an unwanted pregnancy. For as in rural society, there existed unwritten codes of honor, according to which a young worker would not just "dump" his pregnant girlfriend. That is how sailors might behave in the port cities, or soldiers in the garrison towns, or "gentlemen" students in the university centers. For most workers, it was "a matter of course" to get married if a pregnancy occurred, or at least to establish a joint household, if for economic or other reasons marriage was not yet possible. If necessary, colleagues or the family would exert a bit of moral pressure. Such social mechanisms were even stronger in cases where a journeyman started a liaison with the master's daughter. However, we are best informed about the working of these mechanisms in certain rural areas. As the above-mentioned figures on illegitimacy in individual cities of the Reich indicated, there were some surprising differences. This applied even more so to larger regions. The fact that some parts of Catholic Bavaria ranked so high and the Catholic Rhineland so low indicates that confessional factors were not decisive, if we discount the low illegitimacy rate of German Jews. Rates were also low in Protestant Frisia and around Brunswick, but were much higher in Protestant Saxony. To some extent these differences may be explained by "divergent intra-Church currents and the varying effectiveness of the imposition of High Church norms". [26] Most demographers are inclined today to see marriage age and work organization as the decisive factors.

In most of northern Europe the marriage age for women declined from 26-27 years to 24-25 years during the nineteenth century. At the same time the start of a woman's fertility cycle moved back to 14-15 years from an earlier 18-20 years. Unlike in the Balkans and in the Mediterranean with their patrilinear family systems and patriarchal structures, there was no tradition of "child marriages" in central Europe. Consequently women had ten years between reaching sexual maturity and their average marriage age to gather sexual experiences. They lived "dangerously" in this period. At an age when the chance of conception was high, they and their often no more enlightened and experienced boyfriends experimented, if at all, with contraceptives and techniques that were very unreliable. [27] Wherever, following the abolition of the marriage consent, sanctions against sexual intercourse among unmarried people were mild, but outside pressures to honor the promise of marriage or not to "dump" the women were high, we also find high illegitimacy rates. This applied above all to those rural parts of Germany in which

26. M. Mitterauer, *Ledige Mütter* (Munich 1983), 33.

27. J. Woyke, *Birth Control in Germany, 1871-1933* (London 1988).

inheritance laws had prevented a splintering of peasant lands. These larger farmsteads were unable to operate on a family basis and were hence dependent on servants. This pattern, together with an increased sexual freedom among young people, offered greater opportunities for sexual contact. If, in these circumstances, birth control was practiced carelessly or not at all, a high pregnancy rate was the almost inevitable result.

Existing statistics, of course, refer only to actual births. The number of infanticides in the *Kaiserreich* was low, if court records are any guide. The large unknown is the number of abortions, about which we have no more than very rough estimates, running into hundreds of thousands. Contemporary interviews with female factory workers showed that many had had several intended and unintended terminations. Around 1900, about twenty-five percent of pregnancies in Berlin ended in abortion. There are no comparable figures for the rural areas. What presumably prevented a high incidence of abortions in the villages, where everyone knew everything about everybody else, were, apart from a fear of criminal prosecution, the existing instruments of social pressure. Here local traditions and the economic dependence of the female servants had a powerful influence. It was difficult for the father to abandon the mother of his child, and in many cases marriage took place just before or after the baby's birth, or the couple established a common-law household. If this solution proved impossible, alimony payments were due. But even in such cases, the children did not have to grow up in foster families without their natural mother. They would be raised on the farm. Employers in the cities very rarely offered a domestic servant the opportunity to stay on with her illegitimate child. For financial reasons bourgeois households preferred maids that had just arrived from the country. But if these maids brought with them the sexual norms of the village and suddenly became pregnant, the "mistress of the house" would not even hold off giving notice until the child was born. Consequently urban quacks and back-street abortionists were busier than their rural counterparts. Considering that an unwanted pregnancy always meant emotional and material hardship, even if the father stood by his lover, it was no doubt fortunate that high illegitimacy rates were an ephemeral phenomenon. The lower classes, too, began to limit pregnancies by practicing more effective birth control. Urbanization, the lowering of the marriage age by an average of two years, and a higher marriage rate finally contributed to reducing the problem further.

Meanwhile the situation of unmarried mothers and their children did not necessarily improve if the fathers stayed with them. As has been mentioned, [28] infant mortality rates remained high during the first year of life, not least because of the poor living conditions to which these children were exposed. These conditions also contributed to the relatively low life expectancy of women, even though it was slightly higher than that of men (tables 58, 60). What continued was the increased danger to working-class women during pregnancy or birth as well as the progressive undermining of their health due to inadequate nutrition and sheer overwork. Affliction with tuberculosis, the "disease of the poor", provides a good indicator of this. Not only was the rate of affliction higher for females over the age of five than it was for males, but it also experienced no more than a very small decline between 1879/79 and 1914 among people between the ages of twenty and forty.

Nor were chances particularly great that children would grow up with both parents. This was not because of high divorce rates, but rather because, although the average marriage age of women declined, men continued to marry late, and because they died earlier than the male average, if they came from the industrial working class. One factor to account for the late marriage age was that many men had to do military service, but could be drafted only from the age of twenty. Military pay (in 1913) was 23 pfennigs per day, making it difficult to save up for a future family. Not surprisingly, at the end of 1910 no more than 8 percent of the twenty- to twenty-five-year-olds were married. The figure then rose to 50 percent for those between twenty-five and thirty. A good four-fifths of all industrial workers had finally married by the age of fifty, and there was only a modest increase in this figure between 1882 and 1907 from 83 percent to 86 percent. Meanwhile the average life expectancy was still under fifty years.

Since ultimately most women would also get married, the question arises as to why the nuclear family came to be the most common form of living among the lower classes, even though it was exposed to so many emotional and material hardships. Among agricultural and industrial laborers, marriage in most cases became the destination not because the couple was longing to have children or because the wife expected to devote herself exclusively to her family. To begin with, many children either existed before marriage or arrived shortly after the modest wedding. Above all, around 30 percent of all married women had to work in order to make ends meet. This figure does not include those who had small and often irregular jobs to boost the weekly budget. With the decline in the number of domestic service jobs, such jobs included working as a cleaning woman for a well-to-do middle-class family

28. See above pp. 57ff.

or in one of proliferating offices and stores. There were obvious advantages to not having to work the full ten to twelve hours which factory labor then still involved. Working a few hours in the morning or late at night made it easier to find supervision for the children. Unless the economy as a whole did poorly, the wage was in many cases enough to secure a slightly higher living standard. Logistical considerations of this kind also explain why the share of married women in the domestic industries was particularly high. It was clearly easier to look after small children if the workplace was in the home. If one of the children fell ill, factory women stood to lose a full day's pay and perhaps even their job. Moreover, children could be put to work at an early age – finishing garments, making cigars, or wrapping sweets and chocolates. The preparation of meals, washing, and other domestic chores were also more manageable. If there was an elder daughter, she could look after the children or do the cooking.

Those 30 percent of married women who had full-time jobs with relatively low pay had no relief from carrying the triple burden of monotonous and often unhealthy factory work, the bearing and raising of the children, and keeping a household of four to five people on a meager budget. The fact that the patriarchal family structures and attitudes of the preindustrial family survived in many working-class marriages, just as they did elsewhere, only made matters more difficult for the woman. Rarely did the husband bear his share in the running of the household. His wife repeatedly sacrificed her needs to those of the family. Kitchen aids were too expensive to be affordable for the lower classes. If her indispensability provided her with some influence within the existing family hierarchy, the time which she had for herself was strictly limited. We will never know how many of them harbored the modest and secret hope that one day their husband's income would be high enough for these wives to be able to give up their menial jobs. This is when "life" might at last begin. Conversely, it seems that many a lower-class husband too dreamed of the day when he would be able to say that his wife no longer *had* to work. For to have reached this goal could be taken as proof that a working-class marriage had ceased to be no more than an emergency arrangement that offered emotional and material shelter against illness, job loss and political discrimination by the employer and the police, especially when the family's ideological commitment was to the Left. That many working-class women strived to devote themselves to the family, without a job – as was the ideal and in most cases the reality of many a bourgeois and upper-class wife – should not mislead us, however, into thinking that they were being absorbed into the bourgeois universe. Workers and middle-classes lived in different worlds in Imperial Germany, and indeed increasingly so; this was also true of working-class women and their bourgeois counterparts.

Gender role divisions were sharper, even more asymmetrical and polarized, among the middle classes. This applied to the families of shopkeepers and artisans, where the wife might lend a hand with the accounts or behind the counter. It was even more true of civil servants and white-collar workers, whose wives by and large stayed at home minding the "private sphere". If nothing else, the size of this sphere differentiated them from working-class women. Though often stifled by prudishness and sexual repression, this sphere was also larger simply by virtue of the fact that accommodations were more spacious. While the working-class family with its larger number of children and lodgers had little privacy, there were more spaces in the middle classes to which one could withdraw and be undisturbed. The husband acted as the sole "breadwinner"; his wife kept the house and was in charge of the private sphere, while remaining economically and legally dependent on her husband. [29] To some extent the following depended on the size of her household budget: how she would be able to spend her day as homemaker; to what extent she could be a "perfect housewife", concerned mother, and lover who understood the needs of her husband. Among the lower middle classes – whose incomes often barely kept up with inflation – it was virtually unthinkable to have a domestic servant. Here housewives did their own shopping, their own laundry, and their own house-cleaning. Children below school age had to be supervised and kept occupied full-time; school children came home around lunchtime, not, as in other countries, in the mid-afternoon. If there was a small backyard, some time would be spent growing vegetables, thus relieving the budget. Part of the fruit season might be spent making preserves for the winter. The advent of the sewing machine made it easier to save on expenditure for clothes. If all these activities were taken seriously, not much time was left in the day for social life. A longer chat with a neighbor at the local shop or on the street fulfilled an important social function. And on Sunday, after church, one might meet with friends in the afternoon over coffee and cake or in the evening for a glass of beer at the local pub.

Middle-class households that could afford a domestic servant made it easier for the wife and mother to create leisure spaces for herself. If she lived in a town, she might go window-shopping, spend some time at the hairdresser, play some tennis, or meet her friends at a café. Charity work remained important. The advent of department stores went hand in hand with

29. See below pp. 77f.

the emergence of a consumer culture, buoyed by the spending-power of a prosperous urban bourgeoisie. Women who had postponed marriage and had found a relatively well-paid job were also among the new female consumers. Finally the social obligations of their husbands, especially if they belonged to the local oligarchy of notables, could make for a busy life. To be sure, many of the social evenings were males-only affairs. But there were also theaters, concerts, and balls to attend, and receptions and private dinner-parties to prepare. The often strict demands of etiquette required considerable organizational talents to avoid embarrassments. What was at stake here was the ability of the husband to demonstrate his status. On such occasions, some of his public prestige would reflect also upon his wife, just as she would benefit from any of his professional achievements by being addressed as "Frau Doktor" or "Frau Direktor" when out shopping. Still, it was a world set apart from the virile ambiance of men, who engaged in business, gathered in clubs and smoke rooms, and occasionally even challenged each other to a duel.

Social commitments multiplied for women whose husbands moved in court circles, in the diplomatic service, or in the armed forces. The diaries of Baroness Spitzemberg provide good insight into the changing, but often very stiff lifestyle and sociability of the more urbanized and cosmopolitan nobility, where on some days one reception, dinner party, or concert would be chasing another, and where a single new evening dress might cost as much as the annual wage of a factory worker [(30)]. However, these women could also retreat into their own homes and private suites. They could sit alone in the garden. They had most of the comforts of modern life – a bath tub, central heating, gas. The family budget of the upper bourgeoisie and the still wealthy nobility was also large enough to accommodate a vacation which the wife and children would spend, accompanied by the nanny, by the seaside, in the mountains, or in one of the famous spa towns. A horse-drawn carriage might be waiting outside, and after the turn of the century perhaps even an automobile. In short, many women lived a busy life, but it was often also emotionally empty, especially where the genuine love of the early marriage years had been replaced by routine and indifference. Since divorce was viewed as a serious violation of social norms and hence rarely entertained, happiness often proved an elusive thing. Migraine became one of the symptoms and symbols of a neglected female psyche. And in many cases it was also a weapon of refusal used by many "well-situated" women.

Compared with women of the urban upper classes, the wives of the landed estate owners had a more sedate life, which could become one of isolation

30.R. Vierhaus, ed., *Das Tagebuch der Baronin Spitzemberg* (Munich 1960).

during the long winter months. At the same time, there were quite a few organizational matters to attend to. The servants had to be supervised. Church and parish welfare had to be supported. She was required for consultations with her children's private teacher. Hunting parties had to be entertained. In the evening there might be time to read a book or, during the summer, to sit in the garden. But just as in the case of working-class women in comparison with their bourgeois counterparts, the relationship between actual work and tending the private sphere defined the difference in the lives between the ladies of the manor and the peasant wife. On the wealthier farmsteads, the woman was still an administrator of the family sphere. Lower down the income scale, she too would bear the triple burden of hard farm labor, looking after the children and keeping the household. What was common to the situation of all women was that they had to operate within a patriarchal society and family structure which did not evolve with the rapidly changing economy around it. To be sure, many partners had deeper emotional and sexual ties than did those in the average marriage. But they also ran up against the legal, political, and social obstacles that existed in order to secure male dominance. Sometimes marriages would break up over the strains that the unequal relationship imposed. In 1895, some 8,300 marriages were legally dissolved. Six years later the number had actually declined to 7,892. By 1913 some 152 out of 100,000 marriages ended in divorce, with considerable variations between Catholics and Protestants, and between city dwellers and rural folks. But as has been indicated before, this was probably no more than the tip of the iceberg. No doubt the number of unhappy marriages was considerably higher; but like other legal provisions, divorce laws also disadvantaged women, and many therefore found other solutions to their difficult predicament.

7. Issues of Generation and Socialization

A. The Young and the Aged

As a result of rapid population growth the percentage of children and young people was particularly high during this period. In 1913, youngsters under the age of fifteen made up 34.4 percent of the total population. At the other end of the spectrum, the increase in life expectancy had led to a slightly larger number of elderly people (table 55); [31] but as long as average life expectancy remained at 47.7 years for men and 50.7 years for women, it is not surprising

31. See above pp. 57ff.

that in 1910 no more than 5 percent of the population were over 65. At the same time, the young and the aged were among the most defenseless groups of the population and the ones who especially suffered from existing inequalities.

With infant mortality being as high as it was, for the newly born it was first of all a question of getting through the danger zone of the first twelve months (tables 59-62). This in turn depended in large measure on the social group into which the child happened to be born. To be sure, chances of survival of an infant born to an upper-class family were lower by international standards, and it is also true that infant mortality rates experienced ups and downs. Still the fact remains that the survival rates of working-class children or of illegitimate babies born to unmarried mothers were depressingly low. Thus the social background of the parents, legitimacy, and housing as well as nutritional standards remained important factors. For example, infants who were not being breast-fed died most frequently of diarrhea and vomiting caused by milk which had not been pasteurized and had gone sour during the hot summer days for lack of cool spaces or refrigeration in the overcrowded apartment blocks of the big cities. And more generally, it tended to make a difference between life and death for a child whether or not the mother had a basic medical or nutritional knowledge. Finally, there was the question of whether the family could afford to call a pediatrician.

It is now also common knowledge that the early years of childhood can be decisive for a person's later psychic, intellectual, and even physical development. Nor can there be any doubt that emotional warmth and close human contact are no less important than proper nutrition. In the late nineteenth century, many people had at least a rudimentary appreciation of these aspects of child-rearing, which were promoted by doctors and social reformers. Yet this knowledge rarely and, if so, incompletely reached the lower classes. The educated and well-to-do middle classes were most likely to pick up the growing information on child development. It was put into practice more rarely among the upper classes, where wet-nurses and nannies were more common and where other social commitments of the mother kept her away from the children, while the patriarchal father remained remote. The detrimental effects of an aristocratic upbringing have been studied most closely in respect of the development of Emperor Wilhelm II. [32] That the use of wet nurses was less common in bourgeois families, even if the mother did not breast-feed, is related to middle-class perceptions of family life and the fear that wet nursing might interfere with the bonding between mother and child.

32. J.C.G. Röhl, "Kaiser Wilhelm II. Eine Charakterskizze," in: idem, *Kaiser, Hof und Staat* (Munich 1987), 17-34.

Although preconditions for a happy childhood were less favorable in working-class families, this does not mean that loving and warm relationships did not develop between parents and children in this milieu. However, material hardship and the difficulty of articulating feelings toward family members, spouses, or children, put up considerable obstacles. The father, who spent ten to twelve hours in the factory, would not be present during the day. When he returned to the overcrowded apartment of no more than a kitchen and a bedroom and often after a detour to the local pub, he was often tired and irritable. He did not have to be a particularly brutal or authoritarian person to grab a coat-hanger or a leather belt to give his boisterous children an intemperate thrashing. Even without this, his tone and language were frequently harsh. There were no long discussions; authority was not to be questioned and any argument was liable quickly to degenerate into a shouting match. If the father had a drinking problem, all members of the family were liable to fall victim to his violent outbursts. However, it must be stressed that we have virtually no reliable data on the extent of battering and child abuse in any strata in this period. Some have argued that the increased consumption of bottled beer indicates more frequent socializing within the family circle, and it would be quite wrong to assume that love and warmth simply did not exist in this milieu. While her husband was at work, the wife was fully preoccupied with the household and, in many cases, with improving the family income with a part-time job. If she was lucky, there might be a nearby grandmother to take over as a baby-sitter. Older daughters also had to help watch the other children. Even if the mother had to work full-time, crèches or baby-sitters might be too expensive and difficult to come by. In 1914, there existed in Germany around 1,400 kindergartens with no more than 85,000 places. Consequently, in many cases the children were just left to themselves. A neighbor might agree to keep an eye on them, as they played in the backyards and stairwells of the apartment buildings. In Berlin alone there were an estimated 20,000 of these unattended children in 1912.

By comparison, children of middle-class families must be considered fortunate. Whether it was their mother or their nanny, someone was around them all day. There were toys and children's books; they were encouraged to play imaginatively. At bedtime stories were read to them. There was no need to give them – as frequently happened in working-class families – tranquilizers like beer or a lump of sugar dipped in brandy so that there would at last be peace and quiet in the small apartment. However one-sided and monotonous the food that lower-class children were served may have been, it had to be eaten. Their bourgeois counterparts were offered greater variety and more choice all around. One could think of other aspects of a child's life to provide further illustration how much of a head start was given by having the "right" family background and by having parents who were well-to-do and pedagogically enlightened. The beginning of school was the next major step in child development, and one which working-class parents looked forward to, if only for economic reasons. Whatever the benefits and drawbacks of primary schooling for their education and socialization, children starting school were now old enough to contribute to the family income. However, this was no longer the kind of child labor involving long hours in the mines or the factories with which we are familiar from earlier periods of industrialization. In Prussia the minimum age had been fixed at twelve as early as 1853. The *Gewerbeordnung* of 1869 had outlawed the employment of children in jobs that were dangerous to their health. Further legislation in 1891 raised the minimum age to thirteen and imposed a general ban on child labor in the factories. The maximum hours for fourteen- to sixteen-year-olds was fixed at ten hours, und this also applied to apprentices and agricultural servants, most of whom were taken under contract at age fourteen.

The changes in the law led to a drastic decline in the number of children working in industry, whose number had doubled to 27,500 during the 1880s. By the mid-1890s this figure slipped to fewer than 5,000, but rose once more to 10,900 in 1906. Yet, however progressive labor legislation may have been in Wilhelmine Germany, abuses continued to occur, especially in the treatment of apprentices and agricultural servants. (33) In 1904, the Berlin Insurance Association reported a high incidence among apprentices of illness that was related to the workplace. According to the 1905 annual report of the factory inspectorate at Minden in Lower Saxony, many employers tried to flout regulations by obliging their apprentices to stay on after their ten-hour workday to clean the machinery. Moreover, behind the vague term of "supplementary work" lurked an even bigger problem: hundreds of thousands of children under thirteen or fourteen years of age had "small" jobs. Around the turn of the century some 540,000 school-age children were registered as having part-time occupations. This was well under ten percent of primary school students. But the actual number must have been much higher. This is reflected in a survey by the Prussian government, according to which forty percent of all school children worked for at least three hours six to seven days of the week. Many of them carried out papers or fresh rolls at six in the morning. Or they were up late at night setting up pins in bowling alleys and washing

33. See below pp. 88ff.

dishes and glasses in restaurants and pubs. However, the largest number of these part-time child laborers worked in domestic industries.

The Child Protection Law which came into force in 1904 tried to regulate the hours of work permitted and to outlaw the employment of children in particularly dangerous jobs. The problem was, though, that this Law protected children from other families more effectively than the natural children of a family. The position of the latter was governed by Paragraph 1617 of the Civil Code of 1900 in which the rights of parents had been given precedence over the interests of children. Nor was it easy to police families who employed their own children. It was not the parents who complained about this type of child labor, but the teachers. The power of the law notwithstanding, every day they faced children who had clearly had too little sleep either because they had gotten up hours before the start of school to run errands or because they had not been able to get to bed much before midnight. To be sure, these children had not been sent out to do part-time work in order to further their education or apprenticeship; rather they took on these jobs to make an important contribution to the family budget. These children too were therefore part of that emergency arrangement which constituted the primary *raison d'être* of lower-class families.

This type of child labor was so deeply rooted in agriculture that the government, faced with the sharp opposition of agrarian pressure groups, was forced to exclude rural children from the law's sanctions altogether. It just was not possible politically to introduce in agriculture a clause similar to what industry grudgingly accepted. Opposition was particularly vocal in East Elbia, where day laborers in some cases even had a contractual obligation to the local lord to send their school-age children into the fields. In Prussia alone the number of children working in agriculture was estimated to be just under 1.4 million in 1904. Thanks to the Prussian bureaucracy's penchant for meticulous record-keeping, we possess some interesting statistics relating to the approximately 1.8 million children who worked outside their own families. Some 445,000 of them were under ten; 717,000 were under twelve, with the rest distributed in-between. How many children within the family were employed in agriculture is not known. We do have some official statistics, though, concerning the total number of hours worked. Thus around 446,000 were temporarily employed for over six hours per day. Demand was particularly high during harvesttime, when a minimum of 1.5 million children who came from other families worked in agriculture.

The sons and daughters of the middle and upper classes were rarely exposed to the health-damaging circumstances that children from the lower strata experienced. It was on the whole economically possible for wealthier parents to grant even slightly bigger wishes for toys and entertainments, at least at Christmas time and on birthdays. These parents were also educated enough to help their children, and, if necessary, could ask a private tutor to take over. However, few children, and certainly not those who went to a public primary school, would have been totally ignorant of the poverty in which some of their fellow pupils lived. True, the concentration of certain social groups in specific parts of town promoted separation. But at least in more mixed neighborhoods, it was more difficult not to notice the differences. Rarely did this lead to closer social contact or even friendships, though. In short, there were several different types of childhood, depending on whether one's parents were factory workers or belonged to the middle classes, whether they were small peasants or estate owners. In many ways the situation of children of bourgeois background came closest to the prevailing notions of the ideal family espoused by family politicians and child psychologists, who wrote about the psychic and intellectual needs of young people. With regard to the children of the rural or industrial proletariat, one is often left to wonder how many of them had any childhood at all.

Very young boys from this milieu fared no better than their female counterparts. But as children grew older, differentiations occurred. Thus daughters would be asked to help in the kitchen and with the supervision of younger siblings. Later on, when they had their first jobs, girls were more likely to have to surrender a larger share of their earnings to the family budget than boys. The latter also began to insist more loudly on their economic independence. Thus we have reports from the region around Eßlingen in the southwest about "young insolent lads, who gave improper expression of their sense of freedom on Sundays at the local alehouse". [34] Some parents were glad if they got hold of the weekly wage "without deductions and were able to determine the amount of their sons' and daughters' pocket money". Siblings were also treated differently when it came to further education or training. Here sisters often had to defer to their brothers – a treatment that even daughters of middle-class parents might find themselves subjected to, especially if the fees for high school exceeded the financial power of the family.

34. Quoted in: W. von Hippel, "Industieller Wandel im ländlichen Raum," in: *Archiv für Sozialgeschichte*, 1979, 105.

Among the lower classes, however, even the boys lacked many opportunities to stay on beyond primary school. Most of them therefore tried to find apprenticeships and the girls signed up as servants. These were careers that were typically taken up by children from the lower strata. Still working-class youths usually lived a somewhat happier life than they had had in earlier childhood. In respect to their developing adolescent sexuality, it may even be said that they were less inhibited in expressing it than their bourgeois counterparts. The latter were often also restricted by the norms imposed by their parents' religion. On the whole, however, our knowledge of sexuality among middle-class teenagers is limited and generally confined to what can be gleened from memoirs and is found in the way of contemporary advice and sanctions against the "sins" of puberty. In the memoirs of educated women we may find references to the start of menstruation or to the long years of waiting and celibacy at a time when the average marriage age for women was twenty-four to twenty-five. For many of these women, these were the years of further education or preparation for eventual marriage.

The quite high illegitimacy rates [35] reflect at least in part a lack of an elementary sex education. On this point most parents tended to be mute and too embarrassed to talk. In lower-class families, where life was centered around the kitchen and one or two bedrooms, children could not avoid becoming witnesses to their parents' sexuality. Or they by chance observed their elder sister, a lodger, or, on the farm, servants engaging in sex. The idea that children were brought by the stork was therefore a notion that was least likely to be undermined by the observation of sexual situations among boys and girls from middle, and upper-class backgrounds. However, sooner or later even they began to pick up the basic information from their older friends or in the schoolyard. While parents and teachers warned against the dangers of masturbation and venereal disease, advice on unwanted pregnancies was most easily available outside the family. Also largely excluded from public discourse would be questions of homosexuality. After the turn of the century, adolescents organized in the Youth Movement started to raise these topics as a serious issue, unleashing a debate on the advantages and disadvantages of separating the sexes in schools and elsewhere.

In the rural areas, the sexual behavior of young people was furthermore regulated by traditions that varied from region to region. In the South, *Fensterln* (climbing through the window into the woman's bedroom) was practiced as a courting ritual, ending, not always, but frequently, in sexual

35. See above pp. 70ff.

intercourse. If an unwanted pregnancy resulted, the couple would marry, which in many cases had been previously agreed. In this respect, it was often safer to engage in *Schwärmen* (swarming), a practice by which young men would roam through the village and visit the young women in their bedrooms in groups. The so-called *Spinnstuben* (spinning sessions) were similarly policed by the adolescents themselves, but, at a time of increasing sexual freedom, occasionally got out of hand. This may partly also explain the survival of the "cat music," a ritual meant to humiliate and condemn members of the village community who were suspected of having violated local sexual mores. Much of this was, of course, impossible to uphold in the anonymity of the large industrial cities. And yet it might happen even there that workers would perform a "cat music" for a colleague who had reneged on a marriage promise. In some parts of Upper Bavaria around the towns of Miesbach and Bad Tölz the custom of well-organized *Haberfeldtreiben* (charivaris) continued, which were directed against "fallen maidens" and young couples who had diverged from local sexual norms. However, there are also signs that before 1914 these practices were sometimes the result of conflicts between young people and the irritated local police authorities.

Conflicts between parents and their teenage children also happened, not least because the low life expectancy frequently produced early widowhood and remarriages. Conflicts across three generations, on the other hand, were rare, because not many children ever got to know both their grandparents. Where the grandparents did survive, the relationship was more often one of respect and mutual support. Only after the turn of the century did the hitherto positive image of the elderly change. Help from the younger family was vital for many of the aged. The benefits of the old age insurance schemes were still meager for the insured and even more so for their widows [36] (tables 75, 77). In 1907, no more than 17 percent of all men over seventy actually received a pension. Among the retired self-employed and rentiers this figure was at least thirty-two percent. The middle classes also had a higher capacity to put some of their money into savings. All this meant that many elderly people had to carry on working for as long as they could manage, preferably in occupations that did not require much physical exertion. This was also the age when men and women began to suffer from many smaller ailments, if not from more serious complaints, for which medication was either unavailable or too expensive for a low-income person. Some had to think twice about whether they could afford to pay a visit to a doctor. If one

36. See below pp. 250ff.

had been permanently disabled by a work-related accident, the insurance system which had been established under Bismarck might pay a small pension. Apart from the well-to-do who did not have to worry about getting the best treatment or about a spa cure afterwards, civil servants, whether still active or retired, probably enjoyed the most generous benefits. Their medical care and their retirement pensions had been taken over entirely by the state.

Furthermore there was the problem of loneliness, from which many elderly people suffered. Chances were high that anyone who lived beyond the age of fifty would lose his or her spouse early. In the villages, custom and tradition made it relatively easy to integrate the elderly into the community. The "rental barracks" of the cities made this much more difficult, though not impossible. Many a widow became an ersatz granny to the young family next door. At a time when affordable leisure activities for the elderly were few and boredom could be devastating, these relationships were welcome, and they gave a sense of purpose to a widow's life. Since economic factors were so crucial to a retired person's life-style, older people from the middle and upper classes generally found themselves in an appreciably better situation. Independent peasants had greater security because they remained landowners until the farmstead was either handed over to an eldest son or divided up among his children. But even thereafter they continued to live on the farm and, if possible, gave a helping hand. Meanwhile retirees of the urban bourgeoisie had plenty of time to meet with their friends in clubs, in restaurants, or at the *Stammtisch*, the table for the regular notables in the local pub. For well-to-do widows an afternoon out among her friends with coffee and cream cake in one of the more posh cafés in town was a welcome distraction. Noblemen could count on the continued respect of the younger members of their family, and among the high aristocracy the senior member of the clan had, as the "head of the house", far-reaching powers with respect to the disposition of family property and to marriage policy.

B. Generations and Generational Conflicts

Many of the elderly found the rapid pace of change in society and the economy in the *Kaiserreich* understandably worrisome. If the young impatiently pushed toward new frontiers, the elderly wanted to preserve "what had proven its worth". Since Karl Mannheim, generational researchers have started from the assumption that it is historical experiences and socialization into a certain era which binds members of several cohorts together as a generation. [37] Since later generations have undergone a different social and ideological experience, conflicts will arise. To some extent, the history of the German Empire may be illuminated with the help of this model. Certainly, there was something like a *Gründergeneration* which had supported the founding of the German Empire and the great compromises that were forged during the 1860s and 1870s. Faced with the period of retarded growth in the 1880s, this generation continued to be convinced that the main task was to consolidate what had been achieved in 1871. However, it must be added that this view was not shared by all large social groups. Industrial workers of this generation, especially if they were Social Democrats and subject to constant police harassment, would hardly have agreed that consolidation was the most important objective.

Above all, there was a younger generation growing up in the 1880s that was keen to move to new shores in domestic and foreign policy as well as in culture. [38] Wilhelm II, who came to the throne in 1888 at the age of twenty-nine, has generally been regarded as the embodiment of a different sensibility and Weltanschauung than that of the *Gründergeneration*. Both tendencies can be traced most clearly through the broad spectrum of the middle strata, while our knowledge of generational conflict in the industrial working class remains rudimentary. This does not mean that tensions did not emerge in the latter between fathers and sons, mothers and daughters. But the subject matter was different. Faced with innumerable forms of social, economic, and political discrimination, young workers, it appears, began to rebel against what was to them the excessive caution and conservatism of their fathers and of the Social Democratic leadership in particular. Spurred on by much bitterness and youthful fervor, some of them were even prepared to accept further persecution for their acerbic criticism of conditions under the Hohenzollern monarchy. Many of the older generation, who had more experience with police brutality, and who moreover had to think of their families, thought this radicalism dangerous and self-destructive. They also had high hopes, which soon turned out to be illusory, that the young emperor, as the representative of the Wilhelmine generation, would be a Kaiser of reform and of the workers of Germany. Indeed, Wilhelm II, in his desire to set

37. K. Mannheim, "Das Problem der Generationen," in: *Kölner Vierteljahrshefte für Soziologie*, 1928; H. Jaeger, "Generationen in der Geschichte," in: *Geschichte und Gesellschaft*, 1977, 429-52; A. Spitzer, "The Historical Problem of Generations," in: *American Historical Review*, 1973, 1353-85.

38. See below pp. 142ff., 270ff.

himself apart from the Bismarckian generation, had at first presented his reign as a fresh start. Young workers had always been more skeptical of the Kaiser's determination to initiate fundamental change, and they turned out to be correct in their doubts.

After the turn of the century yet another generation began to raise its voice against the spirit of the Wilhelmine age, albeit with different arguments from those that were advanced by working-class activists. However, this generation did not reach the positions of power before the outbreak of World War I, so as to be able to influence events in any tangible way. Instead it became the "Generation of 1914," [39] whose world of ideas - hardened and partly transformed on the battlefields on the Western front - helped to shape the ideological climate and the political culture of the Weimar Republic. Still, their critique of the status quo began before 1914 and - at least as far as middle-class adolescents are concerned - found a focus in the Youth Movement. They felt particularly alienated from the self-satisfied materialism, the profit-oriented rationality, and the plush life-style of the Wilhelmine generation. Some of Germany's middle-class youth set out on the search for alternatives. They tended to emphasize the romantic and the irrational; they discovered nature and longed for human warmth in what they saw as an age of heartless technology. Some of them found themselves in the flight from reality. But much of it remained confined to the weekend when they went on their hiking trips and, in the evening by the fireside talked about eros and eternity or, accompanied by the guitar, sang songs from the *Zupfgeigenhansl* collection. Many of them also rebelled against the age of the masses and democracy. They displayed a strong elitism and were, as many youngsters at that age are, receptive to charismatic leadership. With respect to this elitism and their social background, members of the bourgeois Youth Movement were distinctly different from their proletarian age-mates, who became organized in Young Socialist associations.

C. Agents of Socialization: Family, School, Churches, Apprenticeship, Military Service, High School, University

As in other societies, agents of socialization such as family and school, religion and occupational training, universal military service and the education system played an important role in partly mediating and partly exacerbating generational tensions. Historians have pleaded, however, that we not apply the concept of socialization too widely and that we differentiate

39. R. Wohl, *The Generation of 1914* (Cambridge, Mass. 1979).

between divergent levels and phases in the socializing process. [40] If the family is the first institution for the transmission of general societal norms, the younger generation is introduced to the sphere of politics during the school years. The consolidation of all these and other influences into a more systematic Weltanschauung is then assumed to occur only thereafter during a third phase. Above all, while it cannot be stressed too strongly that in the *Kaiserreich*, social origin made a considerable difference in people's lives, it must also be emphasized that the various agents of socialization had contradictory impacts upon the young. On the one hand, they promoted the integration of the next generation into the existing society; but on the other we are also dealing with institutions whose rough edges the young rubbed themselves against. Indeed, in many cases it was the latters' explicit or tacit critique of their experiences with these institutions that incited their resolve to do things differently once they had reached adulthood.

For most children, the family was the organization that helped them to adapt to their immediate environment and to the existing order in the widest sense of the word. Children of the rural or urban lower classes, who had to contribute to the family income, were moreover conditioned to the routine of the workday and the regularity of economic processes. The family milieu also left its mark on the way the young learned to interact with others, to eat, to drink, to sleep, to spend their leisure time. Thus solidly bourgeois parents instilled their children with values and conventions of social intercourse which were in many ways markedly different from those of working-class parents. As a rule they would also equip their offspring with a better capacity to get ahead in life, to seize opportunities, and to master a crisis. To be sure, there might be too much sheltering so that middle-class children would be unprepared to weather setbacks. Nor would it be right to draw too idyllic a picture of the bourgeois family as an agent of socialization, with its fundamentally patriarchal structure and marriages that frequently existed merely on paper.

But however effective the mechanisms of integration, family life and the assertion of parental authority also offered many points of tension that reinforced a youthful tendency to rebel as a way of finding one's identity. Frequently, and particularly in those 'fatherless' families in which the 'provider' was present only in the evening, children were liable to feel alienated. In rural areas and in the industrial quarters of the cities this alienation

40. K.H. Jarausch, *Students, Society, and Politics in Imperial Germany* (Princeton 1982), 238.

would find its clearest expression in the fact that many children would leave the home soon after finishing their basic compulsory education or because they had been turfed out by an irate father. If, for whatever reason, they stayed at home, they would put in a fleeting appearance at dinner time. They would spend their free time in loosely organized groups or gangs. Even in those days, adults would complain loudly about the loutish '*Halbstarke*'. The boys among them would be open to the influence of a charismatic ersatz father, whom they would find in those gangs or in one of the religious or secular youth groups that mushroomed especially during the Wilhelmine period. Similar groups emerged for girls or they would 'hang out' among themselves or with one of the male gangs. Occasionally it might also happen that these youngsters who were looking for role models would become fascinated by one of their teachers.

Most schools, however, tended to project a different model in which the teacher appeared as the stern drill-master. School was not merely the place where basic rote learning was systematically instilled by repetition, with the effect - inter alia and in this case no doubt positive - that illiteracy rates were reduced to practically zero; (Table 49) but next to the family, school was also a major agent of socialization. The dramatist Gerhard Hauptmann has given a vivid description of the military style in his primary school with its rigid discipline. Even Wilhelm II complained bitterly in his memoirs how in his youth the uninspiring approach with which his private tutor Georg Hinzpeter dissected the classical texts of antiquity had killed off any interest that he may have had in them. And Willhelm did not have to sit in overcrowded classes. Indeed, to some extent, the stress on discipline was a function of very unfavorable staff-student ratios and one-class schools. Almost 20 years after the founding of the Empire, over half of Prussia's 4.5 mill. pupils attended village schools in which all age-groups were instructed in a single room. (Table 50) Meanwhile class-sizes in the cities were in many cases over 100. As late as 1911 the average student-teacher ratios in the new industrial cities of the Ruhr and in Upper Silesia were between 50-60:1. Only in towns like Wiesbaden or Wilmersdorf near Berlin with strong middle-class populations had class-sizes meanwhile dropped to 43 and 37 respectively.

Apart from purveying a knowledge of the Three Rs, the state had traditionally used schools as institutions for ideological indoctrination. The educational policies adopted after 1871 continued this practice. It reached a new level of intensity after the ascendancy of Wilhelm II to the throne. In May 1889, he issued a Cabinet Order which warned of the Social Democratic dangers threatening society and politics and demanded that efforts be redoubled to instil a conservative image of existing conditions in the young. Shortly thereafter discussions began on a new curriculum which were unveiled two years later. German was to be given greater emphasis vis-à-vis other languages. The revamping of History and Religious Studies, it was hoped, would lend support to traditional values and to the Hohenzollern monarchy. The successes of these policies may have been greater at the beginning than they were in later years. This raises the question of whether primary education remained no more than a 'school for the production of subjects' ('*Schule der Untertanen*'). [41] The question of whether school had a more ambiguous effect on pupils seems pertinent also in the light of a growing teachers' rebellion against the political interference from the top. As Marjorie Lamberti has shown, teachers developed their own professional ethos and standards. [42] Many of them, confronted day in day out with the poverty and poor preparation of their pupils, also turned toward a reformist Left Liberalism. They questioned the wisdom of crude patriotic indoctrination and tried hard to gain the trust of working-class parents.

Meanwhile the struggle was well underway to provide opportunities for advanced education for middle-class girls. The female teachers who, through their work, were committed to this idea also acted as role models for their students that contradicted prevailing notions of femininity and of the position of women in society. Finally, the success of indoctrination through school also depended on whether the family was able to reinforce these policies or acted as a counter-weight to them. The latter is obviously more likely to have been the case in households where the father (and perhaps also the mother) were Social Democrats than in families of the upper bourgeoisie who were loyal monarchists and church-goers.

Nor should we underestimate the contribution which the churches and regular attendance of Sunday School made to the socialization of children. In the Protestant parts of Germany it was the peculiar link between Church and State, the alliance of throne and altar, fostered a conservative orientation of the young who were searching for a *religio*. Although the *Kulturkampf*, the struggle of the Liberals and Bismarck in the 1870s against the 'ultramontane' influences of the Catholic Church, had complicated relations between religious institutions and the secular authorities in Germany, this was more true

41. F. Meyer, *Schule der Untertanen* (Hamburg 1976).

42. M. Lamberti, "Elementary School Teachers and the Struggle against Social Democracy in Wilhelmine Germany," in: *History of Education Quarterly*, 1992, 73-97.

in Prussia than it was in, say, Bavaria. The church communities there did not see a contradiction between being a good Catholic and being a loyal adherent of the Wittelsbach monarchy. Moreover, the Catholic priest remained in most cases the representative of a conservative institution whose influence on the formation of norms and values in children should not be underestimated. Lay Catholics, who began to organize in the hope of affecting reforms within the Church and of promoting a new relationship between Church and State, could not seriously undermine the prevailing conservative mood in which ritual and a mechanical piety were important elements. Nevertheless, the fact that this lay movement gained increasing support in the years before 1914 indicates a generational change. Many, who had still been raised in a very strict and hierarchical Catholic milieu now pushed for a modification of what they had been taught on Sundays or in preparation for their first communion. Although anti-clericalism never became as strong as in France, the move of many Catholic workers toward the Social Democrats may also be taken as a sign that the Church as an agency of socialization triggered contradictory responses among a younger generation. The tensions which this induced probably affected men more than women. Certainly the latter remained more firmly attached to the orthodoxies of both the major Christian denominations and also continued to be more regular church-goers. The Jewish experience also reflected these tendencies. Here the strict regime of rules and rituals among orthodox congregations was increasingly challenged by the proliferation of liberal ones, and many intellectual Jews abandoned all institutional affiliations. In short, generational change and the contradictory impact of religious conservatism were clearly interrelated.

After finishing primary school, many young people underwent an apprenticeship through which they were socialized into the world of work. In the workshops adolescents would not only learn the rules of precision and craftsmanship, but also of behavior in a time-honored hierarchy. Still, many a apprentices, faced with the petty authoritarianism of their master or journeyman, must have sworn themselves to organize things differently once they had a workshop of their own. Whether this rebellious determination was eventually put into practice was another matter. Later the weight of tradition and the greater convenience of rulings from the top may have proved stronger. There was also the problem that many handicrafts were threatened by the rise of the factory, and more generally an apprenticeship presumably never had the same importance as family and school for the socialization of the young. Industry and commerce, it is true, jumped into the breach by developing their own training systems. But they and the network of occupational training schools

(*Berufsschulen*) that was set up, were more interested in expert knowledge than in conservative indoctrination. Nor was the mind-set of those who saw further training as an avenue for upward mobility ever such that they would be open to rebellion and radical ideas.

Finally, universal military service channelled thousands of young men year after year for 24 months into an organization that was permeated by conservative traditions. No doubt the effect of this experience on many of them was profound. Here obedience and punctuality was drilled into them. Men from very different regional and social backgrounds were thrown together in the confining spaces of a garrison and forced to find a modus vivendi. A large proportion of them came from the rural parts of the country, once the Prussian War Ministry showed an increasing reluctance to draft the urban young who were suspected of Social Democratic sympathies. Meanwhile many sons of the bourgeoisie succeeded in getting a deferment. And so the Army came to be seen as the 'school of the nation' where poorly educated young men from the provinces were filled up with conservative values about the Hohenzollern monarchy and national unity. 'Whoever has influence over the youth, has command of the Army' was a later Social Democrat slogan; but as an insight and motto it applied conversely to the officer corps that considered itself charge with upholding the existing order in its conservative and monarchical form. (43)

For a long time the Army relied on the quasi-automatic formative influence of military service as a 'duty to the Fatherland'. By the 1890s, however, this indirect style came to be regarded as insufficient. For a number of years a formal patriotic instruction was introduced in which officers gave their recruits rather one-sided interpretations of the course of German history and of contemporary politics. Soon some of the students, who had experienced a different reality in the slums of the big cities and who had come into contact with Social Democratic ideas, began to ask pointed and embarrassing questions. They were questions which left the mostly upper-class officers either helpless or led them to give provocative answers. Slowly, even the politically less sophisticated recruits started to think about what they were hearing. The infamous 'Zabern Affair' of 1913 was in fact triggered by an indoctrinational lesson that went badly wrong. (44) Meanwhile, the contradictions of socialization through the military also came to the surface as more and more details about the 'maltreatment' of soldiers were made public and

43. See below pp. 257ff.

44. See below pp. 274f.

became a matter of public debate. Suspecting an ubiquitous revolutionary threat, the Army reverted to well-worn methods: searches of lockers for subversive propaganda material; bans on frequenting certain public houses in the vicinity of the garrison.

Overall, the mechanisms of socialization discussed so far nevertheless proved powerful enough to promote a basic identification by a majority of the population with the existing order and its institutions. True, there was a growing number of voters who supported a reform of the political system; but only a few aimed to overcome the Hohenzollern monarchy through revolutionary means. This is also why so many millions joined up, enthusiastically or pensively, when a war broke out in 1914 that had been presented to them as a war in defense of the Fatherland. [45] Nor would one wish to deny that the Army achieved considerable successes with its methods of training and socialization if we look at its purely military achievements and its capacity to keep millions of men fighting a very costly war until the 'military strike' of the spring of 1918 ushered in the final collapse of the *Kaiserreich.* But ultimately it also helped that these millions had been prepared for the strains of industrialized warfare by other socialization agencies and by the routine that mechanized factory work had increasingly become.

For a small minority high school and tertiary education finally constituted important socialization experiences. (Table 51) All three types of high school that proliferated in Imperial Germany experienced an expansion in the number of students. The figure for Prussian *Gymnasien* increased from 63,200 in 1873 to over 103,000 in 1911. The figures for the second type, the *Realgymnasium,* almost doubled to 48,100. Finally, the *Oberrealschulen* grew ten-fold from 4,120 in 1882. Of course, such rises must be correlated to the population explosion in this period. In this respect inequalities diminished, but participation rates still remained very low. If in 1870 0.4 per cent of the total population went to high school, the figure for 1900 was 2.7 per cent rising to 3.2 per cent by 1911. High schools remained dominated by the middle classes, the more so since school fees were high enough to remain beyond the reach of many lower-class families. This was also true of the high schools for girls. While the impact of the latter on their charges may have been more ambiguous, high schools for boys remained agencies of socialization that influenced most of their students in a conservative and elitist direction, especially where the emphasis was on the value of a 'humanist' education centered on Greek and Latin. Only the *Oberrealschulen* may be said to have provided their stu-

45. See below pp. 282ff.

dents with an education that was more geared toward a future in an industrial-technological society. It was also the type of high school that was frequently seen by lower middle-class and middle-class parents as an avenue of upward mobility for their sons. If their daughters made it to a girls' high school, the expectation was that they would come out as better educated mothers who would be able to offer their children a more nurturing environment.

The dividing lines that the school system introduced were reinforced by the tertiary sector. In 1891, there were just under 34,000 students in the Reich. By 1912, that number had risen to 71,710. (Table 52) In 1871, some 0.5 per cent of the population had an academic education. By 1900 this share had increased to 0.9 per cent, rising further to 1.3 per cent in 1910. This small minority received first of all a systematic scholarly training in a chosen field, which would be the spring-board for a comparatively well-paying position in the private or public sectors later on. The exclusiveness of higher education also strengthened in university students an elite consciousness that had already been instilled by their parents and in high school. This was the third phase of socialization during which many of them consolidated their ideological commitments and most of them ultimately became defenders of the status quo. Nor were the lectures of their professors free from ideology and politics. (46) To be sure, higher education also bred rebels, who, if nothing more, advocated social and political reforms. But they must be juxtaposed with those large numbers of students who, when it came to their political beliefs, adhered to an aggressive nationalism toward the outside world and to a dichotomous view of domestic politics which divided society into large blocs of Right and Left. (47)

The fraternities represented an organizational focus for these nationalist tendencies, attracting a considerable, though declining percentage of the students. (Table 86) At Marburg University over 50 per cent were members in 1873. In 1913, the share was a little over 45 per cent. At Bonn, the share slumped from around 56 per cent in the late 1880s to 40 per cent during the final years before World War I. In Berlin, by contrast, around 75 per cent of the students never joined a fraternity throughout the same period. Yet, however interesting these latter figures may be, because they undermine the widespread later impression that virtually all German students were members, the ideological force of the student 'sub-culture' radiated well beyond the fraternities. By the turn of the century, even the sports fraternities (*Turnerschaften*)

46. See below pp. 176ff.

47. See below pp. 239ff.

which had their roots in the liberal era of the first half of the 19th century had moved away from their earlier ideals and had adjusted in their styles and outlook to the more conservative *Korps* and *Landmannschaften*. By 1914, many of their members propounded an integral nationalism and supported illiberal policies at home. Meanwhile the largely conservative 'old boys' paid for the maintenance of fraternity houses and tried to be helpful when it came to career-planning of younger fraternity 'brothers'. Their presence also saw to it that new recruits integrated themselves into the conservative consensus which permeated higher education in the *Kaiserreich*. Contemporary critics of the tertiary sector as a socialization agency never tired of pointing to its role as a breeding-ground for a profound disdain of the 'masses'. This is where social divisions were in fact deepened 'from above'.

8. Majorities and Minorities

A. Basic Problems

In trying to understand the development of German society during the decades before 1914 it is helpful not only to study the situation of women, young people, and the elderly, as we have just done. No less telling is how those individuals and groups were treated who lived in Germany as minorities and how ordinary citizens and those who held positions of power and influence reacted to them. On the one hand, this raises the question of how far the majority was prepared to permit the integration of minorities, a process not to be confused with assimilation; or, alternatively, how far the majority tried to ostracize the minorities in their midst. Integration, in short, implies acceptance of difference, of the 'other'. The second question is related to the willingness of the minorities to assimilate and adapt to the majority society around them. In other words, the concepts of integration and assimilation are not being used interchangeably here, but as complementarities, as a way of looking at the relationship between majorities and minorities from opposite angles. However, until now our knowledge of certain marginal groups like homosexuals is so limited that they cannot be dealt with here. All we can say is that in principle their interactions with the majority society could also be analyzed within this framework. This also applies to the criminal 'underworld', with reference to which recent social history, though still in its infancy, has reminded us that many crimes were in effect poverty crimes. Certainly they cannot be explained by invoking biologistical theories concerning the criminal behavior of marginal groups that were popular at the time. [48]

---

48. R.J. Evans, ed., *The German Underworld* (London 1988).

B. Catholics

The Catholic population of the *Kaiserreich* represented by far the largest minority. In 1871 over 62 per cent of the population were Protestants, and 36 per cent belonged to the Catholic Church. (Table 38) Until 1910 a slight shift occurred in this imbalance in favor of the Catholics. There were considerable regional variations, however. In Hamburg and Saxony the number of Catholics per 10,000 population was a mere 503 and 491 respectively. In Bavaria, Baden and Alsace-Lorraine, on the other hand, the Catholics were in the majority, and so they were in a number of Prussian provinces (West Prussia, Posen, Silesia, Westphalia, Rhineland, and Hohenzollern). Our analysis of denominational developments would be badly flawed, if we used these examples to construct a majority position for Catholicism. Both within the whole of Prussia and the Reich, the Protestants did not only hold the numerical majority; they also enjoyed predominance in the qualitative aspects of power and influence. In Prussia Protestantism was recognized as the official church. The alliance of throne and altar turned the Protestant Church into an instrument of the state, although it would be wrong to overemphasize the discriminatory leverage which this gave to the Protestants. Still, it is difficult to deny that the victory of the Prussian army and state over Catholic Austria was also seen as a triumph of Protestantism. In the Catholic South, the sense of defeat was temporarily overcome by the wave of enthusiasm that swept through these states at the time of the Franco-Prussian War. But soon thereafter Bismarck and his Liberal allies launched the *Kulturkampf* in the expectation of welding the new Federal Germany together on a Prussian and Protestant basis by turning the Catholics into 'enemies of the Reich'.

In the eyes of many Catholics this struggle, whose political dimensions will be discussed later, [49] temporarily assumed very menacing proportions, and its traumatic memory lived on long after Bismarck had quietly abandoned the conflict. After this inauspicious start, whose aim on the part of the majority had been to exclude rather than to integrate the Catholic minority, the denominational question remained on the agenda. The difficulties which Catholics continued to have may be illustrated by comparing patterns of social mobility. In the educational sphere, the participation rate of Catholics high schools and universities was significantly below that for Protestants. The fact that this held not only for Prussia, but also for Bavaria indicated that other factors came into play that had more to do with the prevailing Catholic

49. See below pp. 206ff.

social milieu than with actual discriminations by the Protestant majority. Thus most Catholic high school students and even more so pupils at Catholic girls' schools were oriented toward rather more traditional personal objectives. Of the Catholic women who were registered as freshers at Prussian universities in 1910, only 7.1 per cent were Catholic, with the Jewish share being more than twice as high. (Table 54) A noticeable gap also remained when it came to signing up for science and economics courses. All in all, it may be said that the professional ethos of Catholics was more 'pre-industrial' than that of the Protestant bourgeoisie. Although toward 1914 this ethos also came under the pressure of change, not many Catholics seem to have geared their life to the currents of modernity. The consequences of this attitude can be gleaned from data on the professions and on industry. As late as 1910, the Catholics' share of attorneys was still a mere 12 per cent. They were also strongly underrepresented in the group of entrepreneurs. As to the civil service not only social background and lower educational attainment proved a handicap, but also discriminations of a political and ideological kind. Thus in 1907, Catholics, in terms of the total population, were lagging behind Protestants by as much as 17 per cent when it came to positions in the higher civil service and in the professoriat. Of the cadets who entered the Navy between 1895 and 1914 only 14 per cent were Catholic.

There are many indications that these discrepancies had socio-economic and political causes. In promoting civil servants, it was quite clear that the Protestant superiors, guided by their latent anti-Catholicism, quietly discriminated against Catholics. The latter were faced with the blanket accusation that they were ideologically unreliable and not sufficiently loyal to the Reich. Their loyalties were allegedly with the Vatican, that power beyond the Alpes (hence 'ultramontane'), and not geared to the secular German national state. Social background was important both subjectively and objectively. The statistics show unambiguously that the majority of Catholics lived in rural and small-town parts of the Reich, and we have already seen that the opportunities for upward mobility were poor for such people generally. [50] Denominational discrepancies in respect of upward mobility were thus less stark for groups at the bottom of the social pyramid. However, they were more marked when a comparison is made between the two denominations in the middle classes. Here discriminations for political and ideological reasons were probably strongest. But again there was a difference which cannot be reduced to 'extra-religious facts', but rather resulted from different 'value notions, mentalities,

---

50. See above pp. 50ff.

[and] behavior'.[51] Such intangibles were, as Thomas Nipperdey has argued, partly responsible 'for a measure of a stronger motivation among Protestants to be mobile and dynamic, [to be interested] in science and [a better] education'. Catholics, by contrast were less 'individualized and professionalized, more traditionalist and less oriented toward upward mobility and success and toward career planning'; but they were also 'better integrated into social groups and more affirmative toward life'. Apart from highlighting the differences in professional ethics between Catholics and Protestants, scholars have also pointed to Catholics having larger families and a lower suicide rate.[52]

What is at stake therefore is not just a lack of preparedness on the part of the Protestant majority and its leaders in state and society to integrate the Catholic minority. There is also the question of how far the latter was capable and willing to adapt to the majority that was so eagerly promoting industrialization, urbanization and secularization, i.e. forces which the Vatican eyed with great suspicion. Especially with regard to secularization the Catholic Church in Germany remained conservatively dogmatic, defensive, and authoritarian. Seen in this perspective, the *Kulturkampf* was more than a political conflict. It represented a clash with the forces of modernization which labored for the 'demystification of the world' (Max Weber) and whose spearhead were the Liberals. The Church found it difficult to conclude as little as an armistice with these particular forces even after the end of the *Kulturkampf.* It proved more flexible when it came to the problem of industrialization and its consequences, above all with regard to the 'workers' question' and how it might be organized. The majority of middle-class Protestants had little sympathy with the workers' desire to form associations and to represent their interests. The Vatican adopted a different stance, even if took until 1891 to enshrine it in a papal encyclical. Thenceforth Catholics were called upon to be conscious of their social responsibility, and the welfare work that Catholic priests had been engaged in among the poor and in the industrial regions of the Reich became a task sanctioned at the highest level.

There were two sides to the 1891 Encyclical, though. On the one hand, it marked the Church's step toward accepting the industrial revolution which seemed unstoppable; on the other, it drew a line not only against Marxist recipes for solving the 'social question', but also against Protestantism. Here

51. T. Nipperdey, "Religion und Gesellschaft: Deutschland um 1900," in: *Historische Zeitschrift*, 1988, 612.

52. M. Kaplan, *The Jewish Feminist Movement in Germany* (Westport, Conn. 1979), 96f.

lie the other roots for the growth of a sense, that Catholicism was confined to a 'beleaguered tower' which the Center Party politician Julius Bachem wanted it to come out of when in 1906 he made public his famous appeal. After the turn of the century this striving for greater openness was no longer an enterprise without hope, not least because Protestant pressure had been declining. To be sure, the Kaiser but also many conservative politicians remained convinced that Catholicism and the Center Party (its increasingly more important political arm) received their orders from the Vatican. Meanwhile the Center Party's leadership sought cooperation with other political forces in the hope of breaking through the isolation which, it must once more be added, had also been a consequence of its self-retreat.

Nothing was more supportive of the Bachem line than the impressive growth of Catholic associations to a size where they could no longer simply be ignored or ostracized. If the Protestant majority showed a willingness to integrate the Catholic minority, it was, of course, also because it was so sizeable and, in the age of universal suffrage, accordingly influential. Conversely, the Catholics very strongly felt the pressure to adapt themselves. This pressure was generated in the final analysis by constant change in society and economy which eroded traditional hierarchies. The old clericalism was on the retreat; the lay movement was gaining ground. Now it became clear how deep the traces were that industrialization, urbanization, and secularization were leaving on all parts of German society. A small rift began to run through Catholicism. The warnings of the hierarchy went unheeded. Illegitimacy rates edged up in some Catholic regions. [53] There was a decline in the attendance of services, even though Catholic priests on the whole were more successful in upholding church discipline than their Protestant counterparts. The share of female church-goers was considerably higher than that of male Catholics. Between 1900 and 1912, the share of young males is estimated to have declined from 90 to 60 per cent. In Munich attendance at Easter communion had dropped to around 50 per cent during the late 1880s. Few, however, officially declared that they had left the Church. Similarly, for many Catholics it was a matter of course that their children would be baptized and receive first communion at the appropriate time. Over 90 per cent of the Catholics did not wish to hold a wedding or a funeral without the assistance of a priest.

Taking a bird's eye view, it appears that the old tensions between the Protestant majority and the Catholic minority did diminish over time. Where

53. See above pp. 70ff.

there existed a preponderance of the one denomination over the other, competition was less fierce than in mixed areas. The Catholics began to catch up with Protestants as regards their position in the social and economic sphere. The bitter struggle of the 1870s slowly faded from memory. A new generation came along. Ideologically speaking, 'God-less' Marxism appeared to be the greater danger in the last years before the War. State and Church moved more closely together when defending the German Empire against internal and external enemies. These developments which indicate a better integration of Catholicism into the mainstream, must not mislead us into thinking, however, that the cultural characteristics of the Catholic minority also began to disappear. There was some adaptation to the political and social currents of the time. Like other groups, Catholicism tried, from the 1890s onward, to create a mass base for itself. This was the hour of the 'People's Association for Catholic Germany' which, when it was founded in 1890, had the struggle against the Social Democrats as one of its major objectives. The main target shifted away from the Liberals toward the Social Democrats. The latter now replaced the Liberals as the main target of Catholic political propaganda.

In the long run, therefore, Catholicism in Imperial Germany became more modern and less tightly knit. But there was never any question as to whether it should allow itself to be absorbed into the Protestant majority culture. The Catholic minority culture may have become more similar to that of Protestantism, and yet it had no wish to be assimilated by it. A clearly identifiable Catholic milieu continued to exist in which tradition and innovation combined into a distinctive cultural mix, and not even this mix was uniform. In the more remote rural parts, tradition remained the stronger element. There the position of the old-fashioned parish priest lost little of his prestige, and many devout parishioners adhered to a dogmatic piety that acted as a brake on the encroachment of modernity. In the cities and industrial centers – especially in the diaspora or in regions where the numerical balance between Catholicism and Protestantism was fairly even – the priest would appear in a more modern guise. He knew that only if he responded to the changing circumstances and attitudes of his flock, would he be able to preserve his customary position at the head of local associational life. In these regions loyalty to the Church and piety had a different content from the Catholicism that lived on in rural Upper Bavaria or the isolated Eifel region south-west of Cologne. A glance at intermarriage rates provides a good insight into the changing balance between assimilation and self-assertion among German Catholics. As a result of the deep-rooted historical tensions, exacerbated by the *Kulturkampf*, the rate had traditionally been low, hovering around 8 per cent at the turn of the century. But although the Vatican continued to oppose such marriages as vigorously as before, by 1910 the rate had gone up to 12 per cent.

C. The Jewish Minority

The relationship between Imperial Germany's Jewish minority and the Christian majority may similarly be fruitfully analyzed in terms of the questions of integration and assimilation. The emancipation of the Jews had reached its final conclusion in the 1860s. Their life as social, economic and political pariahs was officially over. Baden and Württemberg had passed the legislation that gave the Jews complete equality before the law in 1861-64. The same policy was adopted by the North German Confederation in 1869 and then taken over by the newly-founded Reich. Even before 1871, the Jews had made good use of the opportunities which this equality gave them. At that time some 512,153 of them lived in the Hohenzollern monarchy; by 1910, the figure was 615,021. The latter figure subsumed some 79,000 foreign Jews, 13 per cent of the German total, who had moved to Germany, mainly from the East. Some 416,000 of all Jews lived in Prussia. Bavaria was home to 55,000, followed by Baden (25,896), Hesse (24,063), Hamburg (19,472), Saxony (17,585), and Württemberg (11,982). A little over 30,000 Jews lived in Alsace-Lorraine.

In the light of a rising anti-Semitism, which will be dealt with later, [54] it is also significant that the Jewish share in terms of the total population actually declined from 1.25 per cent in 1871 to 0.95 per cent before World War I. In large measure, this development is due to the fact that the excess in births over deaths among the Jewish minority declined more rapidly than among the rest of the population. On average Jews married later and practiced more effective birth control. What prevented an even steeper decline was a lower mortality rate among Jews, especially in respect of infants. Another factor was that Jews immigrating from the East tended to have larger families. In the face of these statistics there were even some pessimists in the Jewish community, who predicted the eventual disappearance of this minority, also because the rate of mixed marriages with Christians kept moving up. In the last years before the War, around 13 per cent of all Jewish women had taken a Christian husband. Conversely, between 1911 and 1915 the share among Jewish men was even 22 per cent. In some cities and regions at this time the share reached as much as 62.6 per cent (Saxony) and 73 per cent (Hamburg).

---

54. See below pp. 106ff.

Finally, those ca. 15,000 Jews who converted to Christianity between 1871 and 1909 must be included in these statistics.

Looking at the residential structure of the German-Jewish minority opens a window to an analysis of the occupational structure. Before Germany was seized by the great wave of industrialization and urbanization in the second half of the 19th century, most Jews lived in the rural or small-town areas of Central Europe. They made a living as traders and money-lenders, while the legal restrictions that were still in force at that time prevented them from acquiring landed property. Thus even after 1871, Jews were strongly represented among the cattle and hops dealers of Bavaria. In Baden and Hesse, they excelled in the grain trade, and among the wine-growers of western Germany they acted as 'buyers'. Many Jews also sold haberdasheries, kitchen utensils, and foodstuffs to the local peasantry. Finally, they emerged as money-lenders particularly in those areas where the peasants tried to hide their indebtedness and hence were reluctant to go to the bank or other financial institutions.

In the towns, peddlers who went from door to door were a familiar sight for many years. However, by 1895 the share of Jews in this trade had declined to 8.7 per cent. This change did not merely hint at shifts in the occupational structure overall, but also at a considerable occupational mobility among the Jewish minority. (Table 24) Those who as peddlers had once pushed a rickety cart from house to house, would soon be wholesalers, or sales representatives covering an entire region. The move to the big city became imperative. In 1871 not even 20 per cent of the Jewish population lived in cities; by 1910 the share had grown to 53.8 per cent; in Prussia it was almost 60 per cent. (Table 39) In 1871, some 36,015 Jews lived in Berlin; by 1910 their number had risen to over 90,000. During the same period the Jewish minority of Cologne quadrupled from 3,100, and increased two-and-a-half-fold from 10,000 in Frankfurt. Breslau and Hamburg also witnessed sizeable increases. Overall the change happened more slowly in the South than in Prussia. As late as 1910, around 30 per cent of the Jews of Bavaria and Württemberg still lived in communities of under 5,000 inhabitants. In Prussia the share was much less; by 1910 it had fallen to 28 per cent in towns of over 20,000 inhabitants.

In line with these changes, the share of Jews in industry and crafts rose from 19.3 per cent to 21.9 per cent between 1895 and 1907, amounting to 0.5 per cent of all Germans employed by this sector. Many Jews continued to work in trade and commerce. But in comparison to the total number of employed in this sector, the share of Jews likewise declined, from 10.5 per cent to 8.0 per cent. The really striking findings concerning the occupational mobility of German Jews emerge only if we look at their share among the self-employed. In crafts and industry this share was 43 per cent. This was considerably higher than the percentage of all self-employed in relation to the total working population. Some 54 per cent of the Jews worked in commerce in 1907, compared to the 29 per cent which constituted the share of the self-employed among all people working in this sector. Jews became pioneers in the development of department stores and the mail-order business. They were also strongly represented in private banking, even if the rise of the joint-stock banks led to an overall decline of the Jewish share among the directors of privately owned institutions by 6 per cent to 37 per cent between 1882 and 1895. At the same time many Jews moved up onto the management boards and supervisory boards of the large banks and industrial trusts, though officially they were employees of these companies.

Social historians have tried to refine these statistics. By evaluating Prussian data on millionaires which Rudolf Martin, a former civil servant with the Reich Office of the Interior, had published before 1914 in 21 volumes, Werner Mosse succeeded in identifying 29 families, whose total wealth was over 50 mill. marks each. (55) No less than 9 of these families (31 per cent) were Jewish or of Jewish descent. Among the 25 wealthiest individuals, the Jewish share was 44 per cent; among the top 800 rich people it was still as high as 23.7 per cent. Beyond these percentages at the very top of the income scale, Jews in Imperial Germany generally had a higher income than the population average. The reports of the Inland Revenue Service of Breslau show that 15 per cent of the Jewish tax-payers in the cities fell into the highest tax categories; the figure for Hamburg was even 27 per cent. The Inland Revenue Service reports are warped in two ways, though. Firstly, large-scale landowners rarely appeared in the upper ranks because wealth locked up in landed property was not assessed, even though land prices had risen. Moreover, most landowners were less honest than wealthy Jews and the rural tax officials, who were responsible for checking their returns often did not pursue even the most blatant dishonesties. Their reasons were political and ideological at a time when the *Junker* were 'ailing' economically and in the eyes of the conservative bureaucracy any means to prop them up seemed justified. (56) Secondly, when assessing tax liabilities, an adequate yardstick

55. W.E. Mosse, *Jews in the German Economy* (Oxford 1987).

56. P.-C. Witt, "The Prussian *Landrat* as Tax Official, 1891-1918," in: G.G. Iggers, ed., *The Social History of Politics* (Leamington Spa 1985), 137-54.

can be gained only if we compare Jewish middle-class tax-payers with their non-Jewish counterparts, rather than with the total population. Unfortunately, such data are as yet unavailable.

What can be said, however, is that German Jews, their minority position notwithstanding, fully participated in the expansion of the country's industrial economy, and made a contribution to it which was well above the average. Their occupational mobility was remarkable. Their rise into the well-to-do bourgeoisie opened up better educational opportunities, as many Jewish parents found that the fees for high school and later the costs of a college education for their children were no longer beyond their means. Education and certainly immersion into the religious texts had long had a special importance particularly for Jewish men. Jewish mothers also played a major role in transmitting the values of learning and education. There hence existed few psychological or cultural barriers against going to high school or university. As early as 1863 the share of Jewish pupils at Prussian high schools was 16 percent. As the *Abitur* certificate was an entry-ticket to the tertiary sector, the percentage of Jewish men at first also saw a rapid rise at German universities. In 1886/87 around 9.6 percent of the students at Prussia's universities were Jewish; it was still 8 percent in 1911, although total numbers had increased markedly and the percentage of Jews in the population had declined. After women had finally been admitted to Prussian tertiary institutions, the share of Jewesses was over 14 percent a mere two years later.

Those German Jews who did not take over their father's firm after graduation or otherwise sought a career in industry and commerce, would go into the professions. In 1907, some 14.7 percent of all private attorneys and notaries were Jewish. The figure for physicians was 6 percent, and another 8.1 percent of Jews registered in the occupational census of 1907 gave their profession as 'private scholar, writer, and journalist'. Like in industry and commerce, many of them achieved positions of influence in these professions, above all in the press. This gave them a high visibility, especially in the large liberal newspapers for which they worked. Since the civil service officially adhered to the principle of qualification and merit, one would have expected to find a correspondingly large share of Jews in the bureaucracy and the armed forces. Since the 1860s, the law had established equality in the competition for these careers. However, time and again Jewish applicants found themselves turned down through various tricks and under all sorts of flimsy pretexts. The barriers were particularly insurmountable in the armed forces. Only the Bavarian army officer corps was prepared to make a few exceptions. The allegedly liberal Navy, like the Prussian army did not have a single Jewish officer, though a few converts. A few also succeeded in climbing to the top of the ladder in the civil service. Entering the transport, library, and public health services proved somewhat easier.

To obtain a promotion often proved no less arduous. In 1907, some 4.3 percent of all judges were Jewish, 906 of them in all. Since the number of qualified attorneys of Jewish background was much higher, however, many of them were pushed into private practice, even if they preferred the judiciary. Scholar, many of them highly qualified, had similar experiences. They would be kept waiting for a tenured professorship for years. In 1909 some 2 percent of all full professors were Jews, with a noticeable concentration in the sciences. During the *Kaiserreich* no Jew was ever given a full professorship in German literature or in classics. Among the associate professors (*Extraordinarien*) the share was 7 percent, and again an important statistical point should not be overlooked: This percentage should not be related to the share of Jews in the total population, but rather to the pool of qualified candidates. Jewish school teachers also found professional life a struggle. They were virtually excluded from Christian church schools. Public schools, too, were under a mandate to offer an education that was guided by the principles of Christianity which Jewish teachers were presumably unable to provide. Fortunately, this mandate was handled more flexibly at high school level. Following a decree by the Prussian Minister for Cultural Affairs, Jews could be admitted as teachers from 1872 onward, and the first of them served in Breslau with its large Jewish community. Finally, there were also a few Jewish schools, and here there was even a chance to rise to the headmastership. The material presented so far demonstrates that, their rise in the economy and the educational system notwithstanding, Jews were subjected to an array of discriminations which in turn reinforced their concentrated appearance in other professions. Finally, they experienced many handicaps when it came to honors and decorations, and membership in various clubs and associations was also denied to them.

The reasons for these realities cannot be found among the Jews themselves. Rather their difficulties indicate that this minority had many obstacles put in the way of its integration into the majority society which originated in a widespread anti-Semitism. Innumerable studies have been undertaken on this topic. [57] They are all concerned with divergent types of anti-Semitism, often specific to a particular non-Jewish group. They also deal with the

57. See, e.g., the studies listed in the Bibliography.

organization and proliferation of anti-Jewish prejudice in the decades before 1914. There existed a strong social anti-Semitism which was largely confined to the upper classes as well as the rural and court nobility. Its adherents simply considered Jews inferior socially, and hence totally unsuited to be invited to court. Aristocrats would try to obtain useful advice from Jews in business matters, but even now they would display the inimitable condescension with which they would approach other people of unequal birth. The treatment of Gerson Bleichroeder is a good case in point, who, as Bismarck's private banker, had done much skillfully to increase the Reich Chancellor's wealth. This did not prevent Bismarck's son Herbert from cracking ugly anti-Semitic jokes, the moment Bleichroeder had left his father's house after one of his visits. Although there were some Old Prussian conservatives who were unhappy about these prejudices and about how they were used in Conservative agitation as a means of rallying support from among the peasantry, a vicious type of anti-Semitism also flourished in the entourage of the crown prince and later Kaiser Wilhelm II, which was merely different by degree from the anti-Semitism that existed in Germany after 1918.

Parts of the lower middle classes and the peasantry adhered to a religious anti-Semitism. Promoted by the churches (or at least not opposed by them), this type had deep roots in the history of Christianity and in the early persecutions of the Jews all over Europe. Particularly powerful was the notion that the Jews were allegedly the 'murderers of Christ'. Long before the 19th century, such arguments had repeatedly been accompanied by an economic anti-Semitism that blamed the Jews for harvest failures and other disasters. Now, in an age of rapid socio-economic change, peasants, artisans and shopkeepers time and again found themselves faced with economic ruin, whose larger structural causes they had difficulty in understanding. [58] In these circumstances it was certainly simpler and more comforting to find a scapegoat for these ills. The Jews were a small and easily identifiable group to be thrust into this unhappy role. The prejudice never disappeared even in better times in those regions where Jews appeared as traders and money-lenders. This type of anti-Semitism had a dangerous attraction, and political agitators knew how to play on these feelings.

During the final decade of the 19th century, a racist-biological variant of anti-Semitism began to spread, whose emergence must be seen in connection with the more or less simultaneous rise of an intolerant integral nationalism and a missionary imperialism. It divided the world into 'superior' and 'inferior' nations and 'races'. These currents were reinforced by the spread of

58. See above pp. 11ff.

Social Darwinist ideas. Here history was viewed as a 'struggle for survival' in a power-political jungle, in which those nations and 'races' would win out that were deemed to be better equipped biologically for dominating the weaker ones. The pseudo-scientific foundations of this world view endowed it with a special plausibility. It is thus not too difficult to see why many non-Jews, threatened by socio-economic decline, ideologically confused and predisposed by the above-mentioned religious and economic anti-Semitism would be open to the plain lie that the Jews were not only an inferior, but a particularly menacing 'race' that tried to undermine the biological fibre of the Germans in order to dominate them. After this practically no limits existed to the invention of the most hare-brained conspiracy theories. Already before 1914, such theories were being debated in various splinter associations and propagated in obscure journals and pamphlets. After 1918, the National Socialists added scarcely a new thought to this anti-Semitism. Ultimately, the explanation for the strength and prevalence of such feelings must be sought in the social pathology of the anti-Semites themselves. The Jews played their role only insofar as their high-profile minority position made them an ideal scapegoat. Thus many Germans who subscribed to one type of anti-Semitism, or to all of them, not only came to reject an integration of the Jews; they wanted to eject them from all spheres of life.

The growth of a racist nationalism and its political organizations will have to be discussed in a later chapter. [59] At this point an attempt is made to view the evolving situation from the Jewish perspective. On the one hand, the unfolding of a vicious scapegoat mechanism points to the limited capacity of the majority of Germans to integrate its minorities. On the other hand, there is the question of Jewish assimilation and its possible limits. The case of the German Jews appears to provide an even better illustration than that of the Catholics for the conceptual differentiation proposed at the very beginning of this chapter. The emancipation of the Jews of Central Europe had been predicated on the assumption that they represented a religious community and not a 'nation'. Most Jews agreed with this and accordingly they saw themselves as 'Germans of Jewish denomination' ('*Deutsche israelitischer Konfession*') once a German nation-state had been created in 1871. Under the impact of a growing anti-Semitism and in particular of its racist variant, Germany's Jews began to widen their self-definition. However much they rejected the biological arguments of their enemies, many of them came to realize that their religion was but one important element of the social persona. What also

---

59. See below pp. 228ff.

molded them into a group, was their long history, much of which had been marked by persecution, their cultural institutions and their perceptions of the environment in which they lived. All these elements taken together in fact made them an *ethnic* group, rather than merely a religious community within German society at large.

This consciousness was strengthened by the fact that many German Jews were captivated by the general process of secularization that began to permeate society. They became estranged from their religion, especially in its very strict orthodox varieties. However, this did not prevent them from identifying with their Jewishness in a broader sense and to see themselves as a cultural minority. Because of these developments, which offered the Jews both self-confidence and a sense of belonging, very few of them were prepared to assimilate themselves to the majority to such a degree that their ethnic identity would disappear completely. Nowhere else did this emerge more clearly than in the fact that only a small number actually converted to Christianity. This was a line that many Jews were unprepared to step over. At the same time, the majority environment contained many cultural elements toward which they felt a strong attraction. Indeed, many of these elements could be reconciled quite easily with the Judaic system of values and with their own traditions.

As pressure on this minority mounted from the anti-Semites and other groups and Jewish children experienced open prejudice from their classmates in the school play-grounds, currents arose within the Jewish community which rejected an adaptation that stopped distinctly short of absorption. The supporters of these tendencies worked for a separation and, in the case of the Zionists, even for the founding of a Jewish national state. [60] However, the latter always remained a small minority within the German-Jewish community. More significantly, foreign observers were frequently struck by how 'German' even these more radical elements were in their attitudes and behavior. Theodor Herzl, one of the fathers of modern Zionism, provides a telling, if somewhat amusing case in point for how this 'German-Jewish ethnicity' worked as a hyphenated identity that was in fact synthesis of partial adaptation and reinterpretation of what it meant to be a Jew in Central Europe in the late 19th century; for in 1895 it did not strike Herzl as incongruous when he received the astonished Chief Rabbi of Vienna at his home under the Christmas tree! Similarly, German Jews also had no problems with the ideals and attitudes of the Central European educated bourgeoisie, the

60. See below pp. 232ff.

Bildungsbürgertum. Nor did it cause liberal Jews much headache to reform their own services and to integrate Christian traditions into them. Old Hebrew songs were accompanied by organ music, while the texts were recited in German. Under the impact of secularization, the position of Jewish women in family and community also began to change and the rigid patriarchism that pervaded orthodoxy softened. On the one hand, the role of the mother remained important; on the other, the share of working Jewish women rose by 47.8 percent to almost 49,000 between 1895 and 1907. This was 18 percent of all Jewish women and hence a smaller percentage than the 30 per cent of all German women who had a job in the *Kaiserreich*. But it must also be remembered that most Jews had by this time risen into the middle class. Those 18 percent should therefore be compared with the share of non-Jewish bourgeois women, and in the absence of precise statistics it may be speculated here that the Jewish share was at least the same if not higher. The high share of Jewish female students at universities points in the same direction.

As these social and cultural processes unfolded, Germany's Jews understandably felt challenged by the anti-Semites, whose numbers appeared to be rising, indicating a disturbing socio-pathological potential. They did not want to leave uncontested the lies that were being spread. Nor were they prepared to put up indefinitely with discriminations against them that were based on anti-Semitic prejudice. They also wanted to assert their independence as an ethnic group. These tendencies finally found an organized expression in the founding of the 'Central Association of German Citizens of the Jewish Faith' (CV). The name of this organization, which rejected Zionism, says it all. In speeches and articles, its members insisted thenceforth that they saw themselves as both – as Germans and Jews – and that they fully identified as such with the society into which they had been born. To them being a Jew and being a German were not alternatives, but complementarities. How seriously they took this position, became evident during World War I, in which around 100,000 Jews participated. No fewer than 2,000 of them were promoted to the rank of officer. It did not help them much. Anti-Semitism and the policies of exclusion continued to rise after 1914.

C. The Polish Minority

Cultural synthesis without losing one's own identity was also a strategy of those German citizens who were of Polish origin and of whom large numbers moved from the eastern provinces to the Ruhr area. It was a strategy that ultimately worked no better for them than it did for German Jews.

Conversely, the attitudes of the majority and the policies of the Prussian government put very tangible limits upon their integration. Their experience in turn led to defensive reactions that were typical of ethnic minorities. The development of the German-Polish relationship therefore bears many similarities to that of Germans and Jews. It merely proceeded along a different social level. Whereas most Jews belonged to the middle class, the Polish minority was made up mainly of agricultural workers. Those who subsequently moved West and North, settled in industrial communities and experienced an increasingly proletarian-industrial life. Moreover, the Polish minority lived in clearly identifiable concentrations in both East and West. These circumstances as well as the fact that Poland, until its destruction by Russia, Prussia, and Austria in the late 18th century, had been a sovereign state put the German Poles in a somewhat different setting from German Jews. Zionism remained a marginal force among the latter. Geography and memories of a period of national independence make the history of this minority under the *Kaiserreich* more comparable to that of the Danes or Alsace-Lorraineans than to the Jews or Catholics. Above all the Danes were not merely a culturally distinct ethnic minority, but also a national one. And the more this minority felt ostracized, the greater its desire to separate. The Poles occupied an unusual position somewhere in the middle between Jews, on the one hand, and Danes, on the other, in this spectrum of minority experiences in Imperial Germany. For a long time they stood right at the crossroads, and it depended on the larger domestic development inside the country whether they would take a separatist-nationalist road or the path toward a German-Polish symbiosis.

From what we know about the ca. 3 million land laborers and small-holders in the Prussian East, at the time of the founding of the Reich, they did not possess a strong Polish national consciousness. This consciousness was much more highly developed among the Polish-speaking aristocracy and bourgeoisie. Those who joined the trek to the West in search of a better job were too apolitical to have a clearly articulated ideological position. In the first few years after 1871 it was just a few thousands who migrated to the Ruhr region. According to Reich statistics, their number, including the Masurians, rose to 34,000 by 1890. Twenty years later this figure had grown ten-fold. It is fairly certain now that the Poles who went to the Rhineland numbered 300-350,000. To this figure must be added a string of smaller settlements, e.g. in Wilhelmsburg just south of Hamburg. Remaining statistical uncertainties notwithstanding, it appears that there were around 400,000 Poles outside the eastern provinces of Prussia. Most of them went to the Ruhr area and found employment in the mines. This occupational pattern explains to same extent why they settled in colonies. Especially in the eastern Ruhr there emerged a number of '*Polenzechen*', mines with a high share of Poles among the workforce. Many of these Poles were married. Once a few families had found their feet in the new heavy-industrial environment, they would act as magnets for friends and family who had stayed behind. Single men would be recruited by agents of the mining companies and would be put into company-housing. The number of overnight lodgers was large among the Ruhr Poles. As early as 1881 a survey found that some 735 predominantly Polish households had no less than 1,377 such lodgers. A count for Essen in 1902 even found an average of three per household. The important point is that networks were created in this way through which the long-distance migrants could be channelled. Newcomers were given a bed not only because the rent was needed to improve the family budget, but also because there were the solidarities of the extended family and ethnicity.

Since the number of Ruhr Poles was initially small, the majority population was not confronted with the question of integration. The strangers could simply be ignored. But when they arrived in large numbers, the question of their position within society became more acute. At first sight, there appeared to be a considerable potential for tension between the majority and the Polish minority. Stereotypes and a superiority complex among the native population had existed before their arrival. Language and culture were different. The migrants tended to come from regions in the East with very low wage levels, while Ruhr miners were among the best paid. The Poles therefore acted as a 'reserve army' which made it easier for the mining bosses to push down wage levels. This created bitterness among the indigenous mining community. In short, there were a number of neuralgic points where conflict between the newcomers and the natives might break out. Nevertheless, recent research has shown quite reliably, that the integration of the Polish minority into its *immediate* environment proceeded unevenly, yet more smoothly than earlier historians had assumed. The organization of work down in the mines no doubt helped in this respect. Here German and Poles were exposed to the same dangers, and the work in gangs and teams promoted a sense of sitting in the same boat. Finally, and unlike Germany's Jews, the German Poles did not outpace the majority as regards occupational mobility. Majority and minority shared the very limited opportunities to move up, which existed for all industrial laborers during the *Kaiserreich*. Among native miners intergenerational mobility was 14 percent higher. Meanwhile the Polish miners were hardly ever promoted to a supervisory position which carried with it a period of study at the Mining Academy.

Similar conditions obtained in the textile factories of Wilhelmsburg, where many Polish migrants found employment. Here native workers gained a slight advantage on the ladder to becoming a skilled worker or foreman. However, both groups rarely succeeded in rising to master positions. Better opportunities developed for Poles in the crafts sector; but like their native fellow-workers they were virtually excluded from the lower civil service and white-collar jobs, except for a few Polish 'railroad civil servants' who were promoted to the position of engine driver. This meant that sources of friction due to the one group receiving preferential treatment over the other were few. Accordingly, as marriage patterns demonstrate, the integration of the newcomers was making progress. A survey of the Dortmund Mining District Office showed that in 1893 some 40 percent of immigrant miners whose main language was Polish had married German-speaking women. Until 1914 there was a further rise in the absolute number of these mixed marriages, but the actual share rose only slightly between 1908 and 1912 from 2.8 percent to 3.2 percent among Polish men and from 2 percent to 2.2 percent among Polish women.

Promoted by the expansion of the system of company-owned mining colonies, Polish miners tended to live closely together. This was also true of other regions. Wilhelmsburg experienced 'tendency toward ghetto formation', though not 'in the sense of a concentration that resulted from a discrimination of the minority'. [61] Thus, Polish workers were rarely disadvantaged when it came to accommodation. In this respect only large families had difficulties in Wilhelmsburg. The rest suffered more or less equally with the natives from the poor housing conditions. Wherever 'Polish quarters' emerged in Wilhelmsburg, they were not isolated from the rest of the town; but they did provide stability to an emergent ethnic culture. Christoph Klessmann's findings for the Ruhr have been less favorable. He discovered 'social discrimination, ... above all as a consequence of native prejudices'. [62] As in the case of the Jews, this raises in turn the question of the assimilation of the Polish minority and its openness to this process.

Their language alone made former Polish land laborers from the East who had migrated to the cities of northern and western Germany well aware that they were culturally different from the majority around them. In the Rhineland Catholicism initially still provided a bridge. And yet, just as in the

61. E. Hauschildt, *Polnische Arbeitsemigranten in Wilhelmsburg bei Hamburg während des Kaiserreichs und der Weimarer Republik* (Dortmund 1986), 67.

62. C. Klessmann, *Polnische Bergarbeiter im Ruhrgebiet, 1870-1945* (Göttingen 1978), 93.

case of the Jews, the Polish desire to adapt to their environment never went so far as to be totally absorbed by the native society. Name changes are a good indicator of this. True, between 1910 and 1912 there was a rise in the number of applications to change a Slavic sounding name from 382 to 764. But apparently most of the applicants were Masurians, who, for various reasons, were less resistant to losing their cultural identity. Moreover, even this doubling of applications remained low in comparison to the total number of Ruhr Poles. Their preparedness to be absorbed by their environment also had clear limits when it came to eating habits or to the question of having Polish priests to head their church communities. Above all, it was the mushrooming and colorful associations that pointed to a clear desire to preserve their ethnic culture. Indeed, these associations acted as pillars of a slowly evolving Polish minority culture that became a psychically stabilizing element. In 1906, there were no less than 106 singing clubs with 5,225 members. By 1912 the total number of the mostly cultural Polish clubs in the Ruhr was 875 with some 81,500 members. The range of activities was astounding and included a 828-strong temperance society, probably one of the less popular among the Polish associations. By contrast, the rosary brotherhoods counted over 16,000 members, and even the lottery associations had some 1,500 supporters. Although the new urban environment had begun to change many of the attitudes that the immigrants had brought with them, their cultural heritage was not so easily forgotten. Like the Polish language, it was upheld collectively and passed on to the next generation. At the same time indigenous traditions and patterns of behavior were picked up as well. The new blend that developed is perhaps most strikingly reflected in the closing ceremony of the 5th Festival of the Catholic Associations of Dortmund on 31 May 1885, which had brought Poles and Germans peacefully together. It was a matter of course that the assembled would issue a joint salute to both the Emperor and the Pope and finish the meeting by singing the Leo as well as the Kaiser Hymn. A year later the Stanislaus Association participated quite happily in the public celebrations of Sedan Day, to commemorate the defeat of France in 1870.

If it had been up to the Ruhr Poles, it is perfectly plausible that they would have continued to develop without major tensions as an ethnic minority within their industrial environment and would have seen themselves as German citizens of Polish descent. Unfortunately, the *Kaiserreich* was not a country, and did not have a leadership, that was prepared to tolerate such a minority with its specific culture. Its basic structure was too illiberal and authoritarian. Even more important was that both Germany's elites and larger sections of the population became more intolerant in their outlook toward 1914. Their Germanic nationalism which was unwilling to allow minorities the preservation of their own culture grew into an ever more dynamic and ultimately self-destructive force. It was further deformed before 1914 by additives of a racist and imperialist character which pushed for brutal domination and submission. This nationalism, which to be sure was not a German monopoly, aroused resentment and ultimately a nationalist defense. Over time, this reaction developed into a centrifugal force, and in the case of the Austro-Hungarian multinational empire Slav counter-nationalism became so powerful that it threatened the survival of the Habsburg Monarchy. Incapable of initiating life-saving reforms, the government in Vienna began the open ethnic struggle against the different Slav minorities within their sphere of power. On the Polish side resistance against the repressive policies in Vienna at first came mainly from the nobility and the middle classes, who dreamed of the restoration of the former Polish national state.

Prussia which had annexed parts of Poland during the divisions of the 18th century was bound to feel threatened by these developments. If Polish nationalism succeeded in building up a genuine popular movement, the eastern provinces with their large Polish-speaking populations were no longer secure. This explains why the Prussian government tried to smother the rising Polish nationalism with ever more brutal means. Numerically, the Poles already constituted the majority in some of the provinces. Fears arose of a 'flooding' of the 'German East' with Poles, partly because of immigration from Austrian Galicia and from Russia, partly because the Polish birth rate was higher than the German one and many Germans themselves began to migrate West in search of better jobs in industry. In these circumstances it was not too difficult to see that repressive measures would fail in the long run, unless they were complemented by 'positive' policies. This, however, meant in the minds of the Prussian government and its supporters that the provinces concerned should be 'Germanized'. Thus Bismarck started a *Kulturkampf* of a special kind in the East. The first drastic measures were taken by the authorities in 1885 when they unceremoniously expelled some 32,000 Poles whose German citizenship could not be immediately proven. Since even some hard-line Prussian conservatives reacted negatively to these expulsions, a 'constructive' program began a year later: With the help of a financially well endowed Settlement Commission, large Polish estates were bought up for distribution in smaller parcels to German peasant settlers. Bismarck, who as Prussian Prime Minister was ultimately responsible for this program apparently also hoped to foster the integration of the parties and of domestic politics with this 'national' initiative. [63] However, in his conception of things this integration did not include the Polish minority; it aimed to ostracize the Poles.

The activities of the Settlement Commission had a somewhat paradoxical effect. In the twenty years after 1886 it used its fund of 250 mill. marks more for the purchase of German estates than Polish ones, raising the suspicion that heavily indebted German landowners were saved from bankruptcy under the guise of a 'Germanization' program which enabled them to sell land at vastly inflated prices. Although this was a welcome effect for the 'ailing' *Junker*, the program proved a disaster from the demographic point of view. For however strenuously the government and various private associations, which barely veiled their racist intentions, tried to sell their 'Germanization' policy, by 1914 a mere 22,000 German peasants had actually settled on the bought-up land. One reason for this depressing result was that the Poles applied the rules of the Settlement Commission to their own benefit. Since they were German citizens, they, too, could acquire land, as long as they paid for it. Accordingly they founded some 85 credit cooperatives which financed the acquisition of land by Polish peasants. The advocates of 'Germanization' had the tables turned upon them. In 1904 the frustrated Prussian government made an attempt to block these developments by an unconstitutional move that turned Poles into second-class citizens in respect of their right to acquire land. But soon a decision by the Prussian Administrative High Court put a judicial stop to this policy. Unrelenting in its desire to weaken the economic position of the Poles in the East, another law was ratified in 1908 which made the forcible expropriation of Polish property easier for the purpose of 'strengthening the Germandom in the Provinces of West Prussia and Posen'. This fresh discrimination greatly increased tensions between Poles and Germans when, in 1912, the new law was used against four Polish landowners.

The memorable settlement policies of Prussia were complemented by discriminations in the field of language and education that similarly aimed at 'Germanizing' the Poles. As to educational policies, the measures which had been introduced in the course of the *Kulturkampf* against Catholics in general also offered a lever against the Poles, many of whom were Catholics. Thus the Schools' Supervision Law of 1872 had curtailed the influence of the clergy in the class-room. Since many of these priests in the eastern provinces

63. H.-U. Wehler, "Von den 'Reichsfeinden' zur 'Reichskristallnacht': Polenpolitik im Deutschen Kaiserreich, 1871-1918," in: idem, ed., *Krisenherde des Kaiserreichs, 1871-1918* (Göttingen 1970), 187.

were of Polish background, the Prussian authorities were able to hit the instruction of Polish children at the same time. In October 1873 a degree was added that made German the sole language in schools. For the moment, Polish could continue for several hours per week as a foreign language. Further laws followed in 1876 and 1877 which declared German to be the exclusive language in the administration and in the courts. The year 1908 then saw the final phase in this process of escalation, when a paragraph was inserted into the new Reich Association Law which banned the use of the Polish language in private clubs and associations. In the following year, a number of public servants were dismissed because they had voted for the Polish party in a municipal election.

It is not too difficult to imagine, how 'German citizens of Polish descent' reacted to these measures. A Polish national consciousness now also began to take root among the lower classes who were embittered by the discriminations in education, administration, and landownership. They, too, began to speak up for the preservation of their ethnic identity, sometimes underlined by the use of physical force. Thus the introduction of the language policies led to open clashes between Polish parents and German teachers. In 1906/7 tens of thousands of parents temporarily refused to send their children to school. Prussian 'Germanization' policies and the agitation of German associations, above all the '*Hakatisten*' movement (HKT), gave a boost to the founding of Polish counter-organizations. Faced with discriminations of the kind described above, these organizations were no longer content to pursue cultural objectives. They demanded a restoration of a Polish national state. Polish nationalism became a mass movement and differences became more and more irreconcilable. The government proved incapable of solving the 'Polish Question' in the East and the situation there became badly polarized.

After this it was virtually inevitable that the separatism among the eastern Poles that German ostracism had unleashed would spill over into the Ruhr area. Here, too, the deterioration began when the authorities exerted pressure on the educational front. Faced with small numbers, local officials at first still believed that the problem of ethnic minorities would solve itself. As the *Landrat* of Bochum put it [64], 'in the long run, the Germanization of the Polish elements in this area' will be effected 'through primary schools, marriages, and the constant social intercourse with the German population'. But then the Polish-speaking pupils became so numerous that the authorities lost hope in the success of this long-term strategy. Suddenly, Polish private

64. Quoted in: C. Klessmann, *Polnische Bergarbeiter* (note 62), 66.

schools had their accreditation refused. Public schools no longer took account of ethnic peculiarities. Where the percentage of Polish-speaking students became too high, classes were divided up. Parents who organized private lessons for their children would find the police on their doorstep. Other administrative obstacles were put up. Teachers and officials were instructed that it was their special duty to promote a German national consciousness. In January 1899 the Mining Police issued a degree which expected a sufficient knowledge of German of all miners – for reasons of safety. Discriminations began which affected existential questions. The 1904 Settlement Law made it more difficult for Poles who wished to return to East to use their savings for the purchase of land. And finally, in 1908, came the Association Law, whose intolerant language clauses applied to the entire Reich.

The reaction of the Polish minorities in the Ruhr area or in Wilhelmsburg was predictable: They resisted these repercussions of the 'Germanization' policies in the East upon their own lives. The associational life that, as we have seen, had been predominantly cultural and oriented toward a Polish-German synthesis, became politicized and took on a nationalistic tone. There was a closing of the ranks. The Catholic Church of Rhineland and Westphalia learned this lesson when the Ruhr Poles suddenly began to demand Polish priests and services. Unions and parties underwent a similar shift. The local Polish newspapers which had begun to report regularly on Prussian government policies in the East distanced themselves from what was happening. Meanwhile the German press launched attacks on the Polish minority in their midst. And yet it would probably go to far to speak of a Polish separatism in the Ruhr area. What certainly acted as a counter-weight to such tendencies was the fact that many Polish families had become rooted in their industrial-urban environment that was so different from the rural conditions they had originally come from. They now identified with the Ruhr and their main concern was to get the majority and the authorities around them to recognize their culture and to provide them with equal opportunities for advancement and self-expression. However, official and popular suspicions of the 400,000 Ruhr Poles had meanwhile grown so strong that they could not visualize anything less than a minority that would allow itself to be fully 'Germanized'. It did not matter that defining this Germanness continued to be difficult; but presumably it meant giving up one's ethnic identity, just as the Jews were expected to. A majority of Germans and their spokesmen were unwilling to allow their minorities to continue along the path of cultural synthesis on which they had set out with considerable optimism in the 1870s.

E. Alsace-Lorrainean and Danish Minorities

If a comparison is to be made at all, the experience of the people of Alsace-Lorraine, whose territory the Reich had annexed from France in 1871, is more likely comparable to that of the Poles in the East than to that of the Ruhr Poles. There were no Alsatian or Lorrainean minorities outside the '*Reichsland*', where they in fact constituted the majority. There were also differences between the East and Alsace-Lorraine, the most important among them being that the gradual integration of the population into the Reich developed more happily in the latter region until the truncated constitutional reform of 1911 and the infamous Zabern Affair two years later. [65] This was all the more remarkable since the German civilian administration that had been installed in Alsace-Lorraine in 1871 started its job in most difficult circumstances. The indigenous bourgeoisie was strictly anti-Prussian and culturally, economically, and linguistically oriented toward France. The peasant population of Alsace along the Rhine Valley was predominantly German-speaking and had many ties with Baden, just across the river to the East. The French element was dominant in most of Lorraine. Just under 80 percent of the inhabitants of the territory were Catholics; 17 percent were Protestants, with a slight shift toward the latter occurring by 1910.

Some forty years later, around 1910, major changes had taken place. Thus the elites of the '*Reichsland*' no longer looked toward Paris, but toward Germany. The bulk of the population continued to hope that further constitutional reforms would bring them the same rights and privileges enjoyed by the other Federal States. It is tempting to explain the reorientation toward Germany in purely economic terms and to invoke the magnet effect that the prosperous industrial *Kaiserreich* exerted upon the inhabitants of Alsace-Lorraine. No doubt, the region experienced a moderate expansion of its indigenous industries, once trade had increasingly begun to flow across the river Rhine. Between 1882 and 1907, the share of people employed in agriculture declined by 8 percent to 37.4 percent. Meanwhile the share of industry rose from 36.4 percent to 38.6 percent and that of the tertiary sector from 18.6 percent to 24 percent.

The economic reorientation toward Germany was a painful process which was to some extent forced upon the business community by France. The high French tariffs of 1892 hit the economy of the region hard, particularly the textile industry which was concentrated around Mülhausen near the Swiss

65. H. Hiery, *Reichstagswahlen im Reichsland* (Düsseldorf 1986); D. Silverman, *Reluctant Union* (Philadelphia 1972).

border. German trade policies contributed little to creating an alternative outlet. Attempts to send more products to southern Germany, encountered opposition from vested interests there. In 1871 Bismarck had temporarily granted Alsace-Lorraine special tariff protection; but when this came to an end, local industries had to face the stiffer competition from across the Rhine. The wine-growers of Alsace also had a hard time. For a while the local tobacco industry harbored high hopes that Bismarck would succeed in getting them a monopoly position. When the Reichstag rejected this project in June 1882, this branch also found itself struggling. Only the iron and steel industry of Lorraine posted a tangible rise in production. Between 1898 and 1909 it increased its output from 374,000 tons to 1.2 million tons. Nevertheless, the overall conclusion must be that the rest of German industry and its interest groups did not do a lot to integrate Alsace-Lorraine, however keen the region's businessmen were on this after the virtual loss of the French market. There were other factors in the early years after 1871 that might have facilitated the integration of the '*Reichsland*'. Thus resistance against the annexation was decisively weakened by the westward migration of some 300,000 people. Among them were many who identified very strongly with France and French culture so that practically one fifth of the most anti-German population disappeared. They were replaced by some 176,000 men and women who, as so-called '*Altdeutsche*', settled particularly in Alsace and hence contributed to creating a basic mood that was pro-German.

Alsace-Lorraine is also a good example that clear policies by the administration which aimed at gradual change and reform were capable of winning the support of the indigenous population. The measures taken with regard to school and the French language offer a case in point. Given Berlin's irreconcilable differences with the French 'arch-enemy' as well as the prevalence of a basic intolerance toward ethnic minorities, it might have been expected that Alsace-Lorraine would also be subjected to a dogmatic language policy that was geared to 'Germanization'. The German language, it is true, became the official language of the bureaucracy in 1872 and a year later the same rule applied to the school system. There were also the effects of *Kulturkampf* legislation on Catholic Alsace-Lorraine. But the implementation of these laws after 1874 made but slow progress and French explicitly remained the second language. In fact, the number of communities in which school lessons continued to be held in French rose during the seven years after 1875 from 385 to 435. As late as 1911, some 16 percent of primary schools had no choice but to use the French language with their first-graders, because teachers would not have been able to teach their charges in German. The newly founded University of Straßburg did adopt the German academic system, but it had almost three times as many non-Germans as the universities in the rest of the country.

That slow change and procrastination on the language front were seen as the best way forward, may be gauged from the way the issue was handled in the *Landesausschuß*, the regional representative assembly. First it took until 1881 before German became the official language in this quasi-parliamentary body of notables. But even thereafter deputies who claimed to have insufficient German were allowed to read their speeches from a prepared manuscript in French. French could be used freely in committees. By comparison with other parts of the Reich, the introduction of German as the language of the courts was also delayed by a dozen years. When the language paragraph in the Reich Association Law of 1908 reached the statute book, the administration of the '*Reichsland*' issued a decree that generally permitted the 'co-use' of the French language in public meetings. In short, the regional bureaucracy implemented the language stipulations quite differently from what the Poles had to cope with. No doubt this approach was more conducive to an integration of the local population into the Reich than that in the eastern provinces. Apparently the German administration calculated that time was on their side. Over one or two generations, they believed, demographic and economic changes would take care of the problem.

Meanwhile the desire of the people of Alsace-Lorraine to adapt also developed in positive ways. No doubt, they wished to preserve their regional cultural identity; but even those who had French roots increasingly saw their future as lying with the *Kaiserreich*. Thus, culturally speaking, there emerged a mix of indigenous elements and others that came from across the Rhine. What ultimately disrupted this trend, however, was a huge stumbling block that increasingly appeared in the way of integration: the peculiar constitutional status of the '*Reichsland*' within the German Empire. Between 1871 and 1874, the region had de facto been under a government in which the Kaiser, with the approval of the Federal Council, held both the executive and legislative powers. Only from 1874 did the centralism of Berlin become modified when the above-mentioned *Landesausschuß* was created. From 1877 onwards, this assembly was given the right to participate in the legislative process. Thenceforth the people of Alsace-Lorraine and its leaders pursued the idea of an extension of their rights of self-government. At the end of this process, the region would be recognized as a Federal State, thus gaining equal status with the other Federal States of the Reich.

Yet, time and again the pressure for constitutional reform encountered two obstacles. The most serious stumbling block was the Army which never stopped viewing the region as a bastion and glacis vis-à-vis the French 'arch-enemy' to the West. In the view of the powerful officer corps, their strategic and security concerns demanded the continuation of Alsace-Lorraine's special constitutional status which guaranteed the ultimate primacy of military interests. Serious problems arose, secondly, over what kind of suffrage would apply, should the region ever become an equal Federal State. All other Federal States had restrictive electoral systems and introducing a similar system to Alsace-Lorraine became a precondition of their supporting the region's admission as a full member of the Federal Council. The citizens of the '*Reichsland*', by contrast, had enjoyed France's universal suffrage before 1871 and now expected to regain it from the Germans. This is where the other Federal States sensed danger. Introducing the universal suffrage in Alsace-Lorraine would have greatly increased the pressure to liberalize their systems for which many of their own citizens, and the Social Democrats in particular, were clamoring. Such and other impasses explain why the constitutional reform of 1911 went to the brink of the region's recognition as a Federal State, but ultimately denied it full equality. To be sure, the reform opened up the chance for further changes in the future. But the disappointment of the population with what had been achieved until that year was profound. Soon thereafter they were hit by the Zabern Affair [66] which made it clear to them that, all advances notwithstanding, Berlin and the Army in the final analysis determined their political life. As in the case of other groups this experience was grist to the mills of those who had always been skeptical of some kind of a synthesis between Alsace-Lorraine and the rest of Germany.

The Danish minority found itself in the Reich as a consequence of Denmark's defeat in 1864 and the territorial gains made by Prussia at the time. Secret negotiations in Vienna in 1879 then removed a clause in the Treaty of Prague which would have allowed the Danes to reunite with Denmark after a successful plebiscite. But even before then, Prussia had begun to 'Germanize' the Danish minority in the North by subjecting it to the same school and language policies that so thoroughly alienated the Poles. Following criticism by Berlin of the slow progress that allegedly had been made until 1877, German was to be used in schools in every subject with the exception of religious studies. Repeated petitions to preserve the Danish language submitted during the 1880s were turned down by the Prussian Ministry for Cultural Affairs. The failure of these policies is indicated by the large number of Danes who refused to accept German citizenship. By 1900,

---

66. See below pp. 274f.

relations had grown so bad that the German authorities began to deport those Danes whom they deemed to be openly anti-German. Finally, the election results also demonstrate that up to 1914 the Danish minority remained alienated from the rest of the population in the Reich. The Germans were reluctant to see them integrated, and few Danes sought anything less than the preservation of their national identity.

As we have seen, many problems arose with the country's minorities whether they lived at the periphery of the Reich or right in the midst of the majority population. It is instructive to analyze these problems. They tell us much about the basic character of official policy and about the development of German society, its level of tolerance and its capacity to cope with cultural difference. It cannot be said that the minorities were, in principle, not available for socio-cultural assimilation. But they wanted synthesis and resisted the idea of total 'Germanization'. It would also be wrong to assume that no attempts were made by the majority to integrate the minorities on a basis other than illiberal domination. But the former were repeatedly pushed aside by the advocates of force. Thus a situation arose before 1914 which many contemporaries viewed with increasing despair. On the one hand, the 'Germanizers' could conceive of only two solutions for the country's minorities: absorption or ostracism. On the other, with the passage of time the moderate spokesmen of the minorities found it harder to convince their followers that Germany was a society that tolerated the kind of synthesis and ethnic pluralism that they were aiming for.

9. Basic Patterns of Social Inequality and Their Milieus

If the findings of this chapter on the development of German society during the *Kaiserreich* can be summarized, it is clear that this society was not only more colorful than earlier studies have suggested, but also found itself in restless movement. This movement was connected with the large-scale processes of industrialization and urbanization, of explosive demographic change and secularization. And yet it was not complete chaos and anarchy. Indeed, it is possible to discern various lines that separated or unified those 65 million people who lived in Germany in 1911. There were structures within which it made a difference as to whether a person was male or female, young or elderly, Jewish or Protestant, banker or maid, Bavarian or Berliner. The question that must now be asked is whether we can recognize within this network a basic pattern which would allow us to arrive at more clear-cut answers regarding the character of German society in this period. This question has often been hotly debated with reference to the argument, first put forward in the 19th century, that social classes constitute the framework of capitalist-industrial societies. In the final analysis, so the argument continues, individuals are divided or bracketed together by their class affiliation.

We saw at the beginning of this chapter that the social situation of an individual was strongly determined by his or her position in the market-place. Thus it made a big difference whether a person had cash savings, landed property, or factories or whether he/she earned a living exclusively through employment, with the size of remuneration in turn influenced by qualifications and skills. Max Weber has expanded the concept of social class that Karl Marx had defined primarily in economic terms by the notion of social status which he defined in terms of divergent life-styles and attitudes. He pointed to people who enjoyed a prestige in their community that bore no relation to their position in the economic market-place. The impoverished, but highly respected *Junker* might be mentioned in this context, just as the 'stinking rich' owner of a slaughter-house whose money could not buy him acceptance in the 'high society' of his home-town. However, in most cases one would find a far-reaching congruence between class position and social prestige in Germany.

Webers differentiation has nevertheless remained helpful because he extended the classification of men and women by economic position within a particular society by a notion that brought customs, traditions, and culturally formed attitudes into the equation. He looked for groups that were in a similar situation – and differentiated themselves from others – not merely in respect of their provision with material goods, but also in respect of their 'inner existence'. This extension of perspective has inspired and enriched more recent research on the German Empire. It enabled scholars to move beyond the examination of quantitative data on income, consumption or housing toward topics of a qualitative kind. The study of social history now also included leisure, residential styles, attitudes toward tradition and history, or the interaction with other individuals and groups. It was within this discussion that the centrality of the concept of social class to understanding German society came to be called into question. Thus generational research started from the hypothesis that 'the historical experiences, that unite the members of a particular age-group are more important than any social differences'. [67] In other words, the real conflicts within society occur not between classes, but between generations. At the end of his careful analysis of the 'Generation of

67. R. Wohl, *The Generation of 1914* (note 39), 81.

1914', Robert Wohl ultimately inclined more toward rejecting this position and, although some recent work on veteran's organizations has again emphasized the generational theme, there is no plausible reason not to follow him.

So, if the generational divide is not crucial, after all, what about gender as a category of differentiation? During the past 20 years, women's historians have conducted a lively debate over this question, and some would indeed see gender as being the most fundamental divide. There is little dispute today that a female factory worker and a bourgeois woman shared certain experiences and situations within a society that was patriarchically organized. There is also agreement that class and gender are inseparable and complementary in defining a person *within* a particular class and that the languages of class are gendered. The problem arises when we look at the system of social stratification and structured inequality overall and find that a decision on which of the two relationships has priority can no longer be evaded. And at this point it would appear to be more decisive for the material and psychic situation of those two women that the one belonged to the working class and the other to the bourgeoisie. As this debate unfolded, Thomas Nipperdey and others began to revive the older question that religious affiliation constituted a basic fissure in Imperial German society. Wilfried Spohn then went so far as to postulate that 'the identities of members of the working class were constructed along lines that were essentially based on denomination'. [68] This position, too, has remained controversial, and Nipperdey has been criticized for having given too high a priority to religion and to the denominational factor. [69] If the behavior of voters of the Catholic Center Party, which will be dealt with below, is any guide, it must be concluded that, certain regional 'lags' notwithstanding, class, at least in the long run, proved more important in the behavior of Catholic industrial workers than the conflict between the two major denominations. In other words, just as in the case of gender, the denominational line is not denied, but it is also not seen as overriding the basic division by class. Both have an impact on the peculiar patterns of class formation.

Similar has been the outcome of a debate which stressed the significance of regions in the structuring of German society. Research on the Ruhr area in particular has postulated that regional culture was very powerful in shaping the structures of Imperial Germany at large. This culture was characterized by the fact that men and women living in a region had common bonds on the level of how they interpreted the world around them. They saw these bonds

68. W. Spohn, "Piety, Secularism, Socialism," MS, n.d., 11

69. Review in: *German History*, 1990, 211.

as 'natural' and as a way of setting themselves apart from the inhabitants of other regions. Manfred Brepohl has even gone so far as to argue that 'the people of the Ruhr area regard themselves as "us", because they feel the same, judge in similar categories, and believe that, a lack of structures and a blurring of border-lines notwithstanding, there exists a spatially identifiable sense of togetherness'. [70] There can be little doubt that space and geography play an important part in shaping regional units. They mold human behavior and forms of expression, including language. This was true of the Ruhr region as much as it was of Upper Bavaria, Dithmarschen in south-western Schleswig-Holstein, or in the Magdeburg Basin. Yet however striking regional differences may have been in a Germany that was, after all, a federation of states, in the long-term class lines came more powerfully into play. Language provides a good yardstick here. For an outsider the Baden or Saxon dialect may have lacked class specificity. However, for the natives of those regions it did exist. Thus Hamburgians could instantly recognize, also from the style of speech, from intonation and gesticulation whether he or she had grown up in the working class quarters of Barmbeck or in grand-bourgeois Pöseldorf. Karl Rohe has defined the culture of the Ruhr region as 'essentially a culture of the "little people"'. [71] In this sense we are indeed dealing with a class culture of those workers who, arriving from outside the region, became the backbone of Ruhr industrial society.

Drawing the balance-sheet from many studies of the social history of Imperial Germany, leads us to the conclusion that, in spite of continuing differences of gender, generation, denomination, and region, its society evolved more and more into a class society. This is not meant to imply a drastic downgrading of the significance of the other dividing lines. On the contrary, our detailed treatment of gender in the *Kaiserreich* was designed to highlight its importance for understanding the development of German society and how it was gendered. The same point applies to the question of minorities, of generations, and of regional differentiations. Still, it was in the area of class that, exacerbated by rapid industrialization and urbanization, the sharpest social lines were drawn, bunching or dividing men and women, young and old. Urban-industrial society opened up opportunities for upward mobility,

---

70. W. Brepohl, *Der Aufbau des Ruhrvolkes im Zuge der Ost-West-Wanderung* (Recklinghausen 1948).

71. K. Rohe, "Regionalkultur, regionale Identität und Regionalismus im Ruhrgebiet: Empirische Sachverhalte und theoretische Überlegungen," in: W. Lipp, ed., *Industriegesellschaft und Regionalkultur* (Berlin 1984), 137.

but rarely did the movement, whether intergenerational or connubial, go beyond the slowly consolidating social blocks. This is where the strongest homogenizations and delineations occurred; this is where milieus emerged that were distinctly different from each other. This is why we return at the end of this chapter, after a description of the material and other conditions of the German population, to the question of what daily life within the larger blocks looked like.

At the time of the founding of the German Empire, most men and women were not employed in industry, but in agriculture, and here the landless laborers, servants, and small-holders constituted the largest bloc. The notion that these people constituted a class has been called into question because they lacked, unlike the industrial workers later on, class consciousness and political forms that articulated their aspirations. Nevertheless, it may be said that in the age of agrarian capitalism this group found itself in a similar situation regarding the economic, but increasingly also the social and cultural conditions under which they lived, particularly vis-à-vis the landowners and wealthier peasants who employed them. This division is most noticeable when we come to consider the lives of agricultural servants who were contractually bound by the *Gesindeordnung*, the Code that regulated their lives and remained in force until 1918. To be sure, this Code also imposed certain obligations on the employer which had their roots in a pre-capitalist age. But by the time the *Kaiserreich* was founded, the relationship had in most cases been tacitly transformed into a capitalist wage labor connection (including remuneration in kind). The gradual dissolution of the domestic family community is one tangible expression of this change. Meals were no longer jointly taken, and the servants' food was frequently different, thus sharpening the line which had long existed in respect of accommodation. The resulting tensions were often explosive, even if migration to the cities increasingly provided another way of conflict resolution.

Day laborers, the other large group in this category, may have been slightly better off in that they operated within a 'free' contractual relationship and were able to return to their own cottage or tiny rented apartment in one of the 'reaper garrisons' at the end of their long work-day. Nevertheless, day laborers, too, were tightly controlled by their income situation which was frequently so desperate that whatever positional differences may have existed between them and the servants became less significant than the similarities of their situation. Some of them were able to improve their economic situation a little by tending a small garden in the rear of their cottage. Their wives could take up weaving or other domestic industries. Their children were sent out to take lunch to the fields or to mind the animals. Overall their predicament remained precarious. Slowly leaving the age of deference and resigned acceptance of their fate behind them, they became increasingly aware of the gap that yawned between them and their employers, and, like the agricultural servants especially the young ones among them, resolved the confrontation not by organized resistance, but by migration. In trying to explain why existing conflicts did not assume more radical proportions, it must also be considered that many of these laborers lacked the articulacy to put their grievances into words. And if they did talk back, the well-established mechanisms of social control and even the local police could be mobilized to support the employers. In the face of these realities, it has become problematical to view the village or the estate as a harmonious community. Nor, having given all due consideration to gender and generational differences, could the evolution of social relations in the country-side in this period primarily be explained by reference to those factors. It is important to add that this picture of an agrarian society divided into two blocks remained particularly applicable to the areas of large-scale farming in the East; the division was less marked in the South and South-west where farmsteads were smaller and the social distance between landowning peasants and landless laborers was more easily overcome by the proximity of life in the village community.

At the same time it would be equally wrong to see the lives of hundreds of thousands of men and women on the estates and in the villages as totally joyless and humdrum. In rural Germany, work and leisure in large measure continued to be determined by the rhythm of Nature. The day began at 4 or 5 o'clock in the morning and work was always left to be done even on Sundays. Yet, however, limited the horizons of rural life, there was time to relax and socialize at the end of the day and on holidays. To be sure, this life was still ruled by the strict hierarchies of the village or estate, except where the next town could be reached on foot, by horse-cart or by train. Fairs and other events permitted the younger generation to extend their network of social contacts. They saw different dress fashions, dances and vaudeville. The lucky ones among them might even see a silent movie in the last years before 1914. They would bring back illustrated journals and other reading matter.

Railroad and road construction could push the doors of the secluded world of the village wide open. Construction workers would pass through, whose life-styles were very different and often exacerbated existing generational and social differences. Some villagers took the strangers as models of a more independent life; for others they were invaders without morals, who did not shrink from stealing, from seducing local women, and from spreading venereal diseases. The daily life of those villages that were close to one of the booming industrial regions of Saxony, the Rhineland, or the South-west was even more profoundly affected. Now fresh opportunities offered themselves to find better paying jobs with specified hours of work. Some commuted back and forth, bringing the town with them to their village. Their experiences influenced those who had stayed behind. And if the local agrarian notables had been complaining about their increasingly 'impertinent' servants before, they had only seen the beginning of it. Gradually tensions became politicized, and loud accusations could be heard in the local public house against the 'exploitative masters and gentlemen' and the lack of self-determination.

If the move to the city was permanent, newcomers would not take long to develop a consciousness of the situation in which workers found themselves in the factories: 10-12 hours of work for six days of the week, overcrowded housing conditions, and poor health care. [72] Nevertheless, it would be misleading simply to view life in the working-class quarters as a poverty culture in which long hours of sleep on Sundays were the only recreation. However much factory workers lived under the threat of unemployment, inadequate nutrition, illness, and constant moves, this group of men and women, married or unmarried, developed its own sense of solidarity and were not a 'sullen mass' of people. There was variety in the working-class suburbs, enlivened by customs and traditions that had been brought here from the former homeland. Accordingly, not only material conditions differed substantially from those of the local bourgeoisie, but also life-styles. Language and dress became hallmarks of social classes. It was a sign of social difference whether a person wore a hat, a cloth cap, or a headscarf, a frock coat, an overall, or silk stockings; whether the preferred sport was soccer or tennis; whether on Sunday one was driven by coach or car to a gourmet restaurant or whether one took to streetcar to one's allotment or to a garden café on the edge of town where 'families were able to make their own coffee'. These are just a few examples of how clearly delineated spaces emerged outside the work place, which, on closer inspection, were in effect attitudes of different class milieus and which created a sense of belonging to a larger societal 'camp'.

All these examples cannot be understood unless the dimension of change over time is factored in. Class milieus that were barely discernible in the 1870s, had taken more concrete shape 20 or 30 years later. Although material

72. See above pp. 57ff.

conditions of the industrial working class had generally improved by then, most of its members did not move beyond the ghettoes of the 'rental garrisons' and workers' colonies that have been described in this chapter. This was therefore also the environment in which they developed their life-styles, patterns of social interaction, solidarities, and value system, partly taken from the rural culture they had left behind, partly transforming the latter. The world of the bourgeoisie was on the whole clearly differentiated from this universe. This world, too, underwent change, most tangibly reflected in the rise of the white-collar employee and the civil servant, who became a 'turntable' of social mobility within the large middle class. (73) The milieu of the small town in which the artisans and shopkeepers had set the tone, became overshadowed by the city. Where a provincial milieu survived, it remained largely untouched by the larger shifts at national level. Many craftsmen would have their own house with a workshop next to it, and they would live as solid burghers amidst heavy oak furniture and a landscape in oil on the wall over the settee. Much of small-town life remained tradition-bound, whether with regard to the education of the children or to social life. On the other hand, the lower middle class, whether provincial or urban, was not as restricted to its confines as the industrial working class, from which one kept one's distance materially and socially. People did move up without suddenly finding themselves in a milieu that was completely strange. The middling and upper middle class were not only more secure materially and better networked, but also had a more active cultural life. Their social routine displayed self-confidence. Nevertheless, none of the fine and manifold gradations within the middle class prevented them from seeing themselves (and being seen by others) as another social block which delineated itself from the urban working class, as it did, no less strictly, from the nobility.

The important point concerning this latter relationship is that it was not just the aristocracy that shut the bourgeoisie out 'from above'. The middle class deliberately and proudly set itself apart from the upper class. Only in some regions, like Silesia, was there a symbiosis which led to the creation of a new plutocracy. To have a few titled guests at a dinner party, in most cases did not necessarily reflect an inferiority complex and a desire to be feudalized, but tended to be a display of bourgeois pride. Nor should business interests be ignored. The 'splendid receptions' that Wilhelm and Elly von Siemens held in Berlin, or the 'court' with which the Krupps surrounded themselves at Villa Hügel in Essen must be seen as self-representations of

73. R. Schüren, *Soziale Mobilität* (St. Katharinen 1989), p. 234.

class, buttressed as they were an elaborate etiquette. Meanwhile, although there existed in the capitals of the German Federation an aristocratic leisure class, the main bastions of the ancient upper class continued to be located in the remoter parts of the country. The structural crisis of agriculture forced many of them to live more parsimoniously. But there was also the weight of tradition with its social 'obligations' and expectations that defined the culture of the large-scale estates. This was not as hectic a life as in business or industry. Going on a hunt often constituted the only 'moving and invigorating element' in an otherwise uniform daily routine. [(74)] Upper middle class businessmen who spent part of their newly acquired wealth to buy a stately home and landed property, did not find it easy to make inroads into the rural aristocracy and to be accepted as social equals. Ultimately, that aristocracy remained largely among themselves. Toward 1914 there occurred at most an ideological rapprochement, also with the wealthier peasantry. For the more the propertied strata in the country-side set themselves apart from the rest of rural society, the stronger became their desire to stand together politically. Similarly the bourgeoisie and the industrial working class, economically and socially already more sharply delineated among themselves and vis-à-vis the upper class, began to form themselves into political and ideological blocks whose profile and evolution will be discussed in a later chapter. [(75)] First, more will have to be said about the question of cultural life in the *Kaiserreich*.

---

74. H. Gollwitzer, *Die Standesherren* (note 16), 293.

75. See below pp. 201ff.

Part III: Culture

10. High Culture and Popular Culture

A. Basic Issues

The notion of culture underlying this book is a broad one, as social historians whose interest in cultural topics has been stimulated by anthropology tend to use it nowadays. The focus is not just on individual artistic and intellectual creativity, but on customs and rituals, attitudes and experiences of entire groups, classes, and even nations. This kind of cultural history aims to retrieve the overall milieu that influenced the actions and reactions of men and women in a given period. It includes the study of past conflicts between classes, regions, ethnic groups, and the sexes over what traditions, actions, and cultural goods are acceptable and freely usable. And it raises the problem of resistance to dominant cultural norms and practices.

Of course, this broader framework subsumes aspects of culture which conform more closely to the older themes of cultural history and which will be treated first: the arts, music, literature, the humanities, and the sciences. One main interest here is the analysis of artistic and scholarly creation and the organizational frameworks within which these activities take place. In other words, we will be dealing with what is usually called "high culture," in contrast to "popular culture." However, no sharp line is drawn in this section between the two spheres, since the divisions are often blurred and overlapping. It is well-known that nineteenth-century composers were often inspired by popular tunes. Similarly writers found the material for their novels by "keeping their ears close to the tales of the people." Nor do we wish to promote a notion of culture that is merely interested in "great works" and disdainfully excludes the sphere of the "trivial." Indeed, the latter sphere – even if it is considered "trashy" – may tell us a great deal about a particular society and its development. This is also true of both working-class culture and the emergent "consumer culture" of the late nineteenth century.

There is one final general point. The retrospective observer usually does not find it too difficult to recognize the gradual evolution of artistic styles or of scientific theories and methods. But in tracing such developments we should not forget that time and again, radical counter movements grew out of the struggle between a dominant "orthodox" school or approach and a "modern" one. Thus many cultural debates took the form of a dialectical conflict, and if the year 1890 is seen by many today as an epochal divide, the roots of modernity and modernism go back much farther. What often exacerbated these conflicts was that they broke out between an older and a younger generation of artists or scholars. And in many cases it was not so much the radicalism of the young, but the stubbornness of the established artists and the ruthless ways in which they used their prestige, power, and influence, that made the controversies so acrimonious. In the art world, this opposition between the generations, having gone through various preliminary tussles, could be discerned on a broad front by the early 1890s. This was the turning point of the fin de siècle, when a revolution "transformed culture in all its branches. It utterly changed painting, sculpture, and music; the dance, the novel, and the drama; architecture, poetry, and thought. And its ventures into unknown territory percolated from the rarified regions of high culture to general ways of thinking, feeling, and seeing. A very troop of masters compelled Western civilization to alter its angle of vision, and to adopt a new aesthetic sensibility, new philosophical style, a new mode of understanding social life and human nature." (1)

B. The Bismarckian Period

If we look at the fine arts against the background of these broader developments during the first two decades after the founding of the German Empire, their conservatism, which was manifested by a suspicion of all stylistic innovation, is particularly striking. The aesthetic principles which painting adhered to in this period had been firmly established for a long time. Above all, it was still supposed to be the task of the artist to depict what was good, true, and great in humanity. This concept of art engendered a peculiar mix of exactitude and romanticization which could be found in most works. The political events of the 1860s provided plenty of inspiration for the production of patriotic scenes from history. Thus many battles of the Wars of Unification, as well as the political and social highlights of the period, were portrayed in oil on huge canvases. Georg Bleibtreu, Carl Becker, Christian Sell, and Anton Werner were among the best-known artists. Ferdinand Keller painted the frequently reproduced "Apotheosis of Wilhelm I." Among the painters of historical subjects and portrait artists of the high and mighty were

1. P. Gay, Freud, Jews, and Other Germans (Oxford 1978), 21f.

many whose names were soon forgotten. Apart from those already mentioned, Karl Friedrich Lessing, Karl von Piloty, and Franz von Lenbach were among the successful ones. No doubt they were all technically accomplished and even important masters who showed much affection for precision and detail. In their later years, some cautiously experimented with impressionist elements; but, with the exception of Adolf Menzel, they were shaped by conformism and aesthetic narrowness.

This was especially true of portrait painters, who enjoyed great popularity after 1871. There was a growing number of bourgeois who – having accumulated a respectable wealth – had themselves or their families painted. Portrait sessions were no longer just a pastime of the nobility and of the heads of ruling families, although Wilhelm II loved to be painted in all sorts of fantastic costumes that said much about his mentality. Of course, such works were almost invariably designed to satisfy the patron's desire to recognize himself on the canvas, ideally somewhat beautified. There was also a demand for historical paintings and landscapes, as the expanding museums were anxious to fill their galleries with well-known names. The extension or new construction of ministerial buildings, schools, assembly halls, and opera houses helped to create a considerable market for art. Once ministers and city fathers had their portraits put up in halls and chambers, industrialists and bankers did not want to be left behind. There was always a special place in the lobby of the headquarters building for a bust of the firm's founder, with the current owner, in oil, looking benignly down from the wall. For those who could not afford an original, cheap reproductions could be hung, in expensive-looking gold frames, above the living room settee: these depicted wild Alpine landscapes or storm-whipped tall ships in the North Sea.

Sculptors and architects similarly found themselves in harmony with their bourgeois and noble patrons when it came to commissioned work. They also moved into new fields of activity. There were first of all those innumerable monuments that commemorated the victory of 1870 and other historical events. The intent of patriotic edification and indoctrination was highlighted at both the pompous opening ceremony and at annual festivities like Sedan Day. Until the turn of the century some three hundred monuments were put up in Prussia alone, excluding the war memorials that many communities and cities erected for their fallen soldiers. Among the larger historic monuments were the *Hermannsdenkmal*, built in 1875 near Bielefeld to commemorate the Battle of the Teutoburg Forest, waged against the Romans; and the *Niederwalddenkmal*, built in 1883 near Rüdesheim on the Rhine. These were followed in 1897 by the *Kyffhäuserdenkmal*, erected in memory of the medieval German Emperor Frederick Barbarossa, and the *Deutsches Eck*, erected at the confluence of Rhine and Moselle in Koblenz. The last large construction before World War I was the *Völkerschlachtsdenkmal*, built near Leipzig in 1913 to celebrate the defeat of Napoleon there a century earlier. Second only to Germania, Bismarck became a frequent object of veneration in stone, whether in the shape of the old man himself, like the one sternly gazing across the port of Hamburg in St. Pauli, or of so-called Bismarck towers, like the one that sits on top of the Deister Mountain near Hanover. A "Victory Column" was built in Berlin in 1873. By the end of 1901 no less than thirty-two imposing statues had been put up along the "Victory Avenue" that led up to this column. The statues represented prominent figures in the history of Brandenburg-Prussia, each flanked by two busts of somewhat lesser-known men. Women were not honored in this way. All these pieces of art tell us a great deal about the concepts of art and culture held by the patrons, the artists, and the admiring passers by. The garden became the "central image of the good life" in which architects tried to blend culture and nature. [2] Residential architecture, which displayed pomp, pride, and elegance, also aimed to show how prosperous the Reich was becoming. The artists drew from styles which were familiar – classical and baroque. The facades of town houses and apartment blocks were designed to impress. The stairwells were generously laid out in marble with large mirrors along the walls. The taste of the bourgeois inhabitants for solid oak furniture and heavy draperies has already been mentioned. In short, the members of the well-to-do middle class tried to represent themselves not only in their portraits, but also in the public and private buildings they commissioned. [3] The conservative artistic establishment drew its strength from this patronage.

Meanwhile the interest of the princes in promoting the arts did not diminish. Wilhelm I preferred military scenes and insisted that all details of military dress be meticulously copied, but he also kept himself informed about general developments in the field. Outside Prussia, the Bavarian kings were patrons with a marked preference for the traditional and its exaggerations. Ludwig II constructed Neuschwanstein like a castle straight out of a fairy-tale. His Herrenchiemsee, a palace on an island southeast of Munich, looked like a mini-Versailles. In 1874 the neo-Gothic town hall was completed in Munich, the artistic and cultural center of the south. Museums, galleries, and churches were also put up there. Friedrich III, the son of Wilhelm I and in

---

2. C.E. Schorske, Fin de Siècle Vienna (Cambridge 1981), 302, 310.

3. See above pp. 7f.

1888 Kaiser for one hundred days, had personal contact with painters like Werner, Menzel, Piloty, and Bleibtreu. He appointed himself guardian of the Prussian museums and tried to influence their acquisition policies. Friedrich's son, Wilhelm II, probably had the most pronounced views on the arts. He thought the statues along *Siegesallee* were more beautiful than those of the Renaissance. Hermann Knackfuss, Max Koner, and Hermann Prell were his favorite painters. He also loved the work of the maritime painter Willy Stoewer, especially those that showed the monarch on the bridge of one of his warships. In architecture the Kaiser developed a passion for the Romantic period and for the neo-baroque. Above all, in his conception of things art had a pedagogical function. As he put it during the unveiling of further *Siegesallee* statues, art was supposed to contribute to filling the laboring classes with ideals. All Germans, he added, had the task of upholding these ideals. They would inspire the lower strata of the population and help them to liberate themselves from the restrictions of ordinary thoughts and attitudes. [4]

That art was to elevate the people and to serve a conservative stabilization of society was a view which the fine arts establishment shared with him. Above all, they had already in Bismarck's time used various institutions to promote their ideas. Werner played a key role here. As a young artist he had caught the eye of those in power with his large paintings of historic scenes, like his depiction of the proclamation of the Reich at Versailles in 1871 and his representation of the 1878 Berlin Congress. He was an accomplished and careful painter, without much depth. His organizational talents were all the more remarkable. In 1875, when he was only thirty-two years of age, he became the director of the powerful Berlin Academy of the Arts. He also assumed an important role in the German Arts Association and the Association of Berlin Artists, whose chairman he became 1877. The latter, founded in 1841, had been granted a royal charter in 1867 and at the end of the 1880s had some six hundred members. Many of these painters were of no more than average talent and became Werner's foot soldiers in his fight against stylistic innovation. Partly financed by the government, this association staged annual exhibitions, and since all painters wanted to show their pictures, there was invariably a great deal of kowtowing toward the chairman and the selection committee. Werner, who hardly ever changed his own style, also saw to it that younger artists who were more prepared to experiment and who had begun to develop different aesthetic ideas would not get their work exhibited. This regime remained in power for many years, supported by the

4. J. Penzler, ed., Die Reden Kaiser Wilhelms II., vol. 3 (Berlin 1907), p. 61f.

cultural bureaucracy and the high aristocracy, spearheaded by the Hohenzollerns and the conservatism of the general public. But around 1890, the time was ripe for revolts and secessions.

Literature underwent a development similar to that of the visual arts, except that the book was less dependent than the painting on the support of academies and artists' associations. Accordingly, nonconformists among the community of writers had a better chance than similarly rebellious painters of achieving a breakthrough, and often did so much earlier. Hence changes in this sphere came less abruptly than in painting. One reflection of this is that a number of women gained recognition and popularity in an artistic world that was otherwise dominated by men. Among them were Marie von Ebner-Eschenbach, Clara Viebig, Gabriele Reuter, Helene Böhlau, Bertha von Suttner, Hedwig Courts-Mahler, and Eugenie Marlitt. At the same time it must be remembered that the narrative style that was dominant after the founding of the German Empire first emerged in the middle of the nineteenth century from a critique of the humanist educational novel that the previous generation had developed. As early as 1853, Theodor Fontane had demanded in an essay that literature must mirror real life. But his appeal was rarely heeded in subsequent decades. Books by Joseph von Scheffel and *A Struggle for Rome* by Felix Dahn were popular. Meanwhile real life in an age of rapid industrialization and urbanization looked rather different and more depressing than what was portrayed in historical novels and in quite traditional, patriotically inspired short stories. The realist novel began with the assumption that there were clear limits to human action and that moral codes should be viewed with skepticism. This position may have contributed to facilitating the introduction of new themes later on. For the moment, however, it tempted writers to worship the power, if not of the state, at least of history, where good would win out over evil. An alternative position that was no less conservative was to highlight the contradiction of the human existence and to end up in a noncommittal sentimentality.

It was partly for this reason that novels and short stories with a regional flavor gained great popularity – a development which can be seen in the context of a growing movement of *Heimatkunst* (regional art). Theodor Storm became one of the towering figures of this kind of regional literature in gale-torn northwestern Germany. Hermann Sudermann took up East Prussian themes, and Paul Keller Silesian ones. Hermann Löns wrote about the rural parts of Lower Saxony, while Dietrich Speckmann dealt with Rhenish motifs. Like Ludwig Thoma, Ludwig Ganghofer wrote highly successful novels set against the background of the untamed landscape of the Alps.

Gustav Freytag, Friedrich Spielhagen and the Swiss writers Gottfried Keller and Conrad Ferdinand Meyer are known to this day, but none of them left the confines of traditional novel and short story construction. They displayed a quietistic joy in writing on the small-scale themes that they had inherited. Paul Heyse, on the other hand, is largely forgotten today, although he wrote some one hundred fifty novels and received the Nobel Prize for Literature in 1910. He and his bourgeoisified classicism occupied a position among the writers of the cultural metropolis of Munich similar to that which Werner and Adolf von Menzel occupied among painters in Berlin. Thus the literature of the Bismarckian era was neither subjectively nor politically radical. It was a literature that could be found on the coffee tables of the well-to-do middle and upper classes. Its readers included the young ladies of the nobility and the *haute bourgeoisie*, who seized any opportunity to become better educated. [5]

Similarly, the plays that were put on the stages of the many court and town theaters were intended to please and uplift. Suburban stages specialized in farces, comedies, and sentimental pieces mostly for the lower middle classes. Outside Berlin, which became the theater metropolis of Imperial Germany, Saxe-Meiningen under Duke Georg II developed a type of theater that was characterized by its "veneration for the text, the inquiry into the historical-geographic ambiance, verbal precision, the use of prominent actors even in smaller roles, intensive rehearsals, training of supernumeraries, and careful selection of costumes and sets." [6] This "style-shaping model stage" performed primarily Schiller and Shakespeare, and it is indicative of the general development of culture and society that the latter – once shown with frequent noisy interruptions before lower-class audiences – had meanwhile been integrated into the culture of the upper classes. Of course, these groups would sternly frown upon audience participation. The classical repertoire was concerned with beauty and the victory of good over evil. Meanwhile other theaters offered, apart from light society plays, historic dramas from antiquity or the nineteenth century. No effort and money was spared when it came to the reputedly genuine reconstruction of expensive historic sets and costumes. Theater thus became an experience for the audience. But rarely did they leave a performance feeling disturbed by its message. Opera was even better at putting on the stage a pompous fairy-tale which had little connection with real life outside. Only popular theater might contain the occasional social criticism and mockingly take on the rule of the clerics, as in Ludwig

5. See above pp. 67ff.

6. H.A. Frenzel, Geschichte des Theaters (Frankfurt 1984), 490.

Anzengruber's *The Fourth Commandment* or *The Priest of Kirchfeld.* Although the *Gewerbeordnung* of 1869 had opened the way for entrepreneurial initiative in the arts, for many years privately owned stages were no less conventional than the public ones.

In contrast to the visual arts, however, there were from the start exceptions to the basically conservative style of writing and theater of the Bismarckian period. And the works of the nonconformists became well-known enough to pose a genuine challenge to prevailing artistic canons. This challenge came less through a change in form than in content, and next to Wilhelm Raabe and Max Kretzer, Theodor Fontane is of course most closely associated with this shift. As he grew older, Fontane increasingly went back to his postulate of 1863 that literature must reflect real life. In his later works, he used the depiction of real life to criticize both sources and himself; this encouraged a younger generation to abandon the dominant themes. Indeed, if Fontane's *Irrungen und Wirrungen* (1888) and *Frau Jenny Treibel* (1892) are compared with the novels of his contemporaries, it becomes understandable why conservatives were appalled by his subtly indirect attacks on the upper classes and his "objective" descriptions of the life and survival of ordinary people. Even if he never integrated the predicament of industrial workers in the cities into his genre plays, the full range of human problems, societal fissures, and gender conflicts is nevertheless to be found in them. Eduard von Keyserling was another writer who portrayed a rural world that was coming apart at the seams.

The young Gerhard Hauptmann similarly turned his back on idealism. In 1889, his *Before Sunrise* – a play about immorality, alcoholism, and avarice – was recommended to Otto Brahm, the director of the recently founded Free Stage in Berlin, by none other than Fontane. What fascinated the latter about Hauptmann and led him to compare his work with Henrik Ibsen's naturalist dramas was, to be sure, anathema to what the audience expected to see on stage and until now had regularly been presented with. Brahm could afford to put on controversial plays, including Ibsen's *Ghosts*, only because they were performed in front of the members of the association that subsidized the Free Stage. Government censors could not ban plays shown to private audiences, and indeed it was for this reason that leading Berlin intellectuals like Theodor Wolff and Maximilian Harden had founded this theater. It was as misleading as it was typical that the Brahm's opponents, who sometimes disrupted performances, immediately condemned the Free Stage as a platform for the spread of social democratic ideas. Still, Brahm certainly belonged to the artistic opposition that emerged at this time. As he put it 1891, "the new literature is revolutionary, the theater is conservative. Among all factors, none clings more obstinately to tradition and none is in its entire essence as hostile to innovation as the stage." [7]

Like a number of other directors of private stages, Brahm worked hard to change this conservatism. When in 1889 he put on Hauptmann's *Before Sunrise* he had his first scandal on his hands, surpassed four years later by the first performance of the same dramatist's *The Weavers.* No public stage was able to show such plays at this time. In 1874 a Reich Press Law had been ratified that required all periodicals and papers to be submitted to the local police for scrutiny. Prior notification also applied to theater performances. If a particular issue or play was deemed to violate existing legal or moral norms, it would be confiscated. Worse, author, publisher, and producer could be prosecuted under criminal codes that had been sharpened by the 1878 anti-Socialist laws. Among the most frequent charges were *lèse majesté*, obscenity, and blasphemy. The lapse of the anti-Socialist laws did not ease the use of these codes in the 1890s. Authors were frequently hauled through the courts. The young Kaiser intervened repeatedly, first in 1890 when he ordered the Prussian Minister of the Interior to the Palace after he had lifted a ban on Hermann Sudermann's *Sodom's End* – a play whose title alone made it suspect enough. But it also became clear in this period that the advance of the new theater could not be stopped and that Imperial Germany was not an art dictatorship. A verdict by the Prussian Supreme Administrative Court of 1894 declared censorship of Hauptmann's famous play illegal, and soon thereafter it was performed in the Deutsches Theater in Berlin.

It should be added that Hauptmann never arrived at a clear-cut definition of his naturalism. On some occasions, as in the case of *Florian Geyer*, he took his material from a historic period of disruptive change. In *Hanneles Himmelfahrt*, his naturalism appeared not in the shape of an open social criticism, but of a psychologizing dream poem. For the historian the reactions of the audiences of that time are of particular interest. When *Before Sunrise* was performed, there were loud protests from the audience, especially against the key figure of the socialist Loth. We have a diary entry about *Hanneles Himmelfahrt* by the later Reich Chancellor Clodwig von Hohenlohe-Schillingsfürst, who was not a reactionary in matters of the arts. He wrote in December 1893: "A monstrous, wretched piece of work, social-democratic-realistic, at the same time full of sickly, sentimental mysticism, nerve-racking, in general abominable. Afterwards we went to Borchard's to get ourselves

7. Quoted in: H. Schanze, "Theater - Politik - Literatur," in: H.-P. Bayerndörfer, et al., eds., *Literatur und Theater im Wilhelminischen Zeitalter* (Tübingen 1978), 285.

back into a human frame of mind with champagne and caviar."[8] Powerfully projected by Hauptmann as well as Halbe, Arno Holz and Johannes Schlaf, naturalism, like the criticism of dehumanization and double standards that accompanied it, could no longer be ignored. The shift in literature and theater had occurred. Its first rumblings could be heard earlier than in the case of the visual arts. Once the latter had also succumbed to naturalism, there were few barriers against further artistic revolution; indeed, naturalism would soon be overtaken by other and newer stylistic directions.

The same may be said with respect to music – with an important qualification relating to the work of Richard Wagner. The revolution in tonality which he triggered as early as the 1870s was obscured by the backward-looking worlds that he put on the stage in his operas. His audiences loved him as a Germanomaniac mythmaker, who perpetuated the canon of classic drama with his final victories of good over evil. If Wagner's music alone had been performed in a darkened concert hall, it may be doubted whether he would have found so many bourgeois and aristocratic admirers. The schizophrenic attitude of Wilhelm II was probably not untypical of many contemporaries. The Kaiser could be heard raving about the heroic themes of Wagnerian operas; but when it came to passing judgment on the music, he thought that it made "too much of a noise." This was a somewhat simple-minded response to what Wagner had in fact dared to do, i.e., to abandon, albeit not completely, the dogmas of classic harmony. He combined this departure with visions of a *Gesamtkunstwerk*. The expressionists also dreamt of this later on, as they rebelled against the growing specialization in the arts and in modern society in general.

Despite the increasing chromaticism of Wagner's music, to which we shall come back in a moment, musical life in the Bismarckian period remained conservative. Like the theater and the museum, the concert hall was part of the furniture of urban and court culture in central Europe. To be sure, music lovers did not go merely to hear the great composers of earlier ages or to be seen in black tie and evening dress. What also attracted them were the virtuosi on the program or their favorite conductor. Occasionally, a conductor might even succeed in smuggling a modern piece into a traditional program of Haydn, Bach, Mozart, Beethoven, and Mendelssohn, as, for instance, Johannes Brahms would do when he took the baton. Indeed, the reception of Brahms' work is typical of the obstacles which more experimental compositions encountered. For however much Beethoven was his

8. P. Gay, Weimar Culture (Harmondsworth 1968) 4n.

model and however much his work is characterized by a dualism between orderliness and romanticism, for a long time the critics and audiences denied him recognition of his genius as a composer. Thus Louis Ehlert remarked on Brahms' Symphony No. 1 when it was first performed in 1876 that the author was "a far-flung, speculative mind, a mixture between a musician of the good old days, who had the sound of harmony in him and whose cradle cover had a contrapuntal pentagram embroidered into it, and a universally trained man of the modern age. What differentiates his music from that of all his contemporaries is that he introduces another world into it, [a world that] gently and movingly knocks [at the door of] our heart." (9) Only toward the end of Brahms' life, in the 1890s, did the once polite applause change into enthusiastic cheering. Hamburg, his birthplace, made him an honorary citizen, and he ended up as a wealthy man whose work was used to counteract the effects of Wagner.

Significantly, Brahms never saw himself as a radical. He hoped to advance no more than a bit beyond the great master, and even in his Symphony No. 1 shrill dissonant sequences are to be heard only in the first movement. In this respect, Wagner was a very different person. During the revolution of 1848, he had still been on the wanted list of the Saxon authorities. Thirty years later he was no longer a political revolutionary. Nevertheless, his gigantic ego gave him the self-confidence to see himself as the herald of an artistic revolution. That his bombastic operas gained him an enormous reputation no doubt tells us a great deal about the mentalities and dreams of his audiences. But even his enthusiasts left the long hours of his performances somewhat exhausted and dazed, whether or not the revolutionary claims of the work had escaped them. After this, the animated light-heartedness of an Italian opera was a wonderful relaxation. It was no less characteristic of the durable catholic tastes of the musical world that operettas enjoyed great popularity. These depicted the rosier sides of life, and any problems raised in them would by the time of the last act dissolve into a superficial happy end. For a long time operetta lovers in Paris or Vienna may well have outdone their German counterparts; but when Franz Léhar came to Berlin, he met with more enthusiasm there than he had found in the Austrian capital.

C. The Emergence of Modernism

Although the debates on a revolutionary change in arts and society and a new beginning in Europe went back to the 1880s and earlier, the shift became very

9. F. May, *Johannes Brahms* (Munich 1983), part II, 167.

clearly discernible after 1890. In terms of cultural developments, this year marked the farewell to the nineteenth century and the beginning of the twentieth. Any analysis of this development, which accelerated tremendously toward 1914 and beyond, must bear in mind that it occurred not merely in Germany, but in France, Austria-Hungary, England, and Italy as well. For this reason it is quite difficult, even with the benefit of hindsight, to decide where the initial impulses came from. Nor is it easy to discover the mainstream along which the transition proceeded. At this time, many currents of thought emerged that were often moving in very different directions. They might criss-cross later on, as their adherents tried to find answers to what all of them perceived as a cultural crisis. The debates that will be examined in a moment often took place in relatively small circles of artists and intellectuals, who were usually ignored or rejected by the divergent elite groups. Large sections of the population remained untouched by the arguments about modernism. At most the proletarian culture movement represents an exception in so far as it also posed the question, albeit from different ideological premises, of a "new culture" that would overcome the culture of the bourgeois age of the nineteenth century. [10] The diagnoses and solutions that were offered by this latter movement were correspondingly removed from those that Germany's artists contemplated during the Wilhelmine period.

In light of our discussions below, [11] one further point must be mentioned here: many of the artists who participated in the march toward modernity pursued aesthetic and often highly individualistic concerns; but this did not prevent their constant talk about a European cultural crisis from spilling over into the political and ideological sphere. There they captivated elements of the middle class that were already deeply unsettled by the process of rapid industrialization and urbanization. The belief in the idea of Progress and the confidence in the rationality of human beings that had permeated much of the nineteenth century were lost. Developments in economy and society appeared to make life more anonymous and more difficult to fathom. The globalization of politics and economics went hand in hand with the internationalization of high culture. While foreign avant garde artists settled in Germany, a nationalist cultural philistinism proliferated. The rise of new mass movements on the ideological Right must therefore also be seen against the background of the cultural shift of the 1880s and 1890s. [12] This is why,

10. See below pp. 159ff.

11. See below pp. 146ff.

12. See below pp. 228ff.

next to the evolution in economy and society, the developments in the cultural-intellectual sphere that will be analyzed in a moment provide the backdrop to the treatment of the new political movements later on in this book.

If the innovations in the sphere of high culture had any common source, it lay in the conviction of many artists and intellectuals at this time that the certainties of the nineteenth century had been destroyed or at least become questionable. Now the argument was gaining ground that bourgeois Europe was sick and that its values were in a state of decay. Friedrich Nietzsche was among the first to make this point, and his ideas and aphorisms were picked up by the artistic avant garde a generation later. [(13)] Many intellectuals were equally convinced that the seeds of the European sickness had been sown long ago and that its visible symptoms had merely been downplayed until now. To unmask bourgeois hypocrisy, to destroy as an illusion the idea of a world that constantly improved itself – this was the decisive impulse behind the cultural debates which now also started in Germany with full vigor. Modern man – women only figured in rather peculiar ways in the mainly male world of artists – would have his mask torn from his face; he was to be forced to show his true physiognomy.

The powerful feelings and perceptions of reality that have been described here could be viewed as part of a generational phenomenon whose significance has already been discussed. [(14)] True, there were a number of older artist and intellectuals among the avant garde who had been early representatives of the "revolution" before 1890. Others had allowed themselves to be convinced that a new beginning had to be made. But on the whole, it was "the Young Ones," as they were called in Vienna, who joined the movement. It must remain an open question, whether these young artists and intellectuals were driven by oedipal complexes. No doubt their rebellion was one against the "authority of the paternal culture"; [(15)] for in the meantime a generation of intellectuals had grown up that felt alienated from traditional values and notions of aesthetics. They believed that they had sharply diagnosed the ills of the age and now made their insights part of their creative wrestling with the world around them. Earlier art had been assumed to be the expression of universal values and order through which it was possible to achieve a harmonious balance between one's inner self and the outside world. Now artistic creativity was seen as a violent explosion and a revolutionary accel-

13. See below pp. 180ff.

14. See above pp. 86ff. See also below pp. 270ff.

15. C.E. Schorske, *Vienna* (note 2), xxvi.

eration toward a state of disorder and nihilism. Value systems seemed fragmented and transitory. In this way, the changed consciousness of intellectuals after 1890 first revolved around emotion and imagination, the construction of the self and its dissolution, its sexuality, and its ultimate destruction.

Given these tendencies, it was no doubt logical that the revolt in the fine arts defined itself as a "secession." The term alluded to the model of the *secessio plebis* by which the people of ancient Rome announced their withdrawal from the Republic and its mismanagement by the patricians. The only question was how far this rejection should go, and this is where further controversy began. Many intellectuals and artists conceived of nothing less than the creation of a new world in which human beings would live according to principles different from those of the nineteenth century. Others were less concerned with building an alternative world than with establishing a situation of pluralistic chaos, which they thought was the only true reflection of the human condition. Culture was supposed to mirror life in the full spectrum of its possibilities, good and bad, without cosmetic operations to show only its beauty.

The chaos solution to the crisis can be traced most easily in the development of music. In discussing Wagner and Brahms, we have already indicated that the rules of tonality that had been observed since the Renaissance had been extended step by step in the direction of dissonance. Nevertheless, composers eventually returned to the prescribed order of consonance and harmony. It was Claude Debussy who once stated that "music is not just harmony that caresses the ear and has a pleasant, narcoticizing effect – something that can easily be absorbed because so much and, one believes, so much that is different peacefully chimes together." [16] The question was how far artists were to move away from this peaceful kind of musical experience. In this connection it is significant that Richard Strauss at first did not break with the established principle of harmony. Later he wrote with reference to his tone poem *Tod und Verklärung*, composed in 1889, that the soul of the patient, who had long been tortured by terrible pain and shaken by fever, in the hour of death left the body "in order to find in the eternal universe in most perfect form what could not be fulfilled in this world." [17] His tone poem *Ein Tod* on the other hand made a deliberate break with classical dogma. Thenceforth his operas also began to move into dissonances that badly hurt the ears of audiences

16. Quoted in: P. Gradenwitz, *Kleine Kulturgeschichte der Klaviermusik* (Munich 1986), 242.
17. Quoted in: W. Schuh, *Richard Strauss* (Munich 1976), 183.

used to Mozart or Puccini. And in his *Salomé* he finally broached themes on stage that had hitherto been taboo subjects for bourgeois morality.

It was Arnold Schoenberg who finally pushed chromaticism and the disintegration of harmonies beyond Wagner to its logical conclusion, although one does not have to go as far as W. Mellers, who has called Schoenberg's use of the full range of the twelve semi-tones of the scale "a technical and intellectual necessity." (18) Schoenberg's hesistancy in the face of his own radicalism, which reflected the uncertainty of his age, is evidenced by the fact that he took the step into atonality only in his piano pieces of 1908 and in his Quartet No. 2 of 1922. Up to that point he preferred to generate an overall mood through the use of long modulations of the chromatic scale. In this way, the listener was given a feeling of endless suspense of the kind that Strauss had been trying to provide as early as 1896 in his tone poem *Thus Spoke Zarathustra* and which Gustav Mahler had attempted to create in a different way again in his Symphony No. 5. Schoenberg, too, therefore hoped to create through his music cosmic visions which, incidentally, can also be found in his paintings. It is especially his "gazes" that gain a central importance in this respect – those eyes that, though they may not have seen everything, had nevertheless taken in much: the ugly and the beautiful, the good and the evil. They are eyes that give us an inkling of the unfathomable complexity and the inner chaos of the human situation; for they speak and are mute at the same time.

Other artists and intellectuals did not want to take the path into permanent disorder. They tried to reestablish a balance in a world that appeared to be falling apart, though they hoped to do so not by repairing what was left, but through a fundamental renovation resulting from a search of the self. Since reality had become problematic to them, they set out on a long inner journey on which the search of the self would not be constrained by objective limits. It was not surprising that this search should include the sexual sphere which the churches and bourgeois morality had banned from public discourse. While the liberating experience of eros may have opened up new dimensions, sexuality also generated anxieties stemming from the supposedly unfathomable female soul. If vitality and a male fear of being swallowed up became too difficult to separate, retreat into narcissism and the escape into pure art alone promised salvation beyond reality. Thus some artists lapsed into a world of illusions, in which they loved only their own disorderly selves.

---

18. W. Mellers, *Man and His Music*, vol. 4 (London 1969), 186.

Not surprisingly, this kind of journey into the unknown was unacceptable to other intellectuals. Reality had not become blurred, fluid, and meaningless to them. They refused to retreat from reality through introspection and to create a totally individualized and fragmented culture. They were not interested in narcissistic self-exploration which ultimately threatened to end in an adaptation to a real world that, after all, was still out there. Instead they set out to change this world and to create a tangible new culture. To them creativity was not *l'art pour l'art*, but a judicial investigation that uncovered social injustice and condemned it in order to bring about social change. The question was, though, whether the great task of cultural reconstruction could be achieved through radical revolution alone, or whether it was possible to take the route of modernizing reform and functionalize the structures and norms that had already been built in the process of industrialization and urbanization.

Before we give concrete illustrations for the emergence of these divergent and coexisting currents, it is important to remember again that initially all protagonists of change found themselves in the same boat. Differences between them took shape only slowly. The reason for this is that at first there was a common opponent who was then still powerful and who was best confronted jointly. After all, the *secessio*, the departure from the cultural edifice of the artistic patriarchs of the Bismarckian age, was not just about abstract aesthetic positions; it was also about whether artists would be able to exhibit work that had broken away from the orthodoxies of their elders. The question of power and influence had thus been posed. The "Young Ones" were not content merely to stack up their work in studios. They, too, craved for recognition. They wanted their ideas to be taken seriously.

As early as the 1880s, there had been signs of a growing dissatisfaction with the authoritarian conservatism and the lack of imagination of the older generation. As far as the fine arts are concerned, the year 1892 was an important turning point. In the spring of that year some 106 artists decided to leave the local chapter of the Allgemeine Deutsche Kunstgenossenschaft in Munich. Dissatisfied with Lenbach, the dominant figure in the Bavarian artistic community, and also dissatisfied with the funding policies of Werner in Berlin, the secessionists founded their own association, the Verein der bildenden Künstler Münchens. The repercussions of this "Munich Secession" could soon be felt in the Reich capital. The Munich artists had seceded partly due to their fear of competition from Berlin and their disapproval of mass exhibitions that pleased all and sundry. The crisis in Berlin also involved the more basic question of how far new styles should be represented. In September 1892, the exhibitions committee of the Association of

Berlin Artists had resolved to invite the twenty-nine-year-old Norwegian painter Edvard Munch to present his work at a special exhibition in the rotunda of that association's building. This was a great honor for the artist. But when the show opened in November of that year, the conservatives among the membership were scandalized by Munch's disturbing colors and motifs. They demanded a closing of the exhibition. Some 250 members turned up for an extraordinary meeting of the association in mid-November, and at the end of a heated debate there was a small majority in favor of cancelling the show.

Many of the opponents of this decision thought of immediate secession. But those who wished to leave had no money with which to set up an alternative organization. Moreover, the dissidents were split among themselves. In the end they followed Walter Leistikow's advice to continue work inside the existing association and to try to change the attitudes of the majority. When it became clear that this was impossible, partly because of strong animosities between Leistikow and Werner, the "Berlin Secession" was finally effected in 1897. Max Liebermann, who was now fifty-one, became the new chairman. His work enjoyed a considerable reputation, but he also had many enemies. His themes were taken from the life of ordinary people, and later also included that of upper-class people, whose faces fascinated him and whom he portrayed without pathos. For this reason he was seen as an open and conscious social critic. This may have been a question of perception. One critic professed to being absolutely horrified by the ugliness of one of Liebermann's paintings. [19] His picture Jesus in the Temple, whose portrayal of Christ offended the religious feelings of Catholics and Protestants alike, led to charges of sacrilege and anti-Semitic attacks.

Beyond this kind of obnoxious criticism, it is not easy to classify Liebermann stylistically. It is certain that he abandoned his peculiar type of realism for a while and, influenced by France, turned to impressionism. Some of his later works seem to point in the direction of a completion of his naturalist phase. Perhaps it was because he painted so imaginatively that Liebermann first gained highest recognition abroad, and only later in Germany. His prestige enabled him to become one of the spokesmen and advocates of modernism outside the art community. Among the secessionists, a group with a variety of disparate outlooks and temperaments, he acted as an integrating force. And now that they had left Werner's association behind them, there were no limits to their experimentation with styles and motifs.

---

19. See P. Paret, *The Berlin Secession* (Cambridge, Mass.), 44.

On the one hand, there were "poor people's painters," as Wilhelm II called them, who advanced their societal concerns more or less openly. Among these were Hans Baluschek, Arthur Kampf, and Käthe Kollwitz, whose ideological position was close to Social Democracy. Heinrich Zille should also be listed in this connection, although his street and backyard scenes, taken from the milieu of the Berlin working-class quarters, contained his accusations in rather more subdued form. Some of his vignettes made reference to the desperate situation of the proletariat only in their ironic captions. Most of his artwork confined itself to the loving portrayal of men, women, and children, who, though living in a desolate environment, had against all odds succeeded in preserving their humanity.

At the other end of the artistic spectrum were those who had developed what came to be known as German Impressionism, above all Lovis Corinth, Wilhelm Trübner, and Max Slevogt. The contours in their work often disappeared completely in a soft carpet of colors. No ideological aims could be discerned. Like their French counterparts, the German Impressionists did not intend to inform the viewer about the subject matter. They postulated subjectivity, the primacy of what impressed itself upon the individual's artistic senses. Other painters concentrated on the landscapes and people of the different regions of Germany, while a fourth group took up the ideas of the *Jugendstil*, first developed in Vienna, and then turned to decorative art. *Jugendstil* also tried to challenge artistic orthodoxies and was looking for the new in "simplified, stylized forms that were decorative and ornamental." Above all, its adherents saw themselves as "bearers of those utopias of happiness, youth, vitalism, and harmony which secretly" one still hoped to achieve through art. [20]

Yet, there was little time for consolidating the new currents. Change came ever more rapidly. Corinth, one of the leading members of the Berlin Secession, briefly toyed with Expressionism, to which Lyonel Feininger, Max Beckmann, and Emil Nolde had firmly committed themselves when they joined the Secession in 1905. In the summer of 1907, Ernst Barlach finally showed two of his beggars who were supposed to represent the nakedness of lonely and shivering human beings between heaven and earth. Conservatives promptly criticized them as obscene. It was probably

20. H. Kramer, *Deutsche Kultur zwischen 1871 und 1918* (Frankfurt 1971), 219 (for first quotation); F. Trommler, "Theorien und Programme der literarischen Bewegungen," in: H.A. Glaser, ed., *Deutsche Literatur* (Reinbek 1987), 62 (for second quotation).

inevitable that, just as the role of the artist in society became the subject of heated debate, divergent styles would also be at loggerheads inside the Secession. It was not just a question of Impressionism or Expressionism, but also of whether artists had a collective responsibility to society or whether, removed from politics and ideology, they should take only their individual creativity as their point of orientation. Finally, the secessionists had to contend with the competition of older cultural centers in Dresden, Dessau, Hamburg, Düsseldorf, and Frankfurt – centers that, thanks to the prosperity of the local bourgeoisie, had seen a renaissance.

The Berlin Secession, like the Association of Berlin Artists before it, became threatened by schism. Open conflict broke out in 1910, when the selection committee for the big annual exhibition rejected no less than twenty-seven artists who had submitted their work. Among them were Emil Nolde, Ernst Kirchner, Karl Schmidt-Rottluff, and Max Pechstein. Not without some justification, these artists felt that they were now subjected to the same treatment that Werner had meted out to the Secessionists half a generation earlier. Pechstein and others thereupon founded the "New Secession" which organized two exhibitions a year later. A similar split occurred at about the same time in Munich, when the local Association of Artists rejected a picture by Wassily Kandinsky. In December 1911 the so-called *Blaue Reiter* group staged a first exhibition of its own. After the arguments of 1910-11, the disintegration of the Berlin Secession could no longer be halted. Conflicts over styles were exacerbated by personal animosities, and in the fall of 1913 the whole enterprise finally collapsed when the majority of its members left. Worse, the visual arts in general presented a picture of growing fragmentation. Thus the *Die Brücke* group that had been established in 1905 in Dresden by Kirchner and Schmidt-Rottluff also broke apart in 1913.

It is conceivable that these centrifugal tendencies might have come to the surface much sooner, had the bastions of conservatism not remained strong, buttressed as they were by official policy and by Wilhelm II in particular. Werner's attacks against modern art continued relentlessly. He was certain to be of one mind here with the Kaiser whose silliness in matters of the new styles was difficult to match. When the monarch was shown a painting of the Grunewald by Leistikow, he remarked that he had been to this forest and knew for certain that the trees there did not look like that. No doubt this was the kind of incomprehension with which other critics also viewed the new styles. They just never got the point of modern art. The Kaiser's views might have safely been ignored, if he had not used them for political purposes. He believed that art should uplift people and educate them in a patriotic sense.

Consequently, "poor people's painters" like Kollwitz quickly became a threat that was perceived to be real. When, in 1896, she received a gold medal for her work, the honor was not handed over to her. Liebermann was compelled to turn down a decoration which the French Legion of Honor had offered him in 1889. Even the German Impressionists incurred the wrath of the Kaiser – however apolitical their works may have been.

After this it is not too difficult to visualize how Wilhelm II reacted to Expressionism, whose aesthetic concerns ran counter to the pedagogical definition of art which the monarch labored so hard to construct. This had far-reaching consequences for the acquisitions policies of the Prussian museums. It was also thanks to the Kaiser's and Werner's interventions that the German art show at the World Exhibition in St. Louis in 1903 was very conventional and unrepresentative of actual trends. At the same time, the Kaiser was not powerful enough to dictate art policy. True, faced with growing tensions in politics and society at large, the monarch was deeply disturbed by the talk of a cultural crisis and the need to revolutionize the arts. Occasionally, he intervened impulsively in the decisions of the cultural bureaucracy. But he could not stop the advance of modernism. Indeed, his conflict with Hugo von Tschudi, the director of the Prussian National Gallery, demonstrated the constraints upon the Kaiser's power. Tschudi thought the new directions in painting too important to exclude them from his collections; so when he asked for a supplement in his budget in order to buy several paintings of the Barbizon school and the Kaiser denied the request, the director got the missing 400,000 marks from private patrons. Following this impertinence, the monarch had Tschudi dismissed, but the latter went to Munich to continue his important work in the Bavarian capital.

It may also be taken as a sign of changing power balances and of a greater acceptance of modern art that the liberal press became more and more scathing about the Kaiser's interventions into the arts. While works by Liebermann, Corinth, and others continued to be banned from the National Gallery in Berlin, the Hamburg *Kunsthalle* proudly acquired and displayed them. The ministerial bureaucracy, eager to portray Germany as a culturally modern country, pleaded for greater pluralism. Hildegard von Spitzemberg, who came from the more liberal southwest, although she had become increasingly conservative with age, went to see the summer exhibition of the Berlin Secession in June 1900. As she recorded in her diary, she did see some objectionable pieces, but also many others that caught her enthusiasm. [21]

21. R. Vierhaus, ed., *Das Tagebuch der Baronin Spitzemberg* (Munich 1960), 396.

The prices that works by Liebermann, Kandinsky, or Kollwitz fetched on the art market may be taken as another indication of growing recognition. By 1906, their drawings cost as much as an industrial worker would earn on average in six months. A few years later catalogues listed oil paintings by Liebermann or Trübner at 20,000 marks. However, it would be a mistake to deduct from Werner's gradual marginalization in the art world that he and his supporters had abandoned the fight. They also had on their side broad sections of the educated middle classes who continued to prefer the catholic tastes of the Academy to the paintings of the Berlin Secession. What both factions had in common was that art had meanwhile become part of a culture of consumption which was reflected in the founding of organizations that tried to represent the economic interests of artists.

In reference to the avant garde's forays into Expressionism, another polarity must be noted. A glance at the newspapers and journals of the Right will show that they used the widely perceived "ugliness" of modern art as a lever for ruthlessly politicizing intellectual and artistic debates. Toward 1914 the attacks against what was said to be "un-German" in Wilhelmine culture were conducted in a language against which there was hardly any protection. This means that, when looking at the greater pluralism of cultural activity in this period, we must not overlook the polarization of opinions that occurred at the same time. This was a seemingly paradoxical development that had its parallel, as will be seen, in the realm of politics. [22] Even if the Berlin Secession ultimately won its victory over the conservatives around Werner, the country's elite and other groups who got involved in the debate over art had certainly not been won over to an unconditional liberalism and an art that knew no taboos.

The shift in literature and theater that has already been examined was a rebellion against a common enemy, but it also involved fragmentation. Like some of the visual artists, some writers categorically asserted that the autonomous creativity of the individual was answerable to no-one and shunned political commitment. As a representative of this orientation, Stefan George comes to mind who, surrounded by his disciples, championed the retreat to the inner self and cast himself into the role of a poetic visionary of another world. Accordingly, his circle was preoccupied with the ritualistic. Rainer Maria Rilke's aesthetic was deeply concerned with the interpenetration of the inner and the outer worlds. Ultimately, Rilke's attitude towards life displayed an optimism that the George Circle had lost. But he also articulated a

22. See below pp. 210ff.

modernist approach when he wrote in a letter of October 1907 that art must see life in "what is horrible and seemingly repulsive" because these aspects of life were just as valid as all others. [23] Meanwhile reality remained something perfectly tangible for those who were engaged in social criticism. Since naturalism, having risen early to an influential position, continued to occupy that place, the fragmentation in literature and theater proved as irreversible as the fragmentation in the visual arts.

In a more general sense, Thomas Mann's novel *Die Buddenbrooks* (1901) may also be said to fit into the modernist mode. In it he portrayed the slow decline of a patrician family in the Hanseatic town of Lübeck and, more broadly, the fragility of the bourgeois world. Mann also displayed a strong interest in the psychology of his characters, even if he tried to distance himself from them through irony. This was also true of his relationship with art and its contemporary postulates. Basically of a conservative mindset, Mann was in the final analysis an advocate of preserving the unique cultural artifacts that the bourgeoisie had produced. He therefore remained a burgher among his often eccentric fellow artists, which in turn made his books more accessible to an educated readership. The antihero who perishes with and through the world remains a marginal figure in his writings. Thus the middle-class reader could recognize himself in Mann, as – in this period of economic boom – he nursed his fin de siècle mood. For *Die Buddenbrooks* does not just deal with Lübeck; this was *the* novel of this epoch. Not surprisingly, its author found himself among the most widely-read German novelists before 1914 – unlike his brother Heinrich. Certainly, the middle-class reader had much greater difficulty identifying himself with Heinrich Mann's antibourgeois and politically committed critique of society. Perhaps his characters were not as subtly constructed as those of his brother; indeed to some extent they were grotesquely overdrawn; but sociologically his books captured basic features of Wilhelminism more accurately. His criticism was not so much of the bourgeois world per se, but rather of its deformation (e.g., in *Professor Unrat*), of the emptiness of the Wilhelmine conventions that had become petrified, and of the brutality of the middle class, especially toward the weak and those who spoke up for them. In *Der Untertan* he put the following words into the mouth of his protagonist, the businessman Diederich Heßling, when the latter learns of the shooting of a worker suspected of a petty crime: "For me this event reflects something really great, something majestic, so to speak, that someone who cocks a snook can simply be gunned

23. R.M. Rilke, *Gesammelte Briefe*, vol. 2 (Berlin 1939), 432.

down, without a court verdict out in the street." Carl Sternheim's plays that put the small-town bore on the stage tended to elicit a condescending laugh from his urban and urbane audiences. That petty bourgeois was indeed despicable, but the audience never really noticed that the mirror was also held up to them.

Like the satire of Heinrich Mann and Carl Sternheim, the sarcasm of Ludwig Thoma went straight to the bone, especially when he dealt with basic problems of the bourgeois marriage. Thus in his *Moral*, Frau Beermann in one place remarks to her husband that both of them had been "playing theater for many years" – he as the "Christian head of the family" and herself as the "pious onlooker." Yet, she added, no ideal had been "shattered." Their marriage simply did not have one anymore. It was difficult enough to cope with this kind of female impertinence, which many contemporaries took to be a sign of a general decline of morals and of the growing demands for an emancipation of women. [24] Even harder to stomach was the open literary discussion of sexuality, including such topics as sex without love, erotomania and prostitution. Just as the visual arts began to shock people with their modernist treatment of nudity, literature was not far behind. Here Frank Wedekind became one of the *enfants terribles* whose works dealt with sexual murder, homosexuality, masturbation, and procurement. Wedekind's *Lulu* took its audiences into the sphere of the nocturnal and sensual, evoking deep male anxieties. Lulu for him was the "primordial figure of woman," shown in this case in its most devouring and at the same time most narcissistic embodiment.

Women appeared more often in a less disturbing guise which was closer to the traditional image of them in a patriarchal society. In some writings woman was presented as the sensitive female who enables man to discover his own sensuality. As the critic and dramatist Rudolph Lothar put it in 1885 in *The Psychology of Literature*, as "woman's striving for power, and the competition between man and woman" found expression in the fact that "female hypersensitivity is transmitted to man in [the process of] looking, enjoying, thinking, and touching." [25] Lothar's statement, which displays an interest in psychology typical of the time, is significant because he defines this alleged role of the woman as "feminism." However, there were limits to the discussion of sexuality in pre-1914 Germany that existed not merely because of the watchful eye of the censor. Even those artists who counted

24. See below pp. 234ff.

25. R. Lothar, *Kritische Studien zur Psychologie der Literatur* (Munich 1895), 19.

themselves among the avant garde adhered to a concept of gender relations that was by no means "free." Although interest in the self and subjectivity were great, the female psyche left all men bewildered. Nor was the removal of this barrier achieved through the works of Franziska Reventlow, Lou Andreas Salomé, and Ricarda Huch, who took up the theme of the emancipated woman. Because they were assumed to be different, women, in the eyes of men, continued to have something frightening about them and the postulated dissolution of individuality in an orgiastic sexual union was seen as a deterrent. In these circumstances the widespread stereotypes about women rampant in society at large offered a stability that the male artist, however radical his ideas may have been in other respects, did not dare to undermine. At most he might deal with the misery of a marriage entered into for financial reasons; or he might raise the question of equality in marriage. As far as gender relations were concerned, the last literary taboos concerning sexuality and gender were broken much later in the twentieth century. What is now judged to be great literature was still considered pornographic before 1914 and thus existed outside the realm of art. Meanwhile the older tradition of the sentimental *Heimat* novel or love drama continued virtually untouched by modernist and postmodernist experimentation.

In many other respects the social boundaries of the arts in Wilhelmine Germany were fast disappearing. The more Expressionism left Naturalism behind, as it had done in the visual arts, the more shrill its messages became. Although we still possess little detailed knowledge of the intellectual preconditions of this genre, there were some quite amazing eccentrics among its representatives. As a French observer wrote in an essay on "Youth Searching for a German Culture of Modernism": "The thronging in the streets, the fermenting of ideas in literary circles" put the artists "into a state of drunkenness, the more so since it hit them with an empty stomach." Thus "a new messiah" presented himself to the inebriated older bohème "at regular intervals": "Conradi began to swoon when he visited the bordellos; Arno Holz, standing between smokestacks, played the prophet; in the Würzburger Hof [a beerhall], Karl Bleibtreu announced his royal rule over the waitresses and the literature which had been toppled." [26] Among the younger generation, the titles of their journals, like Sturm (1910) or Aktion (1911), published by a circle around Jakob van Hoddis, Kurt Hiller, and Erwin Loewenson, indicated that by now more was at stake than modest linguistic experiments. In the

26. F. Berteaux, "Die naturalistische Revolution in Berlin und München," in: H.P. Bayerndörfer et al., eds., *Literatur* (note 7), 440f.

case of some, like Franz Pfempfert, it was not just the artistic intellect, but the entire mind that was in a state of pathological disorder. The disciples of Hiller and Loewenson, like those of Walter Hasenclever, worshipped an activism that was oriented toward the ideas of Friedrich Nietzsche and his "transvaluation of all values." [27]

Hasenclever's work, which often deals with the theme of the rebelling son, is also permeated by a celebration of life, a cult that spread after the turn of the century. As he put it retrospectively, his writings were designed to take him close to life. It was only in his later work that, following Hiller, he left this narcissistic vitalism behind and turned toward an activism that ultimately led him to promote the idea of an anti-Wilhelmian cultural revolution. He expected a new spiritual man to be born from this upheaval, but he lived long enough to be witness to an age of destruction. And when, in 1949, he looked back upon this age, suicide seemed the only way out. Thus destruction and self-destruction were never far apart in the thoughts and actions of the avant garde. However, these intellectuals not only pursued radical objectives; their language, too, was that of an experimental literature and theater whose roots had much in common with another art form that flourished before 1914: cabaret.

In dealing with cabaret, it is important to realize that it was not just the type of political cabaret that later reached its prime in the Weimar Republic. Rooted in Parisian Montmartre, in the carnivals of central Europe, and in the travelling entertainers on the fairgrounds, this art form saw itself as an alternative to the great theater and established a different relationship between itself and the audience. Like experimental theater, cabaret was anything but an orderly performance watched from numbered seats. The stage was not set apart from the audience. Cabaret tried to create intimacy. Its lyrics were both sung and spoken. Its short sketches presented parodies and caricatures of the human predicament often without reference to the politics of the day. Thus artists who, like Hauptmann, took the struggle for modern art very seriously might be satirized by their cabaret colleagues. The names of the cabaret groups point in the same direction. In Munich the "Eleven Executioners" emerged as the first German cabaret in the wake of the opposition to the restrictive Lex Heinze. [28] They lasted for no more than a few years before the authorities disbanded them. Later groups in Berlin called themselves "Echo and Smoke," "Colorful Plank," "The Nasty Boys"; in Vienna there was "The Bat."

---

27. On F. Nietzsche see below pp. 180ff.

28. See below pp. 248f.

Although political themes were occasionally taken up by all groups, "Echo and Smoke" was the only one to develop a regular series concerned with contemporary politics. In it the archconservative notions of art held by Wilhelm II and other German princes were mocked. Art censorship was another favorite topic, even if the bureaucracy's presence loomed sufficiently large to engender caution. If the political criticism in cabaret frequently appeared in a cultural guise, this was not just because of a fear of the police, whose methods became harsher toward 1914; it was also because cabaret was a kind of counter-theater that tried to provoke, fascinate, alienate, and attract at the same time.

D. Popular Culture, Workers' Culture, and Industrial Design

Cabaret, as has been indicated, originated in the bohemian pubs and cafés, on the one hand, and in the semiprofessional fairground performance, on the other. At the same time, publishers in the nineteenth century began to put out texts and songs that had been handed down from earlier decades and centuries. Amateur recitations of these works became a popular entertainment which enlivened family reunions and club festivities. Reclam and other publishers issued cheap softcover editions for the private occasion. Not surprisingly, this literature had a wide appeal, even if the cultural histories of the *Kaiserreich* rarely include it in their discussion of artistic life.

This neglect is unjustified, as these art forms were rooted in peasant and small-town culture before the advent of industry and now gained considerable significance in the leisure pursuits of the middle classes. The same is true of "trivial literature," whose importance has been underestimated partly because it was thrown together with the "trash and filth" that was also published, and partly because all this literature was disdainfully identified with the "masses." To be sure, the bulk of trivial literature, which included adventure novels, murder mysteries, and love stories, was not of great and lasting literary value. Nevertheless, this literature reached millions of people and should therefore not be ignored in a history of German society in this period. During the lifetime of Karl May, who died in 1912, his books — especially those on North American "Red Indians" and trappers — already had a large and enthusiastic following. Many people also enjoyed science fiction, such as Bernhard Kellermann's *The Tunnel*, which was translated into twenty-three languages. Murder mysteries, with their simple linguistic, but complex narrative structures, could mostly be found by the bedsides of men. The love story, normally written in accordance with a rather conventional basic design, appealed to bourgeois women with time on their hands. Trivial literature was not so much guided by artistic axioms as by what authors and publishers thought to be the prevailing popular taste. This was also why existing social taboos continued to be observed, particularly in romantic novels that packaged all allusions to erotic situations very carefully. It was rare that a "trashy" novel would slide into the pornographic. Still, these books satisfied certain sociopsychological needs and in this sense were more than entertainment and distraction. As the popularity of Hedwig Courts-Mahler or Eugenie Marlitt demonstrate, this was also a genre in which female authors could make their mark.

Of interest from a sociological point of view is the growth of "trivial poetry," many of whose authors can be found in an anthology entitled *Neu-Deutschlands Dichterschatz*, published in 1910. The percentage of female poets in this collection was surprisingly high, probably reflecting a desire for self-expression on the part of bourgeois women for whom other outlets were not available within a patriarchally organized society. Among the literature of *Heimat* and of the regions, there were many works whose authors were quickly forgotten, while others continued to be listed in the handbooks. Both "trivial poets" and *Heimatdichter* frequently took their raw material from folklore. This also applies to music where there often existed a similarly fine line between what became "great" art and what remained "trivial." During the time when Schoenberg began to experiment with atonality, amateur orchestras and provincial brass-bands continued to play old favorites. The old melodies continued to be heard in the coffeehouses of the major cities.

Even in theater we can recognize various links between "high" culture and "mass" culture. However, unlike "trivial literature," the old suburban stage experienced a decline that is not entirely attributable to the competition of the boulevard theaters. An industrial working class that was working for ten to twelve hours per day for six days of the week was not an amenable audience, as townspeople of all backgrounds had been before the advent of the factory system. Change came not long before 1914, when the masses had gained more leisure time and some had slightly more money in their pockets. People did return to the theater, although by this time the cinema had appeared on the horizon as a medium of cheap popular entertainment. Before World War I, the Reich contained some 2,500 movie theaters, each screening a new and usually foreign silent film per week. [29] Around 1914 daily cinema attendance was at around 1.5 million. In some cities viewers were able to

29. D. Welch, "Cinema and Society in Imperial Germany," in: *German History*, 1990, 29.

choose between up to thirty theaters by this time. In Berlin the figure was as high as 139. The long debates about "filthy literature" which the conservatives and other guardians of public morality had unleashed in earlier decades were now expanded to a discussion of "filthy movies" which the masses had begun to consume so eagerly. Meanwhile the traditional theater, often subsidized by the city fathers, attracted primarily the better-off and the educated bourgeoisie. The lower classes became involved in theater again later on via the *Volksbühne* movement. This movement, related to the rise of the Social Democrats, offered discounted subscriptions.

At this point there emerged a working-class cultural movement which aimed to reshape the cultural consciousness of both its members and the industrial working-class as a whole. This movement, which was in some ways similar to the *Volksbühne* movement, developed from a Marxist critique of the increasingly commercialized "trashy art" that was offered to the masses. The impact of this movement on politics will be given a more detailed treatment in a later chapter.[30] The task that it set for itself vis-à-vis the art world, however, was to create the preconditions for the establishment of a new culture that would replace bourgeois culture once socialism had prevailed over capitalism. We will examine in a moment whether this working-class culture was a subculture or an alternative culture.

It is against the background of these working-class aspirations that the emergence of an extensive network of cultural organizations after the lapse of the anti-Socialist laws in 1890 must be seen. None of these organizations was directly related to any of the secessions that have been mentioned, and all of them identified more or less strongly with Social Democracy. The roots of this network of associations predate 1878. Due to legal harassment, however, it was only after 1890 that the Social Democratic cultural movement became a factor of significance to the cultural history of the *Kaiserreich*. Modernism which came into its own at about the same time, was not directly linked to it. Their cultural radicalism notwithstanding, only a few avant-garde artists openly professed their allegiance to the Social Democrats. More links between artists and workers existed at the level of issues. The working-class movement – very much the product of industrialization and urbanization – was highly critical of the existing socioeconomic and political order and, while accepting the idea of a modern industrial society, searched for new forms of human organization. This means that there existed a common intellectual bond between this movement and those in the artistic avant-garde

30. See below pp. 210ff., 247ff.

who were not driven by a phobia of industry and urban life. If the relationship between the two was never free from tension, this was to no small extent due to the fact that many working-class men and women remained wedded to conventional ideas about art and found the aesthetic concepts of modernism alienating. This in turn led to dispute within Social Democracy and to contradictions that will be dealt with in a moment. First we must look at the remarkable quantitative dimensions of the working-class cultural movement.

When Social Democracy again took off in 1891, it initially had not many more than the 26,000 members in the books that it had in 1875. But just before the outbreak of the Great War, this figure rose to a little over one million. The growth of the Social Democratic trade unions was even more momentous: in 1891, the total had been a meager 278,000; by 1913 the membership had increased to 2.5 million. However, what is decisive for the purposes of this chapter are the cultural activities that were developed by the Sozialdemokratische Partei Deutschlands (SPD). The first workers' singing clubs had emerged in the 1860s. Many of these and other organizations survived the harassment under the anti-Socialist laws while others, according to the police, were mere fronts for the Socialists were forced into liquidation. As soon as the anti-Socialist laws had disappeared in 1890 and the working class was once more permitted to organize, cultural associations experienced an explosive expansion. In 1892, a congress was held at Berlin in which some 319 singing associations participated. Representing over 9,000 members organized in fourteen regional associations, they founded a roof association, the Liedergemeinschaft der Arbeiter- und Sängervereinigungen Deutschlands. By 1914, this organization had grown to some 200,000 members. Between 1907 and 1912 slightly less than 100,000 new members joined. In Berlin, the membership rose from 1,200 in 1890 to 7,000 in 1905, divided among some 194 local branches. In 1899, the roof organization began to publish its own series entitled *Der freie Sänger* which printed evergreens and new compositions. Later a newspaper, the Arbeiter-Sänger-Zeitung was added; its print-run in 1913 reached 113,000 copies.

By contrast, workers' associations devoted to the promotion of sports did not exist before 1890. But thenceforth they sprang up all over the country. The movement was spearheaded by the gymnasts, whose number rose from 3,500 in 1893 to 187,000 in 1914. They published their own paper, the Arbeiter-Turnzeitung, whose circulation reached approximately 119,000 copies in 1913. Their main activities included innumerable athletics trips, competitions, and parades. With a total membership of 150,000 by 1914, the workers' cycling clubs also grew respectably. Their roof organization, founded at Leipzig in 1893, had counted no more than 10,000 members as late as 1902. In 1913, some 168,000 copies of the association's paper were printed. The workers' rowing clubs and swimming clubs remained much smaller. The same was true of workers' chess clubs and workers' shorthand associations, which formed their roof organizations in 1912 and 1909 respectively. Finally, by 1914 there were some 6,400 organized "Proletarian Free-Thinkers."

We have no exact membership figures for proletarian amateur theater groups. More is known about the above-mentioned *Volksbühne* movement, which offered its members reduced subscription tickets for professional stages. It operated more or less successfully in a number of cities, with Berlin becoming the main stronghold. There the "Free People's Theater" had been formed in 1890. This organization had some 17,500 members in 1910 and was prosperous enough to establish its own stage four years later. The "New Free People's Theater," which seceded from the Berlin organization in 1892, even reached a membership of 48,000 by 1910.

Finally, we must mention the workers' educational movement, which for financial and ideological reasons was probably closest to the SPD and the trade unions. After many years of fragmentation, this movement in 1906 finally established a Zentralbildungsausschuß (Central Education Committee) which looked after the expansion and coordination of the program of lectures and seminars. It employed an impressively large number of migrant lecturers who, travelling all over the country, offered either one-shot evening lectures or a series of seminars. According to the Central Committee's annual report, in 1907-8, 323 talks and 44 courses were held in which close to 5,000 men and women participated. In 1912-13 there were 941 talks and 206 courses with 29,836 participants. During that year, the Central Committee spent some 51,674 marks in support of these events. The remaining expenses (about 80 percent of the total) were covered by fees which varied from around twenty pfennigs for a one-shot lecture to one mark per seminar course. If other cultural events are included, such as poetry readings, concerts, and lieder evenings, the 244 local workers' educational associations spent over 680,000 marks in 1911. During the following year, the total reached 732,000 marks. Meanwhile the Workers' Educational School, which had been founded in Berlin 1891, offered smaller courses of a more strictly ideological and political content. This was even more true of the Party School that was established in 1906. The latter, from which some 240 students had graduated by 1914, was charged with the training of party cadres. Those attending the trade union schools, which were also created in 1906, received a more pragmatic education than their counterparts at the Party School.

Finally, there were the party and trade union libraries which opened their doors to all members at the local level. Up until 1914, there were some 1,100 such institutes in 748 cities and working-class neighborhoods. Their total holdings included 834,000 volumes. The trade union library in Berlin alone increased its holdings from 11,500 in 1896 to 50,000 volumes fourteen years later, and its books could be taken out at thirty-three local branches. The library of the Woodworkers' Union spent some 5,000 marks on books per annum. Some eighty-seven of the larger workers' libraries had their own reading room.

As far as the membership structure of the workers' cultural movement is concerned, there appears to be general agreement that its active elements came from the younger generation. Thus in 1909 over half of the members of the proletarian singing clubs in the district of Leipzig belonged to the age groups 26-35. Similarly, during the first decade of the twentieth century between 66 and 69 percent of the students at the Workers' Educational School were between 20-30 years of age. The share of passive members, many of whom were presumably elderly people, was particularly high in some singing clubs. Women participated in growing numbers. In 1910 some 277 of the 2,818 workers' choirs were female, and another 8 percent were mixed. The remaining 82 percent continued the tradition of purely male choirs, however, perhaps occasionally organizing an "evening with ladies." Women's sections were added to the gymnastics associations. Still, here too the weight of tradition and of patriarchalism proved powerful when it came to the question of whether or not women should be wearing athletic shorts. The share of women at the Berlin Workers' Educational School vacillated between 10.9 and 12.1 percent around the turn of the century. It dropped to 5.6 per cent in 1905/6 before rising to 7.6 percent again in 1909/10.

In light of the statistical material presented so far, there can be little doubt that the two decades after the lapse of the anti-Socialist laws saw the emergence of a colorful and sizeable cultural movement that attracted above all Social Democratic industrial workers. Differences of opinion have arisen, however, as to how this movement should be seen within the larger cultural development of the *Kaiserreich*. Guenther Roth has argued that the milieu that defined the cultural life of the working-class neighborhoods in the cities was a subculture; [31] Vernon L. Lidtke, on the other hand, has gone well beyond this view and has spoken of an "alternative culture." [32] He believes

31. On the "subculture" position see G. Roth, *The Social Democrats of Imperial Germany* (Totowa 1961); on the "alternative culture" position see V. Lidtke, *The Alternative Culture* (Oxford 1985).

32. See note 31.

that a deep divide existed between the politico-economic and cultural institutions of the country and those created by the Social Democrats. The proletarian model of society, he added, rejected existing notions of culture and developed a "credible alternative" to it. According to Lidtke, this alternative comprised more than politics and economics; it slowly evolved in all spheres of life, including family, leisure, religion, and education. Socialists and nonsocialists alike knew that the working-class movement was forging "a world of its own" and lived in a "peculiar sociocultural milieu." (33) This process was both subjectively perceived as a danger and posed an objective threat to the rest of society. These realities, Lidtke argues, were independent of the much debated question of whether or not the Social Democrats really wanted to overthrow the existing order by revolutionary means. In this sense the alternative vision was radical and could not easily be integrated into the majority society and culture.

What, in Lidtke's view, lends strong support to the notion of an alternative culture is first of all that the persecution of the Social Democratic movement, including its cultural organizations, did not stop after 1890. The Reich Association Law of 1908, it is true, gave greater precision to various rules and thus limited the room for hostile government action against workers; it also standardized a large variety of laws in the federal states. And yet, according to Lidtke, harassment continued. Time and again difficulties arose concerning the membership of young people in Social Democratic sports and cultural organizations. Nor did the police ever abandon its restrictive practices when it came to granting licenses for rallies and demonstrations. Surveillance never stopped. Social Democratic associations were treated somewhat more generously in some localities; but just as in the case of the artistic avant garde, the higher levels of government increased their attempts to muzzle the cultural and political activities of the working-class during the last years before World War I. The fact that associational life in Germany became increasingly stratified as society in general became segemented seemed to confirm Lidtke's notion of an alternative culture. The Social Democratic cultural movement was, moreover, but a fraction of a rich associational life that comprised literally thousands of organizations. Yet it would have been quite unthinkable for a factory worker to join the same club as his boss, just as they would not have celebrated the Munich Oktoberfest sitting next to each other in one of the large beer tents.

This stratification of cultural life explains why, for example, there existed no less than five singing clubs in the small town of Weinheim north of

33. V. Lidtke, *Alternative Culture* (note 31), 9.

Heidelberg. One of these attracted the local workers; another one the town's civil servants. Artisans dominated the third one, and the shopkeepers and traders the fourth. Finally, there was the "Singverein," the oldest organization in town, whose membership was made up predominantly of the local elite. A similar segmentation of associational life appears to have occurred in other towns. Thus in 1896 no less than 74.4 percent of the membership of Hamburg's ninety-seven singing clubs were card-carrying Social Democrats. Some 52.1 percent were trade unionists, and a mere 10 percent belonged to none of these organizations. In 1910, 85-90 percent of the membership of Leipzig's singing clubs were Social Democrats. Some of the associations made membership in the SPD a condition of acceptance. Initially the share of non-workers or non-Social Democrats appears to have been higher in some of the cultural clubs; but soon so many Social Democrats applied for membership that the sociology as well as the ideological orientation of the organizations underwent a marked shift. Conversely, complaints could occasionally be heard at the level of the roof organization that some local branches were too bourgeois.

While the attitude of the authorities and of other social groups as well as the sociology of the cultural associations seem to confirm Lidtke's concept of an "alternative culture," organizational forms and the substance of associational life must also be considered. Certain forms, such as constitutions and written rules of procedure were required by law, even if they took bourgeois practices as their model. On the other hand, there are indications that some of the daily practices of the older bourgeois associations, normally criticized as petty *Vereinsmeierei*, began to rub off on the style of the proletarian movement. Sports clubs were especially prone to develop rigid hierarchies. Social events frequently also copied the rituals of bourgeois associations, and if group photos are any guide, there was a more general trend toward the propriety of mainstream associational life.

The critique of such adaptive behavior pinpoints the dilemmas of a Social Democratic cultural movement which operated in the trend-setting milieu of a bourgeois society. The dilemma was even more acute with regard not to the styles, but to the content of associational life. Thus the sports clubs came under fire because they were charged with having fallen for the competitive ethos of the middle classes. By 1911 this criticism was taken seriously enough for the roof organization of the Social Democratic gymnasts' movement to pass a resolution that, while competition between individuals was acceptable, there should be no competitive encounters between clubs. Internal opponents were also unhappy with a tendency to adopt the traditions of

Friedrich Ludwig Jahn, the revered founder of the bourgeois gymnasts' movement. However, Lidtke is right in pointing to the many indications that substantive elements were incorporated quite selectively. Thus the patriotic theme of the Jahn movement became marginalized by the concepts of freedom and liberty. The names which the Social Democratic associations gave themselves also hint at a self-image of separateness. Some choirs called themselves "Among Us," "Freedom," or "Forward." An analysis of the collections of songs used in these choirs shows that they had been chosen with the aim of generating a sense of solidarity and of political consciousness. Texts of a religious or patriotic kind were excluded. The focus was on workers' songs, while popular tunes were given a new text. On social occasions one would intone the "Workers' Reveille" and the "Workers' Marseillaise." It appears therefore that language was used largely to create internal cohesion and distance from nonsocialist associations.

An examination of theater and literature will show, however, that the developments in bourgeois culture and proletarian culture were not as straight-forwardly parallel as Lidtke has made out. There emerged, it is true, various theater groups that were close to the working-class movement; but their performances remained largely naive and amateurish. A number of committed socialists, among them Willi Münzenberg, Manfred Wittich, and Ernst Däumig, also produced plays. But these works tended to suffer from an unresolved (and probably insoluble) tension between art and agitprop. This was also the problem with a five-volume collection of poetry which appeared under the title of *Deutsche Arbeiterdichtung* in 1893 and to which Karl Frohme, Adolf Lepp, Max Kregel, and others contributed. The debate that inevitably ensued among Social Democrats became quite sharply polarized. Some, like the dramatist Otto Krille, took the position that "tendential art" was valuable not merely from an ideological point of view, but also from the standpoint of aesthetics. Franz Mehring above all objected to this notion, postulating that politics and great art were irreconcilable. He accorded a universal timelessness and applicability to the aesthetic principles of the classical period and its literary giants. In his view, Goethe and Schiller were the models to be emulated, however much they represented the tradition of the bourgeois theater. At the same time, and with the support of August Bebel and Wilhelm Liebknecht, he rejected Naturalism, because it was too pessimistic for his taste. Having criticized "tendential art" and opted for the aesthetics of the classical period, the SPD leadership tried to curb an openly ideological theater. Enlightenment and education remained confined to the political arena rather than the stage. It was therefore also logical that the party promoted the

Volksbühne movement, which offered plays that lived up to Mehring's rather than Krille's standards.

At the same time it may be wrong to assume that *Volksbühne* audiences left the confines of an alternative culture and were absorbed by the hegemonic force of bourgeois culture whenever they saw a play by Goethe or Schiller. To begin with, it seems important to find out what plays were selected for subscription. Even more crucial is the question of what working-class audiences took away from a particular *Volksbühne* evening. We shall probably never know for certain, as no exit polls were ever conducted. We move on firmer ground when considering reader responses to literature, because some documentation on the borrowing habits of members of workers' libraries has survived. We also have some information on lecture offerings. The official Party School, not surprisingly, concentrated on politics and ideology, and Rosa Luxemburg was among the most popular lecturers in 1909-10. The other lectures and seminars had a more practical content or were devoted to general topics of a more historical-political nature. In the last years before World War I, poetry readings responded to a preference for Goethe, Ferdinand Freiligrath, and Heinrich Heine. Programs also included Reuter, Wilhelm Busch and the great Russian poets.

The librarians of SPD or trade union libraries mostly tried to have a good selection of the classics of Marxism on the shelves. They bemoaned their readers' poor taste which forced them to make "trivial literature" available. Accordingly, Marx's *Das Kapital* rarely appears in the borrowing lists. Bebel's book *Die Frau und der Sozialismus* was more popular and also sold well in the shops. All in all, novels were most in demand. At the top of the 1908 list for Leipzig was to be found adventure story writer Friedrich Gerstäcker, whose books were taken out 2,844 times. Goethe and Charles Dickens followed in twelfth and thirteenth place. According to the annual report of the Berlin Transport Workers' Union Library, Alexandre Dumas's books were taken out some 800 times, and his *Count of Monte Christo* was especially popular. Emile Zola's books came in second place. Other popular authors at Social Democratic workers' libraries between 1908 and 1914 were Ludwig Ganghofer, Clara Viebig, Maxim Gorki, and Jules Verne. These lists can be compared with those of public libraries. We have a public library list for the period from the fall of 1903 to the fall of 1904. Here Clara Viebig was at the top, followed by Edward Stillgebauer, Elisabeth von Heyking, Franz Adam Beyerling, Gustav Frenssen, and Thomas Mann. Apart from the ranking differences, the preferences of Social Democratic borrowers seem to indicate that works, whatever their literary merit, were read not merely because of their thrilling plot, but also with a view to their critical portrayal of society. This may be particularly true of Zola and Dickens, but probably also applies to Dumas's *Count of Monte Christo*.

In general it may therefore be assumed that patterns of stratification in German society were reflected in the sphere of culture. (34) Indications of this can be found not only in the separatism that marked the behavior of Social Democratic associations, but also in the hostility with which other groups and the police viewed the workers' cultural movement. It also seems that works of art that were clearly products of bourgeois culture were absorbed through the filter of the class experiences of industrial workers. They were taken in selectively and partly reinterpreted. However, Lidtke's concept of an alternative culture for workers should perhaps not be understood in terms of a ghetto culture that existed in isolation on the margins of the majority culture. The workers' cultural movement was sufficiently immersed in its national environment to be influenced not only by its aesthetic, but also its ideological norms. This is strongly reflected in the increase of reformist moods and tendencies within the labor movement at large as well as in the desire among workers to gain recognition from the rest of society and in the growing stress on respectability. The fact that this recognition was persistently denied by the majority has already been dealt with in our analysis of social stratification and will be taken up again when we consider the political sphere. (35)

In this connection it is also relevant that, though anxious to preserve their organizational autonomy, working-class cultural associations always insisted on equal treatment, not least by the authorities and the police. If these demands had been fulfilled, a growing number of members might even have been prepared to integrate themselves into the mainstream of Wilhelmine culture, or at least into those of its currents that were not backward-looking and did not proclaim a cataclysmic "transvaluation of all values." The currents for which the workers' cultural movement felt an affinity were those that rejected a cultural pessimism and took a positive view of industrialism and its urban culture. The labor movement as a whole welcomed in principle industrial and technological change and its cultural implications. What it criticized were the ways in which economic, social, and political power were distributed in society. In this respect the movement, of course, differed fundamentally from those conservative and bourgeois groups that viewed the

34. See above pp. 49ff.

35. See below pp. 201ff., 221ff.

processes of industrialization, urbanization, and secularization with deep skepticism. If the labor movement was becoming more mainstream, it was developing in the direction of those liberal forces that were themselves wedded to a fuller exploitation of the potentials of industrial society through gradual reform. As these forces perceived industrialization as a cultural phenomenon no less than a socioeconomic one, they too were searching for norms and values deemed to be appropriate to the age of the machine.

The movement that represented this optimistic position within the dominant culture rallied in a number of organizations, among them the *Werkbund.* This association which was founded in 1907 had 492 members a year later and around 1,870 in 1914. Its founders hoped that it would fulfill a number of functions. They started from the basic premise that in the twentieth century a bourgeois culture outside the industrial sphere would be unthinkable. Accordingly, the *Werkbund* saw itself as a mediator between industry and the arts. In particular it was concerned with promoting the applied arts by interesting entrepreneurs in modern design and industrial architecture. Thus two of the key figures in the movement, Hermann Muthesius and Friedrich Naumann, believed, in marked contrast to the cultural pessimism of other intellectual circles, that the dawn of the machine age would usher in a higher stage in man's cultural development from which society in general would benefit. This is why they hoped to bring about a synthesis between high culture and popular culture which would ultimately also create and foster a democratically organized society.

This latter idea was taken from the British and American models which the founding fathers of the *Werkbund* had in front of them. In Great Britain, there was the "Arts and Crafts" movement that William Morris had inspired. The Germans adopted the artisanal tradition, popularized by this movement, though they did not adopt Morris's anticapitalism. On the other hand, they took up his criticism of the production of inferior goods that merely undermined the producer's joy in crafting them. The emphasis was therefore on high quality, which would also motivate workers and raise their self-esteem. In the United States, the architect Frank Lloyd Wright had been trying since the 1890s to unite artists and entrepreneurs within the framework of a democratic industrial culture. Similar professions of democracy notwithstanding, the *Werkbund* continued to display elitist traits. The average consumer, it is true, was to be educated to develop a new sense for style and quality; yet the no doubt beautifully designed products that the movement began to offer were hardly for mass consumption. Only the wealthy could afford them.

One reason for this apparent contradiction was that many members saw an unbridgeable gap between the unique creativity of the individual artist and the standardization of industrial products. Consequently, when Muthesius raised the question of standardization on the occasion of the opening of the *Werkbund* exhibition at Cologne in July 1914, he unleashed major conflicts and barely avoided a secession. His critics were not opposed to the creation of a coherent modern style; but they objected to his demand that this idea be purposefully implemented by the collectivity of artists. Standardization was to be based on the stylistic decisions of the individual artist, not on those of the group. As Henry van der Velde, one of Muthesius's critics, put it, his aim was the mass reproduction of a "singular creation" under the strict personal control of the artist. [36] The stress, he added, was on the "singular creation" and uncompromising quality. In these circumstances it is not surprising that the efforts of the *Werkbund* were directed less toward educating the consumer than toward cooperating closely with industry as a first step toward generating a new sense of quality and art. The main task was the introduction and development of a modern product design. These ideas met with a positive echo among some entrepreneurs, even though most of them came from the new branches of the second Industrial Revolution, like electrical engineering or chemicals and were more used to thinking in social and political categories similar to those of the movement.

Thus Peter Bruckmann, a silverware manufacturer from Heilbronn, made himself a spokesman for a number of modern entrepreneurs at the time of the founding of the *Werkbund*. During the same year, Walther Rathenau's AEG appointed Peter Behrens to become the company's chief product designer. Two of Behrens's most famous students were Walter Gropius and Mies van der Rohe. A large trust like AEG, of course, could afford to be more open to experimentation than many of the smaller firms. AEG was also in the forefront of developing completely new kinds of electrical household products that facilitated the introduction of unusual styles. It was more difficult with established goods to change the catholic tastes of the consumer and to combine art with engineering science. Nevertheless, there are many examples of *Werkbund* artists being able to realize their ideas for industrial production before 1914. Behrens designed electric teapots and streetlights for AEG. In 1910, he was responsible for the styling of a sewing machine by Pfaff. Meanwhile van der Velde was designing modern chairs. August Endell and Walter Gropius created interiors for railway sleeping cars. Like other

36. Quoted in J. Campbell, *The German Werkbund* (Princton 1978), 67.

Werkbund members, they were anxious to leave behind the playful ornaments of the decorative art of the *Jugendstil*. Their aim was to create functional forms and clear lines. Meanwhile the movement also exerted a considerable influence on industrial architecture. In 1909 Behrens designed the building for an AEG turbine factory. There is also the electric motor factory building in Berlin's Brunnenstraße in 1910-11, whose facade powerfully stressed the vertical and the horizontal. Mention should also be made of Alfred Messel's imposing design for the Wertheim department store in Berlin. New ideas were also developed in interior design and garden architecture. There was finally a strong interest in the design of housing estates and suburban settlements for industrial workers. In short, even a cursory glance at these creations makes one realize where the "New Sobriety" movement and the *Bauhaus* of the Weimar period had their roots. Some of the features of the *Werkbund* may have been close to the mainstream of the time, like its nationalism and the missionary zeal with which its members wanted to flood the world market with modern German goods of high quality. On the other hand, they were united in their criticism of the educational ideals of the German university not only with the progressive entrepreneurs and engineers with whom they collaborated, but also with the representatives of the Technological Institutes and the applied sciences. (37)

11. The Sciences and Humanities

A. Basic Issues

Whoever speaks of the development of culture under the *Kaiserreich*, cannot avoid dealing with the human and natural sciences and their organization during that time. As in other countries, most research took place in the institutions of higher education. But there were also many independent institutes which either undertook research themselves or were concerned with promoting it. Among these the Kaiser-Wilhelm-Gesellschaft, which was founded in 1910-1 to stimulate basic research, must be given an important place. (38)

All these institutions were primarily devoted to expanding the frontiers of science through theoretical discussion and empirical research. The colleges and universities had the additional task of providing a basic training in scholarship. The ideas and practices underlying this system gained Germany high

---

37. See above pp. 37ff.

38. See above pp. 40ff.

prestige abroad and were partly adopted by other countries in the late nineteenth century. Even if many students preferred a superficial *studium generale* and the social life of fraternities, for the serious young scholar there was ample opportunity in the labs and lecture halls for learning about the rules of advanced research. Asserting that research and teaching were inseparable, institutions of higher learning transmitted these skills through a finely graduated system of large lectures at one end of the spectrum and the very small seminar at the other. Professors had themselves received an arduous training. Following their admission to the doctorate, they were expected to submit a second – habilitation – thesis. Only after passing this and a colloquium before the appropriate faculty would they be allowed to give lectures. However long and exhausting the years of preparation for this second qualification and the subsequent period as *Privatdozent* might be, there was no guarantee of a much-vaunted professorship. Such an appointment not only depended upon the faculty, but also on the approval of the Ministry for Cultural Affairs of the federal state concerned, and both were time and again guided by massive prejudices of a methodological or ideological kind. Thus there were only a few professors of Jewish background, however highly qualified as scholars the aspirants might be. To be a Social Democratic professor was virtually a contradiction in terms. Werner Sombart was falsely suspected of being a closet socialist and as a result found his career adversely affected. Gustav Mayer, who openly professed his Social Democratic beliefs and who, after long hesitations, decided, with the support of the highly respected Friedrich Meinecke, to submit to the habilitation ordeal, could not marshall the requisite number of votes in the Berlin University faculty after his colloquium. He did not gain the right to offer courses.

The atmosphere in institutes of higher education was no less conservative. Even men like Max Planck, who pursued revolutionary ideas in his research, were not consistently liberal. Conscious of the prestige which they enjoyed both in German society and abroad, they tended to be rather full of themselves and displayed a marked elitism. With a good deal of justification, they have therefore been called "the German mandarins." (39) But all too often this was a facade behind which there existed a human wreck who had long passed the prime of his scholarship. Worn out by the long years of initiation prior to gaining a professorship, they would often teach the knowledge of the previous generation, while being intolerant of the ideas of the next. Thus in the discipline of History, the 1860s and 1870s were a period of an arid and modest

39. F. Ringer, *The Decline of the German Mandarins* (Cambridge, Mass. 1969).

empiricism which was highly specialized. The orthodoxies of the Prussian School dominated the field, which adhered to an uncritical glorification of Bismarck's work of unification. The literary sciences were barely less traditional. For Albert Bielschowsky, a student of Wilhelm Scherer and Erich Schmidt, "the phenomenon of Goethe amounted to a collection of anecdotal-biographical facts which were lovingly, pedantically, and sentimentally reported" by him. [40] Analysis was replaced by solemn exegesis. The Prussian legend emerged between the lines even in Wilhelm Dilthey's highly acclaimed book *Das Erlebnis und die Dichtung*. Just as in the arts, the 1870s were not a period when the humanities advanced into uncharted waters, and the prevailing conservatism was felt for a long time thereafter. However, by the late 1880s new developments had gotten underway, leading the famous theologian Ernst Troeltsch to conclude that all aspects of life had begun to "sway." [41]

B. The Natural Sciences

Troeltsch's dictum was borne out in the fields of chemical and electrical engineering. There, research led to major breakthroughs. A number of phenomena which had puzzled scholars before now began to generate serious doubts about the hitherto unshakable world of classical physics. Was it really tenable that the universe was composed of a limited number of molecules and atoms whose firm structure existed for all eternity? The metaphysical dimension was raised by the assumption that there existed a God who had created this universe. The viability of prevailing scientific conceptions became undermined at the end of the nineteenth century partly because of new research and partly because of fresh theoretical and philosophical considerations. In 1889, Heinrich Hertz demonstrated the identity of light, heat, and electromagnetic waves. Wilhelm Röntgen and others discovered the existence of ultraviolet rays and the phenomenon of radioactivity in certain elements at the upper end of the periodic table. Together with the discoveries by Ernest Rutherford and Niels Bohr, this research put a question mark behind the assumed immutability and indivisibility of atoms. Further investigations showed that during the disintegration of inherently unstable (radioactive) elements very small amounts of energy were set free. Suddenly matter and energy appeared as the two sides of the same coin. Around the turn of the century and on the basis of his research on thermodynamics,

40. W.-H. Friedrich and W. Killy, eds., *Das Fischer-Lexikon: Literatur*, vol. 2/1 (Frankfurt 1965), 327.

41. Quoted in: G.G. Iggers, *Deutsche Geschichtswissenschaft* (Munich 1971), 230.

Planck developed the hypothesis that transformations of energy occurred in bursts. Finally, in 1905, Albert Einstein postulated that time and space, like energy and mass, were interrelated. Meanwhile the laws of Euclidean geometry had also begun to crumble. According to Einstein, the proximity of large masses of matter invalidated these laws. Here space would no longer be straight, but curved. However difficult it may have been for the average person to grasp such notions, it was clear that a revolution had been set off that ultimately became condensed in Einstein's neat mathematical equation $E = mc^2$. The four-dimensional space-time continuum of modern science beyond Euclid had been born. With it the received image of the universe also began to come apart. The former fixed points of a supposedly static universe, whose particles and movements were governed by the laws of mechanics, began to fade. Particles were ephemeral and could in principle also appear in other guises. In the end it even became doubtful if there were *laws* of nature in the traditional sense. Everything seemed relative.

Physical chemistry made important contributions to the revolution in science. In 1906, Walter Nernst developed his heat theorem which subsequently became the Third Principle of Thermodynamics. Developments in organic chemistry may not have been quite so dramatic; but thanks to the research of men like Emil Fischer major breakthroughs were also achieved in this field. Germany gained a leading position in the world in dyes. While Fischer's work established a link to biochemistry, biology made rapid advances of its own. No more than brief reference can be made here to developments in medicine, particularly in the fields of serology and bacteriology. In 1882, Robert Koch discovered the tuberculosis bacillus and two years later the carrier of cholera. In 1890, Emil Behring developed a serum against diphtheria, while Paul Ehrlich became the founder of modern chemotherapy. Although shunned as a rigorous science by some, psychology also emerged in this period, at first on a strictly experimental and quantifying basis. Though mostly practiced by fully trained physicians, it turned to the possible societal causes of pathological human behavior and subsequently moved to the margins of the natural sciences. Sigmund Freud's hypotheses concerning female hysteria and the interpretation of dreams were controversial even in their day. And last, but not least there was Otto Weiniger, whose book, *Gender and Character*, published in 1903, went through six editions during the following three years. In it he asserted that the female psyche was determined by women's biological functions.

In the field of physics, the contributions by other countries can hardly be overestimated; but major impulses were provided by scientists from Central

Europe. This was also true when it came to drawing the philosophical consequences from the new vision of the universe. Among the first to do so was Ernst Mach in Vienna who in the face of recent developments proposed a total separation of metaphysics and the sciences. In his book *Die Mechanik in ihrer Entwicklung* (1883) he even went so far as to see time and space as metaphysical concepts that should be thrown overboard. Nature, he wrote, did not know such confines. The temporal and spatial position of a body was determined only in relation to other objects. Influenced by Mach, Einstein took the final step on this journey into uncertainty when he replaced the idea of particles by the notion of "events" that unravelled within the atom. Matter was thus no longer something tangible, but a process which had physical properties.

Not surprisingly, all these discoveries and hypotheses caused heated debates in the scientific community. Mach's rejection of metaphysics ran into trouble, since he did not put forward an alternative unifying principle which supposedly held the universe together. Many of his colleagues did not wish to abandon the search for such a principle. However, the question of a *prima causa* which would have led them back to metaphysics remained in the background. What now propelled physicists was the prospect of finding a "world formula" of the kind which Werner Heisenberg was arduously working on a generation later. If it was correct that the processes of Nature evolved independently of humankind, Mach appeared to be heading in the wrong direction in arguing that reality merely consisted of perceptions and that modern physics could be constructed exclusively as a sensual experience. If Nature – as he postulated – was indeed no more than the most rational adaptation of the human mind to the world of human experience, all research was bound to end up emphasizing what was individual and limited. For many of Mach's colleagues this kind of degradation of the physical and mechanical world went too far. They did not expect anything good to come from the attempt to link imagination to experience alone and thus to lapse into a pure positivism. The image of the universe that they were developing might never match reality completely; but at least there was a chance of approaching it asymptotically in the course of an incessant refinement of ongoing research.

In short, researchers asserted the continued legitimacy of asking questions about the structure and the evolution of the world beyond what was purely human. The imaginativeness of the researcher was to be given free rein, as long as there was a guarantee that the results of his experiments correlated with those of other scholars who had independently undertaken their work in another part of the globe. In this sense, the quest was also for the creation of a common platform on which, irrespective of their sensibilities, all physicists would be able to move and interact rationally. The internationalization of modern science would thus be promoted. The "hard sciences" – physics, chemistry, and mathematics – might come together, just as the various branches of physics were being unified. The ultimate dream was that one day all scientists would be united under one roof.

Whatever the future may have held in store, even now space, time, and energy had ceased to be immutable categories. Einstein's relativity theory became the core and the symbol of a new theoretical understanding of the universe. Scientists had not yet officially declared God to be dead, but their explanations of what held the world together were far removed from metaphysical explanations, referring instead to the human capacity for reason. It is no less significant that all researchers in the laboratories and scholars debating in the academies were instilled with an optimism that it would be possible one day to know the hitherto veiled structures of the universe in all their dimensions. Relativism, it is true, had complicated the process of scientific cognition; but it had also opened up new opportunities that generated great hopes for the future. This scientific optimism was reinforced in Germany by a sense that researchers were working in the most favorable milieu imaginable. Tertiary education attracted the best talents and was assumed to offer them optimal room for intellectual development. State funding of scientific projects, augmented by donations from industry, was thought to be generous. The small scientific elite, several of whose members appeared to be candidates for the Nobel Prize, was well looked after in terms of its economic status. In 1913, Einstein, for example, was offered the following as incentive to come to Berlin: a professorship without teaching obligations, the directorship of a still to be established Kaiser-Wilhelm-Institut for Physics, and a lucrative membership in the Academy of Sciences. Small wonder that most professors – however revolutionary their research – were politically conservative and monarchist. It was not inconceivable that there might be a connection between the fluid and complex cosmic order that they were investigating and the notion of a pluralistically organized and colorful human society on planet Earth. However, a few exceptions always granted, most scientists did not make this connection with its implications for social and political change. They did not see a tension between their own revolutionary work, on the one hand, and their life in a strictly divided, hierarchical society on the other. It was the monarchy which, in their view, would lead the country toward a golden age, both in science and in regard to politics and economics.

C. The Humanities

The scientists' optimism and self-confidence was not widely shared by their colleagues in the humanities. It would nonetheless be misleading to assume that the cultural pessimists, who – as we have seen – were so influential in the arts, dominated the universities. (42) The influence of Kant, Hegel, and Ranke remained too strong in Germany even at the end of the nineteenth century. What continued to unite the humanities was their somewhat arrogant view that the insights to be gained from their disciplines were more profound than those to be gained from the sciences. They thus affirmed not merely a notion of "Two Cultures" (C.P. Snow), but in fact insisted on the primacy of the humanities. Thus the historian Max Lenz, in a condescending wisecrack, called his *Naturforscher* (natural science researcher) colleagues "*Naturförster*" (nature foresters). (43) In arguing their case, the humanities insisted, as they had always done, that the difference was due to the divergent methodologies and vantage points with regard to the object of research.

The humanities were also united by the use of categories that were much less fixed than those the scientific community worked with. Certainly by the end of the nineteenth century many scholars were no longer confident that there existed a reality behind phenomena and that the world was held together by a well-ordered system. This relativism was particularly marked among the idealists. Hegel had seen History as the expression of a universal reason, which assumed concrete form in institutions and through which the dialectical march toward the Absolute Idea proceeded. However, although the late nineteenth century saw a Hegelian Renaissance, few people supported the view that the world historical process moved rationally according to laws. Similarly, the determinism of the Marxists, whose materialist interpretation of History was supposed to have put Hegel's idealism on its feet, also lost much of its orthodox rigidity. Many Marxists continued to adhere to the idea that History ran through different stages. Yet after the death of Marx in 1883 the belief began to fade in parts of the working-class movement that the evolution of capitalism would inevitably end in a revolution from which a new and ultimately communist social order would be born. Instead political forces gained ground which stressed democratic action on the part of the masses and a reformist transformation of capitalism from the inside.

---

42. See above pp. 142ff.

43. Quoted in J.L. Heilbron, *The Dilemmas of an Upright Man* (Berkeley 1986), 10.

Among the cultural philosophers and historians, Karl Lamprecht was almost alone in his particular search for laws of historical development. His determinism, like Hegel's, met with skepticism and rejection. His work was directed against those among his colleagues who equated scholarship with the straight-laced presentation of "facts." The natural sciences, he wrote, had "long overcome the age of a descriptive method of phenomena that merely differentiates on the basis of striking individual characteristics." (44) He also turned against the dominance of political history and demanded that the cultural, economic, legal, and intellectual aspects of human history be included in the analysis. In this sense he may be called a relativist. A rejection of the earlier certainties also marked the neo-Kantianism of the late nineteenth century. It pervaded the work of the Freiburg University philosopher Heinrich Rickert, who, together with Georg Simmel, Max Weber, and Georg Jellinek, has been counted among the "fathers of scientific value relativism." (45) In the eighteenth century, Immanuel Kant had started from the firm assumption that logical and ethical judgments possessed a universal and timeless validity and that humans were guided by a transcendental reason. Rickert, writing a century later, saw the pluralism of values during different epochs and of values that often contradicted each other. However, he did not abandon the belief that they were nevertheless all an expression of an eternal morality. In this sense, his theory of knowledge did not take the final step into a nirvana. This step was taken by other philosophers who will be discussed in a moment.

First, mention must be made of the metamorphosis that Rankeanism underwent when, toward the end of the nineteenth century, it once again began to overtake the above-mentioned Prussian school. Ranke's religiously founded historicism had seen nations and states as "divine thoughts." Writing from a universal-historical perspective, he was also convinced that world history was moving toward a higher, divinely sanctioned and ultimately harmonious order. His epigones in the philosophical faculties of the *Kaiserreich* were more inclined to operate with a secularized notion of power. They started from the assumption of a colorful quilt of nation-states. But over time this conception of history became infiltrated by Social Darwinist and imperialist ideas that once again undermined the relativist starting point. For Ranke the peak of historical development was that superior order in harmony with God. For the Rankeans of the Wilhelmine period it was the victory of the most

44. Quoted in: G.G. Iggers, *Geschichtswissenschaft* (note 41), 256.

45. Quoted in: *Ibid.*, 199n.

viable nation in the international struggle for survival. No doubt this interpretation of the fate of nations was also colored by the nationalist expectation that, given Germany's cultural and other achievements, she would win this victory. This, as Hans Delbrück kept hoping, is where marriage of "power and culture" would ultimately occur.

Thus the humanities moved away from the certainties of Hegel and Marx, of Kant and Ranke toward a more relativistic view of the world which, it should be noted, was in principle still optimistic. This shift had implications for the theory of knowledge, whose initiates slowly became aware of the difficulties they were running into. How, for example, was one to explain rationally man's irrationality which could no longer be denied? The debates that these and similar questions unleashed in the humanities also reveal a shift into subjectivism. It was a mood that corresponded strikingly with the proliferating relativism. There was a growing suspicion that cognition was dependent on the viewer's vantage point and that humans would never have access to absolute truths. As Wilhelm Dilthey put it, it might be possible to describe and to develop taxonomies. But whatever the explanations advanced, they would all rest on subjective life experiences.

This shift was remarkable because the humanities, in typical overestimation, had long adhered to the view that man's capacity for cognition was limited only with regard to the physical world. Here, so it was assumed, one observed no more than the external, which would never open the door to deeper insights. The humanities were thought to be in a position superior to the one held by the natural sciences. The former facilitated objective cognition because the researcher was able to acquire a firsthand knowledge of humans and society. The main difficulty was seen in the scholar's capacity to transmit his or her insights to others. Thus Dilthey was at first convinced that man was in principle capable of "recogniz[ing] himself and the society and history created by him." (46) However, since he also believed in the subjective sources of cognition, he had obviously begun to argue himself into a corner when he simultaneously postulated that knowledge was objectively possible. He tried to resolve this contradiction by hypothesizing a common denominator for object and subject which he called life, though this was to be understood not in the sense of organic nature as in Henri Bergson's work, but in the sense of historical existence. This solution was hardly satisfactory, but nevertheless characteristic of the age. Now the "objective spirit" could no longer reside in Reason, but in the somewhat more nebulous "structural links

46. Quoted in: *Ibid.*, 179.

between the vital units" that made up human "communities." [47] With this, an irrational element had been taken into the theory of cognition. In this respect Max Weber was certainly more logical when he took the final step in this debate. He denied the possibility of an objective search for universal values and retreated into the examination of value systems within a particular cultural epoch.

The Marxists meanwhile did not allow themselves to be dragged into these theory-of-knowledge problems that liberal and conservative scholars agonized about. For them non-Marxist ideologies and value systems were at heart reflections of tangible material interests and as such easily accessible to analysis. The neo-Rankeans continued to believe for a long time that they could escape the dilemmas of a scholarly subjectivism with the help of their peculiar notion of *Verstehen*, or empathetic "understanding." They assumed, like Ranke, that humans were endowed with a unique capacity to detach themselves from their own time and to immerse themselves in an earlier epoch which would be reconstructed and brought to life through their in-depth interpretation of the primary sources. However, others disagreed with the belief, held by both Marxists and Rankeans, that History was a purposeful process. With veritable fascination they seized upon the irrationalities of that process and of human agency within it. Having spied the dark impulses in the human soul, they lost hope in a better future and lapsed into a deep cultural pessimism. Progress in a rationalist sense appeared to them to be a totally questionable concept. And so they proclaimed the crisis of all existing value systems and retreated into a misanthropic relativism. They were no longer interested in investigating the relationship between societal reality and human norms. Rather what they ultimately aimed at was the radical transvaluation of both. As far as the possibility of cognition was concerned, they nurtured a pure subjectivism and abandoned the idea that humans could make a scientifically founded choice between basic values.

Arthur Schopenhauer, who had died in 1860, was among the most important thinkers to stand at the beginning of this seismic shift. He thought that, thanks to spontaneous intuition, he had broken through the world of superficial phenomena, whose laws the natural sciences were trying to discover. For it was beyond the barrier of these phenomena that the will could be found as the actual reality. This will comprised not only conscious aims and desires, but all unconscious and subconscious impulses as well. According to Schopenhauer all human thought and action consisted of restless acts of will.

47. Quoted in: *Ibid.*, 182n.

What determined the development of humankind was not logic, but creative ingenuity. By the end of the nineteenth century then, the idea had made great strides in the humanities that reason was controlled by "life" and that great achievements were not the result of a determined intellectual inquiry, but of a heroic deployment of the will. The most compelling advocate of this position was Friedrich Nietzsche (1844-1900), poet, musician, essayist, and classical philologist, who had to give up his professorship at Basel University in 1879 for reasons of poor health. He influenced above all a younger generation of intellectuals and artists who supported the "transvaluation of all values" that Nietzsche had proclaimed. [(48)]

If Schopenhauer had insisted on the connection between voluntaristic irrationality and humanity, Nietzsche now broke them apart. He proclaimed the collapse of the great metaphysical systems that science had brought about in the eighteenth and nineteenth centuries. What was more, since Nature and Life were at heart irrational, the task was in his view to affirm the concomitant irrationality of mind and morality. As far as morality was concerned, Nietzsche would merely recognize the existence of relative yardsticks. What was right for one person at a particular point in time could be wrong for another at a later date. Since humans were blindly driven by their impulses, the real value of life did not lie in an ascetic retreat from the world, but in the affirmation of the will through struggle. There were no other values. The central figure, Nietzsche maintained, was not the person who strove for universally applicable norms, but the hero who – following only his self-set standards – transcended himself. God was said to be dead; the superman lived instead. The latter asserted himself in this world because there was no other world, just as there were no value systems. In the Nietzschean world view, the domination of the "herd" was replaced by an aristocracy of the strongest and most brutal. The place of Christian-humanist principles was filled by pitilessness and pride. Pain was given a positive connotation, because it offered the chance to overcome it. Happiness was replaced by heroic creativity.

At first glance, Nietzsche appears to have based his ideas on the belief that humankind and the world were geared exclusively toward conflict and were completely unchanging. Even the hero could do no more than to engage in constant struggle. As there was no hope of salvation, heroic struggle was the only way to realize his potential. And yet Nietzsche's profound pessimism and his disdain for humanity still had an optimistic, though less obvious reverse side. At least in his later works, Nietzsche proposed an alternative

48. See above pp. 142ff.

route to what he believed was the wrong path taken by European civilization during the past two thousand years. Change was therefore not completely out of the question, even if his alternative displayed some of the patriarchal morality of the ancient world. In other words, his utopia contained backward-looking elements, as it extolled the virtues of a time when the "evils" of the present had not yet gained the upper hand.

If we try to understand why Nietzsche was so successful among the younger generation, the fact that his books did not lend themselves in style and content to quiet, contemplative reading is certainly important. His books and essays agitated; they politicized philosophical discourse which had hitherto been viewed as a scholarly discipline. Nietzsche took aim not only at Christianity and utilitarianism, but also at socialism and democracy. Ultimately, there were very few aspects of contemporary politics and culture that did not, in one way or another, become the object of his vitriolic attacks. Often writing in mere aphorisms and enveloping himself in contradictions, he railed at industrialization and capitalism, enlightenment and Jewry, romanticism and sentimentality, historicism and the militaristic Prussian state. And time and again he spoke in favor of creating an elite that was not tied down by existing moral norms, while attacking the morality of the "herd" and, of course, Marxism.

Other intellectuals also recognized the magnetic power of Marxism, viewing it as a danger or a sign of hope. After all, Marxism had never been satisfied with the formulation of abstractions. Its adherents had never differentiated between theory and practice. They thought they had not only an explanation, founded in History and rationality, of existing conditions, but also a guide for changing them through collective action. However far removed the Marxists were from the Nietzscheans, the latter, and other anti-Marxists with them, were no doubt correct in drawing attention to Marxism's advocacy of radical political change. Accordingly, many concepts that were developed in the humanities at this time were intended to be an antidote to this movement and its utopia. As the examples of Gustav Mayer and Franz Mehring show, the academy may have been successful in barricading itself against individual leftists. The penetration of Marxist ideas, however, could not be stopped and hence required an intellectual response.

Some professors, like Weber, Simmel, or Ferdinand Tönnies, took this debate very seriously, and the rise of sociology as a new academic discipline cannot be understood without the challenge which Marxism posed theoretically and methodologically. It was only against the background of this challenge that Weber could develop his thoughts on value relativism, his concepts of "calling" and status, and, more generally, his writings on the influence of ideas on society and on mentality and culture. Having analyzed the rise of capitalism and the "demystification of the world" under the impact of modern rationalism, he became greatly worried about an impending age of highly organized bureaucracies and of the *Fachmensch*, the expert, when humankind would be forced into an "iron cage of serfdom." In his *Philosophie des Geldes* (1900) Simmel tried to deal with city culture in the age of capitalist mass production and mass consumption. He also examined the impact of the changing character of labor upon the psychology of the worker. Meanwhile, Tönnies turned to the tension between *Gesellschaft und Gemeinschaft* (society and community). In economics it was above all the *Kathedersozialisten* around Gustav Schmoller, Lujo Brentano, and Adolph Wagner who were looking for a third way between Marxism and classic economic liberalism. Their *Verein für Sozialpolitik* became an interdisciplinary forum where they met with historians and lawyers.

While these men were much preoccupied with the intellectual challenge of Marxism, most of their colleagues in the humanities barely cast an eye over the relevant literature. Instead they allowed themselves to be guided, on the basis of a very scanty knowledge, by their prejudices and anxieties when they witnessed workers' demonstrations and strikes. With the exception of Ernst Troeltsch, who agreed with Karl Kautsky's interpretation of early Christianity, this was also true of Protestant theology. Meanwhile the Catholic position – officially defined since 1891 in the papal encyclical against liberalism and Marxism – also became increasingly affective. Though theoretically wedded to a notion of *Verstehen* which consciously distanced itself from the present and was devoted to the strict reconstruction of the past, the discipline of History offers a good example of the progressive politicization of the humanities. It has even been argued that historical scholarship became in essence a veiled attack on the Marxist interpretation of the past. Many academic historians undoubtedly believed that their work made a contribution to countering the influence of the political Left when they highlighted the primacy of international over domestic power politics or celebrated Bismarck as the towering figure of his age who had reconciled power and culture. As Max Lenz put it, historical scholarship revolved around the hope "to discover the firm ground upon which a national consciousness can form that is moved by the common idea of eternity." [49] However, there also existed a num-

49. Quoted in: E. Fehrenbach, "Rankerenaissance und Imperialismus in der wilhelminischen Zeit," in: B. Faulenbach, ed., *Geschichtswissenschaft in Deutschland* (Munich 1974), 60.

ber of professors who wanted to complement an imperialist perspective, emphasizing nationalist solidarity and foreign expansion, with the notion of domestic reform that would integrate the working class into the existing social order and ween it away from Marxism. Yet ultimately even these reformist concepts remained subordinate to the primacy of foreign policy. Geopolitical arguments and the demands for greater efficiency abroad served as a cover behind which domestic ideological and political aims could be pursued. In this atmosphere of fear and suspicion it was not surprising that academics like Sombart and Lamprecht, who advocated an expansion of historical methodology beyond the orthodoxies of diplomatic and political history, came to be suspected of being closet Marxists.

The most influential historian of his time was Heinrich von Treitschke, who did not even go through the motions of providing his politicized view of the past with a scholarly mantle. A professor at Berlin University and a member of the Reichstag, he was, before his death in 1896, a prolific writer who took a stand on the major political questions of his time. Unlike that of the neo-Rankeans, his language, when he appeared in the invariably overcrowded lecture halls, was strident. Few academics in the humanities achieved Treitschke's political prominence. Most of them devoted themselves to teaching and research in their increasingly specialized field. Only occasionally would they make a political statement that in most cases would reflect their basically conservative-monarchist attitude. From time to time the better-known among them wrote essays in one of the many non-scholarly journals. In them they would take positions on topical political questions, few of which in retrospect make elevating reading. Moreover, there was a sizeable number of intellectuals operating on the fringes of the academic world who were more regular contributors to these journals and who often used their writings to express their cultural pessimism. [50]

At the other end of the spectrum, however, there was another type of journal that praised the blessings of the machine age and was read by engineers and technicians. Some of the ideas presented there were influenced by Frederick Taylor, the American engineer who wanted to revolutionize industrial production and attitudes toward the factory among employers and employees alike through a more rational organization of the shop-floor. The Taylor movement, which came to Germany soon after the turn of the century, proposed the scientific study of factory organization with the aim of achieving more than mere rationalization of production; rather it wished to

50. See below pp. 185ff.

create a technological-industrial culture which appealed to the material interests of all involved and harmonized the daily routine of industrial labor. It is not surprising that, although they harbored a few doubts about Taylorism, engineers inside the academy and without were generally fascinated by its message. After all, it turned the engineer, rather than the worker, into the key figure of modern industrial society and assured them that the Marxist menace, which engineers were no less worried about than the rest of the middle classes, would be contained by Taylor's system.

Thus the sciences presented themselves in two guises under the *Kaiserreich*. On the one hand, there was the theoretical and empirical research conducted in the studies and laboratories. It put Germany's institutions of higher learning into the top ranks internationally. Of course, the scientific discoveries of the time rarely reached a wider public, and Einstein was anything but a popularly known personality before 1914. One is tempted to correlate the relativization of the classic scientific "truths" with the relativism that began to spread among the humanities at about the same time. But this link, if it existed, was at most indirect. The "Two Cultures" do not appear to have had much knowledge of what was happening on the other side of the fence. Certainly the humanities, in their desire to uphold the notion of the "otherness" of the sciences, perpetuated a very simplistic appreciation of "*Naturförsterei*." The new image of the universe that physicists were developing eluded them almost completely. Of course, few people in society at large appreciated this particular revolution at the time. Nietzsche's hypotheses were no doubt more widely known than Einstein's theories, not least because they were more easily reconcilable with the ideology of the Right.

However, not all natural scientists remained in the ivory tower. Some saw their work not as a contribution to the international community of scholars but as part of a national task. Meanwhile many of those in the humanities, who viewed their work the same way, pursued themes and hypotheses whose ideological charge they were frequently unaware of. The Germanist Rudolf Unger, for example, in his book *Hamann und die Aufklärung*, presented the theoreticians of the *Sturm und Drang* period in the early nineteenth century as opponents of the eighteenth-century Enlightenment. But he failed to mention that he presented his own anti-rationalism and opposition to the eighteenth century in the same forum. Others were either less naive or less worried about compromising their reputations as scholars. In articles and speeches they dutifully participated in the debate of the great questions of the time. Their tone, often pessimistic, reinforced notions of a great cataclysm. On the left of the ideological spectrum there was of course much talk of the impending collapse of capitalism. Meanwhile the Right predicted the demise of a decadent bourgeois world. True, there were also optimists, and not just among the engineers and scientists. If cultural pessimism gained a wider audience toward 1914, this may have been due in part to the anxieties that proliferated with regard to the future viability of the Hohenzollern monarchy. It must also be related to the fact that the academic and intellectual elites were now using an emergent mass press to articulate their pessimism and peddle their solution of the crisis to the general public. For the colorful debate about Germany's future, which nonetheless became more polarized, was reflected in all its forms in the wide variety of papers which, on closer inspection, were similarly divided into two large camps.

12. The Press, Its Readership, and the Role of Intellectuals

In an age of radio, television, and electronic mass consumption, it is not easy to imagine how much the culture of the *Kaiserreich* was a culture of the written and spoken word. Going to the cinema, it is true, became much more popular just before 1914, but the press remained the most important medium through which people informed themselves about their locality or the wider environment and through which ideas and opinions were spread. However highly developed the art of public speech in parliaments, associational life, or political rallies may have been, the spoken word had a larger impact only when it was recirculated in newspapers, journals, books, and pamphlets. That contemporaries realized this is made clear by the behavior of the Social Democratic Reichstag caucus during the period of the anti-Socialist laws. The immunity and freedom of speech of the deputies had not been affected by the proscription of the Party's organizations. However, the privilege of free speech in Parliament was an asset only when statements were more or less extensively reprinted in the bourgeois press. This was a primary reason why Social Democratic deputies were careful not to make speeches that were too radical and might provide the authorities with a pretext to try to suspend their parliamentary immunity.

Against the background of the major structural changes that occurred in the public sphere from the eighteenth century onward, two factors were particularly important for the rise of the printed word as a means of mass communication in the nineteenth century. First, there was a decline in the illiteracy rate to below 10 percent between 1875/6 and 1894/5, as measured by the percentage of military recruits who could read. The percentage of the total population who could read was even higher. This was particularly true in urban areas where it was also easier to obtain printed materials. Secondly, there were technological breakthroughs which, together with the proliferation of the telegraph and the railroads, helped to open up a mass market. Technical progress facilitated cheaper production of newsprint and, with the advent of rotation presses in 1872, a staggering acceleration of printing. The twin rotation machines that first appeared in 1895 were capable of printing 12,000 copies per hour. Typesetting machines were introduced in 1884. This meant that the dailies – linked as they were to the telegraphic news services – could receive news from the farthest corners of the globe and put it on the mass market within hours.

The statistics give a rough picture of the consequences of these developments. In 1912 there existed over 4,000 journals and newspapers (an increase of 1,000 since 1895), some of which appeared in several editions per day. [51] The estimated total of copies per annum is 5-6 billion. In 1903 the *Deutscher Journal-Katalog* listed some 300 titles under the section of critical and literary journals alone. Book production also shot up. In 1875, around 12,000 titles were published. By 1910 this figure had almost trebled (30,317). Soon journals offered something for every taste – from light entertainment to serious literature and intellectual debate. Picture and fashion journalism had emerged in the middle of the nineteenth century in the shape of the *Leipziger Illustrirte* (1843) and *Bazar*, published in Berlin since 1855. Humor and satire were spearheaded at the same time by journals like *Die Fliegenden Blätter* and *Die Lustigen Blätter*. The improvements in photography and reproduction generated competition. The advertising sections of all these papers are no less interesting to cultural historians than the news and opinion pages. Here the reader could find advice on health and fashions, beauty and further education. The advertisements were addressed to a bourgeois consumer society that had come into prosperity and had sufficient leisure time to occupy itself with its exterior and inner condition.

As far as the readership is concerned, it is significant that the large dailies established themselves relatively late. Until then the weeklies and monthlies predominated. These could not provide up-to-date information and therefore specialized in the publication of essays, literary opinion columns, and serialized novels. The German press, including the dailies, was also typically regional in character, even beyond the newsletters of the innumerable local associations and clubs. The *Generalanzeiger* press, which was financed

51. K. Koszyk, *Deutsche Presse im 19. Jahrhundert* (Berlin 1966), also for the following.

through its advertisements and could hence be distributed free of charge, played an important role. *Die Gartenlaube* gained a supraregional readership that was wealthy enough to afford a subscription. Many of its readers were women. Its editor, who pioneered the serialized novel in Germany, succeeded in pushing its circulation to 400,000 as early as 1876. *Die Gartenlaube* presented a mix of "poems by our best poets, always well illustrated," short stories, letters, reports on nature and health, and cultural news. The educated bourgeoisie found this mix particularly appealing, and its success allowed the journal to attract well-known authors, including popular women writers like Courts-Mahler, Hillern, and Marlitt. The new mass media were as lucrative for the contributors as they were for the publishers. Sudermann, for example, received the princely sum of 10,000 marks for the first serialization rights of his novel *Es War*.

The rise of the daily did not undermine the regional roots of the mass circulation press. Only a few papers – most of which were published in Berlin –attained a national importance. As early as 1876 no less than eighty-three newspapers appeared in Berlin alone, among them *Berliner Tageblatt* and *Vossische Zeitung*. Important regional papers whose opinions were taken note of in the capital were *Münchner Neueste Nachrichten*, *Frankfurter Zeitung*, *Kölnische Zeitung*, *Norddeutsche Allgemeine*, *Hamburger Fremdenblatt* and *Magdeburger Zeitung*. The growth of a daily press also reflected the growing social differentiation and politicization of German society. For, although there were 1,900 publications in 1912 that called themselves politically independent, none of the many papers were ideologically neutral. Another 870 openly appealed to right-wing and conservative readers. Some 580 papers were classified as national-liberal or left-liberal. Around 480 publications were close to the Catholic church or the Center party. Finally, the Social Democratic press – forever having to operate under the vigilant eye of the police censor – experienced an impressive expansion. Among the 60 dailies which were published after the lapse of the anti-Socialist laws in 1890, no more than 19 initially appeared on all days of the week. By 1912 this latter figure had risen to 90. Still, by comparing these figures with the number of "independent" papers, which should in effect be counted among the conservative and middle-class press, much can be gauged concerning the readership and the structure of opinion-formation. Certainly no prosperous burgher or East Prussian landowner would ever have dreamed of buying or subscribing to the Social Democratic *Vorwärts*. Conversely it was unthinkable for a Social Democratic worker to open the agrarian-conservative *Kreuzzeitung*. A Catholic worker from the Ruhr area or Silesia most likely read a local paper close in ideology to the Catholic Center Party. All in all, an analysis of the press culture of the *Kaiserreich* provides indirect pointers to the ideological stratification of German society, which will be examined in a later chapter. [52]

The rapid growth of a pluralistic book and newspaper market opened up careers in journalism for thousands of people. Many of them were permanently employed as reporters and correspondents, as editors and typesetters. But there were also opportunities for freelancers of all descriptions. Often academically trained, they may all be described as intellectuals. Many of them defined themselves as apolitical producers of culture. Others rejected the notion of "art for art's sake." However, what united many intellectuals with the proponents of this concept was a widespread elitism and a disdain for the masses. Given the development of German politics and society before 1914, none of them succeeded in escaping from a politicization of their literary activities. [53] And those who saw themselves as members of the revolutionary avant garde were even quicker to recognize that their "revolution" was inseparably connected with the political and societal environment in which they lived.

Beyond this basic attitude began the differences in position. Three of these were noticeable from the 1890s onward, if not before. There were those who understood their writing activity as an affirmation and conservation of the status quo. These conservative intellectuals were confronted, at the other end of the spectrum, by those who ascribed to themselves the role of social critic. In the terminology of the period, most of them had their ideological home on the Left. Whether Left Liberals or Social Democrats, they shared a decisive desire to change the status quo, whether by revolutionary or reformist means. It is typical of their relations with the established powers that their writings were closely watched by the police, while the government and the bureaucracy had no inhibitions in supporting publications of a conservative and monarchist bend. In this respect, the political Left fared no better, and probably fared worse, than the advocates of modernism and an aesthetic revolution in the arts. Eventually the leftist intellectuals gained another competitor from a group of writers on the right, who in speeches, books, and articles advocated a radical transformation of the existing order and of the Prusso-German political system in particular. It may be difficult to find a common denominator in the concepts of societal change that they advanced.

---

52. See below pp. 216ff.

53. See above pp. 270ff.

Some of these intellectuals have been described as forerunners of the fascist movements of the interwar period. [54] Although this view has met with objections from other scholars, it is indisputable that the *Kaiserreich* was increasingly besieged in the last years before World War I by its intellectuals on the Right and Left.

54. F. Stern, *The Politics of Cultural Despair* (Berkeley 1961).

Part IV: The Realm of Politics

13. The Constitutional Framework

A. The Evolution of the Constitution

The Reich Constitution of April 16, 1871, whose basic structure remained unchanged until well into the World War I, was not a completely new document. Rather it incorporated elements of the Prussian Constitution of 1850 and the North German Confederation of 1867. Bismarck held firm ideas about the shape of the Reich Constitution; but other political forces were also involved in its creation. What emerged in the end was a unique framework that has usually been called Prusso-German constitutionalism. It brought together three features - absolute monarchy, representative parliament, and democratic plebiscite. However, it would be wrong to assume that these three basic features were finely balanced. Rather the balance of power was tipped decisively in favor of the monarchical element. The preamble provides a first indication that, unlike the United States, Germany had not been unified through a "revolution from below," but "from above." The unification of Germany was based on an alliance of German princes and was proclaimed by Wilhelm I, "by the Grace of God German Kaiser and King of Prussia, in the name of the German Reich [and] after the consent of the Federal Council and the Reichstag" had been granted. [1] Presented with the document in the spring of 1871, the political parties in the Reichstag, the new national parliament, made no more than a few minor changes to it. Clearly, the compromise of 1871 was in the end an uneven one.

What is particularly striking about the Reich Constitution are the absence of a catalogue of basic rights and the far-reaching powers of the Kaiser. He alone had the right to conduct the country's foreign policy and to make decisions on whether to go to war or to stay at peace. He was also the supreme commander of the armed forces. He nominated and dismissed the Reich

1. For the full text see E. Hucko, ed., *The Democratic Tradition. Four German Constitutions* (Leamington Spa 1987), 121ff.

Chancellor, the state secretaries of the Reich Offices (ministries), and the higher civil service. Apart from executive privileges, the monarch also had legislative rights. They were limited by the Federal Council, which represented the German princes, and by the Reichstag. Both had to approve the bills that the Reich government had drafted with the Kaiser's support. If they refused, the Constitution directed all three organs to seek compromise, and this in turn gave both the other princes and the deputies in Parliament influence and leverage. On the other hand, the monarch and his chancellor had at their disposal powerful means of putting pressure on the deputies to pass the bill in question. There was the permanent possibility that the Kaiser might use his right to dissolve the Reichstag prematurely in the hope that elections would produce a more compliant representative assembly. If this proved impossible, he could also threaten to send the deputies home for an indefinite period and to stage a so-called *Staatsstreich*, which in this context amounted to a coup using the Army to do away with the Constitution altogether. This was no empty threat. Bismarck, in trying to stem all gains in parliamentary influence and power, repeatedly thought of such a coup, and during the Wilhelmine period rumors of an impending *Staatsstreich* circulated at regular intervals. The workings of the Reich Constitution therefore cannot be understood without taking into account that, in principle, the Kaiser had at his disposal the use of military force and could set in motion a violent solution to domestic political conflict.

The Federal Council, as a permanent forum of the German princes or their delegates, could not be bullied, like the Reichstag, into approving a bill whenever the Kaiser waved a dissolution order. However, the threat of a *Staatsstreich* tended to put the non-Prussian princes' nerves on edge and tended to induce them to act as mediators and to work harder toward legislative compromise. There was a flip side to this. The kingdom of Prussia, linked to the Kaiser through a personal union, had a mere seventeen out of fifty-eight votes in the Federal Council. The Reich Chancellor therefore depended on the votes of the federal states, which frequently forced him into long negotiations and modifications even before a bill was put to the parliamentary assembly. When the compromise that had been agreed upon in the Federal Council reached the Reichstag floor in due course, further changes would be proposed by the deputies. The relationship between the Crown and the Reichstag was further complicated by another peculiarity of Prusso-German constitutionalism: because the Reich government was appointed by the Kaiser (and could be dismissed by him alone), the Chancellor, who was not responsible to Parliament, could not automatically count on the kind of reliable majority without which a particular bill could not pass into law – unlike in England where the government emerged from the majority in Parliament and could hence be more sure of its support. All the Reich Chancellor could do was to campaign for parties at election time likely to stand by him. He needed to keep these parties on his side later on during the legislative session. If he failed, he faced a *Staatsstreich*, or risked seeing all state activity grind to a halt.

It is not too difficult to visualize the problems which these triangular arrangements created for the political process. During election campaigns, the constitutional structure furthered demagogic slogans by parties. As they were not *responsible* for the formation of a government, these would try to win over voters by presenting *irresponsible* platforms. Meanwhile the Reich government was under pressure to help those parties and candidates who it knew to be favorably disposed toward its own agenda. And once the elections had yielded such a majority, any pro-government alliance was bound to remain precarious and had to be propped up with ad hoc concessions which the deputies – excluded from responsibility for the Kaiser's unrepresentative government – had recklessly come to expect.

Although the Constitution concentrated a lot of power in the Reich monarch, it should have become clear by now that all in all Prusso-German constitutionalism amounted to a very cumbersome system, the smooth operation of which required great skill on the part of the monarch and his advisors. If tensions rose within society and if domestic and foreign policy options began to shrink, the entire system, unless modified to permit greater participation, was threatened by political paralysis. Because the top leadership was predisposed to resist reform, Bismarck's creation, engulfed after 1890, if not before, by rapid socioeconomic change, carried within it the potential of growing ungovernability. Sensing this threat, the advocates of a *Staatsstreich* repeatedly proposed that the country escape from this nightmare by revising the Constitution in an absolutist direction; others, frustrated by the unwillingness of the Kaiser and his entourage to contemplate even moderate adjustments, demanded a strengthening of the representative institutions and a move toward fuller parliamentary responsibility for domestic and foreign policy. In the eyes of the monarch, who realized what he would lose by this, such demands were tantamount to unleashing a political revolution.

Bismarck always saw and feared this constitutional dilemma and tried to avoid it by resorting to a number of wide-ranging political manoeuvres. One of them was to pinpoint "Reich enemies" and to use them as scapegoats. He also adopted an active colonial policy and introduced social insurance schemes in the hope of appeasing the masses. While we will have to come back to these techniques later on, [2] at this point our task is to examine how the first Reich Chancellor tried to coordinate the executive and legislative machinery and to streamline it without having to resort to comprehensive constitutional reform. One of his approaches was to facilitate the search for legislative compromise in the Federal Council by linking Reich policy more closely with that of Prussia, by far the largest federal state. Initially he tried to engineer this through personal unions, later by merging entire ministerial offices. If these plans ran aground, it was not just because the other federal states feared a "Prussianization" of the Reich; over time the Prussian Ministry of State, the kingdom's actual Cabinet, also developed an aversion to this kind of centralism and possible absorption by the Reich. At the heart of these fears in turn lay the electoral laws, which were reassuringly restrictive in Prussia and other federal states, but menacingly democratic at Reich level. [3] In other words, Prusso-German constitutionalism, for all its monarchist elements, was marked by yet another peculiarity: a male universal suffrage to elect the national assembly.

When Bismarck introduced this suffrage system in the Reich, he expected that conservative majorities would be elected to the Reichstag. But his hopes were soon disappointed. Even before the Chancellor's fall, the Reichstag electoral law, as the historian Hermann Baumgarten put it in April 1890, had begun to threaten "not only the state, but our entire civilization," because it "brought to the fore in all matters the coarse instincts of the masses." [4] Bismarck thought as early as 1879 that if he had to choose "between strengthening twenty-five particularist governments or the power of the Reichstag" he would opt for the former. [5] After his fall, more and more people voted for leftist parties, including the Social Democrats, and these were political forces that the Kaiser and his ministers flatly refused even to consider for inclusion in their constant search for stable legislative majorities. Worse, the more the Prussian government, protected, as it was, by a restricted suffrage, saw a unitary state looming on the horizon that was parliamentary-

---

2. See below pp. 266f., 250ff.

3. See below pp. 210ff.

4. Quoted in: W. Frauendienst, "Der Reichstag im Zeitalter des persönlichen Regiments Wilhelms II.," in: E. Deuerlein, ed., *Der Reichstag* (Bonn 1963), 63.

5. Quoted in: H. Goldschmidt, *Das Reich und Preußen im Kampf um die Führung* (Berlin 1931), 69.

democratic, the more its archconservative members were inclined to distance themselves from the policies of the Reich, whose government could not avoid dealing with the Reichstag and Federal Council. Thus began Prussia's retreat behind the walls of a reactionary particularism, buttressed by a three-class voting system favoring the Prussian conservatives. It is from behind these walls that they worked harder and harder "to put a brake on the democratization of the Reich and to impede its parliamentarization." [6] Worse, "the struggle for leadership" between the Reich and Prussia after the turn of the century exacerbated the country's political and constitutional woes; [7] for without Prussian cooperation the Reich could not really be governed.

Whatever those later troubles, the nightmare of a "democratic-parliamentary unitarism" was frightening enough as early as the 1880s to tempt Bismarck to consider solutions to the constitutional dilemma that went beyond his attempts to simplify the work of the Federal Council. Once or twice he thought of revoking the universal suffrage in the Reich with the help of the Army; he also tried to create economic councils, constituted on the basis of professions. They were to act as a corporatist counterweight to a Reichstag elected on a constituency basis. His plan to establish a Reich Economic Council failed, and the first Chancellor, like his successors, was obliged to govern with volatile party majorities. Meanwhile decision-making in the Federal Council also became more difficult thanks to the above-mentioned obstinacy of Prussia, but also thanks to the reluctance of other federal states to play along, especially after the turn of the century when problems began to mount.

Only within the Reich executive branch was Bismarck relatively successful in promoting centralization under his leadership. The Reich Constitution, it is true, did make him dependent on the monarch who could dismiss him at will. But in actuality the relationship between the Kaiser and the Chancellor had slowly become reversed. Unlike his son and his grandson, Wilhelm I was not particularly interested in ruling personally and in most cases he was therefore only too happy to follow Bismarck's lead. Thus the Reich Chancellor's Office became the most important power center in Berlin. Until 1890 it was directed by Bismarck who did not shy away from using modern means of charismatic leadership and mass propaganda. Whether or not his system should be called "Bonapartist," the Reich Chancellor had certainly learned something from his years in Paris as Prussian ambassador at the time

6. G.A. Ritter, *Die deutschen Parteien* (Göttingen 1985), 36.

7. Thus the title of H. Goldschmidt's study (note 5).

of Napoleon III. But it is also clear that the trend toward charismatic centralization which accompanied the growth of the Reich bureaucracy continued long after Bismarck's fall. [8] However, there was a marked change in the relationship between his successors and the new Kaiser. As was his privilege under the Reich Constitution, Wilhelm II wanted to use his powers fully himself. It is only against the background of these ambitions that we can understand Bismarck's abrupt dismissal by the monarch in 1890 and the latter's persistent attempts in the years thereafter to recast the executive branch of government in such a way that all lines of decision-making ran to him rather than to the Reich Chancellor.

The results of this reorganization, which dragged on until about 1898, have been the subject of divergent assessments by historians. John Röhl has argued that the Kaiser and his advisors succeeded by then in creating a centralized government that was based on Wilhelm's "personal rule." [9] Hans-Ulrich Wehler and others have denied that the "real constitution" of the Reich was successfully reshaped in this way. They have underscored instead the emergence of a leaderless polycracy which – propelled by impersonal forces – consisted of several competing power centers. [10] The weak and erratic Wilhelm II was in this view no more than a "shadow emperor." Other institutions and forces supposedly filled the vacuum left by Bismarck. A resolution of this conflict of views might be achieved by sharply dividing the Wilhelmine period into two phases. Up to the turn of the century, it seems, the Kaiser did succeed in tailoring the governmental machinery to his specifications. However, when it came to deploying this machinery in the fields of foreign and domestic policy after 1900 and when, on top of it all, political difficulties began to accumulate both at home and abroad, the monarch appears to have lacked the imagination, strength, and steadiness to control both the executive and the well-organized movements in the political arena. It was only from this point onward that the civilian and military bureaucracy together with parliamentary as well as extraparliamentary forces began to jockey for strategic positions from which to fill the void that the monarch had left.

---

8. H.-U. Wehler, *The German Empire* (Leamington Spa 1985), passim; M. Stürmer, *Regierung und Reichstag im Bismarckreich* (Düsseldorf 1974), passim, as well as other studies of these two authors.

9. J.C.G. Röhl, "Der 'Königsmechanismus' im Kaiserreich," in: *Historische Zeitschrift*, 1983, 539-77; idem, *Germany without Bismarck* (London 1967).

10. H.-U. Wehler, *Empire* (note 8), 52ff.

While Röhl has continued to defend his position, differences of opinion have erupted among the representatives of the polycracy perspective. The question is to what extent larger centers of power and influence can be discerned in the constitutional development of the Wilhelmine period. While no one denies that such centers came into existence, the disagreement pertains to their actual identity and to how important they were. Manfred Rauh has advanced the hypothesis that toward 1914 the Reichstag emerged a as major power center, so much so that he even speaks of a "parliamentarization" of Prusso-German constitutionalism. (11) Geoff Eley and a number of British scholars of German history have argued that the *extra*parliamentary sphere became the arena in which the major developments of the period were being prepared after the successful mobilization of new political forces "from below." (12) A third group of historians has identified as crucial the growing power of the executive in the wider sense which they relate to the rise of modern bureaucracies and of the interventionist state. (13) All three views of Germany's political development will be examined in subsequent chapters. However, they must also be seen in connection with the economic and financial structures of the Reich.

B. The Economic and Financial Codes

The foundations of the *economic* constitution of the Reich had been laid step by step in the decades before 1871. The gradual establishment of the capitalist market principle in commerce, industry, and agriculture and the abolition of feudal and guild restrictions were of central importance here. The adoption of a free trade policy by Prussia in the 1850s and 1860s fostered economic liberalism. The Commercial Code of 1861 defined the rules which businessmen were expected to abide by. The Reich Constitution of 1871 there-

11. M. Rauh, *Föderalismus und Parlamentarismus im Wilhelminischen Reich* (Düsseldorf 1973); idem, *Die Parlamentarisierung des Deutschen Reiches* (Düsseldorf 1977).
12. R.J. Evans, ed., *Society and Politics in Wilhelmine Germany* (London 1978); G. Eley, *Reshaping the German Right* (New Haven, Conn. 1980).
13. This is above all H.-U. Wehler's position (note 8). For a while he and some other scholars tried to conceptualize the problem not only with the help of Max Weber's sociology of domination, but also with Rudolf Hilferding's notion of "Organized Capitalism." See H.A. Winkler, ed., *Organisierter Kapitalismus* (Göttingen 1974).

    J. Kocka, "Organisierter Kapitalismus im Kaiserreich?," in: *Historische Zeitschrift*, 1980, 613-31.

fore contained no more than a few articles which regulated, in rather global terms, questions of tariffs as well as of railroads, postal and telegraphic services, and shipping. The Reich was given legislative responsibility for refining the law with respect to these specific areas. This means that the economic code of the Reich cannot be found in a single document like the Constitution of 1871. It was made up of a multitude of successively ratified laws and of court decisions. The 1897 verdict of the Reich Court concerning cartels is a good case in point. In it cartels and syndicates – i.e., horizontal cooperative agreements between independent companies to fix prices, production quotas, etc. – were declared to be binding contracts in private law. Breaches of cartel agreements that various branches of industry had meanwhile concluded in larger numbers [(14)] were thereby open to litigation. It was a crucial verdict which moved German industry and commerce away from the principle of market competition in the direction of a protectionist capitalism. This capitalism differed from that of the United States, where the Sherman Act of 1890, notwithstanding various subsequently ratified exceptions, explicitly defended the principle of competition against restrictive economic practices.

Still, as a regulatory agency the state advanced but slowly into the economic field. Meanwhile governmental interest in the *financial* constitution had long been strong, and Bismarck made sure to incorporate earlier clauses in the 1871 document. He knew the population and its representatives would support his side; they were no less anxious to see firm rules under which taxes were raised and state expenditure allocated. After all, "freed from all ideological sloganeering and empty phrase-making, the sober figures of the state budget" more than any other official material told the "bare facts of the political and social condition" of the *Kaiserreich.* [(15)] Article 69 of the Reich Constitution accordingly stipulated that income and expenditure of the Reich were to be estimated in advance on an annual basis, and that a law approving the budget was to be ratified by the Federal Council and the Reichstag before the beginning of the new financial year. Only the Army budget was fixed on a more long-term basis. It was put before the legislature every seven and later every five years, and even then only proposed additional expenditures could be subjected to parliamentary scrutiny. Similar rules for the annual submission and debate of a civilian budget existed in the federal states and the local communities.

---

14. See above pp. 29ff.

15. P.-C. Witt, "Finanzpolitik und sozialer Wandel," in: H.-U. Wehler, ed., *Sozialgeschichte Heute* (Göttingen 1974), 565.

In the federal states the restrictive suffrage systems, often based on an income tax qualification, guaranteed the dominance of the wealthier classes and hence the passage of conservative budgets, drawn up by conservative state governments. [16] The universal suffrage at Reich level and the different social composition of the national parliament, however, made it much more likely for finance bills to run into trouble. There was even the possibility that a more radical majority might change appropriations or cut expenditures beyond what the Reich government found acceptable. If compromise proved impossible to achieve and the government was not prepared to withdraw its bill, Germany faced the same deadlock as Prussia did during the constitutional conflict of the 1860s: the executive would be forced to carry on with an emergency budget in the hope that a compromise could be struck at a later date leading to a retroactive approval of the budget by a more pro-government Reichstag. The other alternative was to undo the constitutional structure altogether by staging a *Staatsstreich*. Although it never came to this crisis point, the Reich budget did become a major annual battleground between an unrepresentative government, on the one hand, and an "irresponsible" Parliament, on the other, ultimately culminating in the very bitter struggle over the 1913 budget. And since the budget was "the realization of a program of political action" that deeply affected the future of society at large, the above-mentioned constitutional dilemma and the threat of ungovernability can be studied particularly well by looking at the huge conflicts over successive Reich finance bills. [17]

First, however, we must inquire into how the power to raise different types of taxes was divided up between the Reich, the federal states, and the local communities. The Reich Constitution gave the central government the ultimate power over all tax legislation. Yet Article 70 also specified that the sources of Reich income were restricted to tariffs, postal and telegraphic services, and to whatever indirect taxes on consumption the legislature agreed to levy. Loans could only be taken out to cover "extraordinary expenditure." The powers to raise potentially very lucrative direct taxes, by contrast, were given to the federal states. The local communities and cities were left with taxes on land and buildings, local duties, and profits generated by commercially run public utilities. They could also expect some funds from the federal states, e.g., for education. In Prussia a law ratified in July 1893 provided guidance to the local communities on how to deal with their finances. Even

16. See below pp. 210ff.

17. Thus G. Jèze quoted in: P.-C. Witt, "Finanzpolitik" (note 15), 565.

more important was the question of fiscal equalization in case of deficits or surpluses in one of the three accounts. The solution found to this particular question contained further potential for major conflicts, because of the above-mentioned division of direct and indirect tax rights between the Reich and the federal states. Some 80-90 percent of Reich expenditure was for the armed forces and was distributed among the four independent military contingents of Prussia, Saxony, Bavaria, and Württemberg (table 73). This budget line proved particularly vulnerable to sharp increases. If Reich income from tariffs and other indirect taxes could not cover armament expenditures, the federal states were expected to chip in with so-called "matricular contributions" to balance the Reich budget.

The reasons for this system are not too difficult to fathom: the Reich was to be prevented from using its supreme authority for a transfer of direct tax rights from the federal states to the center. If this happened, the propertied classes would be exposed to the threat of a democratically elected Parliament voting progressively higher taxes on income and wealth. It was difficult enough to get the well-to-do to pay direct taxes even when, thanks to their restrictive suffrage systems, they were protected by reassuringly conservative majorities in the legislatures of the federal states. The Prussian Minister of Finance Johannes von Miquel experienced these difficulties firsthand when he introduced a bill that imposed a progressive rate of 0.6 percent rising to 4 percent on declared incomes of over 900 marks per annum. The conservative deputies in the Diet thought this to be an outrageous measure. The prospect of the Reichstag trying to tap a lucrative source of income with even steeper rates greatly alarmed the country's wealthy, including those – and there were quite a few of them – who had become artful tax dodgers.

It is against the background of these realities concerning the distribution of wealth and power in Germany that we can begin to see one reason why Bismarck abandoned free trade in 1879 and resorted to successive tariff increases during the 1880s. His aim was not only to help industry and agriculture as they clamored for economic protection in this period of retarded growth, but also to augment Reich income at a time when the growing activities of a more centralized Reich government inevitably triggered increased expenditures. Apart from indirect taxes on tobacco and alcohol, tariffs presented a good source of income. Indeed, in 1879 tariffs appeared to be so lucrative that some feared the Reich would become too rich and spend-happy. In order to block this development, Parliament ratified the so-called Franckenstein Clause which required the Reich to transfer to the federal states all annual income from tariffs and indirect taxes over 130 million marks. [18] It also meant that the "matricular contributions" which hitherto had been provisional, became a permanent feature of the fiscal code. Thenceforth a peculiar system of moving tax revenue back and forth between the Reich and the federal states fell into place, making both mutually dependent upon each other. The dangers of this system of financial equalization came into full view only when the Reich stopped paying the federal states excess revenue from tariffs under the Franckenstein Clause because its own expenditures had begun to surpass its income from tariffs and indirect taxes. Now the federal states suddenly found themselves in the role of paymaster, obliged to transfer money to the center in the shape of regular and rapidly rising "matricular contributions." Unhappy at this turn of events, they began to push the Reich to increase indirect taxes and tariffs and to take out loans for "extraordinary expenditure," even if they were in fact to pay for the ordinary budget.

As a result the Reich debt rose to 5 billion marks by 1914, placing, together with the debts of the federal states (16.3 billion) and local communities (7.5 billion), a heavy burden on the capital market and adversely affecting private investment. [19] Meanwhile the leftward drift in the political composition of the Reichstag had made it more and more difficult to increase tariffs and indirect taxes. After all, these taxes hit the weekly budget of the low-income groups particularly hard. The penny added to the price of a loaf of bread because of higher grain tariffs was a socially explosive issue and grist to the mills of the Social Democrats, who highlighted the tax system as a typical expression of an unjust Wilhelmine class state. They also pointed to the supreme fiscal authority of the Reich and demanded that the government transfer direct tax privileges from the federal states to the center. The propertied classes were terrified. They feared heavily progressive income taxes imposed by a leftist Reichstag that had been elected by an irate majority of men with low incomes. Of course, there was the alternative of increasing "matricular contributions" to plug the Reich deficit. But this became a dangerous device, especially in the less populous smaller states where the contributions were raised as a per capita tax. Moreover, the annual variations in the size of the required contributions threatened to throw the state budgets into disarray, as reliable projections became impossible. Finally, the financial crisis at the top also undermined communal finance so that as early as 1904 the entire financial constitution was in a real mess. The federal states felt

18. H. Bechtel, *Wirtschafts- und Sozialgeschichte Deutschlands* (Munich 1967), 398.

19. See below pp. 240ff.

besieged from two sides and, led by conservative Prussia, were less and less prepared to make any payments. Although it had become increasingly clear that the financial laws were in dire need of a fundamental overhaul, attempts at reform repeatedly bogged down. The finance bills of 1906 and 1908/9 quickly turned out to be totally inadequate. Above all these bills sparked major domestic conflicts which, as we shall see, greatly exacerbated the growing crisis of the Prusso-German constitutional order as a whole during the final years before World War I (table 72) [20].

However significant the story of taxes may be for the development of the *Kaiserreich*, the ways in which revenue was spent and redistributed into society deserves no less intensive study (table 73). However, we are here dealing with an issue on which the Reich Constitution did not contain any instructions beyond the requirement that both Federal Council and Reichstag ratify an annual plan. In order to understand where the money went, we must investigate how socioeconomic and political power were actually distributed and wielded in Imperial Germany. [21]

14. Parties and Elections in a Period of Change

A. Problems of Parliamentarization, the Structures and Sociology of Parties

During the past thirty years, the question of whether the *Kaiserreich* was on the road toward parliamentarism has generated a good deal of heat among scholars, not least because the problem of the reformability of Prusso-German constitutionalism is closely bound up with it. Alfred Milatz and Ernst Deuerlein have pointed out that it was extraordinarily difficult to reform the Constitution, because any bill that might be introduced to change the existing constitutional structure could be stopped at the first hurdle by a mere fourteen votes cast against it in the Federal Council. Since Prussia commanded seventeen votes, one federal state had an absolute veto, and this state increasingly saw itself before 1914 as the last bastion of monarchism and of the social and political status quo. In view of the deteriorating domestic and diplomatic position of the Reich after the turn of the century, chances of effecting peaceful constitutional change through legislation were therefore virtually nil.

---

20. See above all P.-C. Witt, *Die Finanzpolitik des Deutschen Reiches von 1903 bis 1913* (Lübeck 1970).

21. See below pp. 240ff.

However, a constitutional system can, at least in principle, undergo a silent reform due to a subterranean shift in power relations between the individual organs of the Constitution. In two studies, Manfred Rauh tried to advance "a complete theory of the *reichsdeutsch* constitutionalism" [22] and argued that a "silent parliamentarization" was in fact well underway in pre-1914 Germany. In his first book he traced this alleged development up to 1909. He later extended his analysis of this process in a second monograph until "its (provisional) end in 1917/18." In particular he interpreted parliamentarization as a long-term process which started off with a power shift from the federal states toward the Reich and thereafter from the monarchical Reich executive branch toward the Reichstag. Parliament had effectively penetrated the executive's exclusive sphere of decision-making, he maintained, including the field of foreign policy. According to Rauh, another indication of major shifts is to be found in the changing behavior of Reichstag deputies who, he argued, began to interact in ways typically found in fully fledged parliamentary systems.

Rauh squarely set himself against the then prevalent interpretation of Wilhelmine politics as polycratic and fragmented. More recent studies concerning the power structure of the late *Kaiserreich* have taken a mediating position. The parties, it is true, did display modes of behavior that were "adequate to a parliamentary system," but there were also "considerable tendencies to adapt to existing constitutional conditions and to accept the game rules of political influence-wielding that had been shaped by the constitutional system of government." [23] Ultimately it was thought to be impossible "to decide with certainty" which of the two currents "would in the final analysis prove more powerful."

One way of reaching firmer ground in this debate is to remember, first of all, that Bismarck gave the Constitution its peculiar antidemocratic, *federal* structure in order to make a parliamentarization of the political system more difficult. It also seems wise to differentiate between contemporary perceptions and developments that have become visible only in hindsight. Before 1914 the possibility that the Hohenzollern monarchy might slide into a Western-style parliamentarism was portrayed as the end of all civilization by those political forces that wanted to uphold the status quo or even revise it more thoroughly in an authoritarian direction. Conversely many of those who wanted to reform the existing political order, worked quite hard to turn

---

22. See note 11.

23. G.A. Ritter, *Parteien* (note 6), 86.

the democratically elected Reichstag into the powerhouse of decision-making. The pre-1914 debate on the question of parliamentarization periodically became more heated, giving the impression that opportunities for a silent transformation of the Constitution had improved. One of these phases coincided with the founding of the Reich, when the Liberals dominated the Reichstag and Bismarck could not govern without their support. But this sharing of responsibility did not directly challenge the uneven division of powers that the Constitution had just established. The Liberals were satisfied with simply helping to formulate new laws, since they needed the monarchical state to guarantee stability at home and abroad. The Liberals had not, however, abandoned long-term plans to move the Reich toward full parliamentary government. On the contrary, believing themselves to be indispensable to Bismarck, many of them, among whom their leader Rudolf von Bennigsen was most prominent, came to feel that time was on their side in promoting a slow transformation of the Constitution. All they had to do was to wait for the tide of History to sweep silently into Germany.

The problem was that this strategy of waiting prevented the Liberals from clearly articulating their ultimate claim to power. Even more importantly, Bennigsen underestimated Bismarck's determination not to let time work for the Liberals, but to use it to promote the conservative-monarchical order. This is why the Chancellor, whose personal position had been further strengthened by the state-building effort after 1871, did his best to keep his state secretaries subordinated to him directly and to prevent them from becoming ministers responsible to Parliament. Above all, Bismarck worked tirelessly to resolve in his own favor and that of the monarchy the basic tension within the constitutional structure between parliamentarism and Caesarism, i.e., between representative and charismatic-monarchical government. [24] An opportunity to effect this shift came with the onset of the "Great Depression." There, Bismarck succeeded in dashing the hopes that were held by many Liberals in the 1870s for a more gradual parliamentarization. Backed by political forces that had subsequently organized themselves into powerful pressure groups outside the Reichstag, his model of autocratic rule slowly gained the upper hand over the Liberals. Divided among themselves, frustrated by the success of the "second founding of the Reich" in 1878/79 and now led by a generation of more conservative nationalist deputies, the Liberal parties thenceforth became the mouthpiece of groups that were less interested in larger constitutional reforms and more concerned with economic

---

24. M. Stürmer, *Regierung* (note 8), 9.

and political stability. The higher and more comprehensive goal of parliamentarization moved to the margins of their concerns, represented primarily by the numerically weak Left Liberals. Yet even then, when he could have been more relaxed about the Liberal threat, the Chancellor and many conservatives never lost sight of it and did their level best to remove forever the danger of parliamentarization.

An appreciation of the victory of the Bismarckian system over the liberal-constitutional hopes of the *Gründerzeit* of the early 1870s is vital for an understanding of developments during the Wilhelmine period. The inability of the Kaiser to give teeth to his "personal rule" after the turn of the century and the polycracy that subsequently resulted no doubt increased the opportunities of the Reichstag and the major parties to influence political decision-making. [25] This was particularly true in the wake of the *Daily Telegraph* Affair of 1908, when the British paper published tactless remarks by Wilhelm II that further weakened the prestige of the Kaiser. It has been argued that the state secretaries, unlike in Bismarck's time, now seemingly behaved like ministers in a parliamentary system: they lobbied and consulted with deputies. Naval Secretary Alfred von Tirpitz tried to make members of Parliament more amenable to approving higher naval estimates by inviting them on carefully staged tours of the Imperial shipyards. However, these tactical manoeuvres did not soften the monarchist loyalties of the ministers at all. Furthermore, we should not mistake the growing criticism of "personal rule" by Reichstag deputies as a demand for a parliamentarization of the Hohenzollern monarchy. Factors which must always be added to the analysis include the country's increasing difficulties both at home and abroad, the rise of the "unpatriotic" Social Democrats, and the impact of the universal suffrage for men, all of which promoted political polarization among the parties and made it even more difficult to reach a broad and lasting consensus on basic issues and to draw up proposals for constitutional reform. Indeed, the deepening of ideological differences made it difficult and ultimately well-nigh impossible to forge majorities for even the most ordinary bills. Basically the party system had to be reformed before there could be an effective movement for parliamentary government, and such a reform was not in sight in the last years before World War I. Apart from the Social Democrats and the small band of Left Liberals, the parties showed little inclination, even as the crisis of "personal rule" deepened, to work together to reform the Reich Constitution or to promote parliamentarism as a medium-term goal.

25. See above pp. 194ff.

These realities, whose weight Rauh never fully appreciated, lead us into a more detailed analysis of party structures and sociology

The parties had not been given an explicit role in the Reich Constitution. Deputies were assumed to be subject only to their consciences when they voted on a particular issue. Nevertheless, even before 1871 political parties had come into existence almost everywhere in central Europe. It was tacitly assumed that they would participate in the process of opinion-formation. At the same time, the early party organizations did not have the same stable features as those of the late Wihelmine period. They had started as electoral associations run by local notables, and this is what they continued to be for many years after the founding of the Reich in 1871. It took the conservatives, who were moreover badly split in their attitude toward Bismarck, several years to develop consolidated party organizations. During the early 1870s the Free Conservatives, who had supported Bismarck in his unification policy and who, as a reflection of their attitude, after 1871 operated under the name of "Deutsche Reichspartei," barely consisted of more than a few informal electoral committees and even fewer electoral associations. The Central Committee comprised no more than a fraction of the thirty-seven Free Conservative deputies who had been elected in 1871, and the remaining vacancies were filled by cooptation.

The Old Conservatives, who were convinced that Bismarck's policy of unification had been fundamentally wrong, split again in 1872 after much wrangling in connection with the debate over a new District Code (*Kreisordnung)*. When the remaining Old Conservatives lost no less than thirty-five of their fifty-seven seats in the 1874 Reichstag elections, many of them concluded that the time had come to reconcentrate their forces and to make peace with the Reich Chancellor (table 79). The German Conservative party was born two years later, and during the 1877 Reichstag elections the new party almost doubled the number of its seats to forty. After the 1878 elections it even had fifty-nine deputies in Parliament. Still, the party continued to rely less on a well-oiled organization than on its informal contacts in the higher bureaucracy and at the various courts. Its spokesmen, most of whom were socially connected with the agrarians, had many such contacts. It was only due to pressure from the example of the more successful Social Democrats and the Catholic Center, and also in reaction to their economic decline, that the agrarian Conservatives built up a more effective party machine.

Meanwhile the National Liberals had won no less than 125 seats in the 1871 elections, followed by the Progressives (46 seats) and the Liberal Reich party (30 seats) (table 79). For the moment these groups remained tied to each other in rather peculiar ways. In Parliament they formed three independent caucuses, while running a common network of electoral associations and committees throughout the country. [26] In 1874 the National Liberals gained as many as 155 seats. The Liberal Reich party, in contrast, suffered heavy losses and remained a splinter group until its merger with the Liberal Association and the Progressives. The subsequent history of German liberalism is the story of increased organization, but also of painful divisions, disappointments, and decline. This decline occurred first at Reich level and later also in the regions and local communities, although the Liberals tended to retain strongholds in some major cities. As the parties changed, so did the ways and means by which laws were prepared. As long as the politics of notables predominated and the Liberals were at their peak, it was rare for formal negotiations to be held between the Reich government and the majority parties. Bismarck focused his attention on influential deputies, whom he invited to his famous evening receptions. If a vote had to be prepared at all, the preliminary work took place in so-called Free Commissions, which informally and confidentially brought the leading deputies together. At first there were only a few permanent expert committees. Occasionally these were complemented by ad hoc special committees. But then it happened repeatedly that the compromises that had been struck informally in advance were torn up in the plenary session. The frustration that the party elders felt over such setbacks hastened the introduction of the greater party discipline. This in turn required more stable party structures and clearer procedures.

It was one of the advantages of informal gatherings and consultations that undesirable parties and politicians could be excluded. In the first years after the founding of the Reich, members of the Catholic Center party were treated as the pariahs of parliamentary life. This particular party had its roots in southern Germany in the 1860s. In the summer of 1870 the decisive impulse came from the Rhineland to create a supraregional Catholic movement. The Center captured 63 seats in the first Reichstag elections and commanded no less than 91 three years later (table 79). During the 1880s, the number of Center party deputies hovered between 98 and 100, displaying an impressive stability of support thereafter right up to 1912. The Center, which did not have a particularly strict organization at first, could count on the support of an active associational life and of the church hierarchy. Not surprisingly, the latter favored Catholic notables and the local clergy. However, it is unlikely that

26. T. Nipperdey, *Die Organisation der deutschen Parteien* (Düsseldorf 1961), 24.

they could have operated so smoothly and have succeeded in making tangible inroads into the traditional electoral strongholds of the Liberals, if they had not come under outside pressure from the *Kulturkampf*. It, more than anything else, welded political Catholicism together. When this period of ostracism came to an end, the common bonds weakened. Toward 1914 Catholic industrial workers began to vote for the Social Democrats, as memories of the *Kulturkampf* faded and no longer provided a particularly strong ideological glue.

The experience of being viewed as a dangerous "Reich enemy" also united the political arm of the working-class movement during the 1870s. In 1875 the Allgemeinen Deutschen Arbeitervereine (General German Workers' Associations) combined with the Social Democrats under the leadership of August Bebel and Wilhelm Liebknecht. The first electoral successes were very encouraging. In 1871 there were merely two Social Democrat deputies (Table 79). Three years later this figure had risen to nine and by 1877 to twelve, with almost 10 percent of the voters casting their ballot for the new leftist party. By August this party counted over 38,000 members in 291 local groups. The anti-Socialist laws put a severe damper on the growth of the Left. After their lapse in 1890 the growth of the SPD was arrested only once, i.e., during the 1907 elections. By 1912 the workers' party conquered no less than 110 seats and became the largest party in the Reichstag.

Social Democracy's status as a new type of party, very different from the loose organizations of notables, first emerged at elections during the 1870s. Many years ago Sigmund Neumann tried to develop a taxonomy for this new type of organization by differentiating between representation parties, on the one hand, and integration parties, on the other. [27] In comparison to the parties of notables (*Honoratiorenparteien*), the latter were more firmly set with regard to both ideology and organization. From the start integration parties tried to attract their voters and their families, young and old, on a permanent basis. It was a successful recipe which, according to Neumann, soon began to have an impact on the older liberal representation parties. In order to survive in elections, they too had to transform themselves into integration parties. From the 1870s onward, the *Honoratiorenparteien* thus began a slow decline. Parties now built more durable structures that survived beyond the end of an election campaign. Political work inside and outside Parliament increasingly occurred in formally constituted committees, which had their own bylaws and procedures. To be sure, informal channels of influence and

27. S. Neumann, *Die Deutschen Parteien* (Berlin 1932).

power did not disappear, and even in the Social Democratic party, which in so many ways was the pacemaker of organizational modernization, an ostensibly democratic-representative constitution often became a facade behind which powerful politicians made their deals. This tendency to form oligarchies, which Robert Michels wrote about in connection with the pre-1914 SPD, [28] was even more marked among the parties of the Right. Although they began to put on "democratic gloves" (a phrase coined by Friedrich Naumann), authoritarian rule by a few continued to be viewed as a virtue. All in all, the organization of the country's political parties in 1913 was therefore quite different from that of 1871. Only the basic pattern of four large blocs (Social Democrats, Liberals, Conservatives, and Center), supplemented by divergent minority parties (Poles, Danes, Alsace-Lorraineans, and Guelphs), remained unchanged (table 79). The internal structures and the modes of operation had meanwhile undergone a striking metamorphosis.

A look at the type of politician who could be seen wheeling and dealing in the assemblies of the *Kaiserreich* shows that it would be wrong to equate changes in party organization with a silent parliamentarization. The basic trend, which sooner or later affected all parties, was for the amateur to be slowly replaced by the professional. If nothing else, the growth and complexity of parliamentary business made this shift virtually inevitable. In the early days of the Bismarckian period it was perhaps still possible to take the train to the capital to be present for a crucial vote, but otherwise to look after one's main profession in business or agriculture. Nor were the costs of serving in Parliament so high that they could no longer be met by a deputy's ordinary income. With the passage of time, political work became more expensive and time-consuming. The shift from representation party to integration party observed by Neumann can also be gleaned from a growing debate on whether members of Parliament should be paid expenses and salaries. That this demand should be promoted more and more insistently indicated, furthermore, that the social composition of the assemblies was changing. The conservative opponents of expense accounts rightly argued that in the age of universal suffrage for men any such payments would act as an "incentive for wider circles to put themselves forward as candidates." [29] Of course, conservatives had nothing but disdain for the "mercenaries of

28. R. Michels, *Zur Soziologie des Parteiwesens in der modernen Demokratie* (Berlin 1957).

29. Quoted in: M. Stürmer, "Der Reichstag in der ersten Legislaturperiode, 1871-1873," MS, n.d., 20.

Parliament" who, on top of it all, did not even have the "proper" social background. [30] Such attitudes contributed to delaying the introduction of payments to Reichstag deputies until 1906. But in the long term the tactics of the conservatives and the Reich government could not prevent the rise of the professional politician who had made himself an expert in certain fields and served on specialized committees. [31]

Heinrich Best has collected more detailed information on the social profile of deputies. His material signals that a major sociological change occurred, although it remained incomplete and unfolded in a segmented fashion. Thus the trend toward professionalization was much more prevalent in the SPD than elsewhere. The percentage of farmers and men from small towns among the deputies remained higher than might have been expected from the share of the total population living in urban centers. Sixty to sixty-five percent of the Social Democratic deputies were city-dwellers, while a mere seven to ten percent came from rural parts. None of the other parties had so many urban members. The Social Democratic party also had a larger share of deputies who were party functionaries or lobbyists and hence professionals in a double sense. The greater "modernity" of the Social Democrats is also evident in their religious affiliations, or lack thereof. Compared to their colleagues in other parties, more of them had been seized by the wave of secularization and hence did not list a formal denomination in their resumes. [32]

Other calculations indicate a less segmented process of secularization. Thus the "transition from an ascriptive to a competitive mode of recruitment of political elites" is reflected in the successive drop in the number of aristocratic deputies up to 1912. [33] The share of university-trained deputies remained above 50 percent throughout, but it also began to decline. A similar drop affected members who had received a legal education. Meanwhile the share of deputies who held positions in modern pressure groups increased. With respect to other sociological criteria, our knowledge of the Reich's changing parliamentary elites is still woefully incomplete. As regards Social Democratic candidates for Reichstag elections a few data

30. Quoted in: *Ibid.*, 19.

31. See above pp. 270f.

32. H. Best, "Politische Modernisierung und parlamentarische Führungsgruppen in Deutschland, 1867-1918," in: *Historical Social Research*, 1988, 5-74.

33. *Ibid.*, 34.

point to an underrepresentation of unskilled workers even in this party. Tobacco workers formed an exception here, but even their share declined from 7.1 percent in 1898 to 3.8 percent in 1912. Meanwhile the share of skilled workers in the Social Democratic Reichstag caucus grew from 53.6 percent in 1898 to 66.4 percent in 1912. During this time the percentage of candidates who failed to gain a seat remained relatively constant at around 75 percent. Next to the tobacco workers, workers in the lumber industry, printers, and editors of party newspapers also saw their share of seats decline. The metal and construction workers, in contrast, made gains, and so did party and trade union functionaries.

The gradual displacement of the party of notables by the integration party and of the amateur politician by the professional might be thought to have facilitated communication among the deputies. However, professional homogenization did not mean that social background became any less significant. On the contrary, as political and ideological conflicts deepened before 1914, a continued consciousness of social differences tended to exacerbate the situation, making cooperation more difficult. The coordination of campaign styles at the national level worked in the direction of bloc formation. Both the party system and the social composition of the parties therefore moved in a direction which impeded parliamentarization. The Hohenzollern monarchy's attempts to effect constitutional change were not made easier by the emergence of a number of tightly organized political blocs led by politicians with uncompromising ideological commitments and interests.

B. Electoral Systems and Electoral Behavior

The analysis of electoral systems offers further evidence of the difficulties which Rauh's parliamentarization hypothesis has run into. As was the case in many other European countries, political systems at the local and regional levels restricted suffrage. The most frequently cited example is the Prussian indirect three-class voting system, which was important because Prussia comprised two-thirds of the adult male population of Germany. As indicated by the name, there were three types of voters who were categorized according to their tax bracket. Voters in the highest taxation class (about 2.0 percent of the population, depending on the year) selected one-third of the electors, who in turn elected a corresponding number of candidates to the Prussian Diet. The second third was chosen by the next 4 to 14 percent of taxpayers. The majority of those eligible to vote – some 80-85 percent – ended up in the third category and cast their ballot for the last third of the electors. This meant that a vote in the first category tended to carry sixteen to twenty-six times more weight than one in the third category. A good 10 percent of the eligible voters (i.e., men over twenty-four years of age) fell below the tax threshold and were hence barred from voting altogether. Given these realities, it is not surprising that, for example, during the Diet elections of 1908 the mainly agrarian Conservatives gained 47.9 percent of the seats, although no more than 16.7 percent of the voters cast their ballot for them. Authorities made matters worse by refusing to adjust the borders of electoral districts in response to the tremendous migration from the countryside to the cities. Naturally, there were political reasons for this. Not surprisingly, this stubborness met with more and more persistent protests; only in 1910 did the Prussian government finally respond by producing an electoral reform bill. This bill called for the replacement of the indirect system of electors with a direct one and proposed to merge constituencies whose populations had become very small. It also realigned the tax levels and introduced a partial plural ballot that favored the educated bourgeoisie. It is no less significant that the conservative opposition to this very modest bill eventually succeeded in toppling it. The Prussian three-class voting system remained in force until it was abolished in the Revolution of 1918. It was this difficult to bring about very gradual political change that acknowledged the momentous social and economic transformations that the Reich had meanwhile experienced and to introduce a greater measure of fairness at the ballot box.

There are other telling examples from outside Prussia. Since 1868, the Kingdom of Saxony had had an electoral system that required the possession of a residential building lot and the annual payment of a certain minimum in direct taxes. As a result of these restrictions, no more than half of the male population of this federal state was able to go to the polls. After the turn of the century, pressures mounted to initiate reforms; but with fears of Social Democracy in the "Red Kingdom of Saxony" rising, government and parties maneuvered to achieve not only advantages for themselves, but above all to block a further advance of the Left. In 1909 a system was finally introduced that lifted some of the existing restrictions, but the idea of universality was quickly undermined by a new set of conditions. Under the new requirements, voters had to have been Saxon citizens for at least two years prior to the elections and had to be up to date with their tax payments. Furthermore, wealthy Saxons now obtained up to three additional votes. Anyone who was over fifty-nine years old or occupied an elevated position received one additional vote. Another restriction was that the Chamber was elected every six years and that candidates had to gain the absolute majority, which enabled the conservative parties to form alliances in order to keep the local Social Democratic contender out.

The Bavarian system was similarly based on an income qualification and other restrictions so that about one-third of the men of minimum age were excluded altogether. As in Prussia the polls merely identified electors, and until 1881 ballots were not filled in behind the curtain of a polling booth, but written out in public. Until 1914 a certain degree of democratization occurred in Baden and Württemberg, where the principle of direct elections was introduced in 1905/6. Meanwhile Hamburg, Lübeck, and Brunswick actually tightened their systems. Thus over half of the 192 seats in the Hamburg Chamber were elected by specially protected groups of patrician notables, while the remaining taxpayers elected a mere 84 deputies. By the turn of the century a number of other changes were made. In view of the unstoppable advance of the Social Democrats, the tax qualification was sharply increased in 1906, triggering massive popular demonstrations against this "robbery of the voting right." These outbursts were ruthlessly suppressed by the police. [34] Many other urban communities with tax categories similar to those in Prussia raised their tax qualification levels at the very moment when the existing bourgeois majorities came under threat due to gains by the Social Democrats in local elections. Only in a few cases, like in Barmen or Düsseldorf, were the restrictions actually eased.

Voting inequalities were also perpetuated by the stonewalling tactics of the authorities who were responsible for determining constituency boundaries. In Bavaria they engaged in active gerrymandering, repeatedly changing boundaries in such a way that parties loyal to the government were favored. The Prussian State Ministry and later also the Reich government perpetuated inequality by inaction. The huge migrations from the eastern provinces to the new industrial centers further west ought to have resulted in regular reviews of voting districts, but this never happened. Accordingly by 1914 a mere one-tenth, in some cases one-thirtieth, of the eligible males in the depopulated rural regions of the east elected the same number of deputies as voters in densely populated industrial zones. This explains why the Conservatives, with the exception of the 1881 Reichstag elections, always gained a higher percentage of the seats than was justified on the basis of votes obtained (table 80). Being handicapped or privileged as a voter was therefore not just a matter of one's tax bracket, but also of where one lived, and was hence related to socioeconomic status.

In comparison with the restricted suffrage systems of the federal states and the local communities, the direct, universal, and secret ballot for the Reichstag, which Bismarck had adopted from the Constitution of the North-German Confederation, was a revolutionary innovation. Judging from the initial turnout in the early 1870s, it may have taken some time for eligible

34. See below pp. 254ff.

men to get used to going to the polls. But with turnout at eighty percent and higher, indicating that voters began to take their duty very seriously, participation was not a problem once ordinary voters had a sense that each vote counted (table 79). Where this sense was lacking, as it was in many federal states with restrictive systems, turnout figures were much lower, though even here participation increased over time. Without discussing in detail the first Chancellor's cunning political calculations, it is important to remember that he did not take the step into universal suffrage because he had been won over to the idea of democracy. Worse, his calculations turned out to be badly flawed, later causing Bismarck and even more so his successors many agonies. That Bismarck's strategy of univeral male suffrage had backfired is reflected not only in the fact that the Reich government repeatedly toyed with the idea of a *Staatsstreich*, a forcible revision of the Reich Constitution which would have abolished the universal suffrage, but also in an official passivity with regard to constituency boundaries similar to the one that the federal states had been observing. The system of a second ballot (*Stichwahl*) opened up further possibilities of undermining the principle of equality at the polls. As the rise of the Social Democrats since the 1890s challenged the strongholds of the other parties in many regions, second ballots to determine the winner of a race were held with increasing frequency. This provided the local non-Socialist parties with the opportunity to form alliances and to agree on a single candidate if the first ballot had shown that the Social Democratic contender might win. The combined effect of all these rules and practices was that in the 1890s the share of the Social Democratic vote was twice as high as that of the seats gained by the party (tables 79-80). In the 1907 Reichstag elections it was even three times higher. It was only in 1912 that the proportion once again became more balanced (34.8 percent of the votes compared with 27.7 percent of the seats).

Beyond the question of how universal and equal male Reichstag suffrage was actually practiced, there were also violations of the principle of secrecy, especially in the rural constituencies of East Elbia. Thus, it was by no means an unusual sight that, on election day, land laborers would be marched straight from the fields to the polling station. There they were given the "correct" ballot paper which the local "estate owner, in his role as poll supervisor," would then "graciously" accept, occasionally using as ballot box "an empty cigar case or a soup bowl without a lid." [35] Later the Social Democrats turned the tables and learned to apply gentle pressure in their

35. H. Rosenberg, "The Pseudo-Democratisation of the Junker Class," in: G.G. Iggers, ed., *The Social History of Politics* (Leamington Spa 1985), 106.

industrial strongholds to persuade local shopkeepers or publicans to vote for them. Catholic and Protestant priests also developed techniques of exerting moral pressure to get their flock to vote for a "Christian" party.

Overall, however, the outcome of elections was not determined by various corrupt practices, but by the ideological commitments and the interests of the voter. Nothing demonstrated this more clearly than the fact that the political stratification of German society increasingly coincided with socioeconomic class lines. This applied above all to Protestant industrial workers, for whom it became less and less thinkable to vote for a nonsocialist party. In the 1912 Reichstag elections the Social Democrats obtained over 4.2 million votes (table 79). Most of these came from the reservoir of approximately 5.5 million male industrial laborers who had reached the age of twenty-five. The SPD's share of the voting public was very high in a number of large industrial cities. This is also where most of the 1.0 million members which the party had meanwhile recruited came from.

The partial exception to the rule that class determined party were the many Catholic workers for whom denomination remained the more decisive factor. Politically they inclined toward the Catholic Center party and the Catholic trade union movement. Socially, political Catholicism remained a heterogeneous phenomenon, and the successful integration of so many diverse elements into one party over a long timespan remains a considerable achievement. Unlike their Protestant counterparts, Catholic workers turned toward Social Democracy in larger numbers only in the last year before 1914. [36] In the southwest, the Center proved an effective political force when, after the end of the *Kulturkampf*, it succeeded in challenging the strongholds of Liberalism in that region. Supported by the 800,000 members of the Volksverein für das katholische Deutschland, the party attracted Catholic estate owners from Silesia, Catholic bankers and industrialists from the Rhineland, Catholic peasants and artisans from Bavaria, and Catholic miners from the Ruhr area. For a long time, the support by these groups at the polls remained astonishingly stable at 22-23 percent (table 79). With the rise of the Social Democrats after 1890 it declined to about 19 percent and remained fairly steady at this level until 1911. The 1912 Reichstag elections resulted in a further drop of 3 percent, as

36. K. Rohe, "Die 'verspätete' Region," in: P. Steinbach, ed., *Probleme der politischen Partizipation im Modernisierungsprozess* (Stuttgart 1982), 231-52; idem, "Politische Traditionen im Rheinland, in Westfalen und Lippe," in: Landeszentrale für politische Bildung, Hg., *Nordrhein-Westfalen* (Düsseldorf 1984), 14-34; idem, *Vom Revier zum Ruhrgebiet* (Essen 1986).

Catholic workers now began to move to the Left in larger numbers. Votes were also lost in Upper Silesia, most of which more likely went to the Polish minority movement. [37] The simultaneous decline in Alsace-Lorraine, in contrast, was more probably due to a change in the method of vote-counting in comparison with the 1907 elections.

On the Right, the denominational factor remained of significance in so far as no Protestant estate owner would have voted for the Center. As a rule, such a man would have voted for the German Conservative party. Nor was it thinkable for a *Junker* to support the Social Democrats or, with a few exceptions, the National Liberals. The Free Conservatives found their dwindling electoral support among industrialists and those agrarians who – favoring Bismarck's unification of Germany – had, as in Silesia, links with industry. The numerous secessions and regroupings among the Liberals reflect not only the political-ideological crisis into which Bismarck's policies had thrown them after 1878/79, but also the colorful sociology of the middle classes. Unlike the other large parties or, for that matter, the minority movements, they did not operate in a social or ethnic milieu that was clearly delineated. Meanwhile the Danish minority party usually attracted between 14,000 and 16,000 votes; only in 1912 did this figure rise to 17,000. During the 1870s and 1880s, Alsace-Lorraine regularly dispatched some fifteen deputies to Berlin; these gained the support of 150,000-235,000 voters. This figure declined to just over 100,000 after the turn of the century, before returning to 162,000 in 1912. It is quite likely that this latter surge was connected with popular disappointments over the Reich government's failure to effect tangible constitutional reforms in this region. The move toward minority parties is most marked among the Poles. During the 1870s and 1880s, minority candidates usually obtained no more than 200,000 votes. There was a slight rise over the next decade, although it remained under the 250,000 mark. It then shot up in the 1903 elections to 348,000, later reaching 454,000 in 1907 and 442,000 in 1912. All these results reflect the negative consequences of governmental policies which discriminated against minorities. [38]

The above figures also confirm a picture of growing political mobilization among the population, just as they show the emergence of powerful blocs. Meanwhile the rise of the minority parties, which by 1912 had no fewer than thirty-three deputies in the Reichstag, must be taken as an indicator that Wilhelmine society was losing its capacity to integrate divergent forces in

37. See below pp. 231f.

38. See above pp. 96ff.

support of the status quo. The Jewish minority, which for various reasons never formed a party of its own, mostly voted for Left Liberal candidates. These, in the eyes of many German Jews, were the only politicians that openly dissociated themselves from a rising anti-Semitism.

An analysis of electoral behavior during Reichstag elections explains much about the changing material and psychic condition of German society under the *Kaiserreich*. There were, it is true, many distortions, among which the exclusion of the female half of the population was the most glaring. Nevertheless, thanks to the suffrage for men of all classes, national elections represent a much better barometer of the mood of the male population than the restrictive system in the federal states does. The Prussian and Saxon elections, which guaranteed in advance the preponderance of the wealthy, are therefore less interesting in themselves than they are with respect to their repercussions upon the Reich level. They not only complicated relations between the Reich government and the federal states, for example in connection with taxation and the equalization of financial burdens, [39] but also enhanced the leftward drift of the ordinary voter. This voter noted with bitterness that his vote in Saxony, Hamburg, or Prussia was not worth very much. But this was different at Reich level, so that the rise of the Left toward 1914 was partly fueled by a protest movement against the blatant inequalities at the regional and local level.

C. Ideological Main Currents

The history of the *Kaiserreich* provides many examples of how the majority parties in the Reichstag, in the diets of the federal states, and in the local assemblies ruthlessly exploited the advantages of the electoral laws and their victories at the polls to promote and to uphold the interests of their voters. Nevertheless, it would be wrong to assume that the programs and ideological positions with which they justified their policies were no more than smokescreens to cover up hard-nosed social and economic calculations. The ideologies that they adhered to did have a solid core which leaders and supporters genuinely believed in. Their programs were not just empty propaganda slogans. Rather they served to integrate and mobilize members and helped to distinguish their own party from their opponents.

Although Bismarck was, socially speaking, one of them, the Prussian Conservatives found it very difficult at first to reconcile themselves to his work of unification. Unlike the Free Conservatives, who were enthusiastic

39. See above pp. 196ff.

about the founding of the Reich, the Prussian Conservatives continued to fear that Prussia, as the bastion of archconservative ideas, would become overwhelmed by the more liberal and "democratic" southern and western parts of the new Germany. They were particularly hostile to the universal male suffrage in the Reich. If this principle were ever expanded to Prussia with its three-class electoral system, it would have spelled the end of Conservative predominance in the largest state of the *Kaiserreich.* This is why Bismarck's introduction of universal suffrage for men was seen by them as a revolutionary act. In their eyes he was also a dangerous man because in 1866 he had unceremoniously unseated legitimate rulers, above all the king of Hanover, and incorporated their territories into Prussia. It was a sin against the notion of Divine Law and princely legitimacy for which they never quite forgave Bismarck. Following long internal struggles over its basic ideology, the German Conservative party in July 1876 finally recognized the new realities of a German national state. Still, as the writers of the party platform were quick to add: "We insist that, within this entity, the justified independence and peculiarities of the individual states, provinces, and ethnic groups be preserved." [40] The statement also stressed the importance of the "monarchical foundations of our public life and of a strong state authority." It advocated "orderly" economic and civil liberties. Finally, the task was "to counter the excesses of the false dogmas of Socialism" and to end the struggle against Catholicism in order to initiate the "revival of Christian and religious institutions."

All these elements reappeared in the party's Tivoli Program of December 1892, this time expanded by demands that showed how much rapid socioeconomic and political change had put the agrarians on the defensive. They pledged to defend Divine Law and the monarchy most vigorously against the onslaught of parliamentarism and democracy. The Tivoli Program, which launched a radical attack on the "unpatriotic" Socialists, also assumed a distinctly anticapitalist and anti-Semitic tone. [41] The party demanded the continuation of protectionism in order to maintain "a strong *Bauernstand* [estate of farmers]." Crafts as well as "honest trading and manufacturing" were also to be given state protection. Overall, the program showed clearly that a majority of conservatives had left their earlier aristocratic-elitist positions and were trying to offer, with mixed success, an ideological home to peasants and other social groups in the rural parts of Germany beyond their traditional East Elbian "home base." True, Prussian Conservatives remained

40. W. Mommsen, ed., *Die deutschen Parteiprogramme* (Berlin 1932), vol. 2, 3.

41. *Ibid.*, 47ff.

deeply split over the wisdom of abandoning *Honoratiorenpolitik*. Many of its supporters continued to adhere to what can only be described as an archconservative monarchism and would have no truck with the radical right-wing rabble-rousers in their midst. This was so in 1892 just as it was later during the crisis years before World War I.

Although the party was by no means unanimous in this respect either, it is in light of its quest to broaden its popular base that we must also see its anti-Semitism – hitherto mainly the preserve of a few splinter parties. Nor should we deduce from the later "downfall" [42] of these parties that anti-Semitism as a creed was diminishing toward 1914. On the contrary, hatred of Jews, which had long remained latent among broad sections of the population, became more widespread among social groups that felt fundamentally threatened by the anonymous forces of industrialization, urbanization, and secularization. Searching for an identifiable minority that could be turned into a scapegoat for all social ills, many who were unable to cope with the structural changes around them found solace in anti-Semitism. Catholics tended to relate this phobia to a century-old prejudice of their church against Jews as the alleged "murderers of Christ." Protestant conservatives and the educated and commercial bourgeoisie were more likely to look down upon Jews as "socially inferior." What was new in the second half of the nineteenth century was the development of a strain of biologistic anti-Semitism. Its adherents started from the alleged existence of "inferior races" – a notion which appeared in many rightist organizations after 1900, if not before – and Jews were quickly put into this category. In short, anti-Semitism had become more open and widely acceptable in Wilhelmine society. It frequently used a coded language (comprised of words like "un-German") whose meaning was well understood by most people. [43]

The search for "un-German" behavior increasingly went hand in hand with a radical nationalism. From the 1880s onward this nationalism was reinforced by an imperialist ideology which often appeared in the guise of a cultural mission. A growing ethnocentrism and intolerance can be observed with regard to the Polish minority in the east. It was particularly vociferous in the HKT and in the Pan-German League, which aimed to unite all German-speaking Germans in eastern Europe. Others turned to the growing colonial movements whose members were convinced of the superior cultural and

42. R. Levy, *The Downfall of the Anti-Semitic Parties in Imperial Germany* (New Haven, Conn. 1975).

43. See above pp. OO, and below pp. OO, OO.

moral achievements of Germany, which they proposed to bring to "primitive" peoples in other parts of the globe. Nor did militarism – defined here as the penetration of military attitudes and values into a civilian society – remain confined to a small group of eccentrics. In its special form of "navalism," this militarism acted as an ideological bridge to imperialist ideas that began to spread among the nationalist-liberal bourgeoisie. All in all, the middle classes proved to be particularly receptive to the varying forms of nationalism, militarism, and imperialism.

Disagreements among the welter of middle-class movements arose, however, when it came to the question of the uses to which these ideas should be put in domestic politics. The turn toward conservatism in 1878-79 dealt a serious blow to the earlier hopes for reform and parliamentarization; but this did not mean that all Liberals wanted to use "loyalty to the Reich," colonial enthusiasm, and the notion of a powerful military state in order to preserve the domestic status quo. In addition those inclined toward a reformist position, other groups of liberals advocated the pursuit of a successful foreign policy as a means of undermining the influence of the agrarians. Others even asserted that any lasting successes in the international arena could only be won if, rooted in a democratic constitution, they had the backing of the broad majority of Germans. Such arguments occasionally became blended with state-interventionist ideas and were a switch from the unbridled economic liberalism of the early 1870s. They also led to a limited rapprochement with the right wing of the Social Democrats.

Following the formation of a unified Social Democratic party at the Gotha Congress of 1875, there was too little time until the beginning of proscription three years later to decide on whether the new movement, its radical rhetoric notwithstanding, should move more along the Lasallean path of collaboration with the state, or whether the Marxist ideas of Bebel's workers' party were to predominate. The Erfurt Program of 1891 – published one year after the lapse of the anti-Socialist laws – provided an opportunity to clarify the ideological foundations of Social Democracy. What emerged instead was a contradictory statement. The first part offered an orthodox Marxist analysis of bourgeois-capitalist society, culminating in the postulate that "class rule and the classes" be abolished. [44] The second part was preceded by this: "Starting from these principles, the Social Democratic party demands for the time being . . .;" but, curiously, none of the demands that followed required a socialist revolution for their implementation. Here the Erfurt Program

44. W. Mommsen, ed., *Parteiprogramme* (note 40), 83ff.

spoke of an extension of civil rights, the abolition of the death penalty, free medical care, progressive taxation, secular schools, and improved protection of labor.

The tension between two ideological positions which first became evident in the Erfurt Program thenceforth permeated the debate among Social Democrats during the Wilhelmine period. On the one hand, many radicals worked for a revolutionary transformation of existing conditions with all weapons of political struggle, including that of the mass strike; on the other, the "revisionists" advanced, from their strongholds in southwest Germany and Hanover, the cause of reformist solutions and of a gradualist transition to socialism. The two were held together by an intermediate position, of which Karl Kautsky became a prominent representative. He supported in principle the notion of a revolutionary transformation of the capitalist system, but argued that it would not come as a result of the revolutionary activism of a united proletariat. Instead he counted on the expectation, predicted by "scientific" Marxism, that capitalism would collapse under the weight of its own inherent contradictions. This ideological *attentisme* did much to relieve the pressure on the radicals, on the one hand, and the reformists around Eduard Bernstein, on the other, to secede from the party. Similarly the prestige of Bebel until his death in 1913 remained an important factor in keeping all Social Democrats in the fold.

At the same time, it should be obvious that none of the three interpretations of the future which coexisted within Social Democracy held any attraction for the other parties. The Left Liberals more than once considered cooperating politically with the Social Democrats. But since none of them wished to live under socialism, not even if this was to be achieved by gradual reform, this cooperation could only go so far. A similar reluctance held back the leftist Catholics in the Center party and in the Christian trade unions, even though they repeatedly spoke up for individual Social Democrats and local groups that had been subjected to tough police measures or to unfair sentencing by the courts in connection with strikes. [45] Basically all other political forces were united in their opposition to Social Democracy and labored hard to woo the industrial workers away from its ideological hold over them. Marxism was seen as a fundamental threat, and none of the other movements seriously thought of supping with the devil.

However, in the face of rapid industrialization and urbanization there was no escaping the "workers' question." Catholic priests in the working-class

45. See below pp. 253ff.

district of the major cities were among the first to take up the concerns of the new class, or at least of its Catholic members. During the 1870s, the evolution of Catholic social thought had been hampered by the Church's preoccupation with the *Kulturkampf*. Put on the defensive by the rise of liberalism, the Vatican finally proclaimed its doctrine of papal infallibility in 1870. In the decade thereafter, the foremost task appeared to be to uphold traditional rights concerning the pastoral support and religious education of the Catholic population. Although Bismarck quickly de-escalated the *Kulturkampf*, the fortress mentality that had seized hold of the Catholic population survived the fall of the first Reich Chancellor. In a famous article published in March 1906, the Rhenish Center Party politician Julius Bachem urged his fellow Catholics to leave the "tower," but German Catholicism basically continued to live behind its ideological and political bulwark. While the traditional "social-moral milieu" [46] persisted in the provinces, a Catholic working-class milieu was created in the industrial cities, especially in the Ruhr area. This milieu had its own ideological horizons, and Social Democracy with its comprehensive interpretation of the world was not able to penetrate it until the last years before the First World War.

However deeply rooted the Center party was in the Catholic faith, the social heterogeneity of its voters endowed it with a good deal of flexibility in matters of daily politics. The exploitation of this room for maneuver shows more clearly than the case of other movements that the Center party was not just held together by ideological and programmatic principles, but also by particular interests. These interests were articulated most forcefully by a large number of associations which operated in the extra-parliamentary sphere and which tried to use the political parties as their front organizations.

15. Organizations and Movements in the Extra-Parliamentary Sphere

A. Basic Issues

Extra-parliamentary interest groups developed virtually in parallel with the political parties, and by 1914 they had in effect filled all nooks and crannies of the space ordinarily assigned to them in complex societies. This is why the great variety of these groups must be stressed from the start. The more

46. M.R. Lepsius, "Parteiensysteme und Sozialstruktur," in: W. Abel, ed., *Wirtschaft, Geschichte und Wirtschaftsgeschichte* (Stuttgart 1966), 371- 89. See also above pp. 97ff., and the studies on political Catholicism in the Bibliography.

colorful German society became under the impact of industrialization, urbanization, and increasing social differentiation, the more varied became its associational life. In the end there was hardly a human activity which an interested individual could not pursue with like-minded people in the context of an organization. A number of these associations have already been mentioned in connection with the expansion of culture and science and they will not be covered here. [47] Nor is this a chapter that will be dealing with the activities of the Imperial Automobile Club, groups devoted to sexual reform, occultist sects, or stamp collectors. These associations tended to view themselves as nonpolitical, even if in a very general sense they did have a political effect, and toward 1914 increasingly so. Here the task is to analyze those organizations which were openly oriented toward the sphere of politics and which, as lobbies, directly or indirectly attempted to influence the executive, the parties, and the public at large.

The social sciences usually differentiate between politically active economic pressure groups, on the one hand, and political associations and movements, on the other. This would appear to be a sensible differentiation as far as the *Kaiserreich* is concerned, if we look at memberships, both individual and corporative; for it was in terms of membership that economic interest groups were restrictive, whereas political associations were, at least on paper, open to any person or organization that identified with their goals and laws. It is also important that economic lobbies tended to be geared more toward influencing government officials and deputies. Political associations and the so-called "national associations" saw influencing public opinion as their most important mission.

B. Lobbies

Groups that represented the interests of economic enterprises had existed before 1871. At that time they also fulfilled certain tasks in public law. Thus the chambers of commerce were partly private, but also had a public mandate; for example, they were required to examine and certify trainees. The Prussian *Landesökonomien* and Agricultural Associations enjoyed similar privileges, and after the founding of the German Empire they continued to exploit the opportunities which their special relationship with the state administration afforded them.

The early 1870s and even more so the period of the "Great Depression" saw the emergence of economic lobbies in the modern sense. The

47. See above pp. 133ff.

Association of German Iron and Steel Industrialists was founded in 1873. A few years later the Association for the Preservation of the Common Economic Interests in the Rhineland and Westphalia (because of its long name also known for short as "Langnamverein") rose to become one of the most influential lobbies. The creation of cartels and syndicates must also be seen in this context of a growing organization of commerce and industry. [48] Some associations covered a region, others a branch of industry. Sooner or later it made sense for a group of organizations to form a roof association at the national level –like the Central Association of German Industry (CDI), founded in 1876. In the late 1870s, most of these associations devoted themselves to pressuring the executive branch of government and the elected representatives into adopting measures to protect them against retarded economic growth. Thus the introduction and subsequent increases of external tariffs between 1879 and the early 1890s was due in no small measure to the indefatigable activities of lobbies. Although conflicts among the members and power struggles regularly occurred behind the facade of unity, for a long time heavy industry remained the most influential group in the CDI.

Only when heavy industry proved reluctant to abandon protectionism during the upswing of the 1890s did the strains within the CDI become too great. There was a revolt and secession of the more export-oriented and manufacturing branches, leading to the creation of the League of Industrialists (BDI) in 1895. After the turn of the century, the peak associations and their member organizations continued to focus on articulating the interests of industry and commerce with regard to such issues as trade treaties and taxation. But increasingly these interests were interpreted more widely and ultimately all of these groups were engaged in debates on Wilhelmine foreign and armaments policy and attempted to shape the various reforms of Reich finances. The "Hansabund" proliferated after the bitter debates surrounding the 1908 Finance Bill. Although its members included a number of organizations that were not economic lobbies in the strict sense, it certainly reflected the growing polarization of the aims of the industrial peak associations. The BDI became one of the pillars of the Hansabund.

What kind of groups were mobilized by this new organization in the wake of the defeat of the Finance Bill by the Conservatives and its substitution by a bill that hit commerce and manufacturing industry hard is evidenced by its membership. The Hansabund presidium included the chairmen of the Association of Florists in Hamburg and Environs, the Association of

48. See above pp. 22ff.

Commercial Groups in Württemberg, and the Bremen Chamber of Small Traders. These titles also indicate the great variety of organizations that had meanwhile formed and increasingly came together as large and powerful economic blocs under the roof of one of the peak associations. Meanwhile the artisans had forged their own lobbies outside the Chambers, and ultimately there was hardly a professional group that did not have its own organization and public voice. The repercussions of this hectic activity in the extra-parliamentary sphere could be felt within the political parties which became more sensitive to economic concerns, while their earlier interest in constitutional reform receded into the background.

The rising importance of social policy and the success of the working-class movement also forced the lobbies to deal with these issues. Collective bargaining between employers and workers' representatives began in some branches of industry, accompanied by a recognition of trade unions. Large-scale industry on the whole remained bitterly opposed to this trend. Encouraged by the conservative CDI, employers' associations began to aim at the containment and even the destruction of the trade unions. The first moves to coordinate this activity were made in 1903/4, culminating in the founding of the Main Office of German Employers' Associations in April 1904. The split between BDI and CDI soon also affected the politics of this new association, as the members of the BDI took a more moderate line on the question of an anti-strike fund and its uses. Unable to find a common base, the moderates created the Association of German Employers' Organizations. It was only in 1913 that the two movements were merged to form the Federation of German Employers' Associations. Henceforth this federation was charged with coordinating the interests of industry and commerce with regard to social policy and wages. In all there existed some 3,670 business associations in 1914.

C. Trade Unions and Professional Associations

Trade unions, which were also banned by the 1878 anti-Socialist laws, had recruited some 75,000 to 80,000 members up to that point. They were subsequently forced to continue their work underground. The mid-1880s saw a limited revival of the *Fachvereine* of which there were approximately one thousand with a total membership of approximately 58,000 in 1885. After the lapse of the anti-Socialist laws in 1890, the trade unions as the representation of the economic interests of the urban-industrial working class experienced an amazing growth, while agricultural workers continued to be barred from forming unions until 1908. By the turn of the century, the Social Democratic "free trade unions" comprised some 680,000 members. A peak was reached in 1913 with 2.5 million members (table 81). However, there were big differences in the degree of unionization in different branches of industry. Parts of the metal industry were close to the 50 percent mark, while in other branches around 10 percent of the workforce was unionized. At the same time the number of full-time functionaries rose to 2,867. By 1914 some 10 percent of working women had also joined a union. Syndicalism remained an insignificant phenomenon, spawning a few splinter groups before World War I, mainly among Ruhr miners. In the mid-1890s, a Catholic trade union movement appeared on the scene. By 1900 it had attracted some 77,000 members, rising to 343,000 by 1913. The liberal Hirsch-Duncker unions succeeded in mobilizing no more than 107,000 workers. It is very telling of the general situation of the Poles in the Reich that the migrants to the Ruhr area, who had gone into mining, formed their own union, the "Zjednoczenie Zawodowe Polskie," whose membership reached 50,000 in 1912.

Ideological differences as well as the numerical imbalances between the unions stood in the way of a more long-term cooperation between them, even though all made the improvement of the material situation of the industrial working class their main plank. The question was as to how this was best achieved. The Hirsch-Duncker unions advocated cooperation with the employers. The free trade unions, by contrast, had a notion of industrial relations that started from a conflict model and considered strikes to be a legitimate weapon for obtaining improvements. As a result there were periods when Germany was shaken by massive strikes. [49] But this should not lead us to conclude that the Social Democratic trade unions were very radical. This is perhaps how they appeared in the eyes of politicians and entrepreneurs. However, recent research has tended to highlight the conservatism and moderation of the union leadership. Unlike the radicals on their left, such as Rosa Luxemburg, they refused to deploy the strike weapon for political purposes. They were neither concerned with abolishing capitalism nor with transforming it or the monarchy. Their goal was to boost the living standards of the workers. What caused them to be additionally cautious was the determined resistance of the employers who could count on the repressive machinery of the state to support them in their antiunionism. [50] What finally

49. See above pp. 31ff. See also F. Boll, *Massenbewegungen in Niedersachsen, 1906-1920* (Bonn 1981).

50. See below pp. 253ff.

strengthened reformist attitudes among the free trade unions was a certain pride in their impressive organizational achievements, reinforced by a trend toward oligarchy at the top and routinization at all levels. Meanwhile the employers expected to win their fight not only with the help of the police, the courts, and the Army, but also with that of the company union movement. Significantly, these Werkvereine never attracted more than a few thousand members.

The trend toward organization is also reflected in the behavior of the middle classes as they combined in numerous professional organizations. The artisans assiduously guarded their guild-like *Innungen*. The professionals founded their own interest representations (table 83). The doctors' organization went back to before the founding of the Reich. But in 1900 it gained a competitor, which assumed the expressive title "Association of the Physicians of Germany for the Preservation of their Economic Interests"; "Hartmann-Bund" for short. Similar lobbies developed for dentists, veterinary surgeons, pharmacists, attorneys, and pastors. Teachers had their own pressure groups, among them a League of Academically Educated Teachers of Germany. One of the largest was the German Teachers' Association, which in 1914 had almost 132,000 members. With the expansion of industry, the commercial and technical white-collar workers began to organize as well. However, members of all these organizations aimed for more than the improvement of their material position; they also asked for greater social prestige and a recognition of their contributions to state and society. In this sense, the professional associations were an expression of the upwardly mobile, educated bourgeoisie's desire to set itself apart from the industrial working class, not just socially, but also organizationally. Their activities resulted in a major victory in 1911, when they succeeded in establishing an insurance system that was separate from that of the blue-collar workers. The country's division into classes was now visibly drawn along this particular associational line.

D. Agricultural Associations

Agriculture, for a longer period of time than industry and commerce, relied for its interest representation after 1871 on preexisting corporations and councils whose spokesmen had easy access to the bureaucracy and conservative-agrarian parties. There were also many social connections between the large-scale estate owners and the executive as high up as the princely courts of the federal states. These links opened up manifold ways of influencing policy-making, especially during the "Great Depression" which hit agriculture harder than industry. The Association of Tax and Economic Reformers, it is true, gained some importance during the agitation for higher agricultural tariffs; but its work was probably less important since Bismarck did not really need much persuading. For various political and economic reasons he was already convinced that the agrarians deserved the special protection of the state. It was the peasants who first expanded or built up from scratch a network of associations that took its place beside the older semi-public agrarian self-administration by means of chambers and other institutions. Thus a variety of "peasant leagues" became active in Bavaria and other parts of Germany during the 1880s, replacing earlier particularist and mostly anti-Prussian peasant organizations. These leagues saw themselves not merely as agricultural lobbies in the narrow sense, but also tried to mobilize the peasants of their region during election times with anti-capitalist and anti-Semitic slogans.

The East Elbian *Junker* took the road of public agitation and populist voter mobilization only in the 1890s. Reich Chancellor Leo von Caprivi, encouraged by the economic upswing and pushed by export-oriented industry, proposed to abandon his predecessor's policy of high protective tariffs. If Caprivi was only temporarily successful and was later forced to submit his resignation, this was to no small degree due to an old-style campaign of personal influence-peddling at the Imperial Court that was waged against him by his agrarian opponents, but it was also due to the activities of the Agrarian League. This league was founded in 1893 and immediately took up the fight against a lowering of tariffs. In subsequent years, this new association began to compete against the peasant leagues. It adopted a more modern style of mass mobilization and, as a result, triggered the decline of the latter, at least in the Protestant regions of the country. In the Catholic regions, the Center party, which was also helped by a more effective populist propaganda, slowly replaced the leagues with its own organizational network. Although the denominational line continued to divide the organization of agriculture, it is nevertheless a remarkable political feat that an association founded and run by large-scale estate owners succeeded in convincing many small peasants that their interests were better served by the Agrarian League than by their own peasant leagues.

One reason for this success is to be found in the Agrarian League's style and sloganeering. This organization evolved into more than an economic lobby in the traditional sense, devoted to the discreet influencing of decisions quietly prepared in government offices. Indeed, its main field of action became the provincial marketplace and the village pub. This is where the Agrarian League put into circulation those vague demands that suggested to the owners of farms of all sizes that they were all sitting in the same boat:

higher agricultural protectionism, subsidies, debt reduction, reduced protection for farm laborers. However, these popular demands were combined from the start with a vigorous agitation that claimed to tackle the real evils of the age: capitalism and liberalism, urbanization and Social Democracy, and – of course – "international Jewry." The League proposed that Germans reject these alleged dangers in favor of the values of the old preindustrial society, complemented by patriotism, "Prussian" parsimony, and the maintenance of a strong army. [51]

The propaganda that was crafted from these positions went well beyond what the country had seen in the 1880s. It used the most modern technical means which, ironically, had first been developed by the despised urban culture. The slogans of the Agrarian League were shrill and did not shy away from blatant lies. They deliberately appealed to latent prejudices and resentments in the agricultural population. There has been some debate as to whether the Agrarian League was a prefascist organization. [52] Be this as it may, the Agrarian League regularly participated in election campaigns and built up an elaborate infrastructure. It employed professional agitators who would appear at its many rallies. It distributed emotional propaganda literature and influenced the shape of major pieces of agricultural legislation. Many deputies were in its debt for its support of their election campaigns. In 1898 some 118 Reichstag deputies from five parties were deemed to be connected with the League. In 1907 this figure reached its peak at 138; by 1912 it had declined to 78 in line with the more general weakening of agrarian conservatism in the last years before 1914. The Agrarian League also had many friends in the diets of the federal states. Around the turn of the century, it had no less than 250,000 members, of whom 75 percent were small peasants.

D. Nationalist Associations

If the Agrarian League, at least in part, still operated as an economic pressure group in the traditional sense, the nationalist associations that emerged from the 1890s onward completely shed this image. This may be seen, to begin with, from the social composition of their membership. Whether individual or corporate, membership was no longer restricted to specific occupational groups or economic activities. In principle, anybody could join a nationalist association, although in practice Social Democrats and, in some organizations, Jews were distinctly unwelcome. This peculiar exclusivity points to a

51. See above pp. 216ff.

52. H.-J. Puhle, *Von der Agrarkrise zum Präfaschismus* (Wiesbaden 1972).

fundamental line that separated the nationalist associations from the working-class movement. However, a noisy nationalism initially tended to drown out this anti-Socialist orientation. It was only after the turn of the century that the uncompromising struggle against Social Democracy was openly put on a level with the chauvinistic propaganda that had become unbearable. The fight against the working-class movement turned the nationalist associations, frequent squabbles among themselves notwithstanding, into a powerful bloc. This bloc, operating in the extra-parliamentary sphere, articulated the hopes and fears of the increasingly politicized middle classes in the towns and the provinces.

We are particularly well informed about the Pan-German League, which remained numerically small but wielded much political influence; the Navy League which counted 300,000 members in 1906; and the Army League, which achieved a similar size. [(53)] (Table 84) Initially the propaganda slogans of all three of them, like those of the German Colonial Society, for example, remained vague and amorphous. They demanded a strengthening of patriotism, a vigorous foreign policy, increased armaments, the acquisition of colonies, and the dissemination of an allegedly superior German culture abroad. The early propaganda of the Navy League contained an array of economic slogans which, buttressed by less than reliable statistics, were aimed at gaining the support of industry and commerce. Soon the struggle against the "threat" of the working-class movement was added to the arsenal of arguments. The emergence of the Reich Association against Social Democracy, founded in 1904, was typical of the period. Friend-foe postures proliferated. Germany, in the eyes of the nationalist associations, was encircled by internal and external enemies. The armament nationalism (*Rüstungsnationalismus*) that developed in Germany gradually assumed paranoid features. The demagogy and political lies of the nationalist associations became ever more crude. What made them convincing to many gullible people was that they were packaged as "scientific" insights gained from Nature and History. By 1914, this propaganda reached its first climax both in style and content.

Although the nationalist associations always claimed to be nonpolitical, the gradual radicalization of their political positions was in fact their most distinctive characteristic. This is well illustrated by the outcome of the long struggle between a moderate and a radical wing within the Navy League. At the turn of the century, leaders and members naively claimed that the League

53. R. Chickering, *We Men Who Feel Most German* (London 1984); G. Eley, *Reshaping the German Right* (New Haven, Conn. 1980); M.S. Coetzee, *The German Army League* (New Haven, Conn. 1990).

was a "supra-party" organization devoted to rallying all patriotic forces in general support of the Kaiser's naval and world policy. But more radical elements soon chiseled away at this position. With a mindset that was even more authoritarian and nationalist than that of the "moderates," these elements, who purported to have the support of the ordinary membership and of many other Germans, ultimately advanced a fundamental critique of government policy and of the monarchical system as a whole. They pressed for the most extreme increases in armaments. If German foreign and domestic politics increasingly lapsed into a state of serious crisis before 1914, it was to no small extent due to the agitation of the nationalist associations. In this sense they acted to destabilize the existing political order. However, this impact was counterbalanced by the fact that the *Rüstungsnationalismus* of the associations, and their ardent fight against Social Democracy, clearly succeeded in rallying and to some extent integrating disparate middle-class groups and individuals. Those with *Besitz und Bildung* (property and higher education) thus helped stabilize the existing order by combatting liberal reformism and the Social Democrats.

This ambiguity accounts for the fact that Geoff Eley's hypotheses concerning the destabilizing impact of organized Wilhelmine populism on the radical Right continue to be controversial. Moreover, while he sees behind the radicalism of the nationalist associations the self-articulation and self-mobilization of the lower middle classes, doubts have been voiced by other scholars as to whether he has really offered the sociological and ideological proof for this (table 85) [54]. After all, the ideology of a nationalist rallying (*Sammlung*) continued to be powerful, even if it proved difficult in practice to sustain it beyond the short term. What is beyond dispute is that the nationalist associations greatly accelerated the political mobilization of the population at all levels.

F. The Political Organization of Minorities

By examining the situation of minorities in German society, it has already been possible to identify a number of larger societal trends. [55] Further insights may be gained by analyzing the position of minorities in politics and in the country's political culture. Insofar as such groups created their own associations, they participated in the broader process of popular mobilization that accelerated the decline of the politics of notables after 1890. But much can also be inferred from looking at the reasons behind their organizing effort.

---

54. See above pp. xivf.

55. See above pp. 96ff.

1. The Peace Movement

While the Navy League and other nationalist and militarist associations attracted a sizeable membership, other groups, whose origins went back as far as the founding years of the *Kaiserreich*, devoted themselves to peace and international understanding, working to expand international law and arbitration as part of this effort. In 1874, Eduard Löwenthal had founded the German Association for International Peace Propaganda, which he transformed into the German Association for Obligatory Peace Jurisdiction in 1896. In 1886 Löwenthal's group gained a competitor with strongholds in Frankfurt, Darmstadt, and Stuttgart. Thus the peace movement remained decentralized for a long time, even though the southwest German groups produced a number of activists who succeeded, through their publications and lectures, in sharpening its profile and in attracting national attention (table 84). Still, it was only under the impact of the First Hague Peace Conference of 1899 that a German Peace Society constituted itself at Reich level. This society sought to build up a mass organization equal to or larger than the most successful nationalist associations. It had a number of prominent spokespersons, among them Erich Fried, Ludwig Quidde, Bertha von Suttner, and Otto Umfrid. Merchants and teachers were particularly strongly represented among the membership. The Society's propaganda started from the somewhat vague goal of creating a more humane, just, and harmonious international order. Fried tried to provide the members' hopes and expectations with a firmer "scientific" basis.

Trying to spread the idea of peace, international cooperation, and international law, the German Peace Society hoped to gain the cooperation of families, schools, and youth groups. Attempts were also made to win over the press, the churches, and even the military. The popular response to the movement's ideas was far from encouraging. This is why other members thought it better to try to influence elite groups. For this purpose they finally created the Association for International Understanding in June 1911. Its founders quickly discovered that the elites were no more amenable to their ideas, not least because the Kaiser flatly rejected the notion of peace. His attitude, in turn, put pressure upon the government and the bureaucracy to conform. The support which the Second Hague Peace Conference of 1907 found in parts of the population moreover convinced Reich government leaders that only the Social Democrats would gain from a reversal of Wilhelmine foreign and armaments policy. In the Reichstag, the Left Liberals showed a relatively serious interest in the ideas of the Peace Society, while the parties of the Right rejected them indignantly. There were some rather timid beginnings of a cooperation with the Social Democrats, among whom Karl Liebknecht, above all, promoted a strongly antimilitarist platform. But social and ideological differences prevented this cooperation from being maintained on a more permanent basis, the more so since the SPD's revisionists adopted some of the nationalist and imperialist stances of the National Liberals, while the radical Left continued to believe in revolutionary violence as a vehicle of History. Worse, this was an age of escalating arms races, irrational nationalism, and wild imperialistic dreams. Wilhelmine Germany offered a fertile soil for the growth of nationalist associations, and it has therefore rightly been argued that the weakness of the German peace movement simply mirrored the strength of its opponents. [56] For reasons of foreign and domestic politics, both the elites and the nationalist movement were very hostile to the notion of a "world without war" and to the small band of men and women who propagated this idea.

2. Religious and Ethnic Minorities

Although the Alsace-Lorraineans and the Danes were better organized than the Poles, the politicization and centralization of the associational life of the Polish minority in the Ruhr area and in the east made great strides during the Wilhelmine period. Harassed by official discrimination, the organizations of the Ruhr Poles lost their originally purely cultural character. Links with the Poles in the East were revitalized. The League of Poles in Germany, founded at Bochum in 1894, finally merged in 1910 with the "Straz" movement that had been built up since 1905. Then, in 1913, this group formed an executive committee that worked alongside the Polish National Council that had emerged in the same year. [57] The common task with which the Polish minority and its press were confronted, which was now more urgent than ever before, was the rebuttal of the Prussian government's relentless Germanization policy. [58]

We have already mentioned the political mobilization of Germany's Catholics through the Center party and mass organizations like the People's Association for a Catholic Germany (over 800,000 members). [59] By the 1890s, the Jews – as an ethnic minority not living in regional concentrations

56. R. Chickering, *Imperial Germany and a World without War* (Princeton 1975).

57. C. Klessmann, *Polnische Bergarbeiter im Ruhrgebiet* (Göttingen 1978), 103.

58. See above pp. 110ff.

59. See above pp. 214f.

like the Danes or Poles – similarly began to raise their voices. Unlike the Danes and Alsace-Lorraineans they had gained equality before the law by 1871. Only those 79,000 Jews who had immigrated from eastern Europe, making up some 12.8 percent of the Jewish population in the Reich by 1910, were still subject to the discriminating laws governing aliens. But in the meantime Jews with German citizenship had become the victims of less blatant forms of discrimination that must be seen in connection with the proliferation of anti-Semitic feelings. [60]

Jews were largely excluded from public service and from many private clubs. To the social and religious anti-Semitism of the earlier period was added a racist component. During the Wilhelmine period, the most incredible biologistic conspiracy theories found quite a few enthusiastic adherents. A growing number of Jewish university students tried to escape the prejudice of the fraternities by forming their own groups which were combined in 1896 in the "Kartell-Konvent." When the anti-Semites conquered no less than sixteen seats in the 1893 Reichstag elections, many politically minded Jews thought the time had come to found their own defensive organization, the Central Association of German Citizens of the Jewish Faith (CV). The group ultimately had over 100,000 members and saw its main task in countering anti-Semitic propaganda. Its members tended to come more from the educated middle classes than from the Jewish business elite. As is indicated by the group's name, all the members saw themselves as Germans *and* Jews – even those who tended more toward the left of the ideological spectrum.

While the members of the CV undertook their defensive work in a spirit of patriotism, other Jews denied that the Jewish minority could ever be successfully integrated into German society. They demanded self-determination within their own state. Theodor Herzl became one of the most prominent spokesmen of these Zionists. He was also responsible for calling the First Zionist Congress in August 1897. Shortly thereafter the Zionist Association for Germany emerged, which achieved no more than a fraction of the membership figures of the CV. Initially, many Jews had been members of both organizations. But in the years after the turn of the century, the goals of the two associations were revealed to be incompatible. The CV promoted the political-ideological and economic integration of the Jews into German society, while insisting on the preservation of their special cultural identity; the Zionists, by contrast, advocated separatism and emigration to Palestine.

---

60. See above pp. 102ff.

That the two organizations should emerge at all points to a growing hostility toward Jews among larger sections of the population who made the Jews scapegoats for the ills and tensions within German society and politics. Eventually, the associational mobilization that was reflected in the founding of the CV and of Zionism also affected Jewish women. In 1904, a Jewish Women's League was established which grew to have some 50,000 members. These women lived under a "double jeopardy": [61] like their male Jewish counterparts, they had to cope with anti-Semitism; but they also had to cope with the traditional Jewish family structure and a society at large that was still patriarchically organized.

3. Women's Associations and Politics

If male Jewish adults at least enjoyed full rights as citizens, Jewish women, like their non-Jewish sisters, remained subject to many legal and political restrictions. Until the introduction of the Civil Code (*Bürgerliches Gesetzbuch*, BGB) in 1900, differences in the treatment of the sexes by the law were considerable in the federal states; but as a general rule women's rights to own and inherit property, like their parental prerogatives, were strictly limited. In a law of January 1875, the civil marriage replaced the church marriage as legally binding. However, the intercession of the state did practically nothing to improve the underprivileged position of women in marriage. All property rights fell to the husband, unless a special contractual arrangement to the contrary had been made. Similarly, the husband had the exclusive authority over the children. The legal and financial consequences of a divorce tended to be very serious for a wife, not to mention the social stigma. For this reason alone, the divorce rate remained low. [62] The Civil Code of 1900 did not require more equal treatment for the sexes, and in some cases it even worsened the woman's position, e.g., with regard to divorce. The Criminal Code of 1871 contained particularly severe sanctions against abortion and prostitution, and we have already heard about the restrictions imposed on women with respect to education, career choice, and professional mobility. [63]

Discrimination against women was particularly glaring in the field of civil rights. The Reich Constitution flatly denied women the vote. The federal

61. M. Kaplan, *The Jewish Feminist Movement in Germany* (Westport, Conn. 1979), 14.

62. See above pp. 55ff.

63. See above pp. 65ff.

states and communities had a range of rules, few of which were consistent. Thus wealthy women had the vote in local elections. Elsewhere a wealthy woman could not cast her vote in person, but only through her husband, who under the rules of the Civil Code relating to legal representation was not, however, bound to her mandate. In short, the inequalities and their plain illogicality opened up a wide field for politically conscious women to press for change. Their problem was that this patriarchal society had erected one further barrier which was particularly difficult to surmount: the association laws explicitly prohibited women from being involved in politics. Nor were they allowed to join male organizations that pursued political aims. Again there were exceptions to this rule in southwest Germany, Hamburg, and Bremen. But in Prussia, the largest state, women were not even permitted to attend political meetings. If the watchful eye of the local policeman spotted a skirt at such a meeting, he could disband the rally without further ado. It was only with the advent of the Reich Association Law of 1908 that this rule was abolished for all parts of the country. However, women were no more welcome in nonpolitical associations. Even before 1908 they had therefore begun to found their own organizations.

The poverty of many lower-class families, the problem of prostitution, and the discrimination faced by women in education opened up many opportunities for women to become active in non-political ways and to form groups for the purposes of charity and social reform. The General German Association of Women dated back to before the founding of the *Kaiserreich*. Its leaders were committed to improving the education and training of women. During the 1870s, they also tried – unsuccessfully – to influence the work of the preparatory commission for the Civil Code that was finally adopted in 1900. When the "social question" moved to the center of public debate in the 1880s, many women seized the initiative at the local level to improve relief for the poor and the protection of children.

The following decade saw a marked expansion of organized activity by women. Meanwhile a younger generation of women took a more radical view of existing problems and their possible solutions. They also interpreted gender relations in new ways. The founding of professional organizations for female teachers and commercial employees at this time also had a wide impact, and it is no accident that until 1914 women gained their most tangible advances in the field of education and training. The proliferation of women's organizations of all kinds inevitably made it more difficult to differentiate between charitable and political activity. The organizing effort reached a new plateau in 1894 with the founding of the League of German Women's

Associations, which combined thirty-four associations under its roof. Seven years later, this league had some 70,000 members in 137 associations. By 1914 its membership had risen to 250,000.

With the expansion of the women's movement came a sharpening of disagreements over strategy and tactics. Prostitution and its control by the authorities became a bone of contention. For the radicals in the women's movement, prostitution was not merely a humiliation of the woman that had to stop; they also took the view that the officially sanctioned system of bordellos which the Hamburg authorities had established constituted a violation of a clause in the Criminal Code which banned the promotion of prostitution. The Hamburg police defended itself against the charge of being engaged in criminal activities by wheeling out public health decrees. They also made it more difficult for the activists to present their case at public meetings. This in turn highlighted the absurdity of the prohibition against women in political meetings. All in all, this ban was undermined long before the Reich Association Law of 1908 gave women the green light to engage in political activities.

However much this law was welcomed by many women, in the meantime other differences of opinion had arisen within the movement that were in principle no less political than the problem of prostitution. To begin with, there was the question of female sexuality and sexual freedom. It sparked a movement for sexual reform and enlightenment whose arguments were remarkably modern. Soon the movement's demands began to impinge upon marriage and legitimacy rights. The radicals in the movement made rapid advances in the first years after the turn of the century and succeeded in conquering influential positions within the roof association. But the liberal phase was soon replaced by a period of conservatism and secessions. Now the more cautious tacticians gained the upper hand in the League of German Women's Associations, which, after all, had never been more than a loose federation of associations with very heterogeneous aims. The conservatives, unlike the radicals, started from the assumption that the private sphere was the main realm of female activity, and that women should devote themselves to their families. Insofar as women had a public mission, it was to secure the future of the nation through child-bearing. From this it was but a small step to arguments about the duty to produce "genetically healthy" children, while the sexual freedom of the allegedly degenerate and volatile lower classes was to be restricted. The radical ideas about love and family that had been promoted by the League for the Protection of Mothers in 1905 were anathema to the conservative eugenicists of the last years before

World War I. The issue of preschool education became similarly polarized along ideological lines.

The liberal reformers and feminists met with vigorous opposition from men, but also from their conservative sisters, whose position was not entirely logical; the latter tried to mobilize women in the public realm for political purposes, while simultaneously extolling a passive ideal of femininity in the private sphere. That patriotic and anti-Socialist activity by women became accepted as a legitimate activity outside the home may also be taken as another reflection of the growing crisis in German politics. When it came to such important issues, even fiercely conservative men and women were desperate enough to be prepared to live with that contradiction. After 1908, most nationalist associations added women's auxiliaries that promoted female activism for antifeminist objectives. Not surprisingly, this incongruity did nothing to relieve tensions within the nationalist movements or among the sexes. Men and women continued to live in separate spheres within a larger society that propounded the values of military prowess and heroic virility, while perceiving emancipated women as a threat. By 1914 male chauvinism was no longer just an individual posture, but had become organized. Resistance to the demands of women arose as early as the 1890s in some professional associations that were among the first to feel the effects of female competition. The backlash widened thereafter, and by 1912 there was even a League for the Struggle against Female Emancipation, which counted prominent conservatives like the painter Anton von Werner, the historian Dietrich Schäfer, and the retired general August Keim among its members. Their propaganda presented a poisonous mix of antifeminism with anti-Semitism, anti-Socialism, militarism, chauvinism, and natalism.

Over time the agitation against a removal of the many forms of discrimination against women also became inseparable from fears of a "social revolution" and of Social Democracy. Feminists were alleged to cooperate with the radicals in the SPD, and the debate on female suffrage came to be seen as the test case. Since demanding the vote was a highly political act, which in Prussia, Bavaria, and Saxony might even trigger a police ban, the League of German Women's Associations had always shied away from putting it into its program. Nor were all its member associations in favor of female suffrage, which was all the more reason for the Association of Progressive Women's Groups, which had been founded in 1899, to take up the idea in its publications. Three years later a number of prominent feminists, with Anita Augspurg, Lida Heymann, Minna Cauer, and Helene Stöcker among them, established the German Association for Female Suffrage. While its aims were obvious, it was only after the ratification of the Reich Association Law in 1908 that this organization could launch its campaign throughout the country without fear of the police. Until then its main activity consisted in discreet lobbying among Left Liberal deputies to support the introduction of the vote for women. The Association's success was rather meager, as even the progressive liberals tended to pay no more than lip service to the feminist cause. These experiences merely increased the determination of the radicals to take up the cudgels themselves, as soon as this became possible after 1908. Organizing street demonstrations proved the most effective means to catch public attention.

In 1910 these rallies became tied up with the mass meetings against the Prussian three-class voting system that the Social Democrats were staging at this time. Suddenly the radical feminists faced being identified with the SPD, or worse still with the party's left wing, whose representatives wanted to use the mass demonstrations for their revolutionary aims. It also turned out that, when the Social Democrats demanded equality at the ballot box, their first thought was the abolition of the restrictive suffrage systems in the federal states for males and females. The feminists were more concerned with gaining the vote for women throughout the *Kaiserreich* and for Reichstag elections in particular. Finally, the working-class movement had begun to create sections for women within its own organizations whose political agenda was often different from that of the feminists (table 82). By 1914, some 175,000 women had joined the SPD; they constituted 16.1 percent of the total membership. Most of them agreed with the view of their male comrades that the question of the professional, sexual, and political emancipation of women would be resolved only after the existing socioeconomic and political order had been radically transformed. There could be no genuine equality between the sexes before then. The interests of women were therefore best served if they supported Social Democracy.

Many feminists found it difficult to accept this and some of them asked themselves whether a fully democratized suffrage system was in fact desirable. Had it not been a mixed blessing that Bismarck had given the vote to lower-class men? Was it, in this case, not wiser to retain the restrictive suffrage systems, but to include women with a weighted vote? In short, the suffrage debate opened a Pandora's box and thus began to divide the advocates of women's suffrage along class lines. The doubts and changes of heart that followed were translated into changes in the leadership, finally effected at a decisive meeting at Weimar in December 1912. As in the League of German Women's Associations and elsewhere, conservatives now took the helm of the suffrage movement. The radicals left in protest. Thenceforth these conservatives worked with the middle-class parties and helped to combat the SPD. The suffrage campaign came under the spell of eugenicist notions of a "healthy" family. By 1913 things had gone so far that the journal Frauenstimmrecht published a long article dealing with imbecile and crippled illiterate males. They, the author argued, had the right to vote, while healthy and educated women were deprived of it. In the end the patterns of political mobilization among women coincided with divisions along the lines of social class and ideology. Bourgeois feminists would join the established women's associations. Meanwhile, although the share of women in the SPD and the trade unions remained small at 10-16 percent, most of the female members came from a proletarian background (table 82).

G. Pluralization and Bloc Formation

The emergence and subsequent omnipresence of interest groups is of central importance to the development of the *Kaiserreich*. Associations began to mushroom in all spheres of life, and many were founded with the avowed purpose of exerting pressure on governments, legislatures, and public opinion. They contributed to a growing mobilization of the average citizen and to the high turnout during elections. They accelerated the transition from the liberal representation party of notables to the modern integration party. There is a positive side to all this in that it reflected commitment and an interest in politics. However, the associations did not promote a parliamentarization of the Prusso-German constitutional system. Rather they enhanced the dogmatization of politics. By the turn of the century this was also true of the economic pressure groups.

However varied associational life in Germany may appear to have been on the surface, these increasingly politicized movements in the extra-parliamentary sphere helped to concentrate political life into large and largely immobile ideological blocs. The nationalist associations in particular popularized the attitude that the world was divided into friends and foes. The minorities suffered badly from these changing attitudes, which led them to form their own defensive organizations. The Social Democrats constituted one such bloc, as they were the most ostracized and discriminated against. For however fragmented the majority with its many organizations may have been and however tangible the differences of interest among the anti-Socialists, when it came to the crunch the bogey of the "Red menace" brought them all together, pushing aside the relatively small band of those who tried to mediate between the blocs and searched for ways of integrating the working class into the existing order.

The rise of parties and extra-parliamentary associations also exerted pressure upon the executive. Of course, there was never any question in this branch of government that the organizations of the Left had to be fought hard. But the authorities were also vulnerable to the relentless and ever more extreme demands of the associations to be more active in foreign and domestic politics. They had to proffer solutions. The problem was that the solutions that were ultimately implemented did not defuse the crisis of the *Kaiserreich* before 1914, but rather moved the monarchy more deeply into a political *cul-de-sac*.

16. Structure and Functional Changes in the Executive Branch

A. The Government Apparatus: The Kaiser and his Court; Reich Government; Federal, State, and Local Governments

Beyond the larger structural questions of the Prusso-German constitutional system, which concerned the relationship between monarchy and parliamentarism as well as the development of both the Bismarckian and the Wilhelmine models of "personal rule," [(64)] there is the issue of how the executive organs interacted with one another and of the lines of daily communication from top to bottom and from the bottom up.

As regards the higher Reich administration, the Bismarckian period is marked above all by a tendency to centralize bureaucratic activity. The innumerable bills that had been ratified after the founding of the *Kaiserreich* required a considerable executive machinery if they were all to be implemented and upheld. If the Reich bureaucracy had been relatively small in size in 1871, it now experienced a remarkable growth. According to the Constitution, its members were servants of the Kaiser, on whose "graciousness" they all depended. However, constitutional reality developed in such a way during the 1870s and 1880s that Wilhelm I never filled his powerful position to the letter of the law. He left the government largely to Bismarck so that the latter's office – reinforced by his role as Prussian Minister President – became the actual power center of the executive. The heads of Reich offices with their proliferating staffs were not ministers answerable to the monarch, as they were in Prussia, but state secretaries who reported to the Reich Chancellor. They had no direct access to the Kaiser. Meanwhile the Prussian State Ministry, governed as it was by the principle of ministerial

64. See above pp. 194ff.

collegiality, stubbornly resisted Bismarck's centralizing policies. This led the Reich Chancellor to put "his" state secretaries as ministers without portfolio in the Ministry of State. His approach to government, which, to be sure, was in tune with broader organizational developments in the economy and society, also weakened the role of the Federal Council, which according to the letter of the Constitution was the actual government of the Reich. And as chairman of the Federal Council Bismarck had many other possibilities to push ahead with his administrative centralization. More effective resistance to this trend came only in the post-Bismarckian period when Prussia began to rebel against centralization for fear of its democratizing potential.

The relative passivity of Wilhelm I moreover made it easier for the Reich Chancellor to contain the influence of the Court and the Kaiser's "entourage." There were quite a few civil servants and officers at Court, all of whom had been appointed personally by the monarch himself. The simple fact that they regularly saw him during meals, at receptions, and on frequent journeys, gave them considerable informal influence. In the case of the cabinet chiefs, who were responsible for civilian and military appointments, this influence was even institutionally guaranteed. These realities produced many frictions with civil servants outside the Court who, led by Bismarck as Reich Chancellor and Prussian Minister President, pursued their own personnel policies. Similar patterns of conflict arose in the federal states where an often inflated court bureaucracy existed next to the conventional executive machinery. The political frontlines often ran in parallel to those at Reich level where the Court represented the archconservative counterweight to a state bureaucracy that was much more directly exposed to political forces in the country that were demanding change.

Given his towering position within the political system, Bismarck by and large succeeded in winning his many battles with the Kaiser's entourage. He was able to influence the personnel polices of the cabinet offices and even to contain the *maison militaire*. This constellation became much more complex after his dismissal in 1890. To begin with, the relationship between the Kaiser and "his" Reich Chancellor changed because the former now wished to rule himself. There was also the growing influence of the entourage. These changes had a great deal to do with the personality of Wilhelm II. Although he had many intellectual gifts, he was an inconsistent, nervous person, incapable of working hard, listening to others, or thinking problems through systematically. Over time many of those who saw him in action or heard the monarch make silly remarks during their daily contact with him began to pose ever more seriously the question of whether he was perhaps unbalanced. Those who came to believe this – and his very close friend and advisor Philipp zu Eulenburg was among them – considered it their duty to support the Kaiser emotionally and politically through thick and thin.

They began to "handle" the monarch not only because they felt a deep personal loyalty toward him, but also because they held the firm conviction that the monarchy in its present shape and form was the best possible system of government imaginable. Thus they tried to prevent him from committing blunders. They shielded him from uncomfortable situations and public criticism, constantly fearing that he might have a nervous breakdown. Caprivi, the first Reich Chancellor after Bismarck, still refused to be guided in his political strategy exclusively by his consideration for the monarch's eccentricities. His neglect of this aspect of government contributed to his early fall from power. His successors made the "management" of Wilhelm II one of their central concerns, and Bülow who visited him every morning became a master of "corsetting" him in this way. However, from 1905 onward, if not before, this fixation on one single person became increasingly problematic. Thanks to earlier miscalculations in domestic and foreign policy, the situation of the Reich kept deteriorating, and it now became necessary also to take serious account of the political goals and demands of forces outside the Court. The old and intimate relationship between Wilhelm II and Bülow foundered because of these shifts. The recognition of outside factors at home and abroad became part of a "policy of the diagonal" which Bülow initiated and which his successor Bethmann Hollweg tried to continue, albeit unsuccessfully.

Since the imperial entourage failed to follow this turn of events psychically and ideologically, fresh tensions arose between the court and the Reich bureaucracy. The *maison militaire* in particular found it more and more difficult to accept Bethmann's conservative reformism. The entourage became "militarized," [65] promoting, if only from a sense of self-preservation, the deepening of trenches that had already been dug against Germany's alleged external and internal enemies. The civilian Reich administration was viewed with growing hostility. Within the Reich government, too, it became more difficult to keep the armed forces under control. At first it was Naval Secretary Tirpitz who, though subordinate to the Reich Chancellor, pursued his own policy. Later the Army deviated from the civilian government's line both at home (in the Zabern Affair) and abroad (in the Crisis of July 1914). If one thinks of the end result, i.e., the decision to start a war, the problems

65. I.V. Hull, *The Entourage of Kaiser Wilhelm II* (Cambridge 1982), 43.

created for Bethmann by Tirpitz's independence in questions of naval rearmament pale in comparison to the "preventive war" policies that the Army pursued in 1913-14.

Although the Kaiser's powers gave the Reich executive considerable influence, it should not be forgotten that the *Kaiserreich* remained a collection of federal states. Apart from the pressure that the Reichstag parties, the innumerable associations, and the press were able to exert upon the top leadership, the monarch also had to take the policies and demands of his fellow princes into consideration. That he was the king of Prussia and hence the head of the state which contained two-thirds of the German population may have had occasional advantages. But the personal union also created dilemmas for him, and over time increasingly so. As a federal prince he certainly had to take into consideration the often divergent interests of Prussia. Prussia, in turn, had a large bureaucracy of its own and a diet, whose electoral laws and composition sheltered the propertied classes and the agrarians in particular against political changes at Reich level. There were also the other ruling houses and their representative assemblies to take into account. Although they had lost their sovereignty rights with regard to external representation, their powers over their internal administrations remained considerable. Since the early nineteenth century, the cities, too, had tangible powers of self-government, and many of them had dynamic mayors whose policies had the support of local assemblies elected on the basis of a restrictive suffrage.

In particular the federal states and the communes were responsible for education and culture. They were in charge of the administration of the poor laws and of developing the urban infrastructure. They looked after local policing and the judiciary below the level of the Reich Court. This decentralization of public tasks had its own momentum in the sense that urban and rural communities were themselves involved in the implementation and, in some respects, even the legislation of policies. There was, it is true, the bureaucracy of the individual federal states whose long arm reached into the communities, but even in this era of centralization communities retained a high degree of autonomy – and shrewdly exploited it. Some of the larger cities were led by respected mayors who, in cooperation with the local assemblies and patrician families, took pride in building up an impressive infrastructure. The capitals of the federal states as well as other towns had a long tradition of promoting theaters, orchestras, and museums. The optimism of the *Gründerzeit* gave a fresh boost to these activities. Wealthy local elites demonstrated their commitment to the community by supporting the arts. A sort of tacit competition arose between individual cities over which of them had offered the richest cultural life. Genuine altruism of the patrons became mixed up with economic interests that called for a continuation of the traditional state support for the local and regional economy. Given the class character of German society, it comes as no surprise that there were limits to this civic pride, when it came, for instance, to the provision of better housing for economically weak groups in these communities. The town of Harburg south of Hamburg is a case in point. Here, the local government became prepared to take note of the poor housing conditions of its workers only after much prodding from Berlin. [66]

B. The Emergence of the Interventionist State: The "Positive State" and Repression

After 1871, and with the expansion of commerce and industry, improving the infrastructure became one of the main tasks of the authorities at all levels. The pressure to act was greatest in the rapidly growing industrial cities whose administrators were faced with completely new problems of planning and organization, and even in the higher echelons of the Reich bureaucracy modernizers found themselves locked in conflict with colleagues for whom industrialization and urbanization were a great evil. Public health concerns and the need to attract industry required the expansion or construction of waterworks, waste disposal systems, street cleaning services, markets, slaughterhouses, transportation systems, and savings institutes. Gas, electricity, sewers, and streets had to be provided, as well as schools, hospitals, and public baths. The previously-mentioned statistics on the phenomenal growth of cities give an impression of the size of the projects that had to be tackled. [67] In 1861, the budget of the town of Düsseldorf on the Rhine amounted to 540,000 thalers; by 1913 it had swollen to 62.7 million marks. Since there were no fundamental legal obstacles to the towns providing public utilities, many of them jumped at the opportunity to establish power stations, gasworks, and waterworks that could be shown off by local politicians and that would raise money to relieve the town budget. This at least

66. P.C. Witt, "Die Wohnverhältnisse der Arbeiter, Angestellten und Unterbeamten der Stadt Harburg am Beginn des 20. Jahrhunderts," in: W. Treue, ed., *Geschichte als Aufgabe* (Göttingen 1988), 603-28; idem, "Kommunalpolitik in Harburg zwischen Interessen lokaler Eliten und Entstehung einer modernen Leistungsverwaltung," in: J. Ellermeyer, ed., *Harburg* (Lüneburg 1988), 219-53.

67. See above pp. 43ff.

was the hope which was all too often disappointed by the realities of the marketplace (table 74). At the beginning of the 1860s as many as 75 percent of the gasworks were still privately owned. In the new age of "municipal socialism" (F.C. Howe), by 1914 some 66 percent were public utilities which produced 82 percent of Germany's domestic and industrial gas. By 1906 as many as 94 percent of the water works were publicly owned. Electricity, though it came somewhat later, underwent a similar dramatic development.

Private electric companies quickly discovered that it was unprofitable to supply many rural areas with their product. Again the state was called upon to step into the breach. Utility cooperatives were established, and as late as May 1914 the Prussian Ministry of the Interior, together with the Ministry for Public Works, Commerce and Trade, expressly instructed the regional administrators (*Regierungspräsidenten*) to support the supply of electricity to "economically weaker areas." [68] As the rural laborers migrated to the industrial centers, large-scale agriculture in particular became dependent on electricity for the running of the machinery that replaced them. Close cooperation between the regional and local authorities inevitably also developed with regard to roadbuilding. Postal services and later on telegraph and telephone networks had to be coordinated.

Like road-building, the construction of canals had enjoyed public support since well before the founding of the *Kaiserreich*. At the end of 1877, the Prussian government published a major report concerning "the waterways existing in the Prussian state, their improvement and expansion." But in the face of the "Great Depression" and the structural crisis of agriculture, Prussia experienced growing political tensions with regard to canal construction. Industry and commerce were keen to have more waterways for the cheap transport of raw materials and heavy goods. Some regional authorities saw them as part of an industrial development policy that aimed to prevent the emergence of large conurbations with their social problems. The agrarians, in contrast, regarded canals as a direct threat to their survival. Waterways were also conveyor belts for cheap imported grain. They partially undermined the effect of the carefully erected tariff walls against foreign competition. Accordingly the construction of the *Mittellandkanal*, that was supposed to run from the river Ems in the west via Hanover and Magdeburg all the way into central Germany at a cost to the public purse of 260 million marks,

68. Quoted in: W. Abelshauser, "Staat, Infrastruktur und regionaler Wohlstandsausgleich im Preußen der Hochindustrialisierung," in: F. Blaich, ed., *Staatliche Umverteilungspolitik in historischer Perspektive* (Berlin 1980), 47.

unleashed a major and prolonged rebellion by the Conservatives in the Prussian Diet which delayed completion of the project for years. In the end a watered-down version was ratified in 1904 which extended the system as far as Hanover.

There was no such massive resistance to the construction of railroads. The bankruptcy of many private companies in the "Great Depression" and their division into a multitude of separate entities had strengthened the hand of the advocates of centralization. Bismarck, it is true, could not realize his goal of a unified *Reichsbahn*, but from the late 1870s onward the state began to take over the railroad system on a regional basis. By 1903 most railroads were under state control. From that time on, the authorities could directly intervene into the economic development of individual regions by building new lines. Although he had to consider the military-strategic interests of the Army, Bismarck was motivated by political and economic calculations when he decided to link his tariff policy to the government's takeover of the railroads. Only if he gained control of freight tariffs was it possible to reverse the discounting practices of private companies and to impose higher rates on imported goods than on exports. The state authorities also found it easier than private companies to disregard questions of profitability and to extend lines into economically weaker regions.

Up until World War I, both objectives were pursued by the federal states, albeit with varying degrees of energy. The Bavarian bureaucracy, for example, found it more difficult than the Prussian one to abandon its economic liberalism in designing its infrastructural policies. Nevertheless, it had certainly become easier to open up remote areas through connecting railway lines and special rates. Some authorities even believed that they could control, with the help of their railroad policies, the regional concentration of industry which attracted too many potentially restive workers. In this way weaker enterprises might find themselves favored by the state's infrastructural policy, while booming industries would find their applications for special tariffs turned down.

Although the primary target of such policies were the medium-sized enterprises, agriculture also benefited from them. After the "Great Depression" the federal governments were willing, moreover, to support ailing landowners by providing direct subsidies and tax breaks. Finally, as the Reich Treasury Office discovered in 1907, the regional administrators (*Landräte*) in East Elbia became conscious accessories to extensive tax frauds by the *Junkers* in their district. [69] As in urban areas, the basic principle continued to hold, i.e., that the politically most powerful groups were also the first and biggest beneficiaries of governmental policy-making concerning infrastructure.

The mirror image of this principle is to be found in the treatment of the poor who had no political power. By tradition the execution of the poor laws was in the hands of the federal states and the communities. They defined the extent of the support and the conditions under which it was given. The founding of the Reich in 1871 had brought no major changes to this system, if we disregard the fact that the general trend toward bureaucratization carried some alterations with it. The bureaucratic trend was accompanied by the rise of the social-policy expert who, as time went by, interpreted his role less and less as purely charitable, and increasingly from a eugenic point of view. [70] Doctors as a professional group moved in the same direction. With the development of genetics, biologistic ideas about human society began to take root, which classified ethnic groups as inferior or superior. But they also appeared in a eugenic guise which classified the indigenous population by socioeconomic status. The demographic explosion, which brought with it a numerical increase in the number of poor people, triggered fears of a degeneration of the nation's health and of popular morals, and it confronted the authorities with the question of who would pay for welfare provision. By a long-standing rule, the poor could expect support only at their place of domicile.

The introduction of unrestricted movement in 1867 promoted mass migrations whose implications for support of the poor were covered in a Reich law a few years later. According to this law, the welfare applicant qualified only if he or she had lived in the locality without interruption during the previous two years. In this case the local or regional agency had to offer sufficient welfare, including accommodation and medical services, even if the person concerned had meanwhile left. In other words, in addition to the obligation of supporting the poor in the community, above all widows and orphans, the authorities were also expected to pay for migrants at their new place of domicile. The agrarians were the first to rebel against this system by proposing to restrict the free movement of people once again. For them this was, of course, also a way of trying to solve the problem of a diminishing supply of

69. P.-C. Witt, "The Prussian Landrat as Tax Official, 1891-1918," in: G.G. Iggers, ed., *The Social History of Politics* (Leamington Spa 1985), 137-54.

70. P. Weindling, *Health, Race and German Politics between National Unification and Nazism* (Cambridge 1989).

rural labor which the mass migrations had caused. When this move failed, the rural communities were offered relief by a new rule under which their obligation to support impoverished former residents elsewhere terminated after two years. In the 1880s, Bismarck made another attempt to impose an immediate welfare obligation on the new place of domicile. But the cities were vigorously opposed to this change, and they also refused to budge when it was pointed out to them that the new social insurance system would reduce the burdens on the local communities.

While some of this support for the poor continued to be private, both public and private relief had, long before the founding of the *Kaiserreich*, been motivated in part by a fear of the impoverished masses and by guilt (table 71). In this sense, the poor laws of Germany were attempts, as elsewhere in Europe, to keep the poor under control with the help of the local authorities. The federal states and the communities therefore also had considerable policing powers which were officially to be used against criminal elements. The extent of criminality in Imperial Germany is not easily estimated, because of variations and uncertainties in the rates of detection and prosecution. In any case, the crime rate rose by a little over 14 percent between 1885 and 1900 to 1143 crimes per 100,000 inhabitants, and it subsequently hovered around this mark up to the First World War. There was a steep increase in reported homicide deaths in Prussia from a yearly average of 356 in 1886-90 to 847 in 1911-13. But there were great regional variations and cities were not necessarily at the top of league table. It must also be remembered that the line between genuine criminal behavior and breaches of the law for reasons of economic desperation was often fluid. [(71)] Furthermore, after the introduction of the anti-Socialist laws the authorities were fully occupied with, and probably also more interested in, using their powers widely against suspected Social Democrats and leftist intellectuals. In the context of the 1878 anti-Socialist laws censorship codes were formulated for the whole of Germany. These allowed authorities to deal with alleged breaches of cultural and political norms. A press law required publishers to submit a copy of their publications to the local police, who would then check whether they contained blasphemous, indecent, or otherwise incriminating passages.

Munich, with its reputation for liberalism, offers a good example of how the intellectual and artistic avant garde was treated by law-enforcement agencies. Bavaria may have been liberal in comparison with Prussia, but this did not prevent the Bavarian authorities from harassing the representatives of

---

71. R.J. Evans, ed., *The German Underworld* (London 1988), 14f.

modernism. They prosecuted the modernists for alleged blasphemy, *lèse majesté*, and depiction of obscenities. In 1899, Wilhelm II insisted that the Lex Heinze be sent to the Reichstag. It made punishable depictions or writings that "crudely offended the sense of decency." Similarly, a censorship advisory council which was instituted in Munich in 1908 should probably be seen in connection with increased police surveillance of the local artistic community. Initially Max Halbe and Thomas Mann agreed to be members of this council; but they soon found out that they were surrounded by conservative teachers and academics and withdrew. With the help of Mann and Halbe, Wedekind's *Frühlings Erwachen* was deemed acceptable by the council, albeit only after considerable cuts. His play *Lulu*, like the plays of other authors, encountered sharp opposition. It was banned in 1913, while some of his poetry got him a seven-month prison term which he served in the Saxon fortress of Königstein. Censorship became increasingly politicized. Demands for a stricter prosecution of violations came from the Catholic Center party and from an organization, founded in 1906, which – significantly – called itself the Munich Men's Association for Combatting Public Indecency. Together with the clergy, which was increasingly alarmed by the erosion of the Catholic faith and the church's authority, they fought to intensify the prosecution of the avant garde in the suburb of Schwabing and of the proliferating cheap entertainment business in the Bavarian capital. At the other end of the spectrum, we find the moderate Social Democrat Georg von Vollmar defending artistic freedom. Such differences of opinion indicate that the whole matter involved not merely questions of taste and morality, but also of divergent ideologies and political positions. Similar considerations apply to film censorship which also increased before 1914. [72] The changing ideological climate is also reflected in the authorities' adoption of police and judicial practices that openly violated the principles of justice and *Rechtsstaatlichkeit* (rule of law). In short, Munich was not a haven of cultural liberalism, and reading about the never-ending prosecutions in the Bavarian capital is not a pleasant assignment.

Another example from outside Prussia is presented by the case of Hamburg. Dominated by an oligarchy of patrician families, the city was deemed cosmopolitan and urbanely liberal. But this did not prevent the police, on orders from the local government, from continuing their surveillance of the indigenous workers after the lapse of the anti-Socialist laws. As the

72. G.D. Stark, "Cinema, Society, and the State," in: idem and B.K. Lackner, eds., *Essays in Culture and Society in Modern Germany* (Arlington, Texas 1982), 123-66.

Chief of the Political Police Department reported, between January and April 1892 alone, twice as many meetings were attended by undercover agents and informers than in the same period during 1891. (73) The number of dutifully collected newspaper clippings rose from 3,948 to 12,722. Dressed up as ordinary workers, policemen sat in the pubs of the harbor quarters listening in on what dockers and other workers were talking about. By 1914 they had produced some 20,000 reports. However, none of these measures prevented major scandals. When in the middle of January 1906 large demonstrations broke out against a planned further restriction of the local class-based right to vote, the police were poorly prepared. Embarrassed, they staged a bloody counterattack on the harbor quarters on the following day. Searching for and arresting the alleged ring-leaders of the earlier demonstrations, they inflicted many injuries on innocent people. After this, fears of revolution never ceased among parts of the Hamburgian bourgeoisie. Slowly the legal barriers against a persecution of the working class were also lowered in other parts of the country.

Historians who have emphasized the lack of political uniformity in the *Kaiserreich* are no doubt correct in calling the powers of the federal states and the communities vis-à-vis the Reich capital "enormous." (74) The salient point is, however, that, even outside Prussia, these powers were deployed, in the years before 1914, in ways which brought about even greater polarization. The rate at which the political climate deteriorated may have been slower in the southwest than it was in the north; but one is hard put to detect major currents in any of the federal states that effectively counteracted this general trend.

If the state was becoming increasingly involved in the censorship of society and culture, its influence was also felt in other ways. Against the forces of particularism there developed, starting in the late 1870s and in connection with a growing Reich bureaucracy, what might be called a centralizing interventionist state which appeared in a positive, constructive guise. Certainly, any discussion of the modern German state and its powers would be incomplete without an analysis of one of its distinctive "positive" features, the social insurance system. It has been seen by many as the beginning of the welfare state of the twentieth century, employing by 1914 some 12,000 civil servants in its accident and invalid insurance branches alone. The word "beginning" is important here. For one thing, it occurred in three modest

73. R.J. Evans, ed., *Kneipengespräche im Kaiserreich* (Reinbek 1989), 8ff.

74. R.J. Evans, *Death in Hamburg* (Oxford 1987), 2.

steps: health insurance law was created in 1883, followed by accident insurance in 1884 and old-age and invalid insurance in 1889 (tables 75-77). Initially it merely covered workers and low-ranking employees in industry and commerce, and even they were subject to a number of restrictions. The law of 1889 included rural and forestry laborers; but it excluded all family members so that they, like the poor who were jobless or unable to work, continued to rely on private and public charity

All three laws either had historical predecessors on which they were modeled or were based on experiences with regulations that had proved unsatisfactory. Thus the ratification of the accident insurance bill must be seen against the background of the Reich Liability Law of 1871. The weaknesses of this latter law, which was supposed to regulate claims from a rising number of industrial accidents, had led to innumerable conflicts between employers and injured workers. After this debacle, the employers had come to prefer an all-inclusive accident insurance scheme at Reich level, even if it meant that they had to pay the premiums all by themselves (table 76). The health insurance scheme of 1883, two-thirds of which was funded by contributions from insured workers, genuinely extended benefits to the working population. Up to that point a mere 5 percent of the population and no more than half of the industrial workers had any kind of coverage against illness, and even this coverage was often inadequate. From 1892 onwards, family members were also accepted into the scheme (table 77).

The idea of health insurance was largely inspired by the cooperative *Knappschaft* model in the mining industry. This model offered coverage for accidents, medical support, health benefits, and even pensions for invalids. So-called *Kassen* schemes had also been established in other branches of industry, and their underlying ideas were adopted in 1889 in an insurance for invalids and the aged. In the mid-1880s, white-collar employees began to organize their own movement for the introduction of pension rights, while civil servants had gained their special old-age support long before. Although the insurance system as a whole initially covered few people and the benefits were meager, it could be expanded, and this is what happened after 1890. Whereas Wilhelm II quickly abandoned his early thoughts of becoming a "workers' Kaiser" and hence did not push for an expansion in the 1890s, the desire to reduce the burdens of poor relief ultimately acted as a strong incentive to build on the Bismarckian beginnings. Social policy was also used to facilitate compromises between government and political parties. Thus the Center party negotiated a linkage between the Tariff Bill of 1902 and the introduction of a law to provide benefits for widows and orphans. The financial crisis of later years put a strong damper on the expansion of German welfare policy. Still, in 1912 some 850 million marks were paid out in benefits under the various schemes. The number of people covered by health insurance rose from 4.2 million in 1885 to 13.4 million in 1911. The medical expenses covered by the insurance initially amounted to 47 million marks; by 1911 this figure had risen to 358 million marks. By 1914 over half of the working population was insured and some 51.4 percent of workers between the ages of fifty-five and sixty-nine were able to draw a modest pension (table 75). In 1911 the white-collar employees succeeded in getting their own insurance scheme passed. Meanwhile workers in public service gained recognition of their claims, with the telling justification that the choice was between "strengthening Social Democracy or extending the civil service status." (75)

Not long ago, historians tended to downplay Bismarck's role in the formulation of the insurance system of the 1880s. Instead it was seen as an outgrowth of a number of long-standing welfare institutions. There is obviously some truth to this view in the sense that few, if any, institutions have ever been created in a complete vacuum. Nor should it be forgotten that the Bismarckian system was never the only pillar of the unfolding welfare state. Self-help organizations and cooperatives never stopped their work. Municipalities went on providing poor relief, while moving into the emergent field of local social work. Here they employed a new type of expert who helped to define and resolve changing social problems while dispensing "social pedagogy" and enlightenment. Still, Gerhard A. Ritter convincingly re-emphasized the Reich Chancellor's crucial contribution. (76) He showed that Bismarck had thought of introducing an insurance system since the founding of the Empire, and it is quite possible that without his determination the bills might well have foundered on the rocks of employer opposition. During the 1870s, it is true, social reformers had loudly called for the state to engage in social policy-making. Bismarck was no social reformer, and his motives are fairly uncontroversial today. What propelled him were political calculations and above all his worries about the growth of the working-class movement. Ultimately the first Reich Chancellor aimed at the destruction of the SPD and the trade unions through social policy – a strategy designed to complement his policy of violent repression through the anti-Socialist laws. In the end even hard-line entrepreneurs warmed to the idea that concessions in the field of welfare policy would take the wind out of the sails of the working-

75. Quoted in: J. Ehmer, *Sozialgeschichte des Alters* (Frankfurt 1990), 47.

76. G.A. Ritter, *Social Welfare in Germany and Britain* (Leamington Spa 1986).

class movement. It has therefore rightly been asserted that Germany's social policy program, as proclaimed in the Imperial Message of November 1881, had another and more important "birth certificate": the "Law concerning the Combatting of the Criminal Aims of Social Democracy" of 1878. [77]

So, although we have been talking about the "positive" interventionist state, its negative side must not be lost sight of. With the introduction of the anti-Socialist laws, the police moved into the front line of the struggle against Social Democrats and leftist intellectuals. To begin with, over 600 newspapers and journals were banned and some 318 associations dissolved. Hundreds of members of working-class organizations and other suspects were arrested, convicted, and thrown into prison. A "minor state of siege" was imposed on Social Democratic strongholds like Frankfurt, Berlin, Leipzig, Altona, and Stettin. This enabled the local authorities to exile known activists. In Berlin, some 300 men were separated from their families and source of income by being forced to leave the city under police escort. The example of Hamburg shows just how strong the pressure from the top could be to take a hard line. Pushed by Berlin, which had been alerted by the police chief of neighboring Prussian Altona, the Hamburg city government decided to declare a "minor state of siege" and to exile some 75 Social Democrats. To be sure, not everywhere and on the whole certainly not in the south was persecution as harsh as in parts of Prussia. Even in Hamburg there were cases of well-known merchants quietly handing presents to the workers passing them on their way into exile. It was their way of registering their disgust with the authorities. Even greater solidarity was shown by neighbors in the working-class quarters. The police observed collections of support funds in towns like Wiesbaden, Erfurt, and Breslau, which in many cases led to the formation of some kind of an association. The names of these associations and their members, in turn, aroused the suspicions of the police, who immediately saw a Socialist underground network in the making. Nevertheless, after a first wave of tough measures, the police later relaxed their methods of surveillance. By 1885 there existed in different parts of the Reich some thirty so-called *Hilfskassen* with 264,000 members. There were also around 1,020 *Fachvereine* with about 58,000 members representing the economic interests of workers (table 78). After the renewal of the anti-Socialist laws in 1886 a further escalation of repression occurred. In April of that year the Prussian Ministry of the Interior published its new anti-strike decrees. One month later followed a second decree requiring that officials be notified forty-eight

77. V. Hentschel, *Geschichte der deutschen Sozialpolitik* (Frankfurt 1983), 9.

hours in advance of any assemblies and demonstrations in Berlin and its environs. Once again leading Social Democrats were dragged through the courts and sent to prison because of some alleged violation of the law. The end of the Bismarckian era was a depressing period from the point of view of domestic politics and the treatment of workers.

Although the network of informers that had been created in the 1880s was not abolished after the lapse of the anti-Socialist laws in 1890, the authorities were now no longer as free to move against Social Democrats as they had been before. Given the widespread perception of a growing Socialist threat, it is not surprising that the renewed introduction of special legislation was repeatedly considered. Thus in December 1894 the Reichstag debated an amendment to the Criminal Code that extended the criteria for a number of political offenses and also increased the available penalties. Two months earlier, the Kaiser had made a typically tactless statement regarding the bill, after which it became nicknamed *Umsturzvorlage* (Sedition Bill). No doubt this helped to defeat the move. Four years later the Reich government made another attempt with a piece of legislation that – following another swashbuckling speech by Wilhelm II – came to be known as Penitentiary Bill. At the core of this bill, which likewise failed, was a clause which banned picketing and imposed high penalties on strikers who prevented fellow workers from crossing the picket line. After the success of the Social Democrats in the 1903 Reichstag elections, industry and agriculture pressured the government once more to reintroduce anti-Socialist laws. However, prospects of a bill getting through Parliament were now bleaker than in the 1890s. Recognizing this, the Reich leadership concentrated on a revision of the Criminal Code of 1871 into which it promised to incorporate stricter sanctions that could be used against the Left. Although completion of the comprehensive review of this code was not expected until 1917, the government was able to refute the rightist charge that it was passive in the face of the "Red threat," while declaring at the same time that there was no realistic hope of getting special legislation through the Reichstag. It was an early version of government by procrastination that soon became the hallmark of the Reich executive in the face of the monarchy's growing political paralysis in the last years before 1914.

At the same time, the depth of anti-Socialist fears and hatreds in government circles and among those social groups that strongly supported the existing order may be gauged from the revival of the *Staatsstreich* idea and support for a violent revision of the Constitution. Thus in January 1897, General von Waldersee, the commander of the Ninth Army Corps, submitted a written proposal to the

Kaiser to smash the Social Democrats without delay and before it was too late. After a further rise in the SPD vote in the 1903 elections, unilateral changes of the Constitution and the abolition of the universal suffrage were once again being considered. At one point, Wilhelm II talked himself into a frenzy about "the coming revolution and its repression" before exclaiming: "I have to take revenge for [18]48 – revenge!" (78) Three years later he bragged again about an impending "bloodbath" among the Social Democrats to be followed by a successful foreign war. Finally, in 1913 the monarch forwarded a memorandum by a retired general and prominent Pan-Germanist, Konstantin von Gebsattel, to the Reich Chancellor. The document called for a violent coup against the working-class movement and the Jewish minority. (79)

Since the Reich Chancellor regarded such solutions to the constitutional and growing political dilemma of the Prusso-German monarchy as too risky from both a domestic and foreign policy standpoint (and with the Reichstag majority being opposed to renewed anti-Socialist laws), the executive had to rely on existing decrees and statutes. These continued to provide the police and the courts with extensive powers, particularly if they were prepared to interpret "creatively" not only the relevant paragraphs of the Criminal Code, but also those relating to association, press, and trading laws. Finally, it was always possible to resort to bureaucratic chicanery. In this climate of hostility, many a worker who had made a joke or a critical remark about the Kaiser at the local alehouse found himself denounced to the police for *lèse majesté* by one of the ubiquitous informants. Legal scholars even raised the question of whether it constituted a violation of this paragraph in the Criminal Code if someone did not join in the royal cheer during some celebration. The courts frequently sentenced workers to prison terms which bore no relation to the "crime." Between 1890 and 1914 the number of convictions rose from 508 to 622 per annum. The authorities also liked to invoke the code's blasphemy section. Paragraphs 130 (incitement to sedition) and 360 (causing a serious nuisance) of the Criminal Code were deployed no less extensively, and the latter was also used to curb the socialist press.

The treatment of strikers and strikebreakers became a major preoccupation for the police and the judiciary. The starting point was Paragraph 152 of the Trade Code (*Gewerbeordnung*) which guaranteed the right of coalition. Much of this was undermined, however, by the following paragraph which

---

78. Quoted in: V.R. Berghahn, *Der Tirpitz-Plan* (Düsseldorf 1971), 263.

79. H. Pogge von Strandmann, "Permanenz der Staatsstreichdrohung," in: I. Geiss and idem, eds., *Die Erforderlichkeit des Unmöglichen* (Frankfurt 1965), 7-45.

stipulated that it was illegal to get "others through the use of force, through threats, through violations of their honor, or by damaging their reputation" to participate in a coalition (or a strike) or to deny them the right to leave that coalition. Attempts to participate in these acts were punishable under the Trade Code, if it did not prove possible to invoke the Criminal Code with its higher penalties. Frequently used clauses of this latter code were Paragraphs 185 (violation of honor), 240 (blackmail), and 241 (announcing a crime). Thus striking workers might be prosecuted because they had shouted the word "strikebreaker" or had spat at the feet of fellow workers whom the police had been escorting through the picket line. When employers threatened a lockout in advance of a labor dispute, the authorities regularly conceded that they were merely trying to uphold their justifiable interests and hence desisted from prosecuting them. When announcing a strike, the unions, in contrast, had to word their statements very carefully to avoid charges of blackmail. Like the employers, policemen and strike-breakers found much sympathy in court, even if they had actually violated existing codes. Justice was blindfolded on just one eye.

With the passage of time the police network became more dense and local authorities received ever more insistent instructions "from above" to use their powers and, if necessary, a strong arm. In this atmosphere the police were less and less prepared to look away or to withdraw a prosecution. The state prosecutors, who were likewise bound to follow higher orders, tended to respond with alacrity, knowing that the courts would give more credence to a vague statement by a police witness than to the politically suspect defendant. Verdicts that the prosecution deemed unsatisfactory were appealed without delay. The Court Constitution Law formally protected judges from outside interference. But just as the Kaiser surprised other civil servants, including the director of the Prussian Art Gallery, he occasionally also surprised the courts. In 1898 he removed a judge who had acquitted the well-known journalist Maximilian Harden of *lèse majesté*. No doubt this acted as a reminder for other judges, most of whom were ideologically conservative in the first place and had been socialized into a profession whose outlook was monarchist. They also sensed, or even knew, that their superiors expected certain verdicts, and so opinions were handed down that were often based on very questionable legal constructions and lines of reasoning. Furthermore, many judges held the view that defendants from the lower classes were used to minor penalties and had been hardened by them. Harsher sentences were thus thought to be justified in order for the punishment to have an effect.

And yet policemen, prosecutors, and their superiors could never be certain that trials would have the outcome they believed to be desirable from the point of view of a tight judicial policy. A less experienced or younger judge might issue a mild sentence which grossly diverged from the general norm. In Prussia it was fairly certain that juries would be packed with notables who took a hard line without much prodding. In the south this was not always the case, however, so that the prosecution had to brace itself for the occasional surprise. Such experiences with juries resulted in cases being sent, if at all possible, before a bench of professional judges. Another way of influencing jury selection was to refuse to pay daily allowances. This immediately restricted the circle of potential jurors. It was only in the summer of 1913 that the Reichstag ratified a bill which provided for a payment of five marks per day of jury service.

In the meantime, the police developed a variety of alternatives to public prosecution where their experiences with the courts seemed to make this necessary. A number of authorities successfully used local traffic regulations against peaceful picketing. Picketing was declared a traffic obstruction – an interpretation which the courts were prepared to support. When the unions objected that this violated the freedom of coalition provided under Paragraph 152 of the Trade Code, the police retorted that this freedom was in no way being touched. What was at stake was the free flow of traffic. Consequently it continued to be up to the personal judgment of the local policeman whether or not a picket line was an obstruction, and in many cases he ruled that it was, even if the traffic was not at all impeded.

Yet however much policemen were urged by their superiors to contain and intimidate the working-class movement without the broad powers of an anti-Socialist law, and however unashamedly the courts practiced "class justice," ultimately there was always the Army to back up the police saber or the one-eyed Justice. The Army was not merely an instrument against Germany's external enemies, but the *ultima ratio* in a civil war against the working class that many officers believed to be imminent. It was no accident that shortly after the lapse of the anti-Socialist laws in the spring of 1890 the Prussian War Minister reminded the commanding generals of the powers which they had under the State of Siege Law of 1851. The Reich Constitution stipulated that this ancient law be replaced after 1871 by a Reich Defense Law. But for all too transparent reasons the Reich government never introduced such a bill. With the 1851 law therefore still in place, the commanding generals were free to proclaim a provisional state of siege if they judged such a measure to be necessary for the maintenance of order. Outside Prussia, it is true, the consent of the Kaiser was also required; but neither the friends nor the critics of the officer corps were in any doubt about the far-reaching powers of the military, including the right to suspend basic liberties. And to make certain that there were no misunderstandings about who was seen as the main enemy of the monarchical state, all officers down to the commanders of local garrisons received a further directive in 1890 to keep themselves "constantly" informed about the "organization, the leaders, and the agitators" on the Left. [80]

Further ministerial instructions that followed in subsequent years were designed to keep the Army in a state of readiness for civil war. After the turn of the century, the General Staff began work on a study whose final version was submitted in 1907 under the title of "Fighting in Insurgent Cities." In April 1907 this study triggered an order by the Seventh Army Corps at Münster northeast of the Ruhr area which provided, inter alia, for the arrest of Reichstag deputies. It was withdrawn in a storm of protest after it had been leaked to the press. The civil war measures which General Paul von Hindenburg drew up in February 1908 for his Fourth Army Corps at Magdeburg met with so much approval in Berlin that they were held up as a model to the other military districts. A decree by the Prussian War Minister on December 8, 1912 reminded the commanding generals once more that they should be prepared for an immediate response. Reactions to a number of strikes showed that the officers had no qualms about calling out the troops. As late December 1896 even the hard-liner Waldersee had taken the view on the occasion of the Hamburg dockers' strike that he would be happy if the police proved sufficient to deal with it. "To use armed force against hungry workers," he added, "is certainly no pleasure." [81] But by 1914 the willingness of the military to be tough during a domestic crisis had become noticeably greater. In 1910 a decree, apparently issued by the civilian administrator of the Düsseldorf district, had urged subordinate authorities to rely on troops only "in the most extreme emergency." [82] No such restraint was shown in Halle during the same year, with bloody results. When the Ruhr miners went on strike in the spring of 1912, police were used on a massive scale and the authorities drew on additional units from as far as Berlin, Frankfurt, Wiesbaden, Hanover, Kassel, and Cologne. These forces were complement-

80. Quoted in: W. Deist, "Die Armee in Staat und Gesellschaft, 1890-1914," in: M. Stürmer, ed., *Das kaiserliche Deutschland* (Düsseldorf 1970), 317.

81. Quoted in: *Ibid.*, 319

82. Quoted in: K. Saul, *Staat, Industrie, Arbeiterbewegung im Kaiserreich* (Düsseldorf 1974), 275.

ed by some 5,000 soldiers, including two machine-gun detachments. Finally, in the July Crisis of 1914, the generals thought of moving against the domestic opposition and arresting the Social Democratic leadership before declaring a foreign war.

The growing importance of the Army for the struggle at home had, during the 1890s, raised the question of whether recruits would be reliable enough to fight in a civil war. Industrialization and urbanization had inevitably increased the percentage of young factory workers in the Army. There were growing suspicions that Social Democratic "agitators" might be among them. The military authorities tried to counter the influence that these men were believed to exert on gullible recruits from the rural parts of the country. As we have mentioned previously, they resorted to searches of soldiers' lockers, spying, and bans on frequenting certain pubs in the vicinity of the garrison; they also introduced lessons to foster patriotism. Even reserve officers, most of whom were of middle-class background, came under a cloud when "reliable" and absolutely loyal cadets of noble background were no longer available in sufficient numbers. Faced with this recruitment dilemma, the Prussian War Minister abandoned the further expansion of the Army. As late as 1910, he wrote to the Reich Chancellor that he had "at the present time no intention" of enlarging the size of the Army beyond the twenty-three army corps that had been fixed as far back as March 1899. [83] He added that, apart from military considerations, the reasons for this restraint were also to be found in "the political arena" and were too obvious to require repetition. It was only from 1911 onward that the earlier domestic calculations that had been made in the face of the presumed Social Democratic threat became secondary. As international tensions rose, Germany resumed her rearmament on land. The naval buildup which until then had enjoyed priority came to a virtual standstill. The system of patriotic instruction that had been designed to produce "reliable" recruits was substituted by the older methods of harsh discipline and drill.

While the Army, as the *ultima ratio* of the "negative interventionist state," thus prepared itself for civil as well as foreign war, the civilian government attempted to expand and sharpen its instruments of propaganda. Once the financial crisis made the expansion of the social insurance system more difficult, the leadership worked hard to stimulate monarchist loyalties in the population through emotional appeals. Bismarck had used the press to influence public opinion in matters of foreign policy and, in pursuing this

83. Quoted in: V.R. Berghahn, *Tirpitz-Plan* (note 78), 270.

objective, had skillfully drawn on his slush fund. Bülow's press chief Otto Hammann later worked hard to systematize the flow of official information. Meanwhile the Social Democrats remained the main domestic enemy against whom Hammann's office relentlessly campaigned. Reich Chancellor Caprivi had proclaimed as early as 1890 that all legislative projects and government actions were to be constantly scrutinized in terms of their impact on the "Social Democratic question." For the same reason, the authorities extended their youth work after the turn of the century. The legal requirement that this work had to be nonpolitical was conveniently overlooked in the case of right-wing associations and applied to leftist youth groups alone. Within the educational system it was above all the primary school teachers who came under increasing pressure when the Left Liberals among them were suspected of being closet socialists. In 1898 the so-called Lex Arons made certain that holding a teaching position anywhere in the educational system was treated as incompatible with membership in the SPD. While some teachers' associations courageously resisted political interference with what they saw as their professional task as educators, from 1906 onward Prussia tried to push back what little influence parents had gained in schools by establishing school commissions which were subject to official supervision. The veterans' associations and the works' committees (*Werkvereine*), which employers founded to combat the "Free" trade unions, enjoyed the special favor of the authorities. When the financial crisis forced the government to reduce its subsidies to these organizations, the authorities stepped up the dispatch of prominent politicians to address their annual rallies. Private benefactors who gave money to "patriotic" associations were recommended for the award of decorations or the coveted title of "councillor." In this way private donations also became increasingly politicized, as all measures came to be justified in terms of a need to fight the perceived leftist threat.

In retrospect it may be said that, paradoxically perhaps, the expansion of the "positive" interventionist state had a polarizing effect, because it openly favored the producers and was so reluctant to offer tangible welfare and participatory benefits that might have appeased the workers, many of whom felt that they were held back in their social aspirations by the class system and discriminated against politically in thousands of small ways. The question of fairness became a major bone of contention. This is even more true of the "negative" interventionist state. Police chicanery, the injustices of the court system, and the policies of the Army greatly embittered the workers. Even after the lapse of the anti-Socialist laws, unfair and unequal treatment by the authorities was part of the daily experience in working-class quarters. Faced with outrageous verdicts on the right to form coalitions and to go on strike, even the Christian and Hirsch-Duncker unions found themselves pushed to the side of the "Free" unions. To be sure, some reformers among the liberal bourgeoisie sought the middle road and hoped to build bridges between the entrenched camps on the Right and Left. Reich Chancellor Bethmann Hollweg, even more than his predecessor, labored to forge a "policy of the diagonal." However, it was unthinkable for a monarchist Chancellor to seek cooperation with the allegedly revolutionary SPD. At the same time the conservative forces lapsed more and more into a fortress mentality. In view of this and given the peculiarities of the Prusso-German constitutional system, the executive was left with little choice but to postpone the resolution of serious and conflict-laden political problems.

The trouble was that no complex society and economy can be governed by an executive that sits on its hands and refuses to address fundamental problems. Paralysis threatened, made worse by the fact that powerful organizations in the political sphere had begun to checkmate each other. However far the expansion of the executive may have progressed by 1914 and however much it had changed its functions, by the outbreak of the World War I the most striking feature of the Prusso-German constitutionalism was its failure to produce at least some results. There was little parliamentarization to speak of, and even in the Center party polarization had now set in "between the majority dominated by the bourgeoisie and the workers' movement." (84) The Reich government did not dare to put the vital questions of financial reform on the agenda. The capacity of the political forces to forge compromises had become exhausted as divergent ideologies and interests struggled ever more vigorously for an outright victory. How this impasse was reached on the eve of the First World War will be discussed in a final section which will provide a chronological account of the most important events between 1871 and 1914.

84. W. Loth, "Das Zentrum und die Verfassungskrise des Kaiserreichs," in: *Geschichte in Wissenschaft und Unterricht*, 1987, 213.

Part V: Foreign and Domestic Policy and Politics

17. The Bismarckian Era

A. Diplomatic Balancing Acts

The first major international challenge with which the new German Empire and Bismarck as its prime political strategist were confronted in 1871 was the question of peacemaking with defeated France and of integrating the new power in the heart of Europe into the existing community of nations. Germany's neighbors watched with interest, but also with suspicion, to see which "path out of war" [1] the Reich Chancellor would take. His reputation from the 1860s was, after all, that of a politician of military force who had worked to overthrow the international status quo. Nor did it go unnoticed that the generals and some members of the general public had been prepared to escalate the conflict in order to win a total victory over France. Given these problems, it was remarkable that Bismarck achieved a moderate peace. If any serious misjudgments occurred, it was in the failure to resist widespread calls to annex Alsace-Lorraine. This decision, which some historians have argued may have been unavoidable, created an irreparable rift with France and in later years contributed to the deterioration of the German position within the international system.

After 1871 German diplomacy was faced with two tasks: to keep the French "archenemy" as isolated as it had been at the outbreak of war in 1870 and, secondly, to fit the *Kaiserreich* into the grouping of the major powers of the day in such a way as to make it impossible for other countries to exert political pressure upon it or to pose a direct military threat. With these objectives in mind, Bismarck tried to convince neighboring countries that Germany had no further territorial ambitions in Europe. To this end, he

1. E. Kolb, *Der Weg aus dem Krieg* (Munich 1989).

attempted to reach an understanding with Russia, Austria-Hungary, and Britain. The first successes of this policy came in October 1873, when Wilhelm I acceded to a treaty which Russia and Austria-Hungary had signed in June of that year. However, as became quickly evident, the three emperors had concluded a precarious alliance. Meanwhile Britain was not interested in any such arrangements. She was preoccupied with her overseas empire and merely saw herself as a "balancer" outside the continental European state system. London appeared on the scene only when, in 1875, the threat of another Franco-German war loomed on the horizon. This ephemeral crisis was rooted in the rapid military and economic recovery that France had been making in the early 1870s. The German military were greatly alarmed by this and began to think of a preventive war. This situation and the ratification of a French military bill in March 1875 triggered the so-called "War in Sight" crisis. Russia and Britain immediately launched a diplomatic counter-offensive that made Bismarck realize the limits of Germany's ability to conduct power politics. It was a major diplomatic setback for the new empire.

Determined not to find himself in an isolated position like the one he faced in 1875 ever again, the Reich Chancellor henceforth tried to strengthen the Three Emperors' League. Perhaps this maneuver would have been more successful if the decline of the Ottoman Empire had not produced fresh tensions between the Tsarist Empire and Austria-Hungary. The immediate trigger was a Russian victory over the Sultan's armies and the forced Peace of San Stephano in March 1878 which, among other things, created a pro-Russian Greater Bulgarian state in the Balkans. In Vienna, but also in London, these shifts in the balance of power unleashed anxieties about the future. As late as January 1877 Russia and Austria-Hungary were in agreement with regard to their interests in southeastern Europe. On this occasion the Tsar had promised the Dual Monarchy that he had no intention of building up a larger Slavic state. Now a Greater Bulgaria had been established, and Vienna felt betrayed. In this tense situation, which even threatened to escalate into a war, Bismarck decided to act as the "honest broker." At the 1878 Berlin Congress he tried to pave the way for a solution to the Oriental question which would give the Russians, Austrians, British, and even the French chunks of the Ottoman Empire which had begun to fall apart.

In this process the Tsar was forced to forego the gains made at San Stephano, which, in turn, soured relations between St. Petersburg and Berlin. Bismarck responded to these unwelcome developments by reaffirming his ties with Austria-Hungary. This cooperation finally culminated in the formation of the Dual Alliance in October 1879. However, in order to explain more fully the tensions between Berlin and St. Petersburg, domestic factors must also be taken into consideration. This was, after all, the period when Bismarck, under pressure from the ailing agricultural sector, increased protective tariffs which hit Russian grain exporters hard. He also introduced a number of bureaucratic obstacles against the Russians, such as more rigorous inspections of meat imports. Thenceforth, a contradiction developed in the Russo-German relationship between a sense of ideological and political solidarity, on the one hand and of a sense of animosity, on the other. The latter was rooted in the survival instincts of the Russian and Prussian landowning classes, as they faced the threat of decline. It was a contradiction that was never resolved and, in fact, ultimately became a factor in the origins of World War I.

At the beginning of the 1880s, Bismarck once again succeeded in reducing Russo-German tensions through a foreign policy geared toward international stability and the preservation of peace. In May 1882, vexed by the nightmare of hostile foreign coalitions, he expanded the Dual Alliance into a trilateral accord by including Italy. Following the collapse in 1885 of the Three Emperors' League only one year after its renewal, he pulled off a coup which, given the prevailing international climate, no one would have thought possible: in June 1887 he secretly secured the Reinsurance Treaty with Russia, the rival of Germany's other ally, Austria-Hungary. Thus at least the two German sides of the St. Petersburg-Berlin-Vienna triangle had been restored.

The precariousness of Bismarck's tightrope act emerges if we look at the continuing problems in the Balkans, which probably defied a permanent solution. It was these problems, exacerbated by a rising Pan-Slav nationalism, which time and again brought the Dual Monarchy and the Tsarist Empire into conflict. It also proved impossible to buttress the Reinsurance Treaty with closer economic cooperation, although the Russians were very interested in this. Instead, the Prussian agrarians continued to wage their silent economic war against their Russian counterparts, and Bismarck's tariff increases of 1885 and 1887 only made the situation worse. St. Petersburg responded by putting very high tariffs on German manufactured goods. During the 1880s, tariffs on pig iron went up by 500 percent, on steel by 20-33 percent, on pharmaceuticals by 20 percent, on locomotives by 42 percent, and on electrical equipment by 21 percent. Overall the increases averaged from 11.7 to 20.5 percent for semi-finished goods and from 16.6 to 30.1 percent for finished goods. We have already established that the question of Polish land laborers from the western Russian provinces also did much to corrode Russo-German relations. Faced with mass migration of the German rural population to the industrial centers, the *Junkers* were happy to import cheap labor from the Tsarist Empire during harvesttime, but only if they could send them back across the border in the winter where the Russians were left to care for them. Nor was it forgotten that in 1885, the Prussians, in connection with their Germanization policy in the eastern provinces, had unceremoniously expelled some 32,000 aliens, many of whom were Russian citizens.

It might have been possible to control the damage that was caused by all this if Prussia's policies had not had military repercussions as well. As early as 1885/86 St. Petersburg had attempted to show its military strength along Germany's eastern frontier by staging elaborate maneuvers and troop movements. At the same time the Russian government labored hard to develop the country's western provinces economically through railroad construction. It sought to attract foreign capital to realize this ambitious project. The building of a railroad network, however, alarmed the General Staff in Berlin. They focused on its strategic implications for a German war against both Russia and France. With the French expanding their armed forces, the General Staff had been handed a further argument for the introduction of a German army bill. When, in the spring of 1887, the Tsar finally banned foreigners (primarily Germans) from holding and using landed property along the country's western border, military and economic rivalries became hopelessly entangled. Indignation over Russian policies reached a peak in the German press, and the Army introduced a major bill in 1887. At the same time Bismarck tried to impede the economic (and military) development of western Russia by blocking German capital exports. In November 1887 – a mere five months after the signing of the Reinsurance Treaty – the Reichsbank was ordered to issue a *Lombardverbot*, which barred the Russians from access to the German capital market. It may be that Bismarck, even after all these set backs, continued to believe that the diplomatic, military-strategic, and commercial interests of the Reich could be hermetically compartmentalized. The tough realities of the Russo-German relationship in the 1880s and the divergent interests behind it should have taught him a different lesson. They demanded a resolution of existing contradictions and a synchronization of policies in all three spheres. When this could not be achieved, St. Petersburg set out to find other friends, first in the field of trade and finance. The capital that they needed for the development of their infrastructure was subsequently advanced by Dutch investors and later by the French. The contacts which these loans promoted facilitated a diplomatic rapprochement between the Tsarist Empire and France. The Reinsurance Treaty was not renewed, and in January 1893 the formal alliance between St. Petersburg and Paris was finally signed and sealed. Thereafter, it was not just Reich Chancellor Caprivi who openly braced himself for a war on two fronts.

Within the new system of alliances that unfolded from the 1890s onward, Britain remained the main missing link. However, by the outbreak of World War I she was to be found on the side of France and Russia. If the emergence of the two blocs, the Triple Alliance (Germany, Austria-Hungary, Italy) and the Triple Entente (Russia, France, Britain) is to be plausibly explained, serious attention will have to be given to the anti-British foreign policy which the Wilhelmine Reich adopted at the turn of the century. [2] However, the deeper roots of the Anglo-German antagonism which came to be encapsulated in the naval arms race between the two powers go back to the Bismarckian period. They surfaced for the first time when Germany turned toward colonialism in the mid-1880s.

Up to that point the Reich Chancellor had firmly rejected the demand, advanced by interested circles, for the acquisition of overseas territories. The consolidation of Germany's position in the heart of Europe continued to be his exclusive concern. This –as he once put it – was where his map of Africa lay. For a long time historians therefore puzzled over why the Reich Chancellor suddenly in 1884/85 declared Germany to be the "protector" of larger stretches of territory in southwest and East Africa, in Togoland, in the Cameroons, and in the Pacific Islands. Today it is fairly certain that Bismarck did not embrace this expansion overseas with enthusiasm, but was guided by soberly pragmatic reasons. To begin with, it was not a propitious moment from the point of view of foreign policy and trade. On the other hand, there was some pressure to act because he did not want Germany to be left behind the other colonial powers. Moreover, there were domestic and electoral calculations. [3] It also seems that his moves were part of an attempted reorientation of German diplomacy, by which Bismarck was hoping to augment France's weight vis-à-vis Britain. The successful cooperation between Berlin and Paris during the Congo Conference at Berlin in the winter of 1884/85 appeared to have improved chances of resolving Germany's dilemma as a continental power between Russia and Britain in a rather different way, i.e., with the help of the French. Just as the Reich Chancellor tried to gain greater freedom of action against the Tsarist Empire by using Austria-Hungary as a counterweight, he thought it possible to escape the towering shadow of Britain by propping up Paris. These hopes soon turned out to be an illusion.

---

2. See below pp. 277f.

3. See below pp. 271f.

But the fact that Britain was the intended target of Bismarck's moves was not lost on London. And just as relations with St. Petersburg deteriorated from the mid-1880s onward, the German attempt to play the French card henceforth had an equally deleterious effect on Anglo-German relations. When, having lost his gamble with Paris, Bismarck did another U-turn in 1889 and introduced the idea of an alliance with London, he found the door across the Channel had closed.

A few years earlier, Bismarck had still been the masterful juggler of five balls in his game of strengthening the new Germany's position among the great powers. If three of those five balls now slipped from his hands, this setback with respect to Britain was also due to a number of problems he was having with London. First, there was the above-mentioned, belated German decision to acquire colonies. For London it was bound to be irritating that the *Kaiserreich* became yet another player in the scramble for overseas territories. After the victory of the Liberals under Gladstone, if not before, differences in the political culture and basic ideological outlook of the two countries had also become more marked. In the age of mass mobilization such differences could no longer simply be ignored by the makers of foreign policy, however much they preferred to be guided by a coolly calculated *raison d'état*. In Britain the Liberals took a progressively dimmer view of Prusso-German Constitutionalism and Bismarck's authoritarianism, while hoping that Germany would experience a parliamentary evolution similar to that of their own country. Meanwhile, the Reich Chancellor did his best to erect dams against precisely such this development by resorting to all sorts of political maneuvers, including the threat of a *Staatstreich* to preserve the constitutional order of 1871. Nor should the impact of Bismarck's protectionism on London be underestimated. The tariffs hampered the export of British goods to Germany, while raising suspicions that German industry resorted to dumping practices in the British Empire. The year 1887, one of major crisis in German foreign policy, also saw the ratification of the Merchandise Stamp Act (better known as the "Made in Germany" Act). Britain's requirement that all goods imported into the country be identified by their country of origin was yet another expression of growing tensions in the field of trade policy. As in the case of Russo-German relations, economic, domestic, and foreign policy could no longer be kept apart as neatly as the Reich Chancellor had expected.

B. Domestic Developments, 1871-1890

The major decisions in German domestic politics during the early 1870s were determined by the need to pass legislation on a large number of questions relating to the structure and consolidation of the new Reich. This need also explains why Bismarck conducted a conservative foreign policy which was firmly geared toward the preservation of international peace. He required calm on the diplomatic front in order to unite the country internally and to rally support for his policies among the Liberals and the Free Conservatives, the main pillars of his government in the Reichstag. He would make concessions to get his way; but he also resorted to identifying *Reichsfeinde*, internal enemies, as a means of nudging divergent political forces to his side. The *Kulturkampf* against the Catholics acted as a rallying point in this sense. Certain of Liberal support, the Reich Chancellor adopted a whole range of measures which greatly impeded the work of the Catholic church and the Center party and to some extent even made it altogether impossible. The Jesuits were banned outright in July 1872. This was followed in May 1874 by the Expatriation Law under whose terms priests could be expelled from the country. The Monastery Law was adopted a year later which, with a few exceptions, ousted other religious orders from Prussia. As early as December 1871 the Criminal Code had contained a so-called "pulpit paragraph" that obliged Catholic clerics to abstain from raising political questions "in a manner that endangered the public peace." A few months later, in March 1872, the Schools Supervision Law was adopted; it secured the state's influence over public and private schools. The May Laws of 1873 extended this supervision to training for the priesthood and to the certification of births, marriages, and deaths. In short, the activities of the Catholic church in Germany came under pressure from all sides. It withstood these pressures well.

From the mid-1870s onward the convenient discovery of the Social Democratic "danger" enabled Bismarck to wind down slowly the struggle against Catholicism. The ratification of the anti-Socialist laws in 1878 were the first major step in the instrumentalization of a new *Reichsfeind*. It is significant of the Chancellor's changing relationship with the Liberals and of the mistrust with which the latter had begun to eye him that he failed to find sufficient support in the Reichstag for special legislation after the first attempt on the Kaiser's life on 1 May 1878. But a week later, Wilhelm I was seriously injured in another assassination attempt. This time Bismarck succeeded in getting the public to accept that the "subversive" Social Democrats were to be blamed for this outrage. Yet even then, the Liberals insisted that some rights of SPD members remained untouched, such as running for legislative office. Nor was parliamentary immunity for Social Democratic deputies abolished. The Reichstag finally imposed a time limit on the laws after which they had to be reconsidered for renewal.

The turmoil in domestic politics during 1878 was followed by the introduction of higher external tariffs a year later. Industry and agriculture, to be sure, had loudly clamored for protectionism. But the new laws were also very much to Bismarck's advantage. On the whole, the bills of 1878/79 not only provided him with an opportunity to destroy the fledgling working-class movement, but also to end the era of Liberal predominance in Parliament (table 79). Thanks largely to the protective tariffs, the agrarian Conservatives were now prepared to cooperate with the Reich Chancellor. This enabled him to put domestic politics on a new and more right-wing course. However, the elections of the 1880s and the "irresponsibility" of the political parties vis-à-vis the monarchical government [4] repeatedly threatened the durability of Bismarck's new parliamentary majorities. Consequently the Reich government in both 1884 and 1887 was under diplomatic and internal pressure to overcome domestic difficulties with the fly-wheel of foreign policy. Here lies another reason for Bismarck's turn to colonialism. He knew, as he once put it, that the colonial business was a hoax, but it was a hoax that he admittedly needed for election purposes. Worse, he found that the genie of imperialism which he had released could not be put back into the bottle. It now affected his foreign policy, particularly his relations with Britain. [5]

Three years later, in 1887, Bismarck again exploited the deteriorating international position of the Reich to counter the Reichstag's demand for a greater voice in budgetary matters. Many deputies were prepared to vote for higher military expenditures, but only if the septennial cycle of appropriations was replaced by a triennial review. The Reich Chancellor responded to this attempt to penetrate the sphere of monarchical prerogative over the armed forces by dissolving the national Parliament, hoping that fresh elections would result in a strengthening of the Right. In this situation it proved useful that international tensions were mounting and that the "Russian menace" could be highlighted. Many voters were impressed by Bismarck's arguments, and both the Conservatives and the National Liberals made considerable gains at the polls. The Reich Chancellor now had the support of a "cartel majority" which helped his government to weather the storms of 1888, the year when both Wilhelm I and his son Friedrich III died in quick succession, ultimately bringing Wilhelm II to the throne (table 79). With this generational leap, an immature 29-year-old assumed the powerful reins of German Kaiser and King of Prussia.

---

4. See above pp. 191ff.

5. H. Pogge von Strandmann, "Domestic Origins of Germany's Colonial Expansion under Bismarck," in: *Past and Present*, 1969, 140-59.

There were several political, psychological, and generational reasons for why the young monarch and the aging Chancellor, who under the Constitution was nothing more than the former's servant, failed to establish a close working relationship. There has been a long debate on whether Bismarck, in order to make himself indispensable, actually planned to unleash an era of domestic conflict or whether he merely toyed with the idea of a *Staatsstreich.* [6] What is perhaps more decisive is that the Kaiser and his advisors firmly *believed* that such an era, deliberately prepared by the Reich Chancellor, was imminent. Since Wilhelm II not only intended to rule by himself, but also hoped to introduce himself to the nation as a Kaiser of peace and of all Germans, he finally decided to replace Bismarck with Caprivi, who quite agreeably helped to dismantle the Chancellor's executive powers that his predecessor had built up since 1871.

18. The Wilhelmine Period, 1890-1913

A. Domestic Politics

After the turmoil surrounding Bismarck's dismissal, Wilhelm II had been hoping for a period of calm on the domestic front which would enable him to initiate a "new course" and to reorganize the government machinery to suit the requirements of his projected "personal rule." But things did not become any easier for Bismarck's successor. The Reich government, it is true, succeeded in getting new labor legislation passed in 1891. However, the debate on another Army bill in 1892 caused so many difficulties that Caprivi resorted to the well-worn ploy of calling premature elections and of using foreign policy to try to move voters in a more conservative, pro-government direction. The election served as a boomerang (table 79). Both the extreme Right and the Left were strengthened by the campaign. Worse, at about this time the Reich's commercial treaties with a number of foreign nations came up for renewal, kindling a bitter argument about whether Bismarck's high tariff policy should be continued. The agrarians were all in favor of it and created the powerful Agrarian League to put this point across to the government and the public. Meanwhile larger sections of industry, keen to exploit the upswing in the world economy and as well organized as the agrarians, called for an across-the-board reduction of protective tariffs. With the end of the "Great Depression" many entrepreneurs had gained enough self-confidence to

6. J.C.G. Röhl, "Staatsstreichplan oder Staatsstreichbereitschaft?," in: *Historische Zeitschrift*, 1966, 610-24.

plunge into the international market. The demand for colonies and for an empire "commensurate" with the size and economic importance of the Reich grew even stronger than it had been in the 1880s. The conflict between agriculture and industry thus shifted to the fundamental question of Germany's future development. The liberal bourgeoisie proclaimed the advantages and virtues of modern industrial capitalism for the country's standing at home and abroad. At the other end of the spectrum Otto von Völderndorff aptly voiced the uneasiness many conservatives felt about industry: "We must leave dabbling in world politics to others; we must limit ourselves to securing the country against the two neighbors. We must pursue utmost parsimony in all matters (except for the Army) and a refounding of the Reich upon the only estate that provides a firm base, [i.e.] the rural population. Our industry is not worth much anyway. It is in the hands of Jews; it produces 'cheaply and poorly'; it is the seedbed of socialism." (7) It is thus not surprising that the agrarians developed a visceral hatred of Caprivi, the modernizer and advocate of a reversal in commercial and tariff policy. When, on top of it all, he refused to give his consent to renewed plans to launch a violent strike against the Social Democrats and Parliament, the Kaiser was persuaded to dismiss him.

However, it is important to emphasize that his successor, the aging Prince Clodwig zu Hohenlohe-Schillingsfürst, had no enthusiasm for an era of domestic conflict which was rumored in court circles to be imminent. The future direction of domestic politics was also fueled by a program of naval expansion which Naval Secretary Wilhelm Hollmann had drawn up at the Kaiser's prompting. The majority in the Reichstag immediately criticized the "limitlessness" of his plans and argued that they lacked a systematic approach. Wilhelm II, who was very agitated by the refusal of the deputies to support his naval program, was finally won over by the group around Hohenlohe against the faction of hard-liners who were calling for a *Staatsstreich*. This group succeeded in assuring a concerned public that no unconstitutional moves were in the offing. Hohenlohe and his supporters said that they aimed instead to rally the agrarians and the middle classes on a basis of conservative moderation. The inauguration of *Weltpolitik* and the idea of a grandiose economic and political future for the *Kaiserreich* were key elements in their strategy.

If a policy of violence had, for the moment, receded into the background, the political battles which Hohenlohe and his successor Bülow had to wage

7. Quoted in: V.R. Berghahn, *Der Tirpitz-Plan* (Düsseldorf 1971), 232. See also above pp. 216ff.

were tough enough. By the same token, the outcome of these battles demonstrated that the decisive political forces inside and outside the Reichstag still had the capacity to forge compromises. This factor provides the only possible explanation for the passage of the naval laws of 1898 and 1900, on the one hand, and the majority agreement on agricultural tariffs in 1902, on the other. What greatly helped the ratification of Tirpitz's Navy bills was that they appeared to offer a systematic program which, at least on paper, looked modest. The favorable international situation of the Reich and the optimistic state of finances helped pass these major pieces of legislation. The increase in agricultural (but not in industrial) tariffs in 1902 similarly raised hopes for a more stable domestic future. The radical demands of the Agrarian League were defeated and Bülow negotiated a middle way which was ultimately perfectly acceptable to industry and the bourgeois parties on whose votes he depended. But it was equally clear, as the experience of effective agrarian opposition to the building of the *Mittellandkanal* had indicated a few years earlier, that industry and commerce could not have their prosperity all to themselves. Concessions to agriculture were unavoidable.

The naval laws and the tariffs were of fundamental importance to the future development of the country and provided grounds for political conflict. In light of this, the acceptance of the three pieces of legislation must be regarded as a remarkable political feat. The question of whether the compromises that were struck between government and the majority parties at the time went beyond the actual text of the accords has caused some controversy among historians. Eckart Kehr was the first to establish a direct link between the two naval bills and the 1902 tariffs, arguing that the great compromise rallied the middle classes and agriculture to the detriment of the working-class and its movement. [8] Others have concurred with his view that a comprehensive domestic tit-for-tat took place. [9] Geoff Eley in turn has challenged this hypothesis, asserting that concrete documentary evidence is lacking to sustain it. [10] What is documented are the statements which the Reich Treasury Secretary Max von Thielmann made during the Reichstag debate of the second Navy bill on May 1, 1900. Pressured by the Center party and the Conservatives, he assured them that the Federal Council – formally the government of the Reich – supported an increase in agricultural tariffs

8. E. Kehr, *Battleship Building and Party Politics in Germany* (Chicago 1973).

9. E.g., V.R. Berghahn, *Tirpitz-Plan* (note 7).

10. G. Eley, "Sammlungspolitik, Social Imperialism, and the Navy Law of 1899," in: *Militärgeschichtliche Mitteilungen*, 1974, 29-63.

which would soon be put forward. The Council and the Reich government therefore clearly saw the immediate context, even if that context often disappeared behind vague slogans about the need to rally in support of *Weltpolitik* and against Social Democracy – slogans that Bülow was a master at inventing when he spoke on these subjects and did not wish to let out too much.

There was another connection between the Navy laws of 1898 and 1900 and the tariffs of 1902: in 1900 Thielmann predicted that the naval armaments which industry and commerce welcomed so heartily could be paid for without difficulty from the additional income that higher tariffs would provide and from the further growth of the national economy with its anticipated higher tax revenues (tables 72-73). It appears therefore that the Kehrite position is not completely unfounded. Nor is it undermined by the fact that Thielmann's optimistic prognosis was proved deeply wrong soon after the passage of the Tariff Bill and now triggered another major domestic conflict over the escalating crisis in the Reich's finances. It was above all the costly naval arms race with Britain that undercut all of Thielmann's and Tirpitz's elaborate fiscal calculations and threw the Reich budget and the system of federal matricular contributions into disarray. The federal states and the communes similarly accumulated uncontrollable deficits. In the end the holes in the Reich budget could only be plugged by new taxes. Yet the mere mention of this prospect alerted a welter of well-organized interest groups and parties, all of which tried to save their constituencies from the tax reform proposal that Bülow, recognizing the looming crisis, had been working on since 1904. When a tax bill was finally introduced in 1906, Parliament chopped and changed it so much that hardly anything remained. But at least one innovation survived the tax battle that was to rattle the National Liberals and the Conservatives: the Catholics insisted on the adoption of a small direct tax on legacies. Although most funds were raised, as before, by increasing indirect taxes, thus hitting the mass of the population hardest, to the propertied classes this was the thin end of the wedge and a harbinger of confiscatory taxes that the "democratic" Reichstag might vote on in the future.

The gains of the anti-Socialist parties in the 1907 "Hottentot" elections (so called because of the successful use of colonial agitation by the government) and the formation of the "Bülow Bloc" raised hopes that a major finance bill would soon be accepted (table 79). The proposed additional revenue was all the more desperately required because the naval arms race had further accelerated and the building of dreadnought-class battleships swallowed up even larger sums of money. Bülow, fully aware of these problems, therefore presented his bill as being absolutely vital for the entire domestic and international future of the *Kaiserreich*. However, along with steep increases in indirect taxes, the bill contained a further modest direct tax proposal. Ultimately it was over this item that the Bülow bill failed. An alternative proposal by the Conservatives was adopted that put the new burden primarily on the shoulders of the masses and of commerce. Bülow's defeat, which decisively contributed to his dismissal in July 1909, showed how polarized the situation had become. The capacity to forge political compromises on central issues like taxation had begun to evaporate to a point which deeply worried Theobald von Bethmann Hollweg, Bülow's successor. Sooner or later, Reichstag elections would have to be held, giving voters an opportunity to take revenge. This opportunity came in January 1912.

Embittered by the injustices of the tax system, the restrictive franchise in the Federal states, and Prusso-German constitutionalism in general, over 4.2 million voters gave their vote to the Social Democrats (table 79). The SPD became the largest party in the Reichstag holding 34.8 percent of the total vote and 110 seats (27.7 percent). The Conservatives and the Reich party gained just over 12 percent of the vote, with the Center party (16.4 per cent) and the National Liberals (13.6 percent) also doing less well than previously, while the Progressives increased their vote to 12.3 percent. In April 1913, despite the protection which they enjoyed under the three-class voting system, the Conservatives suffered losses in Prussia as well. The massive demonstrations against this voting system in 1910 had been harbingers of these developments that now affected the stability and future of German society. After 1912 it was not only the finances of the Reich and the Federal states that were coming apart at the seams, but the political system in general. [11] The difficulties with which the Reich government found itself confronted at home were thrown into sharp relief during the Zabern Affair, which was followed by the debates surrounding the 1913 Army bill and its astronomical costs.

In November 1913 the local military provoked a confrontation between the Army and the population of the small Alsatian town of Zabern which resulted in maltreatment of civilians by officers and the proclamation of a state of siege by the local military commander. Suddenly the Prussian military state began to rear its head from behind the facade of civilian government. Indeed, the events at Zabern were more than a regrettable local incident that could be blamed on the inflexibility and stupidity of a few officers on the ground. The

11. See above pp. 239ff.

affair grew into a national scandal when it became clear that the Kaiser, as commander in chief, was not prepared to tolerate the slightest public criticism of the military. It was as if a flashlight had lit up the deep and deepening divisions within German politics. The incident neatly separated those Germans who were inflexibly hostile to any change in the status quo from those who called ever more insistently for fundamental reforms of existing political conditions. As Marie Countess Radziwill observed at the time, there existed a "latent antagonism between two very different Germanies." [12] Although the military had committed clear breaches of the law, Wilhelm II, under the influence of his *maison militaire*, refused to admit that any mistakes had been made. As the monarch's loyal servant, the Reich Chancellor was forced, against his better judgment, to defend in the Reichstag the bad decisions of the Kaiser's generals. Amid the noisy protests of the deputies, he tried his best to stop an erosion of the constitutional privileges of the crown. The Parliament in turn expressed its displeasure by passing a vote of no-confidence in the Chancellor. To be sure, this vote could not directly touch his position. Only the monarch had the constitutional right to dismiss him. But the affair certainly undermined his public standing. Meanwhile the Kaiser gloated that he could ignore the Reichstag vote. In the face of so much myopia, it is not surprising that many more moderate people were deeply depressed by political developments within a country that, as they saw it, had many impressive economic and cultural achievements to its credit.

The growing tensions and the gradual disappearance of the capacity to compromise can also be traced through the debate on the Army and finance bills of 1913. The enlargement of the Army, the first major one since the 1890s, was adopted after a massive campaign in which Russia and France were alleged to pose a lethal threat to Germany's future. The nationalist associations and the press had made an important contribution to putting the Army bill through the Reichstag. But the parliamentary majority that had ratified the program quickly evaporated when it came to finding additional taxes to pay for the increases. It was quite clear that the horrendous costs of the bill could not be covered by additional indirect taxes and higher matricular contributions from the federal states. Direct Reich taxes seemed unavoidable. Bethmann hoped to win over the indispensable Conservatives to this need by offering a compromise: the money was to be levied via a one-shot "military contribution" that could be dressed up as a patriotic deed; it

12. Quoted in: V.R. Berghahn, *Germany and the Approach of War in 1914* (London 1973), 174.

would not be instituted on a permanent basis. The Conservatives were not prepared even to make this kind of minor sacrifice. No matter whether the financial crisis slowly paralyzed all orderly government activity, direct Reich taxes were in their view out of the question. Such taxes would, they argued, open the door to a progressive expropriation of the wealthy by a Reichstag that was, after all, elected on the basis of the universal suffrage and in which the Social Democrats were the largest party. In the end, the one-time "military contribution" was accepted by a large majority *against* the votes of the Conservatives. Among the 280 yes votes were those of 70 Center party deputies and, for the first time, those of many Social Democrats. However, no monarchical Reich Chancellor could afford to rely on such an alliance twice, if he wanted to keep his job. Accordingly, the 1913 finance bill was the last major piece of legislation that was drawn up by the government before the outbreak of the war. Thenceforth Bethmann administered the country rather than governing it. No less important, the 1913 debates on armaments also shed a cold light on the desperate international predicament into which the *Kaiserreich* had maneuvered itself since 1890.

B. Foreign Policy

With the conclusion of the Franco-Russian Military Convention on August 17, 1892, which was followed five months later by a formal alliance between the two countries, Germany faced a scenario which Bismarck had always sought to avoid: a war on two fronts, to which Caprivi's first response was to introduce a large Army bill. In another respect Caprivi, having to cope with further Russian tariff increases in 1891, did learn a lesson from his predecessor's mistakes. He abandoned the notion that commercial policy could be kept detached from traditional diplomacy. With the trade treaties with Austria-Hungary and Russia coming up for renewal, he tried to end the Russo-German trade war of the previous years by proposing to reduce German agricultural tariffs in return for a lowering of Russian trade barriers against German industrial goods. He succeeded in getting the new treaty signed in 1894; but agrarian wrath ultimately cost him his job, and in 1902 agricultural tariffs were increased again, complicating relations with the Tsarist Empire.

Despite the successful signing of the Heligoland-Zanzibar Treaty of July 1890, relations with Britain also never fundamentally improved. It was a complete misunderstanding of the principles of British foreign policy to believe that German-British cooperation in Europe could be achieved with concessions in the colonial field. The war between China and Japan in 1894/95 occasioned renewed frictions between Berlin and London. These exploded into open conflict after the Kaiser, in a telegram to "Ohm" Krueger, had encouraged the Boers of South Africa in their rebellion against the British. Between 1898 and 1901 Colonial Secretary Joseph Chamberlain raised the question of closer Anglo-German cooperation. His approach ended in failure, largely because those around the Kaiser, who were now in charge of German foreign policy, fatally underestimated the precariousness of the Reich's international position; they had concluded that in light of Anglo-Russian and Anglo-French conflicts in the colonial field, Germany did not require new friendships beyond the 1882 Triple Alliance with Austria-Hungary and Italy. Bülow and Tirpitz became eloquent advocates of a "free hand" policy by which they hoped to escape from the grip of British hegemony.

The slogan of the "free hand" tacitly also acknowledged that it was illogical to have an alliance with Britain, when at the same time the Reich government had begun to build up a fleet that, if necessary, would be able to defeat the Royal Navy in a major battle in the North Sea. Nothing less than such a victory was the ambitious objective behind the Tirpitz Plan to expand the Navy in several stages to a total of sixty large battleships. A fleet of this size, the Navy Secretary believed, would be strong enough to respond to a British attack and thus to be able to shift the international balance of power virtually in one afternoon. If, however, the British decided to hold back, the Kaiser and his advisors hoped to deploy the completed Navy as a lever for a "great overseas policy." It would help Germany to obtain its "fair" share, once the redistribution of the globe and the construction of large power blocs had started in the twentieth century. [13] Backed by a sixty-battleship navy, the Reich government expected to be in a good position to carve up disintegrating older empires, like that of Portugal.

These ambitions amounted to nothing less than a "revolutionizing" of the international system. [14] The motives underlying the Kaiser's decision have recently again become a matter of controversy, once Klaus Hildebrand, Michael Stürmer, and Gregor Schöllgen rediscovered Ludwig Dehio's writings of the 1950s. [15] To explain this prewar development, they invoked geopolitical factors and collective psychology. Faced with an international system whose anarchic state raised both hopes and fears for Germany's

13. Idem, *Tirpitz-Plan* (note 7), 157ff.

14. K. Hildebrand, "Imperialismus, Wettrüsten und Kriegsausbruch," in: *Neue Politische Literatur*, 1975, 160-94 (Part I), 339-64 (Part II).

15. See above pp. xif.

future, the Kaiser and his advisors developed, in this view, no more than airy dreams about an overseas empire. Subsequently, these historians have added, the inability and unwillingness of the other established powers to accommodate these dreams inexorably increased international tensions. According to proponents of this theory, this is where the origins of the First World War must be located. Against this interpretation lies a conception of international relations which was first advanced by Kehr. According to Kehr, Wilhelmine naval and world policy remain the decisive cause of what happened in July 1914, inseparably linked to the unresolved and unresolvable dilemmas of the Prusso-German political system and to the rallying, in the late 1890s, of agrarians and the commercial and industrial middle classes against the industrial proletariat. [16]

By contrast, there is little dispute today over the response which the unilateral rearmament of the Kaiser's navy provoked abroad. Although it took the British some time to become aware of the full extent of the Tirpitz Plan with its sixty battleships, they did react quickly once their suspicions had been confirmed. On the one hand, the British Empire engaged the *Kaiserreich* in a naval arms race whose costs, as we have seen, exceeded the monarchy's ability to raise the necessary taxes and greatly exacerbated domestic conflict. On the other hand, the German challenge accelerated the abandonment of Britain's "splendid isolation." London took the first step in this direction in January 1902, shortly after the collapse of the Anglo-German alliance parleys, when it signed an agreement with Japan. The Entente Cordiale with France followed in April 1904. The significance of this latter agreement can be fully appreciated only if we remember that the two countries had almost gone to war with each other in the autumn of 1898 during the Fashoda Crisis.

What was missing from the evolving British-Russian-French triangle was the link between London and St. Petersburg, which was finally forged in August 1907. The Kaiser and an alarmed German public perceived the new international constellation as an "encirclement" of the Reich aimed at throttling an up-and-coming nation. With the benefit of hindsight it seems more accurate to say that the foreign and armaments policies which Wilhelm II had begun in the late 1890s, had isolated the Reich from the community of nations. Meanwhile the small colonial empire of the 1880s, which had later

16. E. Kehr, *Economic Interest, Militarism, and Foreign Policy* (Berkeley 1977), esp. his essay on "Anglophobia and Weltpolitik." See also M. Epkenhans, *Die wilhelminische Flottenrüstung* (Stuttgart 1991).

been expanded by a few islands in the South Pacific and the leasing of Kiaochow, became a source of trouble. Above all, the uprisings in East Africa and the genocidal methods used against the Herero people in southwest Africa ran into much criticism at home. Such setbacks had one advantage, though: they were well-suited for mobilizing conservative and nationalist sentiment, and this proved most useful at election time, as the hastily called "Hottentot" elections of 1907 demonstrated.

By now Germany's main international support came from a fragile multinational Austro-Hungarian Empire and an unreliable and weak Italy. Confronted with these realities, the Reich government made several attempts to destroy the iron ring which the other great powers had begun to put around the dynamic and politically unpredictable *Kaiserreich*. The panic over the Entente Cordiale led to the resumption of contacts with Russia. These contacts quickly collapsed for the first time in November 1904. The Bjoerkoe Accord which the Kaiser thought he had personally clinched with the Tsar in July 1905 was revoked by St. Petersburg as soon as Nicholas II was back home. The fate of the accord made clear that tensions that had been building up since the days of Bismarck could not simply be swept aside by a meeting between two monarchs. Meanwhile the Reich attempted to put pressure on France. In March 1905 Wilhelm II was sent to Tangiers, where he triggered an international crisis designed by Germany to test the strength of the Entente Cordiale and, if possible, to push Britain and France apart.

Berlin achieved the opposite. Germany emerged as the loser from the Algeciras Conference that had been called for January 1906 and ended in the signing of an international agreement. Thanks to British support at the conference table, France emerged strengthened from the conflict. Similarly the Second Moroccan Crisis of 1911 was deliberately unleashed by the German government in the hope of weakening the Entente Cordiale. State Secretary Alfred von Kiderlen-Waechter moreover had his eye on the acquisition of some African colonies. In a memorandum to Bethmann on May 3, 1911 he justified this demand as follows: "With the sole exception of the Social Democratic party, our public opinion would seriously reproach the Imperial government for simply allowing things to happen in the Sherif Empire; on the other hand, it can be assumed with certainty that practical results would change the mind of many a dissatisfied voter and would not insignificantly influence the outcome of the impending Reichstag elections." [17] The affair

17. Quoted in: W. Zank, "Der Panthersprung nach Agadir," in: *Die Zeit*, 19 July 1991, 13.

ended very differently. The dispatch of the gunboat "Panther" to Agadir on July 1, 1911 and the subsequent German demands were countered three weeks later by the British Treasury Secretary David Lloyd George in his famous Mansion House speech. His warnings so frightened Berlin that Bethmann beat a hasty retreat.

Hoping for a deceleration of the ruinous naval arms race, the new Reich Chancellor had initiated conversations with Britain soon after Bülow's dismissal. But he did not get very far in this climate of mounting tensions, not all of which had been caused by Berlin. It was particularly difficult to find a mutually agreeable formula for the relative size of the fleets which the two countries would keep in service. Mandated by the British Cabinet, War Minister Lord Haldane made a final attempt at reconciliation in January 1912. However, as he discovered soon after his arrival in Berlin, the Kaiser and Tirpitz were not prepared to cut their naval building program by even one ship. Bethmann was too weak to assert himself. Thereafter, the Anglo-German relationship quickly approached a "point of no return," if this juncture had not already been reached. [18] Nor were the negotiations which the Reich Chancellor later conducted with London with regard to the Near East and certain Portuguese colonies able to change this. In the meantime Germany's move away from her overseas ambitions and toward the European continent had been effected. It was a shift that relied for its support not on the Navy, but on the Army. Thenceforth the arms race continued on land against the two continental powers, Russia and France.

At the beginning of 1914, German foreign policy therefore found itself in a state which can only be termed as desolate and extremely dangerous. Contained by the diplomatic countermoves and the rearmament programs of the Triple Entente, Wilhelm II and his advisors were tied to a multinational Austro-Hungarian Empire which was less and less able to cope with its own ethnic minorities and with the pressure exerted on its frontiers by Slav nationalism. The results of the two Balkan wars of 1912 and 1913 worsened the position of the Dual Monarchy. In this situation, Berlin began to consider cutting the Gordian knot with the help of a liberating war against the Reich's external enemies. In 1914, the generals believed, such a conflict could still be won by the Reich, whereas such a victory was less likely after the Russian and French military programs which had promptly followed the German Army bill of 1913 had been completed. The year 1914 therefore offered a

18. K. Hildebrand, "Zwischen Allianz und Antagonismus," in: H. Dollinger, ed., *Weltpolitik, Europagedanke, Regionalismus* (Münster 1982), 323.

"window of opportunity" for freeing the *Kaiserreich* from its diplomatic dilemma and its domestic gridlock at one stroke. But the following analysis of the Crisis of July 1914 also provides an opportunity to draw some broader conclusions about why Germany ended up in this catastrophic world war.

Part VI: The Crisis of July 1914 and Conclusions

In the afternoon of August 1, 1914, when the German ultimatum to Russia to revoke the Tsarist mobilization order of the previous day had expired, Wilhelm II telephoned Moltke, Bethmann Hollweg, Tirpitz, and Prussian War Minister Erich von Falkenhayn to come without delay to the Imperial Palace to witness the Kaiser's signing of the German mobilization order that was to activate the Schlieffen Plan and the German invasion of Luxemburg, Belgium, and France. It was a decision that made a world war inevitable.

The meeting took place at 5 p.m. When the monarch had signed the fateful document, he shook Falkenhayn's hand and tears came to both men's eyes. However, the group had barely dispersed when it was unexpectedly recalled. According to the later report of the Prussian War Minister, [1] "a strange telegram had just been received from Ambassador Lichnowsky" in London, announcing that he had been mandated by the British government "to ask whether we would pledge not to enter French territory if England guaranteed France's neutrality in our conflict with Russia." A bitter dispute apparently ensued between Bethmann Hollweg, who wanted to explore this offer, and Moltke, whose only concern by then was not to upset the meticulously prepared timetable for mobilization. The Chief of the General Staff lost the argument for the moment. The Kaiser ordered Foreign Secretary Gottlieb von Jagow to draft a reply to Lichnowsky, while Moltke telephoned the Army Command at Trier ordering the Sixteenth Division to stop its advance into Luxemburg. As Falkenhayn recorded the scene, Moltke was by now "a broken man" because to him the Kaiser's decision was yet another proof that the monarch "continued to hope for peace." Moltke was so distraught that Falkenhayn had to comfort him, while the latter did not believe for one moment "that the telegram [would] change anything about the

1. Niederschrift by Falkenhayn repr. in: A. von Tirpitz, *Deutsche Ohnmachtspolitik im Weltkriege* (Berlin 1926), 18f.

horrendous drama that began at 5 p.m." Lichnowsky's reply arrived shortly before midnight, detailing the British condition that Belgium's border must remain untouched by the Germans. Knowing that German strategic planning made this impossible, Moltke now pressed Wilhelm II to order the occupation of Luxemburg as a first step to the German invasion of Belgium and France. This time he won; World War I had definitely begun.

After many years of dispute among historians about who was responsible for the outbreak of war in August 1914 in which German scholars either blamed the Triple Entente for what had happened or argued that all powers had simultaneously slithered into the abyss, the previously mentioned Fischer controversy produced a result that is now widely accepted in the international community of experts on the immediate origins of the war – [2] it was the men gathered at the Imperial Palace in Berlin who pushed Europe over the brink. These men during the week prior to August 1 had, together with the "hawks" in Vienna, deliberately exacerbated the crisis, although they were in the best position to de-escalate and defuse it. There is also a broad consensus that during that crucial week major conflicts occurred between the civilian leadership in Berlin around Bethmann Hollweg, who was still looking for diplomatic ways out of the impasse, and the military leadership around Moltke, who now pushed for a violent settling of accounts with the Triple Entente. In the end Bethmann lost, and his defeat opened the door to the issuing of the German mobilization order on August 1.

In pursuing this course, the German decision-makers knew that the earlier Russian mobilization order did not have the same significance as the German one. Thus the Reich Chancellor informed the Prussian War Ministry on July 30, that "although the Russian mobilization has been declared, her mobilization measures cannot be compared with those of the states of Western Europe." [3] He added that St. Petersburg did not "intend to wage war, but has only been forced to take these measures because of Austria" and her mobilization. These insights did not prevent the German leadership from using the Russian moves for their purposes by creating a defensive mood in the German public without which the proposed mobilization of the German armed forces might well have come to grief. The population was in no mood to support an aggressive war. On the contrary, there had been peace demonstrations in various cities when, following the Austrian ultimatum to Serbia on 23 July, suspicions arose that Berlin and Vienna were preparing for a war

2. See above pp. xff., and the arguments of the Hildebrand School notwithstanding.

3. Repr. in: I. *Geiss, Julikrise und Kriegsausbruch 1914*, vol. 2 (Hanover 1963/64), 372f.

on the Balkans. [4] The Reich government responded to this threat by calling on several leaders on the right wing of the SPD executive and confidentially apprising them of Russia's allegedly aggressive intentions. Convinced of the entirely defensive nature of Germany's policy, the leaders of the working-class movement quickly reversed their line: the demonstrations stopped and the socialist press began to write about the Russian danger.

It is against the background of these domestic factors that a remark by Bethmann may be better understood. "I need," the Reich Chancellor is reported to have said to Albert Ballin, the Hamburg shipping magnate, "my declaration of war for reasons of internal politics." [5] What he meant by this is further elucidated by other surviving comments. Thus Admiral von Müller, the Chief of the Naval Cabinet, noted in his diary as early as July 27 that "the tenor of our policy [is] to remain calm to allow Russia to put herself in the wrong, but then not to shrink from war if it [is] inevitable." [6] On the same day, the Reich Chancellor told the Kaiser that "at all events Russia must ruthlessly be put in the wrong." [7] Moltke explained the meaning of this statement to his Austro-Hungarian counterpart, Franz Conrad von Hoetzendorff, on July 30: [8] "War [must] not be declared on Russia, but [we must] wait for Russia to attack." And when a day later this turned out to be the sequence of events, Müller was full of praise. "The morning papers," he recorded in his diary on August 1, "reprint the speeches made by the Kaiser and the Reich Chancellor to an enthusiastic crowd in front of the Schloß and the Chancellor's palace. Brilliant mood. The government has succeeded very well in making us appear as the attacked." [9]

While there is little doubt about the last days of peace and about who ended them, scholarly debate has continued over the motives of the Kaiser and his advisors. In order to clarify these, we have to move back in time to the beginning of July 1914. Fritz Fischer has argued in his *Griff nach der Weltmacht* and in *War of Illusions* that the Reich government seized the assassination of Archduke Ferdinand and his wife at Sarajevo on June 28 as

---

4. V.R. Berghahn, *Germany and the Approach of War in 1914* (London 1993), 213ff.

5. *Ibid.*

6. Quoted in: W. Görlitz, *The Kaiser and his Court* (London 1961), 8.

7. Quoted in: K.H. Jarausch, *The Enigmatic Chancellor* (New Haven, Conn. 1972), 169.

8. Quoted in: F. Fischer, *Krieg der Illusionen* (Düsseldorf 1969), 713.

9. Quoted in: J.C.G. Röhl, "Admiral von Müller and the Approach of War, 1911-1914," in: *Historical Journal*, 1969, 670.

the opportunity to bring about a major war. [10] He asserted that Bethmann, in unison with the military leadership hoped to achieve by force the breakthrough to world power status which German diplomacy had failed to obtain by peaceful means in previous years. However, today most experts would accept another interpretation that was put forward by Konrad Jarausch and others and captured by a chapter heading in Jarausch's biography of Bethmann: "The Illusion of Limited War." [11] In this interpretation, Berlin was originally motivated by more modest objectives than those inferred by Fischer. Worried by the volatile situation on the Balkans and anxious to stabilize the deteriorating position of the multinational Austro-Hungarian Empire (Germany's only reliable ally, then under the strong centrifugal pressure of Slav independence movements), Berlin pushed for a strategy of local war in order to help the Habsburgs in the southeast. Initially, Vienna was not even sure whether to exploit, in order to stabilize its position in power politics, the assassination crisis and the sympathies that the death of the heir to the throne had generated internationally. Emperor Franz Joseph and his civilian advisors wanted to wait for the outcome of a government investigation to see how far Serbia was behind the Sarajevo murders before deciding on a possible punitive move against Belgrade. [12] Only the Chief of the General Staff Conrad advocated an immediate strike against the Serbs at this point. Uncertain of Berlin's response, Franz Joseph sent Count Alexander von Hoyos to see the German Kaiser, who then issued his notorious "blank check." [13] With it the Reich government gave its unconditional support to whatever action Vienna would decide to take against Belgrade.

What did Wilhelm II and his advisors expect to be the consequences of such an action? Was it merely the pretext for starting a major war? Or did Berlin hope that the conflict between Austria-Hungary and Serbia would remain limited? The trouble with answering this question is that we do not possess a first-hand account of the Kaiser's "blank check" meeting with Hoyos and of the monarch's words and assumptions on that occasion. Jarausch and others have developed the view that Bethmann persuaded Wilhelm II and the German military to adopt a limited war strategy which later turned out to be illusory. They have based their argument to a considerable

10. F. Fischer, *War of Illusions* (London 1973); idem, *Germany's War Aims in the First World War* (London 1969).

11. K.H. Jarausch, *Chancellor* (note 7), 148ff.

12. See, e.g., V.R. Berghahn, *War* (note 4), 196ff.

13. *Ibid.*, 198f.

extent on the diaries of Kurt Riezler, Bethmann's private secretary, who was in close contact with his superior during the crucial July days. [14] As he recorded on July 11, it was the Reich Chancellor's plan to obtain "a quick fait accompli" in the Balkans. Thereafter he proposed to make "friendly overtures toward the Entente Powers" in the hope that in this way "the shock" to the international system could be absorbed. Two days earlier Bethmann had expressed the view that "in case of warlike complications between Austria and Serbia, he and Jagow believed that it would be possible to localize the conflagration." [15] But according to Riezler the Reich Chancellor also realized that "an action against Serbia [could] result in a world war." [16] To this extent, his strategy was a "leap into the dark" which he nevertheless considered it as his "gravest duty" to take in light of the desperate situation of the two Central European monarchies.

A localization of the conflict since the risks of a major war seemed remote – this is how Bethmann Hollweg appears to have approached the post-Sarajevo situation. It was only in subsequent weeks, when Vienna took much longer than anticipated to mobilize against Serbia – and above all when it became clear that the other great powers and Russia in particular would not condone a humiliation of Belgrade – that the Reich Chancellor and his advisors became quite frantic and unsure of their ability to manage the unfolding conflict. In its panic, the German Foreign Ministry proposed all sorts of hopelessly unrealistic moves and otherwise tried to cling to its original design. Thus on 16 July, Bethmann wrote to Count Siegfried von Roedern that "in case of an Austro-Serbian conflict the main question is to isolate this dispute." [17] On the following day the Saxon chargé d'affaires to Berlin was informed that "one expects a localization of the conflict since England is absolutely peaceable and France as well as Russia likewise do not feel inclined toward war." [18] On 18 July, Jagow reiterated that "we wish to localize [a] potential conflict between Austria and Serbia." [19] And another three days later the Reich Chancellor instructed his ambassadors in St. Petersburg, Paris, and London that "we urgently desire a localization of the conflict; any

14. *K. D. Erdmann, ed., Kurt Riezler - Tagebücher, Aufsätze, Dokumente* (Göttingen 1972).

15. Quoted in: K.H. Jarausch, *Chancellor* (note 7), 160.

16. Quoted in: V.R. Berghahn, *War* (note 4), 201.

17. Repr. in: I. Geiss, ed., *Kriegsausbruch* (note 3), vol. 1, 189.

18. *Ibid.,* 200.

19. *Ibid.,* 228.

intervention by another power will, in view of the divergent alliance commitments, lead to incalculable consequences." [20]

The problem with Bethmann's limited war concept was that by this time it had become more doubtful than ever that it could be sustained. Another problem is that Jarausch's main source, the Riezler diaries, have come under a cloud since the Berlin historian Bernd Sösemann discovered that, for the July days, they were written on different paper and attached to the diary as a loose-leaf collection. [21] This has led Sösemann to believe that Riezler "reworked" his original notes after World War I. Without going into the details of these charges and the defense and explanations that Karl Dietrich Erdmann, the editor of the diaries, has provided, [22] their doubtful authenticity would seem to preclude continued reliance on this source unless other documents from early July corroborate the localization hypothesis. This would seem to indicate at the same time that the strategy was not just discussed and adopted in the Bethmann Circle, but by the entire German leadership, including the Kaiser and the military. Several such sources have survived. Thus on July 5, the Kaiser's adjutant general, Count Hans von Plessen, entered in his diary that he had been ordered to come to the New Palace at Potsdam in the late afternoon of that day to be told about the Hoyos mission and Francis Joseph's letter to Wilhelm II. [23] Falkenhayn, Bethmann, and the Chief of the Military Cabinet Moritz von Lyncker were also present. According to Plessen, the view predominated that "the sooner the Austrians move against Serbia the better and that the Russians – though Serbia's friends – would not come in. H.M.'s departure on his Norwegian cruise is supposed to go ahead undisturbed."

Falkenhayn's report about the same meeting to Moltke, who was on vacation, had a similar tone. [24] Neither of the two letters which the Kaiser had received from Vienna, both of which painted "a very gloomy picture of the general situation of a Dual Monarchy as a result of Pan-Slav agitations," spoke "of the need for war"; "rather both expound 'energetic' political action such as conclusion of a treaty with Bulgaria, for which they would like to be

20. *Ibid.,* 265.

21. B. Sösemann, "Die Tagebücher Kurt Riezlers," in: *Historische Zeitschrift*, 1983, 327-69.

22. K.D. Erdmann, "Zur Echtheit der Tagebücher Kurt Riezlers," in: *Ibid.*, 371-402.

23. Repr. in: I. Geiss, ed., *Kriegsausbruch* (note 3), 87.

24. Repr. in: *Ibid.*, 86.

certain of the support of the German Reich." Falkenhayn added that Bethmann "appears to have as little faith as I do that the Austrian government is really in earnest, even though the language is undeniably more resolute than in the past." Consequently he expected it to be "a long time before the treaty with Bulgaria is concluded." Moltke's "stay at Spa will therefore scarcely need to be curtailed," although Falkenhayn thought it "advisable to inform you of the gravity of the situation so that anything untoward which could, after all, occur at any time, should not find you wholly unprepared."

Another account of the "blank check" meeting on July 5 comes from Captain Albert Hopman of the Reich Navy Office. [25] On the following day he reported to Tirpitz, who was vacationing in Switzerland, that Admiral Eduard von Capelle, Tirpitz's deputy, was "ordered this morning to go to the New Palace at Potsdam" where Wilhelm II briefed him on the previous day's events. Again the Kaiser said that he had backed Vienna in its demand "for the most far-reaching satisfaction" and, should this not be granted, for military action against Serbia. Hopman's report continued: "H.M. does not consider an intervention by Russia to back up Serbia likely, because the Tsar would not wish to support the regicides and because Russia is at the moment totally unprepared militarily and financially. The same applied to France, especially with respect to finance. H.M. did not mention Britain." Accordingly, he had "let Emperor Franz Joseph know that he could rely on him." The Kaiser believed "that the situation would clear up again after a week owing to Serbia's backing down, but he nevertheless considers it necessary to be prepared for a different outcome." With this in mind, Wilhelm II had "had a word yesterday with the Reich Chancellor, the Chief of the General Staff, the War Minister, and the Deputy Chief of the Admiralty Staff" although "measures which are likely to arouse political attention or to cause special expenditures are to be avoided for the time being." Hopman concluded by saying that "H.M., who, as Excellency von Capelle says, made a perfectly calm, determined impression on him, has left for Kiel this morning to go aboard his yacht for his Scandinavian cruise." That Moltke, clearly a key player in any German planning, had also correctly understood the message that he had received from Berlin and approved of the localization strategy is evidenced by his comment: [26] "Austria must beat the Serbs and then make peace quickly, demanding an Austro-Serbian alliance as the sole condition. Just as Prussia did with Austria in 1866."

---

25. Quoted in: V.R. Berghahn and W. Deist, "Kaiserliche Marine und Kriegsausbruch 1914," in: *Militärgeschichtliche Mitteilungen*, 1970, 45.

26. Quoted in: L. Albertini, *The Origins of the War of 1914* (Oxford 1965), vol. 2, 154.

If, in the face of this evidence, we accept that Berlin adopted a limited war strategy at the beginning of July which turned out later on to have been badly miscalculated, the next question to be answered is: Why did the Kaiser and his advisors fall for "the illusion of limited war"? To understand this and the pressures on them to take action, we must consider the deep pessimism by which they had become affected and which also pervades the Riezler diaries.

In his account of the origins of World War I, James Joll, after a comprehensive survey of various interpretations, ultimately identified "the mood of 1914" as the crucial factor behind Europe's descent into catastrophe. (27) Although he admits that this mood can "only be assessed approximately and impressionistically" and that it "differed from country to country or from class to class," he nevertheless comes to the conclusion that "at each level there was a willingness to risk or to accept war as a solution to a whole range of problems, political, social, international, to say nothing of war as apparently the only way of resisting a direct physical threat." In his view, it is therefore "in an investigation of the mentalities of the rulers of Europe and their subjects that the explanation of the causes of the war will ultimately lie." There is much substance in this perspective on the origins of the war, but it may require further sociological differentiation with regard to the supposedly pervasive pessimistic sense that a cataclysm was inevitable. As in other countries, there were also many groups in German society that were not affected by the gloomsters and, indeed, had hopes and expectations of a better future. They adhered to the view that things could be transformed and improved. After all, over the past two decades the country had seen a period of unprecedented growth and prosperity. German technology, science, and education, as well as the welfare and health care systems, were studied and copied in other parts of the world. There was a vibrant cultural life at all levels, and even large parts of the working-class movement, notwithstanding the hardships and inequalities to which it was exposed, shared a sense of achievement that spurred many of its members to do even better. As the urbanization, industrialization, and secularization of society unfolded, German society, according to the optimists, had become more diverse, modern, colorful, complex, and sophisticated.

However, these attitudes were not universally held. There were other groups that had meanwhile been overcome by a growing feeling that the *Kaiserreich* was on a slippery downhill slope. Some intellectuals, as we have seen, spoke of the fragmentation and disintegration of the well-ordered

27. J. Joll, *The Origins of the First World War* (London 1984), 171ff., 196.

bourgeois world of the nineteenth century. Their artistic productions reflected a deep cultural pessimism, a mood that was distinctly postmodern. Some of them even went so far as to view war as the only way out of the malaise into which modern civilization was said to have maneuvered itself. Only a "bath of steel," they believed, would produce the necessary and comprehensive rejuvenation. If these views had been those of no more than a few fringe groups, their diagnoses of decadence and decline would have remained of little significance. The point is that they were shared, albeit with different arguments, by influential elite groups who were active in the realm of politics. The latter may have had no more than an inkling of the artistic discourse that was pushing beyond modernism, but they, too, assumed that things were on the verge of collapse, especially in the sphere of politics. Here nothing seemed to be working anymore.

The sense of crisis in the final years was most tangible in the field of foreign policy. The monarch and his civilian and military advisors along with many others felt encircled by the Triple Entente. Over the years and certainly after the conclusion of the Franco-British Entente Cordiale in 1904 and the Anglo-Russian accord of 1907 they had convinced themselves that Britain, France, and Russia were bent on throttling the two Central Powers. While the Anglo-German naval arms race had gone into reverse due to Tirpitz's inability to sustain it financially, the military competition on land reached new heights in 1913 after the ratification of massive army bills in Germany, France, and Russia.

However, by then tensions on the European continent were fueled by more than political and military rivalries. As we have seen, in the early 1890s Germany finally abandoned Bismarck's attempts to separate traditional diplomacy from commercial policy. Reich Chancellor Caprivi had aligned the two before Bülow expanded the use of trade as an instrument of German foreign policy following the Tsarist defeat in the Far East at the hands of the Japanese in 1904 and the subsequent revolution of 1905. By 1913 a dramatic change of fortunes had taken place. Russian agriculture had been hit hard by Bülow's protectionism after 1902, and now it looked as if St. Petersburg was about to turn the tables on Berlin. As the correspondent of *Kölnische Zeitung* reported from Russia on March 2, 1914, by the fall of 1917 the country's economic difficulties would be overcome, thanks in no small degree to further French loans. [28] With Germany's commercial treaties coming up for renewal in 1916, the Tsar was expected to do to the Reich what Bülow had done to

28. Quoted in: V.R. Berghahn, *War* (note 4), 189.

the Romanov Empire in earlier years. Accordingly an article published in April 1914 in Deutscher Außenhandel warned that "it hardly requires any mention that in view of the high-grade political tension between the two countries any conflict in the field of commercial policy implies a serious test of peace." (29)

What, in the eyes of Germany's leadership, made the specter of a Russo-German trade war around 1916 so terrifying was that this was also the time when the French and Russian rearmament programs would be completed. Not surprisingly, this realization added the powerful Army leadership to the ranks of German pessimists. Given the precarious strategic position of the two Central European monarchies, the thought that the Tsarist army was to reach its greatest strength in 1916 triggered bouts of depression, especially in Moltke, the Chief of the General Staff, and Conrad, his Austro-Hungarian counterpart. By March 1914 the latter's worries had become so great that he wondered aloud to the head of his Operations Department, Colonel Joseph Metzger, "if one should wait until France and Russia [are] prepared to invade us jointly or if it [is] more desirable to settle the inevitable conflict at an earlier date. Moreover, the Slav question [is] becoming more and more difficult and dangerous for us." (30)

A few weeks later Conrad met with Moltke at Karlsbad, where they shared their general sense of despair and confirmed each other in the view that time was running out. Moltke added that "to wait any longer [means] a diminishing of our chances; [for] as far as manpower is concerned, one cannot enter into a competition with Russia." (31) Back in Berlin, Moltke spoke to Jagow about his meeting at Karlsbad, with the latter recording that the Chief of the General Staff was "seriously worried" about "the prospects of the future." (32) Russia would have "completed her armaments in two or three years time," and "the military superiority of our enemies would be so great then that he did not know how we might cope with them." Accordingly Moltke felt that "there was no alternative to waging a preventive war in order to defeat the enemy as long as we could still more or less pass the test." He left it to Jagow "to gear our policy to an early unleashing of war." That Russia had become something of an obsession not just for the generals, but

29. Quoted in: *Ibid.*, 193.

30. Quoted in: *Ibid.*, 181.

31. *Ibid.*

32. Quoted in: F. Fischer, *Krieg* (note 8), 584.

also for the civilian leadership, can be gauged from a remark by Bethmann, as he cast his eyes across his estate northeast of Berlin. It would not be worth it, he is reported to have said, to plant trees there when in a few years' time the Russians would be coming anyway.

However serious Germany's international situation may have been, the Reich Chancellor and his colleagues were no less aware of the simultaneous difficulties on the domestic front. Surveying the state of the Prusso-German political system in early 1914, it was impossible to avoid the impression that it was out of joint. The Kaiser's prestige was rapidly evaporating. The Zabern Affair had further disillusioned many Germans about the military and the monarchy in general. The government was unable to forge lasting alliances and compromises with the parties of the Right and the center – the only political forces that a monarchical Reich Chancellor could contemplate as potential partners for the passage of legislation. Meanwhile the "revolutionary" Social Democrats were on the rise and had become the largest party in the Reichstag. The next statutory elections were to be held in 1916/17 and no one knew how large the leftist parties would then become. Faced with these problems and fearful of a repetition of the 1913 tax compromise between the parties of the center and the SPD, Bethmann had virtually given up governing. The state machinery was kept going by executive decrees that did not require legislative approval. At the same time the debt crisis continued. Worse, since 1910 there had been massive strike movements, first against the Prussian three-class voting system and later for better wages and working conditions. While the integration of minorities ran into growing trouble, reflecting problems of alienation among larger sections of the population who felt left behind and were now looking for convenient scapegoats, the working class became increasingly critical of the monarchy's incapacity to reform itself. Even parts of the women's movement had begun to refuse the place they had been assigned in the traditional order. So the situation appeared to be one of increasing polarization, and the major compromises that were needed to resolve accumulating problems at home and abroad were nowhere in sight. Even increased police repression and censorship was no longer viable.

Even if it is argued, with the benefit of hindsight, that all this did not in effect amount to a serious crisis, in the minds of many loyal monarchists and their leaders it certainly had begun to look like one. Perceptions are important here because they shaped the determination for future action and compelled those who held the levers of power to act "before it was too late." With the possibilities of compromise seemingly exhausted and the Kaiser and his advisors running out of options that were not checkmated by other political forces, there was merely one arena left in which they still had unrestricted freedom of action. It is also the arena where the broad structural picture that has been offered in previous chapters links up with the more finely textured analysis put forward in the present one. As we have seen, the Reich Constitution gave the monarch and his advisors the exclusive right to decide whether the country would go to war or stay at peace. It was this prerogative that was now to be used in the expectation that a war would result in a restabilization of Germany's and Austria-Hungary's international and domestic situation. The question was, what kind of war would achieve this objective? From all we know and have said about the early response to the assassinations of Sarajevo, this was not the moment to unleash a world war with its incalculable risks. The conservatives in Berlin and Vienna were not that extremist. They expected that war would lead to a major breakthrough in the Balkans and would stabilize the Austria-Hungarian Empire against Serb nationalism. If Moltke's above-mentioned reference to Prussia's victory over Austria in 1866 is any guide, memories of that war may indeed have played a role in German calculations. After all, the Prusso-Austrian had been a limited war in Central Europe, and it had the added benefit of solving the stalemate in Prussian domestic politics, in the wake of the constitutional conflict. [33] Bismarck's "splendid" victory not only produced, after a snap election, a conservative majority in the Prussian Diet that enabled him to overcome the legislative deadlock that had existed since 1862, but it also "proved" that such "shocks" to the international system could be absorbed without further crisis.

And so the Kaiser and his advisors encouraged Vienna to launch a limited war in the Balkans. Their expectations that the war would remain limited turned out to be completely wrong. The Kaiser and his entourage, who under the Reich Constitution at that brief moment held the fate of millions in their hands, were not prepared to beat a retreat and to avoid a world war. The consequences of that total war and the turmoil it caused in all spheres of life were enormous. The world had been turned upside down.

---

33. See, e.g., G.A. Craig, *The Politics of the Prussian Army* (Oxford 1964), 136ff.

Appendix A

Statistical Tables

Introductory Note

It is hoped that, if used with the appropriate circumspection, these tables will be helpful as indicators of major trends.

List of Sources Used

H. Aubin and W. Zorn, eds., *Handbuch zur Deutschen Wirtschafts-und Sozialgeschichte*, vol. 2 (Stuttgart 1976)

R. Bölling, *Volksschullehrer und Politik* (Göttingen 1978)

F. Boll, *Massenbewegungen in Niedersachsen, 1906-1920* (Bonn 1981)

R. Chickering, *We Men Who Feel Most German* (London 1984)

W. Conze and U. Engelhardt, eds., *Arbeiterexistenz im 19. Jahrhundert* (Stuttgart 1981)

D. Crew, *Bochum* (Frankfurt 1980)

H. de Buhr and M. Regenbrecht, eds., *Industrielle Revolution und Industriegesellschaft* (Frankfurt 1987)

J. Ehmer, *Sozialgeschichte des Alters* (Frankfurt 1990)

G. Eley, *Reshaping the German Right* (New Haven, Conn. 1980)

U. Frevert, *Women in German History* (Oxford 1988)

D. Groh, *Negative Integration und revolutionärer Attentismus* (Frankfurt 1973)

W. Grütter and G. Lottes, *Die Industrielle Revolution* (Paderborn 1982)

W.L. Guttsman, *The German Social Democratic Party, 1875-1933* (London 1981)

W.G. Hoffmann, *Das Wachstum der Deutschen Wirtschaft seit der Mitte des 19. Jahrhunderts* (Berlin 1965)

G. Hohorst et al., eds., *Sozialgeschichtliches Arbeitsbuch, 1870-1914* (Munich 1975)

K.H. Jarausch, *Students, Society, and Politics in Imperial Germany* (Princeton 1982)

K.H. Jarausch, *Quantifizierung in der Geschichtswissenschaft* (Düsseldorf 1976)
H. Kaelble, *Industrialisierung und soziale Ungleichheit* (Göttingen 1983)
P. Marschalck, *Bevölkerungsgeschichte Deutschlands im 19. und 20. Jahrhundert* (Frankfurt 1984)
M. Mitterauer, *Ledige Mütter* (Munich 1983)
W. Müller et al., *Strukturwandel der Frauenarbeit, 1880-1980* (Frankfurt 1983)
F.R. Pfetsch, *Zur Entwicklung der Wissenschaftspolitik in Deutschland, 1750-1914* (Berlin 1974)
J. Reulecke, *Geschichte der Urbanisierung in Deutschland* (Frankfurt 1985)
G.A. Ritter, *Social Welfare in Germany and Britain* (Leamington Spa 1986)
J. Sandweg and M. Stürmer, eds., *Industrialisierung und soziale Frage* (Munich 1979)
K. Schönhoven, *Expansion und Konzentration* (Stuttgart 1980)
W. Sombart, *Die deutsche Volkswirtschaft im 19. Jahrhundert und im Anfang des 20. Jahrhunderts* (Berlin 1927)
R. Spree, *Health and Social Class in Imperial Germany* (Oxford 1988)
M. Stürmer, *Das ruhelose Reich* (Berlin 1983)
W. Tormin, *Geschichte der deutschen Parteien seit 1848* (Stuttgart 1967)
P.-C. Witt, *Die Finanzpolitik des Deutschen Reiches von 1903 bis 1913* (Lübeck 1970)

TABLE 1
NET AGRICULTURAL PRODUCTION[a] AT CURRENT PRICES, 1870–1913 (MILL. MARKS)

Year	*Cereals and Vegetables*	*Meat*	*Milk, Eggs, Etc.*	*Total*
1870	1,698	976	1,406	4,080
1871	1,775	1,176	1,507	4,458
1872	2,094	1,296	1,802	5,192
1873	2,173	1,414	1,911	5,498
1874	2,692	1,495	1,622	5,809
1875	2,073	1,417	1,579	5,069
1876	2,061	1,419	1,814	5,294
1877	2,270	1,355	1,933	5,558
1878	2,291	1,454	1,578	5,323
1879	1,994	1,455	1,484	4,933
1880	2,316	1,426	1,677	5,419
1881	2,426	1,428	1,574	5,428
1882	2,206	1,471	1,570	5,247
1883	2,258	1,557	1,732	5,547
1884	2,185	1,634	1,676	5,495
1885	2,085	1,653	1,558	5,296
1886	2,035	1,695	1,484	5,214
1887	2,061	1,670	1,714	5,445
1888	2,078	1,767	1,629	5,474
1889	2,048	1,911	1,744	5,703
1890	2,451	2,019	2,042	6,512
1891	2,304	1,880	1,894	6,078
1892	2,798	1,922	1,782	6,502
1893	2,447	1,950	1,959	6,356
1894	2,206	2,073	2,009	6,288
1895	2,287	2,119	1,787	6,193
1896	2,224	2,282	1,809	6,315
1897	2,397	2,534	2,122	7,053
1898	2,738	2,753	2,251	7,742
1899	2,655	2,704	2,054	7,413
1900	2,842	2,647	2,115	7,604
1901	2,544	2,744	2,142	7,430
1902	2,832	2,640	2,452	7,924
1903	2,827	2,645	2,440	7,912
1904	3,129	2,803	2,297	8,229
1905	3,082	3,275	2,675	9,032
1906	2,845	3,495	2,970	9,310
1907	3,400	3,185	3,041	9,626
1908	3,693	3,539	2,875	10,107
1909	3,470	3,592	3,206	10,468
1910	3,168	3,986	3,545	10,699
1911	3,116	4,110	3,680	10,906
1912	3,931	4,606	3,847	12,384
1913	3,540	4,593	3,607	11,740

[a]After deduction of seeds, animal feedstuffs and processing losses.
Source: Hoffmann, 313.

TABLE 2
INDICES OF PRODUCERS' PRICES FOR AGRICULTURAL PRODUCE, 1870–1913

Year	*Cereals and Vegetables*	*Meat*	*Milk, Eggs, Etc.*	*Total Average*
1870	79.6	55.6	70.1	69.1
1875	80.7	65.4	76.2	74.3
1880	101.8	63.6	78.7	81.3
1885	72.7	63.2	69.3	68.4
1890	88.3	71.5	85.4	81.3
1895	74.2	65.7	68.5	69.3
1900	82.8	65.1	73.7	73.2
1905	92.2	78.0	84.7	84.4
1910	95.8	85.6	104.4	94.1
1913	100.0	100.0	100.0	100.0

Source: Hoffmann, 561.

TABLE 3
AGRICULTURAL UNITS IN REICH BY SIZE, 1882 AND 1908 (000S AND %)

	1882		*1907*	
SIZE	NO.	%	NO.	%
Under 2 hectares	3,062	58.0	3,379	58.9
2–5 hectares	981	18.6	1,006	17.6
5–20 hectares	927	17.6	1,066	18.5
20–100 hectares	282	5.3	262	4.6
100+ hectares	25	0.5	24	0.4

Source: Aubin, 512.

TABLE 4
LIVESTOCK, 1861–1913 (000S)

Year	*Horses*	*Cattle*	*Pigs*	*Sheep*
1861	3,194	14,999	6,463	28,017
1873	3,552	15,777	7,124	24,999
1883	3,523	15,787	9,206	19,190
1892	3,836	17,556	13,174	13,590
1900	4,195	18,946	16,807	9,693
1913	4,558	20,994	25,659	5,521

Source: Aubin, 521.

TABLE 5
PIG IRON PRODUCTION IN GERMANY, BRITAIN, FRANCE, AND RUSSIA, IN ANNUAL AVERAGES, 1870–1913 (000S)

Year	*Germany*	*Britain*	*France*	*Russia*
1870–1874	1,579	6,480	1,211	375
1875–1879	1,770	6,484	1,462	424
1880–1884	2,893	8,295	1,918	477
1885–1889	3,541	7,784	1,626	616
1890–1894	4,335	7,402	1,998	1,096
1895–1899	5,974	8,777	2,386	1,981
1900–1904	7,925	8,778	2,665	2,773
1905–1909	10,666	9,855	3,391	2,779
1910–1913	14,836	9,792	4,664	3,870

Source: Grütter, 16.

TABLE 6
PRODUCTION INDICES OF KEY INDUSTRIES, 1870–1913

Year	*Coal*	*Lignite*	*Iron*	*Steel*	*Shipbuilding*	*Cars*	*Chemicals*
1870	13.9	8.7	7.2	6.0	—	—	—
1875	19.7	11.9	10.5	8.8	—	—	—
1880	24.7	13.9	14.1	10.9	—	—	—
1885	30.7	17.7	14.1	13.4	—	—	—
1890	36.9	21.9	24.1	18.0	—	—	—
1895	41.7	28.4	28.3	22.4	—	—	—
1900	57.5	46.4	43.6	33.4	—	—	—
1905	63.8	60.2	56.9	47.0	—	—	—
1910	80.4	77.5	76.6	75.8	63.8	51.1	80.5
1913	100.0	100.0	100.0	100.0	100.0	100.0	100.0

Source: Hoffmann, 340ff., 353f., 358, 362.

TABLE 7
NET INVESTMENTS IN AGRICULTURE AND INDUSTRY, 1870–1913 (%)

Year	*Agriculture*	*Industry*	*Construction*[a]	*Railroads*	*Total (mill. marks)*
1870–74	10.3	32.6	33.2	23.8	2,040
1875–79	10.8	10.6	53.0	25.5	2,338
1880–84	11.5	37.5	37.5	13.5	2,264
1885–89	13.9	45.3	35.2	5.7	—
1890–94	11.5	34.0	47.9	6.7	—
1895–99	9.0	54.5	30.6	5.9	—
1900–04	11.3	36.1	44.9	7.8	—
1905–09	10.0	43.2	40.4	8.4	—
1910–13	13.8	42.9	35.4	7.9	—

[a]Private non-agricultural and all public construction

Source: Hoffmann, 143.

TABLE 8
EXPORTS/IMPORTS IN CURRENT PRICES (MILL. MARKS) AND BY VOLUME (INDEXED: 1913 = 100), 1880–1913

Year	*Current Prices*		*Volume*	
	EXPORTS	IMPORTS	EXPORTS	IMPORTS
1880	2,923.0	2,813.7	22.4	25.5
1885	2,854.6	2,922.6	25.9	31.8
1890	3,335.1	4,162.4	29.8	44.0
1895	3,318.0	4,119.0	31.7	52.0
1900	4,611.2	5,768.6	44.7	63.2
1905	5,731.6	7,128.8	58.2	75.1
1910	7,474.7	8,926.9	77.4	88.3
1913	10,097.5	10,750.9	100.0	100.0

Source: Hoffmann, 520ff.

TABLE 9
DIVIDEND PAYMENTS OF MAJOR BANKS, 1871–1879 (% OF NOMINAL VALUE)

	1871	*1872*	*1873*	*1874*	*1875*	*1876*	*1877*	*1878*	*1879*
Disconto Gesellschaft	24.0	27.0	14.0	12.0	7.0	4.0	5.0	6.5	10.0
Berliner Handels-Ges.	12.5	12.5	6.5	7.0	5.0	0.0	0.0	0.0	5.0
Commerzbank	7.4	8.4	0.0	3.33	4.75	6.0	6.0	6.33	7.0
Deutsche Bank	8.0	8.0	4.0	5.0	3.0	6.0	6.0	6.5	9.0
Darmstädter Bank	15.0	15.0	10.0	10.0	6.0	6.0	6 75	6.75	9.5
Bayer. Hypoth. u. Wechselb.	9.4	9.8	10.2	10.4	10.4	10.4	10.5	10.5	10.85
Norddeutsche Bank	12.6	13.4	10.8	10.0	6.75	8.0	8.5	8.8	10.0
Schaafhausen 'scher Bankuerein	12.5	14.0	8.0	5.5	0.0	0.0	2.2	3.0	3.33
Württ. Vaseinsbank	13.33	17.2	10.0	8.0	7.0	6.0	6.66	7.5	8.0

Source: Stürmer, 83.

TABLE 10
AGREEMENTS ON WAGES AND CONDITIONS IN THE METAL INDUSTRIES OF BRUNSWICK (A) AND HANOVER (B), 1910–1914

Year	No. of Agreements		No. of Companies		No. of Workers Involved		Workers per Company	
	A	B	A	B	A	B	A	B
1910	5	10	60	262	433	926	7.2	3.5
1911	4	11	57	228	482	982	8.4	4.3
1912	4	11	69	263	438	1,287	6.3	4.9
1913	6	10	105	261	664	1,291	6.3	4.9
1914	8	9	136	251	772	1,024	5.7	4.2

Source: Boll, 78.

TABLE 11
STRIKES AND LOCKOUTS, 1900–1913
(BASED ON TRADE UNION STATISTICS [A] AND REICH STATISTICS [B])

Year	No. of Strikes and Lockouts		No. of Employees (000s)		Working Days Lost (000s)	
	A	B	A	B	A	B
1900	852	1,468	115.7	141.1	1,234.0	3,712.0
1901	727	1,091	48.5	68.2	1,194.5	2,427.0
1902	861	1,106	55.7	70.7	964.3	1,951.0
1903	1,282	1,444	121.6	135.5	2,622.2	4,158.0
1904	1,625	1,990	135.9	145.5	2,120.1	5,285.0
1905	2,323	2,657	508.0	542.6	7,362.8	18,984.0
1906	3480	3626	316.0	376.3	6,317.7	11,567.0
1907	2,792	2,512	281.0	286.0	5,122.5	9,017.0
1908	2,052	1,524	126.9	119.8	2,045.6	3,666.0
1909	45	1,652	131.2	130.9	2,247.5	4,152.0
1910	3,194	3,228	369.0	390.7	9,037.6	17,848.0
1911	2,914	2,798	325.3	385.2	6,864.2	11,466.0
1912	2,825	2,834	479.6	493.7	4,776.8	10,724.0
1913	2,600	2,464	249.0	323.4	5,672.9	11,761.0

Source: Hohorst, 132f.

Table 12
Growth in Expenditures on Sciences by the Reich and Major Federal States in 10-year Averages

Year	*Reich*		*Prussia*		*Bavaria*		*Saxony*		*Baden*	
	IN MILL.	%	IN MILL.	%	IN MILL	%	IN MILL.	%	IN MILL.	%
1870–79	2.3	123	10.4	50	2.8	—	1.4	—	1.3	—
1880–89	5.1	49	15.7	26	3.5	—	1.9	—	1.8	—
1890–99	7.6	97	18.8	90	4.3	—	3.2	—	2.7	—
1900–09	15.0	25	35.9	39	6.3	—	4.2	—	3.7	—
1910–14	18.8	—	50.1	—	10.3	—	6.6	—	4.8	—

Source: Pfetsch, 52.

Table 13
Indices of Nominal Wages, Cost of Living, and Real Wages, 1871–1913, According to A.V. Desai (A) and J. Kuczynski (B)

Year	*A*			*B*		
	Nominal Wages	Cost of Living	Real Wages	Nominal Wages	Cost of Living	Real Wages
1871	74	106	70	78	95	82
1875	98	113	87	97	104	93
1880	82	104	79	82	104	79
1890	98	102	96	100	103	97
1895	100	100	100	100	100	100
1900	118	106	111	115	105	110
1910	147	124	119	139	126	110
1913	163	130	125	153	137	112

Source: Langewiesche, 102; Aubin, 620.

TABLE 14
AVERAGE ANNUAL WAGES AND SALARIES, 1870–1913 (IN MARKS)

Year	All Industries and Handicrafts	Mining		Metals		Administration
		ALL MINERS	EMPLOYEES	WORKERS[a]	LAW, WHITE COLLAR[b]	EDUCATION
1870	506	767	798	—	1,871	1,306
1875	669	929	966	—	2,053	1,647
1880	565	721	750	—	2,416	1,778
1885	622	768	799	—	2,215	1,877
1890	711	966	1,005	1,058	2,515	1,947
1895	738	908	944	1,090	2,540	1,986
1900	834	1,173	1,220	1,287	4,151	2,055
1905	928	1,159	1,205	1,271	3,824	2,115
1910	1,063	1,299	1,347	1,426	3,213	2,409
1913	1,163	1,496	1,667	1,465[c]	3,753[c]	2,607

[a]With Bochumer Verein (Ruhr area)
[b]With Maschinenfabrik Esslingen (southwest)
[c]For 1912

Sources: Hoffmann, 461, 469, 489 f.; Crew, 190; Kaelble, 75.

TABLE 15
AVERAGE HOURS OF WORK PER WEEK IN MAJOR BRANCHES OF INDUSTRY, 1895–1914

Year	Total	Coal Mining	Metals	Chemicals	Textiles
1895	64	51.5	63	60	65
1900	62	53	63	60	62.5
1905	60	46	—	60	61
1910	59	48.5	—	—	59
1914	57	50	60	58	—

Source: Hoffmann, 214.

Table 16
Number of Taxpaying Individuals by Income Group in Prussia, 1882–1910

Annual Income (in marks)	1892	1900	1910
900 – 1,050	658,811	999,270	1,341,497
1,050 – 1,200	437,003	591,485	1,111,000
1,200 – 1,350	234,750	345,466	804,709
1,350 – 1,500	195,459	265,876	679,904
1,500 – 1,650	125,133	152,310	436,897
1,650 – 1,800	120,335	150,541	359,516
1,800 – 2,100	128,037	160,619	326,167
2,100 – 2,400	106,087	132,910	233,807
2,400 – 2,700	71,024	97,307	145,090
2,700 – 3,000	46,328	67,431	99,154

Source: Sombart, 529.

Table 17
Growth in Wealthy Taxpayers and their Average Wealth per Capita in Prussia, 1895 and 1907

Wealth (in marks)	1895		1907	
	No. of Taxpayers	Average wealth per capita	No. of Taxpayers	Average wealth per capita
6,000 – 100,000	1,062,149	24,252	1,608,050	23,295
100,000 – 500,000	86,552	196,279	135,843	198,802
500,000 – 1,000,000	8,375	711,475	13,800	713,612
1,000,000 – 2,000,000	3,429	1,430,700	5,916	1,430,200
2,000,000 +	1,827	4,762,312	3,425	5,321,400

Source: Sombart, 530.

TABLE 18
INCOME DISTRIBUTION AMONG WORKING POPULATION OF BOCHUM, 1875–1907

Annual Income (in marks)	1875		1882		1895		1907	
	No. of Workers	%	No. of Workers	%	No. of Workers	%	No. of Workers	%
Under 420	7,644	44.8	3,079	22.8	—	—	—	—
420 – 660	1,163	6.8	1,851	13.7	—	—	—	—
660 – 900	4,146	24.3	6,277	46.5	7,577	38.8	18,159	35.8
900 – 1,050	807	4.7	381	2.8	8,131	41.6	4,216	8.3
1,050 – 1,200	1,683	9.9	507	3.8	648	3.3	6,150	12.1
1,200 – 1,350	519	3.0	237	1.8	561	2.9	5,203	10.2
1,350 – 1,500	275	1.6	255	1.9	346	1.8	5,583	11.0
1,500 – 1,650	168	1.0	126	0.9	263	1.3	3,880	7.6
1,650 – 1,800	122	0.7	157	1.2	246	1.3	2,220	4.4
1,800 – 2,100	72	0.4	87	0.6	266	1.4	1,479	2.9
2,100 – 2,400	102	0.6	124	0.9	305	1.6	915	1.8
2,400 – 2,700	71	0.4	55	0.4	210	1.1	574	1.1
2,700 – 3,000	69	0.4	112	0.8	157	0.8	414	0.8
3,000+	240	1.4	258	1.9	838	4.3	1,980	3.9
Total	17,081	—	13,506	—	19,548	—	50,733	—

Source: Crew, 32.

TABLE 19
DEVELOPMENT OF SAVINGS BANKS IN THE KINGDOM OF SAXONY, 1870–1914

Year	No. of Banks	No. of Accounts	Total of Savings (in marks)
1870	142	474,272	115,719,834
1875	161	733,951	261,647,201
1880	175	909,787	338,806,699
1885	196	1,274,542	434,048,671
1890	220	1,606,650	581,719,517
1895	247	1,942,533	741,899,912
1900	283	2,237,481	925,294,793
1905	332	2,753,511	1,331,618,482
1910	361	3,196,237	1,716,188,202
1914	361	3,496,430	2,030,323,350

Source: Conze, 453f.

TABLE 20
ANNUAL PER CAPITA CONSUMPTION OF BASIC FOOD ITEMS IN KILOS, 1870–1913

Items	*1870*	*1880*	*1890*	*1900*	*1910*	*1913*
Meat (incl. sausages, offal, bones)	27.6	32.7	37.7	47.0	46.7	44.9
Fish	3.9	4.7	7.1	6.2	9.0	9.3
Rye flour/bread	69.4	76.3	67.0	69.9	63.6	65.2
Wheat flour/bread	35.5	48.2	52.5	64.0	63.9	66.0
Potatoes	186.2	180.2	227.6	271.1	226.6	203.0
Vegetables	49.3	51.9	58.4	61.5	62.5	63.5
Fruit	24.2	10.1	23.2	43.3	38.2	22.6
Sugar	4.2	4.6	7.7	12.6	17.8	20.0

Source: Conze, 61ff.

TABLE 21
UNEMPLOYMENT, 1900–1913

Year	No. (000s)	% of Working Population
1900[a]	183	1.9
1901	631	6.7
1902	272	2.9
1903	268	2.7
1904	211	2.1
1905	166	1.6
1906	128	1.2
1907	175	1.6
1908	319	3.0
1909	307	2.9
1910	211	1.9
1911	215	1.9
1912	239	2.0
1913	348	3.0

[a]Statistics for industry only, excluding handicrafts and only as far as recorded by trade unions. Actual figures probably much higher.

Source: Witt, 384.

TABLE 22
STRUCTURE OF EMPLOYMENT BY OCCUPATION, 1882–1907 (%)

Year	*Self-Employed*	*Helping Family Members*	*Civil Servants*	*Employees*	*Workers*
1882	25.4	9.9	2.6	4.7	57.4
1895	23.3	9.0	2.2	8.6	56.9
1907	18.8	15.0	2.0	10.7	53.0

Source: de Buhr, 66.

TABLE 23
STRUCTURE OF THE LABOR FORCE IN OCCUPATIONAL GROUPS, 1875–1913 (000S)

Sector	*1875*	*1885*	*1895*	*1905*	*1913*
Agriculture	9,230	9,700	9,788	9,926	10,701
Mining	286	345	432	665	863
Industry and handicraft	5,153	6,005	7,524	9,572	10,857
Transport	349	461	620	901	1,174
Commerce/banking	1,116	1,457	1,970	2,806	3,474
Insurance, hotels,[a] domestic services	(1,490)	1,488	1,571	1,541	1,542
Other services	589	659	894	1,159	1,493
Defence	430	462	606	651	864
Total	18,643	20,577	23,405	27,221	30,968

[a]Including restaurants, etc.

Source: Hoffmann, 205.

TABLE 24
OCCUPATIONAL DISTRIBUTION OF JEWISH WORKING POPULATION, 1895 AND 1907

Occupation	*1895*		*1907*	
Manufacturing	46,000	(19%)	63,000	(22%)
Trade/services	133,000	(56%)	146,000	(51%)
Public service/professional	15,000	(6%)	19,000	(7%)
Self-employed	40,000	(17%)	55,000	(19%)

Source: Aubin, 608.

TABLE 25
DISTRIBUTION OF LABOR FORCE ACCORDING TO NUMBER OF EMPLOYED IN CRAFTS AND INDUSTRY (EXCLUDING HEAVY INDUSTRY), 1875–1907 (%)

Year	1–5 Employees		6–50 Employees		50+ Employees	
	Enterprises	Persons	Enterprises	Persons	Enterprises	Persons
1875	—	63.6	—	—	—	—
1882	95.9	59.8	3.7	17.4	0.4	22.8
1895	92.8	41.8	6.5	24.7	0.8	33.5
1907	89.8	31.2	8.9	26.4	1.3	42.4

Source: Aubin, 533.

TABLE 26
DISTRIBUTION OF LABOR FORCE ACCORDING TO NUMBER OF EMPLOYED PER ENTERPRISE IN HEAVY INDUSTRY, 1875–1907 (%)

Year	1–5 Employees		6–50 Employees		50+ Employees	
	Enterprises	Persons	Enterprises	Persons	Enterprises	Persons
1875	—	3.0	—	—	—	—
1882	52.4[a]	1.7	26.0[a]	6.7	21.6[a]	91.6
1895	43.5	0.8	27.4	4.6	29.1	94.6
1907	46.2	0.7	22.0	2.8	31.8	96.5

[a]Including wiring works.

Source: Aubin, 533.

TABLE 27
MALE EMPLOYMENT BETWEEN AGES 45–64, 1882–1907 (%)

Year	Ages 45–54	Ages 55–59	Ages 60–64
1882	97.2	93.6	79.8
1895	96.5	92.6	78.9
1907	96.2	90.5	71.2

Source: Ehmer, 141.

Table 28
Structure of Labor Force by Gender, 1882–1907 (mill. and %)

Year	Male	Female	Total	Employees %
1882	13.42	5.54	18.96	41.9
1895	15.53	6.58	22.11	42.7
1907	18.60	9.49	28.09	45.5

Source: Aubin, 612.

Table 29
Structure of the Female Labor Force, 1882–1907 (no. and %)

	1882	1895	1907
Total no. (000s)	7,794	8,219	9,742
Female rate of employment	24.0	25.0	30.4
Male rate of employment	95.5	95.0	95.2
Employment rate of single women	69.4	67.5	71.7
Employment rate of married women	9.5[a]	12.2[a]	26.3[a]
Women working in agriculture as percentage of all working women	61.4	53.5	49.8
Women working in domestic services as percentage of all working women	18.0	18.2	16.1
Women working in crafts and industry as percentage of all working women	12.8	16.8	19.5
Women in tertiary sector as percentage of all working women	7.7	11.5	14.6

[a]Probably higher because Reich Statistical Office applied rather restrictive criteria to helping family members.

Source: Müller, 35.

Table 30
Number of Female Employees by Sectors, 1875–1907 (000s)

Year	Agriculture, Forestry, Fishing	Mining	Industry, Crafts	Commerce, Banking, Insurance, Restaurant	Transport	Other Services	Domestic Services	Total
1875	—	12	960	376	7	—	—	—
1882	3,935	14	1,200	494	8	116	1,400	7,167
1895	4,153	17	1,536	770	12	180	1,490	8,158
1907	4,599	21	2,154	1,284	36	301	1,430	9,825

Source: Hoffmann, 210.

TABLE 31
PERCENTAGE OF WOMEN IN MAJOR BRANCHES, 1882–1907

Branch	*1882*	*1895*	*1907*
Agriculture	38.7	36.3	40.8
Metal production	2.7	2.9	2.7
Electrical engineering	4.7	12.7	16.4
Chemicals	14.2	17.9	19.9
Paper and printing	10.0	10.1	13.0
Leather, textile, clothing	34.1	42.7	49.4
Food and alcohol	12.1	17.2	22.3
Construction	0.7	1.0	0.9
Commerce	17.4	19.4	28.2
Transport	2.6	1.5	3.5
Banking and Insurance	0.7	2.2	5.5
Education	12.4	36.8	32.4
Health	55.9	57.6	54.3
Cleaning Services	91.8	93.8	87.4

Source: Müller, 132.

TABLE 32
EMPLOYMENT RATES OF MARRIED WOMEN BY AGE GROUPS, 1882–1907 (%)

Age Group	*1882*	*1895*	*1907*
16 – 19	18.1	15.8	22.5
20 – 29	9.3	11.9	22.1
30 – 39	9.1	11.8	25.7
40 – 49	9.8	12.8	28.9
50 – 59	9.5	12.7	29.8
60+	7.1	10.0	23.5
Total %	*9.5*	*12.2*	*26.3*

Source: Müller, 53.

TABLE 33
AGE AND MARITAL STATUS OF FEMALE FACTORY WORKERS IN PRUSSIA, 1875 (%)

Age	*Married*	*Single*	*Total*
16 – 18	0.6	99.4	25.1
18 – 25	11.4	88.6	43.0
Over 25	56.0	44.0	31.9
Over 16	22.9%	77.1%	100.0%

Source: Frevert, 329.

TABLE 34
NUMBER OF INHABITANTS IN GERMANY AND ITS REGIONS, 1864 AND 1910 (000S)

Region	*1864*	*1871*	*1910*
German Empire	39,392	40,997	64,568
Prussia	23,582	—	40,165
East Prussia	1,761	—	2,064
West Prussia	1,253	—	1,704
City of Berlin	633	—	2,071
Brandenburg	1,984	—	4,093
Pomerania	1,438	—	1,717
Posen	1,524	—	2,100
Silesia	3,511	—	5,226
Saxony	2,045	—	3,089
Schleswig-Holstein	999	—	1,621
Hanover	1,926	—	2,942
Westphalia	1,667	—	4,125
Hesse-Nassau	1,388	—	2,221
Rhineland	3,372	—	7,121
Hohenzollern	65	—	71
Bavaria	4,775	—	6,887
Bavaria east of Rhine	4,150	—	5,950
Rhine-Palatinate	625	—	937
Saxony (Kingdom of)	2,337	—	4,807
Württemberg	1,748	—	2,437
Baden	1,432	—	2,143
Hesse	817	—	1,282
Mecklenburg-Schwerin	553	—	640
Saxony (Grand Duchy)	280	—	417
Mecklenburg-Strelitz	99	—	106
Oldenburg	314	—	483
Brunswick	293	—	494
Saxe-Meiningen	178	—	279
Saxe-Altenburg	142	—	216
Saxe-Coburg-Gotha	165	—	257
Anhalt	193	—	331
Schwarzburg-Sondershausen	66	—	90

(Cont.)

Table 34 *(cont.)*
Number of Inhabitants in Germany and Its Regions, 1864 and 1910 (000s)

Region	*1864*	*1871*	*1910*
Schwarzburg-Rudolstadt	74	—	101
Waldeck	59	—	62
Reuß ä.L.	44	—	73
Reuß j.L.	86	—	153
Schaumburg-Lippe	31	—	47
Lippe	111	—	151
Lübeck	46	—	117
Bremen	104	—	299
Hamburg	279	—	1,015
Alsace-Lorraine	1,584	—	1,874

Source: Grütter, 85f.

Table 35
Population Density in the Major States, 1841–1910 (per km^2)

Region	*1841*	*1871*	*1890*	*1910*
Germany	60	76	92	120
Prussia	54	71	86	115
East Prussia	36	49	53	56
West Prussia	36	52	56	67
Posen	42	55	61	72
Pomerania	34	48	51	57
Silesia	71	92	105	130
Saxony	65	83	102	122
Westphalia	69	88	120	204
Rhineland	97	133	175	264
Bavaria	57	64	74	91
Baden	84	97	110	142
Württemberg	85	93	104	125
Saxony	115	171	234	321
Alsace-Lorraine	—	107	111	129

Source: Reulecke, 201.

Table 36
Population in Different-sized Communities, 1871–1910 (%)

Number of Inhabitants	*1871*	*1880*	*1910*
under 2,000	63.9	58.6	40.0
2,000 – 5,000	12.4	12.7	11.2
5,000 – 20,000	11.2	12.6	14.1
20,000 – 100,000	7.7	8.9	13.4
100,000 +	4.8	7.2	21.3

Sources: Hohorst, 52; Sandweg, 25.

Table 37
Growth of Some Major Cities, 1850–1910 (000s)

City	*1850*	*1871*	*1880*	*1900*	*1910*
Berlin	412	826	1,122	1,889	2,071
Hamburg	175	290	290	706	931
Munich	107	169	230	500	596
Leipzig	63	107	149	456	679
Dresden	97	177	221	396	548
Cologne	97	129	145	373	517
Breslau	111	208	273	423	512
Frankfurt/Main	65	91	137	289	415
Düsseldorf	27	69	95	214	359
Nuremberg	54	83	100	261	333
Hanover	28	88	123	236	302
Essen	9	52	57	119	295
Chemnitz	34	68	95	207	288
Duisburg	9	31	41	93	229
Dortmund	11	44	67	143	214
Kiel	16	32	44	108	212
Mannheim	24	40	53	141	194

Sources: Sandweg, 25; Reulecke, 203.

Table 38
Distribution of 10,000 Residents According to Religious Denomination in 1871 and 1910

State	1/12/1871					1/12/1910			
	Evang.	Cathol.	Other Christ.	Jews	Other/ Without	Evang.	Cathol.	Other Christ.	Jews
Prussia	6,497	3,349	22	132	0.3	6,182	3,631	47	104
Prov. East Prussia	8,609	1,278	34	79	0.1	8,434	1,409	84	3
Prov. West Prussia	4,819	4,880	98	203	0.3	4,632	5,182	99	82
City of Berlin	8,904	626	31	436	3	8,155	1,173	53	434
Prov. Brandenburg	9,760	170	14	56	0.1	8,984	734	50	150
Prov. Pomerania	9,761	118	30	91	0.0	9,536	328	70	52
Prov. Posen	3,228	6,374	7	391	0.1	3,079	6,773	20	126
Prov. Silesia	4,749	5,115	10	126	0.3	4,208	5,669	25	86
Prov. Saxony	9,351	603	18	28	0.1	9,161	753	23	25
Prov. Schleswig-Hol.	9,894	60	10	36	0.1	9,556	330	61	21
Prov. Hanover	8,727	1,191	17	65	0.1	8,513	1,372	43	63
Prov. Westphalia	4,543	5,347	13	97	0.1	4,722	5,143	58	51
Prov. Hesse-Nassau	7,056	2,655	28	259	2	6,839	2,824	56	233
Prov. Rhineland	2,534	7,343	16	107	0.1	2,946	6,903	41	80
Hohenzollern	269	9,618	5	108	—	503	9,437	2	57
Bavaria	2,761	7,123	11	104	1	2,821	7,061	20	80
Saxony	9,755	209	19	13	3	9,405	491	53	37
Württemberg	6,867	3,044	21	67	0.2	6,856	3,036	53	49
Baden	3,359	6,449	16	176	0.2	3,856	5,932	62	121
Hesse	6,852	2,803	46	297	2	6,615	3,101	52	188
Mecklenburg-Schwerin	9,921	24	2	53	0.4	9,618	320	20	22
Hamburg	9,044	229	93	407	227	9,163	503	42	199
Alsace-Lorraine	1,744	7,973	14	264	5	2,178	7,629	21	165
Total Reich	6,231	3,621	20	125	5	6,159	3,669	46	95

Sources: Hohorst, 54ff.

Table 39
Jewish Population in Different-Sized Communities in Prussia, 1885–1910 (%)

Number of Inhabitants	1885	1900	1910
under 20,000	53.7	44.8	28.4
20,000 – 50,000	7.7	9.2	8.2
50,000 – 100,000	5.9	5.8	4.0
over 100,000	32.7	49.2	59.5

Source: Aubin, 607.

TABLE 40
FOREIGNERS LIVING IN GERMANY, 1871-1910

Year	*No. (000s)*	*‰of Population*	*% of These from Eastern Europe*
1871	206.8	5.0	43.6
1880	276.1	6.1	48.2
1890	433.3	8.8	50.5
1900	778.7	13.8	56.2
1910	1,259.9	19.4	63.9

Source: Marschalk, 175.

TABLE 41
GAINS AND LOSSES THROUGH INTERNAL MIGRATION BY REGION, 1907 (000S)

Region	*Residents (total)*	*Natives/Staying*	*Natives/Left*	*Newcomers*	*Gains/Losses*
Eastern Germany	12,066.2	11,708.1	2,326.7	358.1	-1,968.6
Berlin, Brandenburg	5,585.2	3,936.1	445.5	1,649.2	+1,203.7
Northwest Germany	6,881.9	6,106.8	495.7	775.1	+279.4
Central Germany	9,719.7	9,001.9	899.4	717.8	173.6
Hesse	3,371.1	2,954.9	348.1	416.2	+68.1
Western Germany	10,171.1	9,080.6	449.4	1,090.5	+64.1
Southern Germany	12,580.5	12,200.0	431.4	380.5	-50.9

Source: de Buhr, 59.

Table 42
Regional Origins of Bochum Workers by Occupation, 1907 (%)

Occupation	*Natives*	*All Migrants*	*Long-Distance Migrants*	*Rhineland/ Westphalia/ Waldeck*	*North/East Germany*	*Others*
Chemicals	10.1	89.9	59.6	24.7	36.9	21.3
Mining/iron prod.	16.2	83.8	46.8	50.1	24.0	9.7
Construction	17.7	82.3	47.0	43.3	15.3	23.7
Food	27.0	73.0	22.7	52.4	5.2	15.4
Textiles	27.1	72.9	28.2	74.1	4.7	21.1
Machines/instr.	27.8	72.2	35.9	40.2	15.1	16.9
Printing	30.1	69.9	36.2	36.1	9.6	24.2
Woodworking	30.4	69.6	34.9	42.0	11.5	16.1
Leather	31.6	68.4	25.6	44.7	9.8	13.9
Paper	33.3	66.7	15.0	54.0	4.6	8.1
Total Industry	21.6	77.4	38.2	44.5	18.5	15.5

Source: Crew, 80.

Table 43
Occupational Mobility Among Male Workers in Bochum, 1880–1901 (%)

	1880–90		*1880–1901*	
	UN/SEMI-SKILLED	SKILLED	UN/SEMI-SKILLED	SKILLED
No mobility	87.1	78.6	78.8	60.9
Down to unskilled	—	11.3	—	15.5
Up to skilled	6.9	—	9.3	—
Up to non-manual	6.0	10.1	11.9	23.6

Source: Crew, 90.

Table 44
Number of Full-Time Primary School Teachers in Germany, 1901–1911

Year		*Male Teachers*		*Female Teachers*	
	TOTAL	TOTAL	OF WHOM CATHOLIC	TOTAL	OF WHOM CATHOLIC
1901	146,540	124,027	—	22,513	—
1906	166,597	137,213	—	29,384	—
1911	187,485	148,217	45,965	39,268	20,239

Source: Bölling, 27.

TABLE 45
SOCIAL ORIGINS OF TECHNICAL EMPLOYEES (A) AND PRIMARY SCHOOL TEACHERS (B) IN BERLIN, PRUSSIA AND BADEN, 1906/7 (%)

	A	B	
Class	*Berlin (1907)*	*Prussia (1906)*	*Baden (1906/7)*
Upper/upper middle class	11	1	3
Middle class	63	87	78
Lower class	17	6	18

Source: Jarausch, Quantifizierung, 294.

TABLE 46
SOCIAL ORIGINS OF HIGH SCHOOL TEACHERS, PHYSICIANS AND ENGINEERS IN PRUSSIA AND WÜRTTEMBERG, 1876–1900 (%)

Class	*Teachers*[a]		*Physicians*[b]		*Engineers*[c]
	PRUSSIA (1887–1900)	WÜRTTEMBERG (1887–1900)	PRUSSIA (1876–1900)	WÜRTTEMBERG (1876–1900)	
Upper/upper middle class[d]	37	30	72	34	23
Middle class[e]	41	66	22	61	64
Lower class[f]	7	1	1	0	5

[a]Based on students of philology
[b]Based on students of medicine
[c]With academic training
[d]Including officers, landowners, higher civil servants, professionals, clerics
[e]Including artisans, white-collar employees, farmers
[f]Including lower civil service, domestics, workers

Source: Jarausch, Quantifizierung, 290.

TABLE 47
SOCIAL ORIGINS OF HIGHER CIVIL SERVANTS IN WESTPHALIA AND BAVARIA, 1851-1914 (%)

Region		*Upper/ Upper Middle Class*	*Middle Class*	*Lower Class*
Westphalia	(1851–1875)	89	10	
	(1876–1900)	90	10	
	(1901–1914)	92	5	
Bavaria	(1851–1875)	54	42	3
	(1876-1900)	60	35	2
	(1901-1914)	56	25	

Source: Jarausch, Quantifizierung, 287.

TABLE 48
NUMBERS OF DIPLOMATS OF NOBLE/NON-NOBLE BACKGROUND RECRUITED 1862–1890 (A) AND 1890–1914 (B)

Background	*A*	*B*
Noble	110	183
Non-noble	20	101

Source: Jarausch, Quantifizierung, 220.

TABLE 49
ILLITERACY RATES AMONG MILITARY SERVICE RECRUITS (%)

Region/State	*1875–76*	*1890–91*	*1894–5*
Germany	2.37	0.54	0.22
Prussia	3.19	0.82	0.32
West Prussia	11.01	3.86	1.22
Posen	13.91	2.58	0.98
Rhineland	0.74	0.09	0.05
Bavaria	1.79	0.03	0.03
Saxony	0.23	0.07	0.07
Baden	0.22	0.03	0.03
France	ca. 20.0[a]	—	—
Russia	—	ca. 70.0[b]	ca. 60.0[c]
England and Wales	ca. 10.0[d]	—	—

[a]For 1873
[b]For 1888
[c]For 1896
[d]For bridegrooms in 1866

Sources: Hohorst, 167; Grütter, 28.

TABLE 50
PATTERNS OF PUBLIC EDUCATION IN PRUSSIA, 1864–1911

	Primary Schools			*Middle Schools*			*High Schools*		
	1864	1886	1911	1864	1886	1911	1864	1886	1911
No. of pupils (000s)	2,825	4,838	6,572	91	135	181	79	152	260
Pupils per teacher	92	75	56	41	34	30	21	17	21
Pupils per 100 pop.	15	17	16	0.47	0.47	0.41	0.41	0.54	0.65

Source: Hohorst, 157ff.

TABLE 51
SOCIAL ORIGINS OF HIGH SCHOOL GRADUATES IN BERLIN, 1882–1911 (%)

Father	*1882–86*				*1907–11*			
	A[a]	B[b]	C[c]	D[d]	A[a]	B[b]	C[c]	D[d]
University graduate or economic upper class	43.1	19.5	28.5	38.3	42.0	24.2	16.7	35.6
New middle class	18.9	15.9	13.3	18.2	25.5	23.7	41.8	26.6
Old middle class	32.7	38.6	51.1	34.3	27.8	43.6	30.9	31.8
Lower class	5.3	26.0	6.7	9.1	4.7	8.4	10.6	6.1

[a]Gymnasium
[b]Realgymnasium
[c]Oberrealschule
[d]Total

Source: Aubin, 674.

TABLE 52
STUDENTS IN HIGHER EDUCATION, 1869–1912

Year	*Total*	*University*	*Technical University*	*Others*[a]	*Ratio*[b]
1869	17,954	—	—	—	8.83
1880	26,254	—	—	—	11.73
1891	33,992	27,398	4,209	2,385	13.87
1902	46,520[c]	35,857	13,151	3,530	16.78
1912	71,710	56,483	11,349	3,878	21.77

[a]Academies of Mining, Forestry, Agriculture and Veterinary Medicine
[b]Students per 10,000 male population
[c]For 1899

Source: Hohorst, 161.

Table 53
Structure of Student Body at Bonn and Marburg Universities (%)

	Bonn (1840s, 1865–1914)	*Marburg (1873–1914)*
Studies		
Protestant theology	6.2	14.0
Catholic theology	9.3	—
Law	33.5	19.9
Medicine	13.0	26.2
Philosophy	24.0	29.4
Other philosophy	8.7	10.0
Cameralia	1.0	0.4
Religion		
Protestant	43.3	82.1
Catholic	52.5	15.9
Jewish	3.5	2.3
Social Class		
High official	19.2	26.6
Professional	8.3	9.3
Bourgeois	24.4	15.2
Old middle class	31.4	24.6
New middle class	15.9	24.1
Lower class	0.7	0.2
Sex		
Female	1.7	2.4

Source: Jarausch, Students, 315.

TABLE 54
STRUCTURE OF FEMALE STUDENT BODY IN PRUSSIA, 1896/97

	No. of Students		No. of Students
1. Age		5. Family Status	
Under 20	14	Single	183
20 – 30	93	Married	23
30+	87	Widowed	3
2. Citizenship		Divorced	1
German	132	6. Purpose of Study	
West European	8	General Cultivation	160
Russian	14	Oberlehrerin Exam	40
American	53	Ph.D.	5
3. Religion		Medical Exam	5
Protestant	158	Legal teacher Exam	1
Catholic	11	7. Subject of Study	
Jewish	29	Science/Mathematics	20
Other	3	History/Philosophy	28
4. Family Status		Modern Languages	65
Single	183	Ancient Languages	5
Married	23	Art History/Literature	76
Widowed	3	Economics	6
Divorced	1	Theology	3
		Medicine	9
		Law	1

Source: Jarausch, Students, 111.

TABLE 55
AGE STRUCTURE OF GERMAN SOCIETY, 1900 AND 1910 (PER THOUSAND)

Age	*1900*	*1910*
0 – 5	129	120
5 – 10	114	114
10 – 15	104	107
15 – 20	95	97
20 – 25	91	86
25 – 30	80	77
30 – 40	132	139
40 – 50	101	105
50 – 60	79	76
60+	79	79

Source: Reulecke, 209.

Table 56
Age Structure of Urban Population According to Size of Town, 1890 per 1,000 Inhabitants

Age	*Population*		
	5,000–20,000	20,000–100,000	100,000 +
Under 15	345	321	291
15–40	417	450	474
40–60	170	169	177
60+	68	60	57

Source: Reulecke, 208.

Table 57
Fertility Rates for Different Age Groups, 1881-1910 (per thousand)

Age	*1881–1890*	*1891–1900*	*1901–1910*
15–19	19.2	21.1	23.3
20–24	179.6	184.9	176.0
25–29	278.0	275.9	260.8
30–34	237.4	231.0	198.5
35–39	181.5	165.9	138.1
40–44	79.8	69.4	59.0
45–49	10.2	8.2	6.4

Source: Marschalck, 157.

Table 58

Average Life Expectancy in Relation to Age in Germany, 1871–1910

Age	*1871–80*		*1901–10*	
	Male	Female	Male	Female
0	35.6	38.5	44.8	48.3
1	46.5	48.1	55.1	57.2
15	42.4	44.2	46.7	49.0
30	31.4	33.1	34.6	36.9
45	21.2	22.8	22.9	25.3
65	9.6	10.0	10.4	11.1

Source: Marschalck, 166.

TABLE 59
MORTALITY RATES IN THE REICH, 1871–1910; NUMBER OF 1,000 LIVE BIRTHS REACHING

Year	Age 1		Age 15		Age 30		Age 45		Age 65	
	MALE	FEMALE	MALE	FEMALE	MALE	FEMALE	MALE	FEMALE	MALE	FEMALE
1871–80	747	783	609	639	545	576	453	485	248	297
1881–90	758	793	624	653	567	596	477	511	269	326
1891–1900	766	801	665	696	613	644	530	568	313	378
1901–10	798	830	720	749	671	698	594	627	361	435

Source: Marschalck, 165.

TABLE 60
AVERAGE INFANT MORTALITY IN PRUSSIA–TOWNS AND COUNTRYSIDE, 1876–1914 (PER THOUSAND)

Year	Legitimate		Illegitimate	
	TOWN	COUNTRY	TOWN	COUNTRY
1876–80	211	183	403	312
188185	211	186	398	319
1886–90	210	187	395	332
1891–95	203	187	385	336
1896–1900	195	185	374	336
1903	183	184	342	332
1906	168	167	303	303
1909	146	160	269	288
1912	130	141	234	262
1914	147	159	261	287

Source: Reulecke, 217.

TABLE 61
INFANT MORTALITY RATES IN DIFFERENT OCCUPATIONAL GROUPS[A] IN PRUSSIA, 1877-1913 (%)

Year	Self-Employed	Public Officials	White Collar	Skilled Workers	Unskilled Workers	Domestics, Household Servants	Total Population
1887–9	18.2	17.5	18.6	18.9	20.6	29.6	20.1
1880–2	18.4	18.0	18.1	19.8	21.6	29.9	20.8
1883–5	18.7	17.8	18.3	20.2	22.3	30.5	21.2
1886–8	18.3	17.0	18.0	19.7	21.8	21.5	20.6
1889–91	18.3	16.3	17.3	19.6	22.2	29.9	20.6
1892–3	18.3	16.2	17.4	19.9	22.8	30.0	20.9
1894–5	17.6	15.6	17.1	19.3	22.6	29.7	20.4
1896–7	17.0	14.9	16.1	18.7	22.5	28.5	19.8
1898–9	17.1	14.7	16.1	19.0	22.2	28.6	19.9
1900–1	17.6	15.3	16.6	19.4	23.7	31.0	20.6
1902–3	16.0	12.5	13.6	17.1	20.2	26.6	18.3
1904–5	16.3	12.9	13.7	18.1	21.7	28.2	19.1
1906–7	14.6	11.0	12.0	16.2	19.7	25.5	17.3
1908–9	14.3	10.0	10.9	15.4	19.4	25.2	16.8
1910–11	14.5	9.9	11.6	15.9	20.0	25.8	17.2
1912–13	12.3	8.3	9.3	13.1	17.4	22.5	14.8

[a]Up to 1901 armed forces excluded. From 1902 groups composed as follows (symbols taken from *Preußische Statistik*): self–employed = Aa, Ab, Ba, Ca (up to 1901 including liberal professions); public officials = Ea, Eb, Ec (after 1901 including liberal professions and armed forces); white–collar = Bb, Cb, skilled workers = Bc, Cc, Cd; unskilled workers = Ad, Bd, D2; domestics and household servants = Ac, D1. Average percentages for two– and three–year periods, including illegitimate children, but excluding stillbirths. Groups determined by father's occupation for legitimate children and by mother's occupation for illegitimate children.

Source: Spree, 194.

Table 62
Mortality Rates for Different Age Groups and Regions of Prussia, 1876–1913 (per 10,000 in each age group)

Year	Age Group	A[a]	B	C	D	E	F	G	H
1876	0–1	2,055	2,181	2,207	1,512	1,680	2,950	1,883	2,015
	1–15	168	190	185	207	185	257	244	240
	15–30	66	58	64	81	80	68	88	75
	30–60	150	164	172	167	164	155	197	178
	60–70	481	520	512	535	494	463	565	490
	All Groups	256	269	275	254	252	301	290	285
1901	0–1	1,997	2,185	2,496	1,590	1,678	2,243	1,907	1,631
	1–15	104	127	151	127	113	104	129	178
	15–30	50	49	54	56	49	46	48	48
	30–60	117	115	111	125	115	122	136	127
	60–70	411	376	370	466	434	410	452	516
	All Groups	207	227	252	199	190	180	204	213
1913	0–1	1,420	1,853	1,951	1,255	1,216	—	—	—
	1–15	58	60	60	67	54	—	—	—
	15–30	41	42	39	47	41	—	—	—
	30–60	94	103	95	95	87	—	—	—
	60–70	380	353	347	420	398	—	—	—
	All Groups	149	177	182	137	125	140	—	—

[a]A= Prussia; B = District of Königsberg; C = District of Gumbinnen; D = District of Arnsberg/Westphalia; E = District of Düsseldorf; F = Berlin; G = Dortmund; H = Essen

Sources: Spree, 191; Conze, 276.

Table 63
Breast-feeding and Mortality of Legitimate Infants in Different Income Groups in the Düsseldorf District, 1905–1911 (%)

Region (Date)	*Breast-Fed Children* Father's Income (in marks)		*Children not Breast-Fed* Father's Income (in marks)	
	≤1500	>1500	≤1500	>1500
Town				
Barmen (1905)	7.3	6.4	31.6	12.5
Mönchengladbach (1909)	9.6	7.3	23.4	13.5
Neuß (1908)	12.2	5.8	43.2	20.2
Rheydt (1909)	7.1	5.7	20.5	11.3
Rural districts				
Geldern (1910)	6.3	3.3	16.7	5.7
Gladbach (1909)	9.5	8.5	29.7	19.2
Grevenbroich (1911)	9.9	8.7	42.1	23.6
Moers (1910)	7.4	4.8	19.7	18.7
Neuß (excl. town, 1908)	9.2	4.9	28.2	19.6
Average	8.7	6.2	28.3	16.0

Source: Spree, 198.

Table 64
Average Number of Children Per Marriage by Economic Sector and Occupation, 1905–1914

Occupational Group	*Year of Marriage*		
	PRE-1905	1905–9	1910–14
Agricultural			
Self-employed	5.5	4.6	4.1
Workers	6.1	5.2	4.7
Agric. pop. in total	5.5	4.7	4.1
Non-agricultural			
Self-employed	4.0	3.1	2.6
Public officials and professional soldiers	3.5	2.9	2.5
Non-manual workers	3.4	2.7	2.3
Manual workers	4.7	3.8	3.3
Non-agric. pop. in total	4.5	3.4	2.9
Total average	4.7	3.6	3.1

Source: Spree, 204.

Table 65
Size of Heatable Apartments by Selected Occupational Groups in Munich, 1895 (%)

Groups	*1 Room*			*2 Rooms*	*3 Rooms*	*4 Rooms+*
	WITHOUT KITCHEN	WITH KITCHEN OR CHAMBER	WITH KITCHEN AND CHAMBER			
No occupation (male)	3.0	6.5	2.5	16.5	26.5	45.0
Self-employed in industry/trade	7.0	13.5	4.5	28.5	23.5	23.0
White-collar employees	22.0	48.5	7.0	69.0	39.0	13.5
Wage laborers	27.0	36.0	3.5	25.5	6.0	1.5

Source: Kaelble, 130.

Table 66
Percentage of Population in Prussian Administrative Districts Resident in Districts with Central Water Supply, 1900

District	Percentage	District	Percentage
Königsberg	20	Schleswig	29
Gumbinnen	9	Hanover	48
Danzig	32	Lüneburg	15
Berlin	97	Osnabrück	16
Potsdam	42	Münster	11
Frankfurt/Oder	18	Arnsberg	83
Stettin	26	Wiesbaden	52
Posen	11	Cologne	60
Breslau	38	Düsseldorf	70
Magdeburg	31	Aachen	39
Erfurt	44	Sigmaringen	22

Source: Spree, 219.

Table 67
Allocation of Resources in Households of 522 Working-Class Families and of 218 Families of Middle-Level Civil Servants and Teachers, 1909

Items	Working-Class Families		Civil Servants' and Teachers' Families	
	MARKS	%	MARKS	%
Necessities (total)	1,478.27	80.6	2,295.32	72.0
Food	883.09	48.1	1,101.50	34.6
Clothing	204.67	11.2	460.41	14.4
Housing/utilities	390.51	21.3	733.41	23.0
Other expenditures (total)	356.79	19.5	892.51	28.0
Alcohol	71.79	3.9	66.89	2.1
Insurance	55.52	3.0	129.05	4.0
Newspapers, books, organizations	51.47	2.8	66.88	2.1
Transportation	25.74	1.4	36.56	1.1
Amusement	21.23	1.2	76.12	2.4
State, municipality, church	19.21	1.1	63.06	2.0
Savings	17.57	1.0	40.58	1.3
Health care	15.26	0.8	106.27	3.3
Education (including materials/fees)	11.63	0.6	75.23	2.4
Miscellaneous	67.19	3.7	231.87	7.3
Yearly total	1,835.06		3,187.83	

Source: Conze, 79.

Table 68
Budgeting for Rent by Different Income Groups in Hamburg, 1874–1901 (%)

Annual Income (in marks)	*1868*	*1874*	*1882*	*1891*	*1901*
900–1,200	19.81	20.87	21.86	24.12	24.67
1,200–1,800	19.89	21.13	18.94	22.22	23.19
1,800–2,400	20.27	20.88	19.50	22.09	21.61
2,400–3,000	19.45	19.21	18.78	20.81	20.53
3,000–3,600	19.59	19.03	17.90	19.15	19.25
3,600–4,200	19.28	18.17	18.33	18.71	18.31
4,200–4,800	18.89	17.38	17.22	17.88	17.36
4,800–6,000	18.55	17.35	18.33	17.71	16.69
6,000–12,000	15.99	15.48	16.72	15.12	14.30
12,000–30,000	11.51	10.75	12.23	10.38	9.61
30,000–60,000	6.68	7.44	8.06	6.21	5.99
60,000 +	3.72	3.78	3.87	3.26	3.04

Source: Kaelble, 131.

Table 69
Number of Hospital Patients and Mortality in Prussian Administrative Districts, 1880 and 1913

Administrative District	*Number of Hospital Patients[a] per 10,000 Inhabitants*		% INCREASE	*Number of Deaths[b] per 10,000 Inhabitants*		% DECREASE
	1880	1913	1880–1913	1880	1913	1880–1913
Königsberg	77	367	377	269	177	34
Gumbinnen	41	146	256	277	182	34
Allenstein	—	146	—	—	169	—
Danzig	138	302	119	310	184	41
Marienwerder	66	144	118	278	169	39
Berlin (city)	386	641	66	292	140	52
Potsdam	62	331	434	262	147	44
Frankfurt/Oder	45	197	338	228	162	29
Stettin	91	248	173	238	166	30
Köslin	37	148	300	213	154	28
Stralsund	139	468	237	239	177	26
Posen	59	180	205	252	162	36
Bromberg	32	156	388	261	166	36
Breslau	176	470	167	289	191	34
Liegnitz	61	267	338	282	176	38
Oppeln	158	208	32	272	191	30
Magdeburg	92	313	240	261	152	42
Merseburg	65	259	298	256	149	42

(Cont.)

TABLE 69 (*CONT.*)
NUMBER OF HOSPITAL PATIENTS AND MORTALITY IN PRUSSIAN ADMINISTRATIVE DISTRICTS, 1880 AND 1913

Administrative District	*Number of Hospital Patients*[a] *per 10,000 Inhabitants*		% INCREASE	*Number of Deaths*[b] *per 10,000 Inhabitants*		% DECREASE
	1880	1913	1880–1913	1880	1913	1880–1913
Erfurt	60	256	327	236	143	39
Schleswig	97	313	223	210	126	40
Hanover	138	372	170	231	125	46
Hildesheim	52	457	779	227	137	40
Lüneberg	70	219	213	215	128	40
Stade	35	165	371	214	131	39
Osnabrück	134	383	186	218	138	44
Aurich	22	272	1,136	184	123	33
Münster	153	562	267	254	157	38
Minden	68	343	404	236	125	47
Arnsberg	86	557	548	257	137	47
Kassel	100	277	177	229	128	44
Wiesbaden	77	496	54	213	126	41
Koblenz	70	373	433	257	145	44
Düsseldorf	132	529	301	252	125	50
Cologne	168	701	317	271	145	46
Trier	79	373	372	225	138	39
Aachen	88	374	325	259	154	41
Sigmaringen	55	152	176	291	165	43
Prussia	104	368	254	254	149	41

[a]Patients treated in general hospitals. Since figures are compared with average mortality rates, specialist clinics can be safely disregarded.

[b]Total number of deaths (not only those in hospitals) excluding stillbirths.

Source: Spree, 217.

TABLE 70
REGIONAL DISTRIBUTION OF PHYSICIANS AND MEMBERS OF STATUTORY SICKNESS AND INSURANCE FUNDS IN GERMANY, 1887–1909

Region (Prussian provinces and selected German states)	Doctors 1887	Members of Sickness Insurance Funds (000s) 1885	Doctors 1909	Members of Sickness Insurance Funds (000s) 1907
East Prussia	396	50	687	171
West Prussia	301	48	518	150
Berlin	1,104	252	1,181	805
Brandenburg (excl. Berlin)	658	206	2,571	645
Pomerania	399	73	644	206
Posen	352	46	627	157
Silesia	1,108	322	1,828	758
Saxony	777	264	1,323	700
Schleswig-Holstein	431	110	787	363
Hanover	812	135	1,316	470
Westphalia	677	191	1,429	571
Hesse-Nassau	735	118	1,575	427
Rhineland	1,509	442	3,087	1,332
Hohenzollern	25	5	26	11
Kingdom of Prussia	9,284	2,263	18,299	6,765
Kingdom of Bavaria	1,916	371	3,451	1,060
Kingdom of Saxony	1,110	556	2,287	1,435
Württemberg	576	152	1,050	413
Baden	618	131	1,157	522
Hesse	388	102	720	285
Mecklenburg-Schwerin	193	26	292	78
Saxony-Weimar	120	21	230	94
Oldenburg	114	15	162	55
Brunswick	149	51	264	161
Bremen	84	18	194	76
Hamburg	302	257	770	356

Source: Spree, 214.

TABLE 71
RECIPIENTS OF PERMANENT AND TEMPORARY SUPPORT IN BOCHUM, 1871-1906 (PER 1,000 INHABITANTS)

Year	Permanent	Temporary
1871	33.1	—
1875	16.5	4.4
1880	35.0	20.9
1885	30.2	21.2
1890	17.1	—
1895	28.2	11.8
1900	22.1	8.7
1903	21.8	24.9
1906	15.4	21.4

Source: Crew, 58.

TABLE 72
ORDINARY REICH REVENUE, 1901–1914 (MILL. MARKS)

Source	*1901*	*1906*	*1909*	*1913*	*1914*
Death duties	—	4.2	38.5	46.4	43.6
Capital gains	—	—	—	15.3	2.8
Property tax	—	—	—	—	—
Stamp duties	84.0	138.6	171.4	258.6	183.1
Tariffs	478.9	557.7	660.2	679.3	560.8
Taxes on consumption[a]	333.2	378.4	485.7	659.7	775.8
Matricular contribution	15.2	24.2	48.5	51.9	51.9
Wehrbeitrag (1913)	—	—	—	—	637.4
Post office/railways	42.2	85.4	24.1	5.5	—
Reich Bank	12.8	29.2	16.4	34.7	—
Special levies	—	—	—	—	43.6[b]
Other	94.4[c]	93.3[c]	196.6[c]	229.9[c]	118.3
Loans	332.8	258.4	639.0	109.3	—

[a]Including tobacco, beer, sugar, spirits.

[b]Including Reich Bank, *Darlehenskasse* levy, export levy, transport levy, post office levy.

[c]Including Reich Stationery Office, administrative fees, fund income.

Source: Witt, 378f.

TABLE 73
GROWTH OF REICH EXPENDITURE, 1872–1913 (MILL. MARKS)

Year[a]	*Armaments*[b]		*Administration*[c]		*Social Insurance Subsidy*		*Totals*
	MILL.	%	MILL.	%	MILL.	%	
1872–75	822.1	98.3	14.0	1.7	—	—	836.1
1876–80	583.0	94.4	34.2	5.6	—	—	617.2
1881–85	460.8	95.0	24.0	5.0	—	—	484.8
1886–90	818.1	95.3	32.8	3.8	7.5	0.9	858.4
1891–95	882.9	93.9	40.1	4.3	17.3	1.8	940.3
1896–00	841.1	90.8	62.4	6.7	22.8	2.5	926.3
1901	1,162.9	90.4	94.8	7.4	28.1	2.4	1,286.6
1902	1,122.8	88.7	112.2	8.8	30.4	2.5	1,265.9
1903[d]	1,105.7	85.6	109.1	8.4	33.7	2.6	1,292.1[d]
1904	1,152.2	87.9	117.6	9.0	40.6	3.1	1,310.4
1905	1,233.5	88.4	116.9	8.4	42.0	3.2	1,394.6
1906	1,358.2	88.4	131.6	8.5	45.8	3.1	1,535.6
1907	1,631.1	88.4	121.7	6.6	90.7	5.0	1,843.5
1908	1,463.7	89.2	122.1	7.5	54.1	3.3	1,639.9

(Cont.)

Table 73 (cont.)
Growth of Reich Expenditure, 1872–1913 (mill. marks)

Year[a]	Armaments[b]		Administration[c]		Social Insurance Subsidy		Totals
	Mill.	%	Mill.	%	Mill.	%	
1909	1,593.6	89.2	134.6	7.6	58.2	3.2	1,786.7
1910	1,771.3	89.5	146.8	7.4	61.9	3.1	1,980.0
1911	1,707.5	88.6	152.4	7.9	66.8	3.5	1,926.7
1912	1,781.3	89.4	146.2	7.3	65.2	3.3	1,992.9
1913	2,406.4	90.1	176.0	6.6	87.9	3.3	2,670.3

[a]1872–1900: Five-year averages.

[b]Including extraordinary expenditure, pensions, invalids welfare, expeditions.

[c]Civilian departments, including debt service for civilian loans.

[d]Including 42.6 million marks not specifically accounted for.

Source: Witt, 380.

Table 74
Share of Public Utilities in Total Debt of Selected Cities, 1908

City	Total debt (in marks)	Expenditure on public utilities (in marks)	%
Altona	36,065.1	19,956.9	52.84
Berlin	397,018.0	160,786.0	40.50
Dortmund	80,445.7	43,759.6	54.40
Düsseldorf	114,343.6	82,686.0	78.32
Frankfurt	222,947.7	69,857.7	31.34

Source: Reulecke, 214.

TABLE 75
WORKERS' PENSION INSURANCE, 1891–1914

Year	Numbers of Insured (000s)[a]	Number of Pensions (000s)[b]		Revenue		Expenditure (millions)		Average Pension in RM per annum	
		Old Age	Disablement	Total (millions)	% of Imp. Govt. Supplement	Total	Of Which Pensions	Old Age	Disablement
1891	11,490	—	—	101	5.9	19	15	123.35	113.38
1895	12,145	—	—	133	12.8	49	41	132.80	123.92
1900	13,015	215	450	187	16.6	104	81	145.54	142.04
1905	13,948	156	858	250	18.8	173	137	159.10	159.45
1910	15,660	114	1,008	307	17.3	219	164	164.31	176.93
1914	16,552	98	1,129	405	15.3	258	200	167.99	200.81

[a]The number of insured is calculated in each case on the total amount of annual weekly contributions divided by the estimated number of weekly contributions, paid annually on a per capita basis. These estimates vary between fifty-two and forty weekly contributions.

[b]For the years 1891 and 1895 figures are available only for pension awards: in 1891, 132,926 new old-age pensions (for people aged 70 or over before the law came into effect) and 31 disablement pensions were awarded; for 1895, the figures were 30,144 and 55,983 respectively. In 1897 the total number of pensions amounted to 226,275 old-age pensions and 237,416 disablement pensions.

Source: Witt, 380.

TABLE 76
ACCIDENT INSURANCE, 1886–1914

Year	No. of Insured (000s)[a]	No. of Persons Registered Injured or Sick[b]		No. of Persons Receiving Pensions or Sickness Benefits (000s)	Expenditure	
		FIGURES (000S)	% OF INSURED		TOTAL (MILL.)	BENEFIT PER RECIPIENT IN RM P.A..
1886	3,822	100	2.68	11	10	178
1890	13,680	200	1.46	100	39	202
1895	18,389	310	1.68	318	68	157
1900	18,893	454	2.40	595	101	145
1905	20,243	609	3.00	893	176	151
1910	27,554	673	2.44	1,018	228	160
1914	27,965	705	2.52	1,000	223	178

[a]Annual averages. It was possible for the same persons to be provided with insurance coverage by several separate agencies administering insurance. According to figures in the relevant volumes of the *Amtliche Nachrichten des Reichsversicherungsamts*, the number of persons insured by more than one agency amounted to approximately 1.5 million in 1895, 1.5 million in 1900 and 1905, 3.4 million in 1910, and 3.3 million in 1914.

[b]Persons registered as injured and sick with accident or sickness insurance.

Source: Ritter, 189.

Table 77
Sickness Insurance, 1885–1914

Year	Members[a]			Contributions		Benefits			
	Figures (000s)[b]	% of Females	Members as % Population	Figures (milions)	Per Member in RM per Year	Figures (millions)	Cash Benefits as %	Benefits in Kind as %	Per Member in RM per Year
1885	4,294	18.1	9.2	56	13.1	47	56.8	43.2	11.05
1890	6,580	19.9	13.3	91	13.4	84	52.6	47.4	12.82
1895	7,256	22.4	14.4	117	15.6	105	48.5	51.5	14.03
1900	9,521	23.1	16.9	166	17.4	158	49.3	50.7	16.74
1905	11,184	25.3	19.6	250	22.4	232	49.0	51.0	21.05
1910	13,069	27.9	20.3	358	27.4	320	46.8	53.2	24.84
1914	15,610	36.9	23.0	524	33.6	445	46.4	53.6	28.49

[a]Insured members' dependents who were covered against sickness have to be taken into account in two respects. In the case of cash benefits, it has been calculated that the payments made to each member of a sickness fund in 1913 also partly protected his, on average, two to three dependants against the economic effects of the breadwinner's ill-health. This meant that financial hardship caused by ill-health was alleviated for around 62.5 percent of the Reich's population. Benefits in kind could be extended to member's dependents who were not themselves liable for contributions through appropriate terms and conditions laid down by the self-managed funds of the insured. This kind of insurance protection, which was made available at first by only a few funds, may well have benefited around 24 million citizens or 36 percent of the Reich's population by 1913.

[b]Annual averages.

Source: Ritter, 187.

Table 78
Growth of Cooperative Movement, 1865–1910

Year	No. of Cooperatives	No. of Members
1865	34	6,647
1870	111	45,761
1880	195	94,366
1890	263	215,420
1900	568	522,000
1910	1,333	1,310,000

Source: Sombart, 491.

Table 79
Reichstag Election Results, 1871–1912 (000s)

	1871			*1874*			*1877*			*1878*		
Eligible	7,656			8,523			8,943			9,124		
Turnout	3,888			5,190			5,401			5,761		
% voting	50.7			60.8			60.3			63.1		
	Votes	%	Seats	Votes	%	Seats	Votes	%	Seats	Votes	%	Seats
SPD	124	3.2	2	352	6.8	9	493	9.1	12	437	7.5	9
Center	742	18.6	63	1,446	27.8	91	1,341	24.8	93	1,328	23.1	94
Left Lib.	361	9.3	47	470	9.0	50	463	8.5	39	451	7.8	29
Nat. Lib/Lib.	1,453	37.2	155	1,597	30.7	158	1,605	29.7	141	1,487	28.5	109
Free Cons.	346	8.9	37	376	7.2	33	427	8.0	38	786	13.6	57
Conservat.	549	14.1	57	360	6.9	22	526	9.7	40	750	13.0	59
RWSp.[a]	—	—	—	—	—	—	—	—	—	—	—	—
Minorities[b]	255	6.6	21	462	10.5	34	519	9.6	34	505	8.7	40
Sp. P.[c]	76	2.0	—	46	0.9	—	28	0.5	—	17	0.3	—

	1881			*1884*			*1887*			*1890*			*1893*		
Eligible	9,090			9,383			9,769			10,145			10,628		
Turnout	5,097			5,663			7,540			7,228			7,674		
% voting	56.1			60.3			77.2			71.2			72.2		
	Votes	%	Seats	Votes	%	Seats	Votes	%	Seats	Votes	%	Seats	Votes	%	Seats
SPD	312	6.1	12	550	9.7	24	763	7.1	11	1,427	19.7	35	1,787	23.3	44
Center	1,183	23.2	100	1,282	22.6	99	1,516	22.1	98	1,342	18.6	106	1,469	19.0	96
Left Lib.	1,181	23.1	115	1,093	19.3	74	1,062	14.1	32	1,308	18.0	76	1,092	14.8	48
Nat. Lib.	747	14.6	47	997	17.6	51	1,678	22.3	99	1,178	16.3	42	997	13.0	53
Free Cons.	379	7.4	28	388	6.8	28	736	9.8	41	482	6.7	20	438	5.7	28
Conservat.	831	16.3	50	861	15.2	78	1,147	15.2	80	895	12.4	73	1,038	13.5	72
RWSp.[a]	—	—	—	—	—	—	12	0.2	1	48	0.7	5	264	3.4	16
Minorities[b]	449	8.8	35	479	8.5	43	579	7.6	33	475	6.6	38	461	6.0	35
Sp. P.[c]	15	0.3	—	13	0.2	—	48	0.6	2	75	1.0	2	129	1.7	5

[a]Right wing splinter groups, e.g., *Christlich-Soziale*

[b]Poles, Danes, Guelphs, Alsatians

[c]Other splinter parties

Source: Tormin, 283ff.

TABLE 79 (CONT.)
REICHSTAG ELECTION RESULTS, 1871–1912 (000S)

	1898		*1903*		*1907*		*1912*	
Eligible	11,441		12,531		13,352		14,442	
Turnout	7,752		9,495		11,262		12,207	
% voting	67.7		75.8		84.3		84.5	
	VOTES	SEATS	VOTES	SEATS	VOTES	SEATS	VOTES	SEATS
SPD	2,107	56	3,011	81	3,259	43	4,250	110
Centre	1,455	102	1,875	100	2,180	105	1,997	91
Left. Lib.	863	49	872	26	1,234	49	1,497	42
Nat. Lib.	971	46	1,317	51	1,631	54	1,663	45
Free Cons.	344	23	333	21	472	24	367	14
Conservat.	859	56	949	54	1,060	60	1,126	43
RWSp.[a]	284	13	245	11	249	16	52	3
Minorities[b]	471	34	559	32	651	29	706	33
Sp. P.[c]	397	18	334	11	528	17	550	16

[a]Right-wing splinter groups, e.g., *Christlich-Soziale*
[b]Poles, Danes, Guelphs, Alsatians
[c]Other splinter parties

Source: Tormin, 283ff.

TABLE 80
CONSERVATIVE AND SOCIAL DEMOCRATIC VOTING STRENGTH AND REICHSTAG REPRESENTATION, 1871–1912

Year	*Conservatives*		*SPD*	
	% OF VOTE	% OF SEATS	% OF VOTE	% OF SEATS
1871	14.1	15.0	3.2	0.5
1874	7.2	8.3	6.8	2.3
1877	9.7	10.0	9.1	3.0
1878	13.9	14.9	7.5	2.3
1881	16.3	12.6	6.1	3.0
1884	15.2	19.6	9.7	6.0
1887	15.2	20.1	10.1	2.8
1890	12.4	18.4	19.7	8.8
1893	13.5	18.1	23.3	11.1
1898	11.0	14.1	27.2	14.1
1903	11.0	13.6	31.7	20.4
1907	9.4	15.1	29.0	10.8
1912	9.2	10.8	34.8	27.7

Source: Guttsman, 80.

TABLE 81
TRADE UNION MEMBERSHIP, 1890–1914 (000S) AND SPD MEMBERSHIP, 1905–1914 (000S)

Year	*Free TUs*	*Christian*	*Hirsch-Duncker*	*Total*	*SPD*
1890	278	—	63[a]	357	—
1895	259	5	67	327	—
1900	680	77	92	849	—
1905	1,345	192	116	1,653	384[b]
1910	2,017	316	122	2,455	720
1913	2,549	343	107	3,024	983
1914	2,076	283	78	2,437	1,086

[a]Figure for 1891
[b]Figure for 1906

Sources: Groh, 724; Schönhoven, 101; Guttsman, 153.

TABLE 82
WOMEN IN TRADE UNIONS AND THE SPD, 1892–1913, IN TOTAL NUMBERS (A) AND % (B)

Year	*Trade Unions*		*SPD*	
	A	B	A	B
1892	4,355	1.8	—	—
1900	22,844	3.3	—	—
1906	118,908	7.1	6,460	1.7
1910	161,512	8.0	82,642	11.5
1913	223,676	8.8	141,115	14.4

Source: Frevert, 332.

Table 83
Membership of Major White-Collar Associations, 1875–1913 (000s)

Year	Commercial			Technical		
	58ers Association	Leipzig Association	German Commercial Employee Assoc. (DHV)	DWV[a]	DTV[b]	Butib[c]
1875	6,371	—	—	—	—	—
1880	10,471	—	—	—	—	—
1885	16,964	4,986	—	4,800	1,716	—
1890	30,067	21,000	—	18,240	2,561	—
1895	49,359	43,311	570	28,037	4,022	—
1900	60,960	55,966	40,205	39,192	9,650	—
1905	72,939	67,277	75,695	43,840	18,243	4,625
1910	102,633	92,301	120,289	54,065	29,499	17,738
1913	127,030	102,124	148,079	62,373	30,207	23,386

[a]Deutscher Wissenschaftler Verein

[b]Deutscher Techniker-Verband

[c]Bund der technisch-industriellen Beamten

Source: Hohorst, 138.

Table 84
Membership of Nationalist Associations, 1881–1914

Year	*Pan-German League*	*Navy League*	*Colonial Society*	*Eastern Marches Society*	*Germandom Abroad Society*	*Defense League*
1881	—	—	—	—	1,345	
1887	—	—	14,838	—	—	
1891	21,000	—	17,709	—	36,000	
1893	5,000	—	17,154	—	—	
1894	5,742	—	16,264	—	—	—
1895	7,715	—	16,474	20,000	26,524	—
1896	9,443	—	17,901	18,500	—	—
1897	12,974	—	21,252	9,400	—	—
1898	17,364	14,252	26,501	—	—	—
1899	20,488	93,991	31,601	—	—	—
1900	21,735	216,749	34,768	20,000	32,000	—
1901	21,924	238,767	33,541	—	—	—
1903	19,068	233,173	31,482	29,300	—	—
1904	19,111	249,241	31,985	—	34,774	—
1906	18,445	315,420	32,787	40,500	—	—
1910	—	290,964	39,025	53,000	45,272	—
1912	c. 17,000	320,174	41,163	—	—	33,000
1914	—	331,493	42,018	54,000	57,452	90,000

Source: Eley, 366.

Table 85
Characteristics of Local Leaders of Nationalist Associations and of German Peace Society after 1900

Category	*Pan-German League*		*Navy League*		*Colonial Society*		*Eastern Marches Society*		*Peace Society*	
	No.	%	No.	%	No.	%	No.	%	No.	%
Retired	36	6.3	24	10.6	109	15.8	38	23.3	2	0.1
Noble	23	3.7	41	16.4	120	16.0	22	11.9	10	2.4
Acad. training	369	68.7	101	61.2	398	67.7	122	74.4	144	45.0
Doctorate	202	32.3	49	19.6	199	26.5	56	30.3	56	13.5
Public administration	303	54.2	159	73.3	510	75.9	122	75.3	144	43.6

Source: Chickering, 314.

Table 86
Student Organizations, 1914

Type	*Universities*		*Other Institutions*		*Abroad*		*Total*	
	No.	%	No.	%	No.	%	No.	%
Duelling	288	31.9	127	49.2	4	—	419	35.0
Corporations	114	12.6	28	10.8	20	—	162	13.5
Religions	102	11.3	24	9.3	2	—	128	10.7
Scholarly	124	13.7	15	5.8	—	—	139	11.6
Political	53	5.9	11	4.3	—	—	64	5.3
Sport	75	8.3	12	4.6	1	—	88	7.4
Social	21	2.3	2	0.8	5	—	28	2.4
Reform	60	6.6	31	12.0	2	—	93	7.8
Women	40	4.4	3	1.2	—	—	43	3.6
Other	26	2.9	5	1.9	—	—	31	2.6
Totals	903	—	258	—	—	—	1,195	—

Source: Jarausch, Students, 303.

Appendix B

Abbreviations

AEG	Allgemeine Elektricitäts-Gesellschaft
BASF	Badische Anilin- und Sodafabriken
BDI	Bund der Industriellen
BGB	Bürgerliches Gesetzbuch
BRT	Bruttoregistertonnen
CDI	Centralverband der Deutschen Industrie
CV	Centralverband deutscher Staatsbürger jüdischen Glaubens
DMV	Deutscher Metallarbeiter-Verband
GNP	Gross National Product
HAPAG	Hamburg-Amerika Paketfahrt-Aktiengesellschaft
HKT	Society of the Eastern Marches
KWG	Kaiser-Wilhelm-Gesellschaft
NDP	Net Domestic Product
PTR	Physikalisch-Technische Reichsa
R&D	Research & Development
RM	Reichsmark
SPD	Sozialdemokratische Partei Deutschlands
TB	Tuberculosis
TH	Technische Hochschule

Bibliography

N.B.: This bibliography contains English-language works only and is organized in line with the basic chapter divisions of this book.

I. General Studies

W. Carr, *A History of Germany, 1815-1945* (London 1987)
G.A. Craig, *Germany, 1866-1918* (Oxford 1978)
R. Dahrendorf, *Democracy and Society in Germany* (London 1968)
G. Eley and D. Blackbourn, *The Peculiarities of German History* (Oxford 1985)
R.J. Evans, ed., *Society and Politics in Wilhelmine Germany* (London 1978)
H. Holborn, *A History of Modern Germany* (London 1969)
G.G. Iggers, ed., *The Social History of Politics* (Leamington Spa 1986)
G. Mann, *The History of Germany Since 1789* (London 1968)
A. Ramm, *Germany, 1789-1919* (London 1967)
E. Sagarra, *A Social History of Germany, 1648-1914* (London 1977)
J.J. Sheehan, ed., *Imperial Germany* (New York 1975)
H.-U. Wehler, *The German Empire, 1871-1918* (Leamington Spa 1985)

II. The Economy

A. Economic Sectors and Structural Change

G. Bry, *Wages in Germany, 1871-1914* (Princeton 1960)
J.H. Clapham, *The Economic Development of France and Germany, 1815-1914* (Cambridge 1936)
A.V. Desai, *Real Wages in Germany, 1871-1914* (Oxford 1968)
W.O. Henderson, *The Rise of German Industrial Power, 1834-1914* (London 1975)
M. Kitchen, *The Political Economy of Germany, 1815-1914* (London 1978)
W.R. Lee, ed., *Industrialisation and Industrial Growth in Germany* (London 1986)
H. Neuburger, *German Banks and German Economic Growth, 1871-1914* (New York 1977)

T. Pierenkemper, "The Standard of Living and Employment in Germany, 1850-1980," in: *Journal of European Economic History*, 1987, 51-73

P. Schollier, ed., *Real Wages in 19th and 20th Century Europe* (Oxford 1989)

A. Sommaria and G. Tullio, *German Macroeconomic History, 1880-1979* (London 1987)

G. Stolper, *The German Economy from 1870 to the Present* (London 1967)

F.B. Tipton, *Regional Variation in the Economic Development of Germany during the Nineteenth Century* (Middletown, Conn. 1976)

T. Veblen, *Imperial Germany and the Industrial Revolution* (London 1915)

P.-C. Witt, *Wealth and Taxation in Central Europe* (Oxford 1987)

B. The Organization of Industry

G. Ahlström, "Higher Technical Education and the Engineering Profession in France and Germany during the 19th Century," in: *Economy and History*, 1978, 51-88

A. Ascher, "Baron von Stumm. Advocate of Feudal Capitalism," in: *Journal of Central European Affairs*, 1962/63, 271-85

K. Barkin, *The Controversy over German Industrialization* (Chicago, 1970)

D. Cahan, *An Institute for an Empire* (Cambridge 1989)

J.P. Cullity, "The Growth of Governmental Employment in Germany, 1882-1950," in: *Zeitschrift für die gesamte Staatswissenschaft*, 1967, 207-17

L.A. Heilman, "Industrial Unemployment in Germany, 1873-1913," in: *Archiv für Sozialgeschichte*, 1987, 25-49

J.A. Johnson, *The Kaiser's Chemists* (Chapel Hill 1990)

P. Lundgreen, "Industrialization and the Educational Formation of Manpower in Germany," in: *Journal of Social History*, 1975/76, 64-80

___, "Educational Expansion and Economic Growth in 19th-Century Germany," in: L. Stone, ed., *Schooling and Society* (Baltimore 1976)

___, "Education for the Science-Based Industrial State?" in: *History of Education*, 1984, 59-67

H. Neuburger, *German Banks and German Economic Growth, 1871-1914* (New York 1977)

L. Schofer, *The Formation of a Modern Labor Force* (Berkeley 1975)

E.G. Spencer, *Management and Labor in Imperial Germany* (New Brunswick, N.J. 1984)

S.B. Webb, "Tariffs, Cartels, Technology, and the Growth in the German Steel Industry, 1879-1914," in: *Journal of Economic History*, 1980, 309-29

F. Wunderlich, *Farm Labor in Germany, 1810-1945* (Princeton 1961)

III. Society

A. Demographic Structure and Development

K.-J. Bade, ed., *Population, Labour and Migration in 19th and 20th Century Germany* (Oxford 1987)

J.H. Jackson, *Migration and Urbanization in the Ruhr Valley, 1850-1900* (San Diego, Calf. 1980)

W. Köllmann, "The Process of Urbanization in Germany at the Height of the Industrialization Period," in: *Journal of Contemporary History*, 1969, 59-76

J.E. Knodel, "Malthus Amiss: Marriage Restrictions in 19th-Century Germany," in: *Social Sciences*, 1972, 40-45

J.J. Lee, "Critics of Urban Society in Germany, 1854-1914," in: *Journal of the History of Ideas*, 1979, 61-83

V.E. McHale and E.A. Johnson, "Urbanization, Industrialization, and Crime in Imperial Germany," in: *Social Science History*, 1976, 45-78 and 210-247

J. Reulecke, "Population Growth and Urbanisation in Germany in the 19th Century," in: *Past and Present*, 1977, 21-32

M. Walker, *Germany and the Emigrations, 1816-1885* (Cambridge, Mass. 1964)

B. Social Stratification and Inequality

D.L. Augustine-Perez, "Very Wealthy Businessmen in Imperial Germany," in: *Journal of Social History*, 1988, 299-321

R.M. Berdahl, "Conservative and Aristocratic Landholders in Bismarckian Germany," in: *Journal of Modern History*, 1972, 1-20

L. Cecil, *The German Diplomatic Service, 1871-1914* (Princeton 1979)

G. Cocks and K.H. Jarausch, eds., *The German Professions, 1800-1950* (Oxford 1990)

K. Demeter, *The German Officer Corps* (London 1965)

R.J. Evans, *Death in Hamburg* (Oxford 1987)

A. Gerschenkron, *Bread and Democracy in Germany* (New York 1965)

K. Gispen, *New Professions, Old Order. Engineers and German Society, 1815-1914* (Cambridge 1989)

L.A. Heilman, "Industrial Unemployment in Germany, 1873-1913," in: *Archiv für Sozialgeschichte*, 1987, 25-49

H.H. Herwig, *The German Naval Officer Corps* (Oxford 1973)

__, "'Allens nur noch Seelenadel.' The Prussian Nobility and the Imperial Navy, 1888-1918," in: *Canadian Journal of History*, 1980, 197-205

D.J. Hughes, *The King's Finest. A Social and Bureaucratic Profile of Prussia's General Officers, 1871-1914* (New York 1987)

K.H. Jarausch, *The Unfree Professions* (Oxford 1990)

M.H. Kater, "Professionalization and Socialization of Physicians in Wilhelmine and Weimar Germany," in: *Journal of Contemporary History*, 1985, 677-701

M. Kitchen, *The German Officer Corps, 1980-1914* (Oxford 1968)

J. Knodel, *The Decline of Fertility in Germany, 1871-1939* (Princeton 1974)

J. Knodel and S. Hochstadt, "Urban and Rural Illegitimacy in Imperial Germany," in: P. Laslett et al., eds., *Bastardy and Its Comparative History* (London 1980)

J. Kocka and A. Mitchell, eds., *Bourgeois Society in 19th-Century Europe* (Oxford 1992)

P.G. Lauren, *Diplomats and Bureaucrats* (Stanford 1976)

H.-H. Liang, *The Social Background of the Berlin Working-Class Movement* (Ann Arbor, Mich. 1980)

W.E. Mosse, *Jews in the German Economy* (Oxford 1987)

J. Perkins, "The German Agricultural Worker, 1815-1914," in: *Journal of Political Science*, 1984, 3-27

R. Spree, *Health and Social Class in Imperial Germany* (New York 1987)

C. Women and Men

C.E. Adams, *Women Clerks in Wilhelmine Germany* (Cambridge 1988)

J.C. Albisetti, *Schooling German Girls and Women* (Princeton 1988)

G. Bernstein, "The Curriculum for German Girls' Schools, 1870-1914," in: *Paedagogica Historica*, 1978, 275-95

G. and L. Bernstein, "Attitudes Towards Women's Education in Germany, 1870-1914," in: *International Journal of Women's Studies*, 1979, 473-88

R.J. Evans, "Prostitution, State and Society in Imperial Germany," in: *Past and Present*, 1976, 106-29

R.J. Evans and W.R. Lee, eds., *The German Family* (London 1980)

J.C. Fout, ed., *German Women in the 19th Century* (New York 1984)

B. Franzoi, *At The Very Least She Pays The Rent* (Westport, Conn. 1985)

M. Kaplan, *The Jewish Feminist Movement in Germany* (Westport, Conn. 1979)

J. Knodel, *The Decline of Fertility in Germany, 1871-1914* (Princeton 1974)

W.R. Lee, "Bastardy and the Socio-economic Structure of South Germany," in: *Journal of Interdisciplinary History*, 1977, 403-25

D.S. Linton, "Between School and Marriage: Young Working Women as a Social Problem in Late Imperial Germany," in: *European History Quarterly*, 1988, 387-408

S. Meyer, "The Tiresome Work of Conspicuous Leisure," in: M. Boxer and J.H. Quataert, eds., *Connecting Spheres* (Oxford 1987)
R.P. Neuman, "Industrialization and Sexual Behavior. Some Aspects of Working-Class Life in Wilhelmine Germany," in: R.J. Bezucha, ed., *Modern European Social History* (Lexington 1972)
R. Orthmann, *Out of Necessity. Women Working in Berlin at the Height of Industrialization* (Hamden, Conn. 1991)
K. Schlegel, "Mistress and Servant in 19th-Century Hamburg," in: *History Workshop Journal*, 1983, 60-77
I. Stoehr, "Housework and Motherhood," in: G. Bock and P. Thane, eds., *Maternity and Gender Policies* (New York 1991)
J. Woycke, *Birth Control in Germany, 1871-1933* (London 1988)

D. The Young and the Aged

H. Becker, *German Youth. Bond or Free* (London 1946)
S. Fishman, "Suicide, Sex, and the Discovery of the German Adolescent," in: *History of Education Quarterly*, 1970, 70-88
E. Heineman, "Gender Identity in the Wandervogel Movement," in: *German Studies Review*, 1989, 249-70
K.H. Jarausch, "Students, Sex, and Politics in Imperial Germany," in: *Journal of Contemporary History*, 1982, 285-303
__, *Students, Society, and Politics in Imperial Germany* (Princeton 1982)
W. Laqueur, *Young Germany* (London 1962)
P.D. Stachura, *The German Youth Movement, 1900-1945* (London 1981)
R. Wohl, *The Generation of 1914* (Cambridge, Mass. 1979)

E. Agents of Socialization

J.C. Albisetti, *Secondary School Reform in Imperial Germany* (Princeton 1983)
G. Eley, "Educating the Bourgeoisie. Students and the Culture of 'Illiberalism' in Imperial Germany," in: *History of Education Quarterly*, 1986, 287-300
R.J. Evans, ed., "Religion and Society in Modern Germany," in: *European Studies Review*, 1982 (special issue)
R.J. Evans, ed., *The German Underworld* (London 1988)
R.J. Evans and W.R. Lee, eds., *The German Family* (London 1980)
D. Fallon, *The German University* (Boulder, Colo. 1980)
K.H. Jarausch, "Liberal Education as Illiberal Socialization," in: *Journal of Modern History*, 1978, 609-30
E.A. Johnson and V.E. McHale, "Socio-economic Aspects of the

Delinquency Rate in Imperial Germany, 1882-1914," in: *Journal of Social History*, 1980, 384-402

K.D. Kennedy, "Regionalism and Nationalism in South German History Lessons, 1871-1914," in: *German Studies Review*, 1989, 11-33

M. Lamberti, *State, Society, and the Elementary School in Imperial Germany* (Oxford 1989)

C. McClelland, *State, Society, and Universities in Germany, 1700-1914* (Cambridge, Mass. 1980)

R.H. Samuel and R. Hinton Thomas, *Education and Society in Modern Germany* (London 1949)

K.A. Schleunes, *Schooling and Society* (Oxford 1991)

J. Sperber, *Popular Catholicism in 19th-Century Germany* (Princeton 1984)

W. Spohn, "Piety, Secularism, Socialism. On Religion and Working-Class Formation in Imperial Germany, 1871-1914," in: B. Strath, ed., *Language and the Construction of Class Identities* (Gothenburg 1990)

F. Majorities and Minorities

1. Catholics

R.M. Bigler, *The Politics of German Protestantism* (Los Angeles 1972)

D. Blackbourn, "Progress and Piety: Liberalism, Catholicism and the State in Imperial Germany," in: *History Workshop Journal*, 1988, 57-78

R.J. Evans, ed., "Religion and Society in Modern Germany," in: *European Studies Review*, 1982 (special issue)

I. Farr, "From Anti-Catholicism to Anti-Clericalism," in: *European Studies Review*, 1983, 249-69

G. Golde, *Catholics and Protestants. Agricultural Modernization in Two German Villages* (London 1975)

V.L. Lidtke, "Social Class and Secularization in Imperial Germany," in: *Leo Baeck Institute Yearbook*, 1982, 21-40

T.M. Loome, *Liberal Catholicism, Reform Catholicism, Modernism* (London 1979)

H. Mcleod, "Protestantism and the Working Class in Imperial Germany," in: *European Studies Review*, 1982, 323-44

J. Sperber, *Popular Catholicism in 19th-Century Germany* (Princeton 1984)

2. The Jewish Minority

P. Gay, *Freud, Jews, and Other Germans* (Oxford 1978)

R. Gay, *The Jews of Germany* (New Haven, Conn. 1992)

E. Hamburger, "Jews in the Public Service under the German Monarchy," in: *Leo Baeck Institute Yearbook*, 1964, 206-38

M. Kaplan, *The Making of the Jewish Middle Class* (New York 1991)
J. Katz, *Out of the Ghetto* (Cambridge, Mass. 1973)
S. Lowenstein, "The Rural Community and the Urbanization of German Jewry," in: *Central European History*, 1980, 218-30
P. Pulzer, "Religion and Judicial Appointments in Germany, 1869-1918," in: *Leo Baeck Institute Yearbook*, 1983, 185-204
F. Stern, *Gold and Iron* (New York 1977)
J. Wertheimer, *Unwelcome Strangers* (Oxford 1987)

3. Other Minorities

R. Blanke, *Prussian Poland in the German Empire, 1871-1914* (Boulder, Colo. 1981)
V. Caron, *Between France and Germany* (Princeton 1980)
J.E. Craig, *Scholarship and Nation-Building* (Chicago 1982)
W. Hagen, *Germans, Poles, and Jews* (Chicago 1980)
T. Kominski, *Polish Publicists and Prussian Politics* (Stuttgart 1988)
J.J. Kulczycki, *School Strikes in Prussian Poland, 1901-1907* (New York 1981)
R.C. Murphy, *Guestworkers in the German Reich* (Boulder, Colo. 1983)
H.K. Rosenthal, *German and Pole* (Gainsville, Fla. 1975)
D. Silverman, *Reluctant Ally* (Philadelphia 1972)

IV. Culture

A. High Culture and Popular Culture

L. Abrams, *Workers' Culture in Imperial Germany* (London 1991)
A.T. Allen, "Sex and Satire in Wilhelmine Germany," in: *European Studies Review*, 1977, 19-40
__, *Satire and Society in Wilhelmine Germany* (Louisville, Kentucky 1985)
W.G. Breckman, "Disciplining Consumption," in: *Journal of Social History*, 1991, 485-505.
S.E. Bronner and D. Kellner, eds., *Passion and Rebellion. The Expressionist Heritage* (New York 1988)
R.M. Browning, *German Poetry from 1750 to 1900* (New York 1984)
J. Campbell, *The German Werkbund* (Princeton 1978)
G. Chapple and H. Schulte, eds., *The Turn of the Century: German Literature and Art, 1890-1915* (Bonn 1981)
C.W. Davies, *Theater for the People. The Story of the Volksbühne* (Austin, Texas 1977)
V. Dürr et al., eds., *Imperial Germany* (Madison, Wisc. 1985)

R.A. Fullerton, "Toward a Commercial Popular Culture in Germany," in: *Journal of Social History*, 1978/79, 489-511
P. Gay, *Freud, Jews an Other Germans* (Oxford 1978)
H. Glaser, *The German Mind in the 19th Century* (New York 1981)
R. Gray, *The German Traditions in Literature, 1871-1914* (Cambridge 1965)
P. Jelavich, *Munich and Theatrical Modernism* (Cambridge, Mass. 1985)
A. Kelly, ed., *The German Worker* (Berkeley 1987)
M. Kennedy, *Richard Strauss* (London 1976)
D.C. Large and W. Weber, eds., *Wagnerism in European Culture* (Ithaca, N.Y. 1984)
V. Lidtke, *The Alternative Culture* (Oxford 1985)
M. Makela, *The Munich Secession* (Princeton 1990)
G. Masur, *Imperial Berlin* (New York 1970)
P. Paret, *The Berlin Secession* (Cambridge, Mass. 1980)
__, "The Tschudi Affair," in: *Journal of Modern History*, 1981, 589-618
R. Pascal, *From Naturalism to Expressionism* (New York 1973)
T.J. Reed, *Thomas Mann* (Oxford 1974)
J. Remak, *The Gentle Critic* (Syracuse, N.Y. 1964)
J.S. Roberts, *Drinking, Temperance, and the Working Class in 19th-Century Germany* (London 1984)
K. Roper, *German Encounters with Modernity. Novels of Imperial Berlin* (Atlantic Highlands, N.J. 1991)
G. Roth, *The Social Democrats of Imperial Germany* (Totowa 1961)
C. Schorske, *Fin de Siècle Vienna* (Cambridge 1961)
__, *German Social Democracy, 1905-1917* (New York 1972)
H. Schulte, ed., *The Tragedy of German Inwardness? Antirationalism in German Culture, 1870-1933* (Hamilton, Ont. 1992)
R.E. Sackett, *Popular Entertainment, Class and Politics in Munich, 1900-1923* (Cambridge, Mass, 1982)
W.D. Smith, *Politics and the Sciences of Culture in Germany, 1840-1920* (Oxford 1991)
G.D. Stark and B.K. Lackner, eds., *Essays in Culture and Society in Modern Germany* (Arlington, Texas 1982)
D. Welch, "Cinema and Society in Imperial Germany, 1905-1918," in: *German History*, 1990, 28-45

B. The Sciences and Humanities

J.E. Craig, *Scholarship and Nation-Building* (Chicago 1982)
J.L. Heilbron, *The Dilemmas of the Upright Man* (Berkeley 1986)
G.G. Iggers, *The German Conception of History* (Middletown, Conn. 1983)

K. Jarausch, *The Transformation of Higher Learning, 1860-1930* (Stuttgart 1982)
J.A. Johnson, *The Kaiser's Chemists* (Chapel Hill 1990)
C. McClelland, *The German Historians and England* (Cambridge 1971)
L. O'Boyle, "Learning for its Own Sake: The German University as 19th-century Model," in: *Comparative Studies in Society and History*, 1983, 3-25
L.S. Pyenson, *Young Einstein* (Bristol 1985)
F. Ringer, "Higher Education in Germany in the 19th Century," in: *Journal of Contemporary History*, 1967, 123-38
—, *The Decline of the German Mandarins* (Cambridge, Mass. 1969)
J. Sheehan, *The Career of Lujo Brentano* (Chicago 1966)
W.D. Smith, *Politics and the Sciences of Culture in Germany, 1840-1920* (Oxford 1991)

C. The Press, Its Readership, and the Role of Intellectuals

A. Hall, *Scandal, Sensation and Society. Democracy, the SPD Press and Wilhelmine Germany, 1890-1914* (Cambridge 1977)
G.D. Stark, *Entrepreneurs of Ideology* (Chapel Hill 1981)
F. Stern, *The Politics of Cultural Despair* (Berkeley 1961)
W. Struve, *Elites against Democracy* (Princeton 1973)

V. The Realm of Politics

A. Constitutions, Parties, and Elections

M.L. Anderson, *Windthorst* (Oxford 1981)
D. Blackbourn, *Class, Religion and Local Politics in Wihelmine Germany* (New Haven, Conn. 1980)
W.K. Blessing, "The Cult of Monarchy. Political Loyalty and the Workers' Movement in Imperial Germany," in: *Journal of Contemporary History*, 1978, 357-75
K.R. Calkins, *Hugo Haase* (Durham 1979)
C.D. Crothers, *The German Elections of 1907* (New York 1967)
K. Epstein, *Matthias Erzberger and the Dilemma of German Democracy* (Princeton 1959)
E. Ettinger, *Rosa Luxemburg* (Boston 1986)
E. Evans, *The German Center Party, 1870-1933* (Carbondale, Ill. 1981)
I. Farr, "From Anti-Catholicism to Anti-Clericalism," in: *European Studies Review*, 1983, 249-69
R. Fletcher, *Revisionism and Empire* (London 1984)
—, *Bernstein to Brandt* (Baltimore 1987), p. 41

J.C. Fout, ed., *Politics, Parties, and the Authoritarian State. Imperial Germany, 1871-1918* (New York 1992)
W.L. Guttsman, *The German Social Democratic Party, 1875-1933* (London 1981)
J.C. Hunt, *The People's Party in Württemberg and Southern Germany, 1890-1914* (Stuttgart 1975)
__, "The Bourgeois Middle in German Politics, 1871-1933," in: *Journal of Contemporary History*, 1978, 83-106
M. John, "The Politics of Legal Unity in Germany, 1870-1896," in: *Historical Journal*, 1985, 341-55
__, "Liberalism and Society in Germany, 1850-1880. The Case of Hanover," in: *English Historcal Review*, 1987, 579-98
L.E. Jones and J. Retallack, eds., *Elections, Mass Politics, and Social Change in Modern Germany* (Cambridge 1992)
R. Koshar, *Social Life, Local Politics, and Nazism: Marburg, 1880-1935* (Chapel Hill 1986)
M. Lamberti, "Liberals, Socialists, and the Defense against Antisemitism in the Wilhelmine Period," in: *Leo Baeck Institute Yearbook*, 1980, 147-62
W. Maehl, *August Bebel* (Philadelphia 1980)
G.R. Mork, "Bismarck and the 'Capitulation' of German Liberalism," in: *Journal of Modern History*, 1971, 59-75
J.P. Nettl, *Rosa Luxemburg* (Oxford 1966)
M. Nolan, *Social Democracy and Society* (Cambridge 1981)
A.J. Peck, *Radicals and Reactionaries* (Washington, D.C. 1978)
J.N. Retallack, *Notables of the Right* (London 1988)
R.J. Ross, *The Beleaguered Tower* (Notre Dame, Ind. 1976)
C.E. Schorske, *German Social Democracy, 1905-1917* (New York 1972)
J.J. Sheehan, "Political Leadership in the German Reichstag, 1871-1918," in: *American Historical Review*, 1968, 511-28
__, *German Liberalism in the Nineteenth Century* (Chicago 1978)
J.L. Snell, *The Democratic Movement in Germany, 1789-1914* (Chapel Hill 1976)
J. Sperber, "The Shaping of Political Catholicism in the Ruhr Basin, 1848-1881," in: *Central European History*, 1983, 347-67
G.P. Steenson, *Karl Kautsky, 1884-1938* (Pittsburgh 1978)
S. Suval, *Electoral Politics in Wilhelmine Germany* (Chapel Hill 1985)
D. White, *The Splintered Party* (Cambridge, Mass. 1976)
C. Zangerl, "Courting the Catholic Vote: The Center Party in Baden, 1903-1913," in: *Central European History*, 1977, 220-40
J.K. Zeender, *The German Center Party, 1890-1906* (Philadelphia 1976)

B. Extra-Parliamentary Organizations

1. Economic Associations

D. Blackbourn, "The Mittelstand in German Society and Politics, 1871-1914," in: *Social History*, 1977, 409-33

__, "Between Resignation and Volatility. The German Petite Bourgesoisie in the 19th Century," in: G. Crossick and H.-G. Haupt, eds., *Shopkeepers and Master Artisans in 19th-Century Europe* (London 1984)

__, "Peasants and Politics in Germany," in: *European History Quarterly*, 1984, 47-75

H. Boehme, "Big Business Pressure Groups and Bismarck's Turn to Protectionism, 1873-1879," *Historical Journal*, 1967, 218-36

E.D. Brose, *Christian Labor and the Politics of Frustration in Imperial Germany* (Washington, D.C. 1985)

R.J. Evans, ed., *The German Peasantry* (London 1985)

R. Gellately, *The Politics of Economic Despair* (London 1974)

A. Gerschenkron, *Bread and Democracy in Germany* (New York 1966)

K. Gispen, *New Professions, Old Order. Engineers and German Society, 1815-1914* (Cambridge 1990)

W.M. Haller, "Regional and National Free Trade Associations," in: *European Studies Review*, 1976, 275-96

D.W. Hendon, "German Catholics and the Agrarian League," in: *German Studies Review*, 1981, 427-46

J.C. Hunt, "Peasants, Grain Tariffs, and Meat Quotas: Imperial German Protectionism Reexamined," in: *Central European History*, 1974, 311-31

I.N. Lambi, "The Agrarian-Industrial Front in Bismarckian Politics," in: *Journal of Central European Affairs*, 1961, 378-96

__, "The Protectionist Interests of the German Iron and Steel Industry," in: *Journal of Economic History*, 1962, 59-70

C. McClelland, *The German Experience of Professionalization* (New York 1991)

R.G. Moeller, ed., *Peasants and Lords in Modern Germany* (Boston 1986)

J.A. Moses, *Trade Unionism in Germany from Bismarck to Hitler* (London 1982)

F.B. Tipton, "Farm Labor and Power Politics in Germany, 1850-1914," in: *Journal of Economic History*, 1974, 951-79

S.R. Tirrell, *German Agrarian Politics after Bismarck's Fall* (New York 1971)

S.B. Webb, "Tariffs, Cartels, Technology, and the Growth in the German Steel Industry," in: *Journal of Economic History*, 1980, 309-29

2. Nationalist Associations

S. Angel-Volkov, *The Rise of Popular Antimodernism in Germany* (Princeton 1978)
D. Blackbourn, "The Politics of Demagogy in Imperial Germany," in: *Past and Present*, 1986, 152-84
R. Chickering, *We Men Who Feel Most German* (London 1984)
M.S. Coetzee, *The German Army League* (New Haven, Conn. 1990)
G. Eley, *Reshaping the German Right* (New Haven, Conn. 1980)
M. Hughes, *Nationalism and Society. Germany 1800-1945* (London 1988)
A. Kelly, *The Descent of Darwin* (Chapel Hill 1981)
P. Kennedy and A.J. Nicholls, eds., *Nationalist and Racialist Movements in Britain and Germany before 1914* (London 1981)
R. Koshar, *Social Life, Local Politics and Nazism. Marburg, 1880-1935* (Chapel Hill 1986)
G.L. Mosse, *The Nationalization of the Masses* (New York 1975)
F. Stern, *The Failure of Illiberalism* (New York 1992)

3. Political Organizations of Minorities

W.T. Angress, "Prussia's Army and the Jewish Reserve Officer Controversy before World War I," in: J.J. Sheehan, ed., *Imperial Germany* (New York 1975)
D. Blackbourn, "Roman Catholics, the Centre Party and Anti-Semitism in Imperial Germany," in: P.M. Kennedy and A.J. Nicholls, eds., *Nationalist and Racialist Movements in Britain and Germany before 1914* (London 1981)
R. Chickering, *Imperial Germany and a World Without War* (Princeton 1975)
R. Gutteridge, *Open Thy Mouth for the Dumb. The German Evangelical Church and the Jews* (New York 1976)
N. Kampe, "Jews and Antisemites at Universities in Imperial Germany," in: *Leo Baeck Institute Yearbook*, 1985, 357-94
M. Lamberti, "From Coexistence to Conflict," in: *Ibid.*, 1982, 53-86
R. Levy, *The Downfall of the Anti-Semitic Political Parties in Imperial Germany* (New Haven, Conn. 1975)
W.H. Maehl, *German Militarism and Socialism* (Omaha, Nebr. 1968)
P.J. Pulzer, *The Rise of Political Antisemitism in Germany and Austria* (New York 1964)
S. Ragins, *Jewish Responses to Anti-Semitism in Germany, 1870-1914* (Cincinnati 1980)
J. Reinharz, *Fatherland or Promised Land* (Ann Arbor, Mich. 1975)
J. Schorsch, *Jewish Reactions to German Anti-Semitism, 1870-1914* (New York 1972)

S.A. Stehlin, *Bismarck and the Guelph Problem, 1866-1890* (The Hague 1973)
U. Tal, *Christians and Jews in Germany, 1870-1914* (Ithaca, N.Y. 1974)
R.S. Wistrich, "The SPD and Antisemitism in the 1890s," in: *European Studies Review*, 1977, 177-97
S. Zucker, "Ludwig Bamberger and the Rise of Antisemitism in Germany, 1848-1893," in: *Central European History*, 1970, 332-52

4. Women's Organizations

A.T. Allen, "German Radical Feminism and Eugenics, 1900-1918," in: *German Studies Review*, 1988, 31-56
__, *Feminism and Motherhood in Germany, 1800-1914* (New Brunswick, N.J. 1991)
R. Chickering, "Casting Their Gaze More Broadly: Women's Patriotic Activism in Imperial Germany," in: *Past and Present*, 1988, 156-85
R.J. Evans, *The Feminist Movement in Germany, 1894-1933* (London 1976)
Comrades and Sisters (Brighton 1987)
A. Hackett, "Feminism and Liberalism in Wilhelmine Germany, 1890-1918," in: B.A. Carroll, ed., *Liberating Women's History*, (Urbana, Ill. 1976)
__, *The Politics of Feminism in Wilhelmine Germany, 1890-1918* (New York 1979)
M. Kaplan, *The Jewish Feminist Movement in Germany* (Westport, Conn. 1979)
__, "Prostitution, Morality Crusades, and Feminism," in: *Women's Studies International Forum*, 1982, 619-27
A.G. Meyer, *The Feminism and Socialism of Lily Braun* (Bloomington, Ind. 1985)
R. Pore, *A Conflict of Interest: Women in Early German Social Democracy* (Westport, Conn. 1981)
J. Quataert, *The Reluctant Feminists in German Social Democracy, 1885-1918* (Princeton 1979)

C. The Executive

S. Andic and J. Veverka, "The Growth of Government Expenditure in Germany since the Unification," in: *Finanzarchiv*, 1963, 169-278
G. Bonham, *Ideology and Interests in the German State* (Hamden, Conn. 1991)
Central European History, 1985 (special issue on censorship and naturalism)
R.J. Evans, "Prostitution, State and Society in Imperial Germany," in: *Past and Present*, 1976, 106-29
__, "'Red Wednesday' in Hamburg," in: *Social History*, 1979, 1-30,
__, ed., *The German Working Class* (London 1982)

A. Hall, "By Other Means: The Legal Struggle against the SPD in Wilhelmine Germany, 1890-1900," in: *Historical Journal*, 1974, 365-86

I. Hull, *The Entourage of Kaiser Wilhelm II, 1888-1918* (Cambridge 1982)

H. Jacob, *German Administration since Bismarck: Central Authority vs. Local Autonomy* (New Haven, Conn. 1963)

M. John, *Politics and the Law in Late Nineteenth Century Germany* (Oxford 1989)

B. Ladd, *Urban Planning and Civic Order in Germany, 1860-1914* (Cambridge, Mass. 1990)

W.R. Lee and E. Rosenhaft, eds., *The State and Social Change in Germany, 1880-1981* (Oxford 1990)

R. Lenman, "Mass Culture and the State in Germany, 1890-1926," in: R. Bullen et al., eds., *Ideas into Politics* (London 1984)

V.K. Lidtke, *The Outlawed Party* (Princeton 1966)

D.S. Linton, *"Who Has the Youth, Has the Future"* (Cambridge 1991)

E. McCreary, "Social Welfare and Business: The Krupp Welfare Program, 1860-1914," in: *Business History Review*, 1968, 24-50

C. Medalen, "State Monopoly Capitalism in Germany: The Hibernia Affair," in: *Past and Present*, 1978, 82-112

L.W. Muncy, "The Prussian Landräte in the Last Years of the Monarchy," in: *Central European History*, 1973, 329-38

P. Paret and B.I. Lewis, "Art, Society, and Politics in Wilhelmine Germany," in: *Journal of Modern History*, 1985, 696-710

G.A. Ritter, *Social Welfare in Germany and Britain* (Leamington Spa 1983)

E.G. Spencer, "State Power and Local Interests in Prussian Cities," in: *Central European History*, 1986, 293-313

—, *Police and the Social Order in German Cities. The Düsseldorf District, 1848-1914* (Dekalb, Ill. 1992)

G.D. Stark, "Pornography, Society, and the Law in Imperial Germany," in: *Central European History*, 1981, 200-29

E.L. Turk, "An Examination of Civil Liberty in Wilhelmine Germany," in: *Ibid.*, 1986, 323-341

P. Weindling, *Health, Race and German Politics between National Unification and Nazism, 1870-1945* (Cambridge 1989)

VI. Foreign and Domestic Politics

A. The Bismarckian Era

K.D. Barkin, "The Second Founding of the Reich," in: *German Studies Review,* 1987, 219-36

J.A. Flynn, "At the Threshold of Dissolution. The National Liberals and Bismarck, 1877/78," in: *Historical Journal*, 1988, 319-40
L. Gall, *Bismarck* (London 1986)
I. Geiss, *German Foreign Policy, 1871-1914* (London 1976)
F.B.M. Hollyday, *Bismarck's Rival* (Chapel Hill 1960)
M. Howard, *The Franco-Prussian War* (London 1961)
G.O. Kent, *Arnim and Bismarck* (Oxford 1968)
A.J. Knoll, *Togo and Imperial Germany, 1884-1914* (Stanford 1978)
I.N. Lambi, *Free Trade and Protectionism in Germany, 1868-1879* (Wiesbaden 1963)
H.P. Meritt, "Bismarck and German Interests in East Africa, 1884-1885," in: *Historical Journal*, 1978, 97-116
G.R. Mork, "Bismarck and the 'Capitulation' of German Liberalism," in: *Journal of Modern History*, 1971, 59-75
O. Pflanze, *Bismarck and the Development of Germany* (Princeton 1990)
R.J. Ross, "Enforcing the Kulturkampf in the Bismarckian State and the Limits of Coercion in Imperial Germany," in: *Journal of Modern History*, 1984, 456-82
W.D. Smith, *The German Colonial Empire* (Chapel Hill 1978)
F. Stern, *Gold and Iron* (London 1977)

B. The Wilhelmine Period

M. Balfour, *The Kaiser and His Times* (Boston 1964)
G. Barraclough, *From Agadir to Armageddon* (London 1982)
V.R. Berghahn, *Germany and the Approach of War in 1914* (London 1993)
G.A. Craig, *The Politics of the Prussian Army* (Oxford 1955)
J.R. Dukes and J. Remak, eds., *Another Germany* (Boulder, Colo. 1988)
R.J. Evans, ed., *Society and Politics in Wilhelmine Germany* (London 1978)
J.D. Farley, "Reform or Reaction: The Dilemma of Prince Hohenlohe as Chancellor of Germany," in: *European Studies Review*, 1974, 317-43
F. Fischer, *War of Illusions* (London 1973)
L.H. Gann and P. Duignan, *The Rulers of German Africa, 1884-1914* (Stanford 1977)
I. Geiss, *German Foreign Policy, 1871-1914* (London 1976)
M. Gordon, "Domestic Conflict and the Origins of the First World War," in: *Journal of Modern History*, 1974, 191-226
B. Heckart, *From Bassermann to Bebel* (New Haven, Conn. 1974)
K.H. Jarausch, *The Enigmatic Chancellor* (New Haven, Conn. 1973)
D.E. Kaiser, "Germany and the Origins of the First World War," in: *Journal of Modern History*, 1983, 442-74

E. Kehr, *Battleship Building and Party Politics in Germany* (Chicago 1975)
Economic Interest, Militarism, and Foreign Policy (Berkeley 1977)
P.M. Kennedy, *The Rise of the Anglo-German Antagonism* (London 1980)
I. Lambi, *The Navy and German Power Politics* (London 1984)
K.A. Lerman, *The Chancellor as Courtier. Bernhard von Bülow and the Governance of Germany, 1900-1909* (Cambridge 1990)
J.A. Nichols, *Germany after Bismarck* (Cambridge, Mass. 1958)
J.C.G. Röhl, *Germany without Bismarck* (London 1967)
__, "Admiral von Müller and the Approach of War, 1911-1914," in: *Historical Journal*, 1969, 651-73
J.C.G. Röhl and N. Sombart, eds., *Kaiser Wilhelm II* (Cambridge 1982)
G. Schöllgen, ed., *Escape into War?* (Oxford 1990)
D. Schoenbaum, *Zabern 1913* (London 1982)
J. Steinberg, *Yesterday's Deterrent* (London 1965)
N. Stone, "Moltke-Conrad: Relations between the Austro-Hungarian and German General Staffs, 1909-1914," in: *Historical Journal*, 1966, 201-28
E.-T.P.W. Wilke, *Political Decadence in Imperial Germany* (Urbana, Ill. 1976)
S.R. Williamson, Jr., *Austria-Hungary and the Origins of the First World War* (London 1991)

Index